ENGLISH G

access 2

Lehrerfassung

Ihr Zugang zum E-Book auf www.scook.de:

nz232-39w3q — Ihr Lizenzcode

Der Code beinhaltet nach Erstaktivierung eine 5-jährige Lizenz zur Nutzung des E-Books auf scook. Für die Nutzung ist die Zustimmung zu den AGB auf scook.de erforderlich.

9783060330713 EG Acc. 2 SB-L kt.

English G Access · Band 2
Lehrerfassung

Im Auftrag des Verlages herausgegeben von
Jörg Rademacher, Mannheim

Erarbeitet von
Laurence Harger, Wellington, Neuseeland
Cecile Niemitz-Rossant, Berlin

unter Mitarbeit von
Dr. Annette Leithner-Brauns, Dresden
Birgit Ohmsieder, Berlin
Mervyn Whittaker, Bad Dürkheim

in Zusammenarbeit mit der Englischredaktion
Dr. Philip Devlin (koordinierender Redakteur), Bonnie Glänzer (Lehrerfassung), Ulrike Berendt, Gareth Evans, Stefan Höhne, Dr. Christiane Kallenbach (Projektleitung), Uwe Tröger *und beratend* Filiz Bahsi, Christiane Bonk, Gwendolyn Düwel, Solveig Heinrich, Renata Jakovac *und* Lothar Teworte (digitales Schülerbuch)

Beratende Mitwirkung
Peter Brünker, Bad Kreuznach; Anette Fritsch, Dillenburg; Uli Imig, Wildeshausen; Thomas Neidhardt, Bielefeld; Wolfgang Neudecker, Mannheim; Dr. Andreas Sedlatschek, Esslingen; Sieglinde Spranger, Chemnitz; Marcel Sprunkel, Köln; Sabine Tudan, St. Georg; Friederike von Bremen, Hannover; Harald Weißling, Mannheim

Illustrationen
Tobias Dahmen, Utrecht/NL; Elke Hanisch, Köln; Burkhard Schulz, Düsseldorf *sowie* Roland Beier, Berlin

Fotos
Trevor Burrows Photography, Plymouth

Umschlaggestaltung und Layoutkonzept
kleiner & bold, Berlin

Layout und technische Umsetzung
Eric Gira, zweiband-media, Berlin

Für die freundliche Unterstützung danken wir der Plymstock School in Plymouth.

Legende zur Lehrerfassung

1 ▶ 12	CD- und Tracknummern
school	Lernwortschatz (produktiv)
°spy	Situativer Wortschatz (nicht produktiv)
Box "when", Voc, S. 197	Verweis auf Wortschatzbox im *Vocabulary*
+(to) groan	Hinweis auf zusätzlichen Wortschatz im *Vocabulary*
were	Grammatische Strukturen
KV 1 · FöFo 1.1 · …	Verweise auf Begleitmedien
['priːjaː, 'priːjə]	Aussprachehinweis
Lernfeld: Die S …	Hinweis auf Lernfelder, die abgedeckt werden
Alternative: …	Didaktische Hinweise, Alternativen oder Zusätze
learned · sat	Lösungen (geschlossene Aufgaben)

www.cornelsen.de

Die Internetadressen und -dateien, die in diesem Lehrwerk angegeben sind, wurden vor Drucklegung geprüft. Der Verlag übernimmt keine Gewähr für die Aktualität und den Inhalt dieser Adressen und Dateien oder solcher, die mit ihnen verlinkt sind.

Dieses Werk berücksichtigt die Regeln der reformierten Rechtschreibung und Zeichensetzung.

1. Auflage, 1. Druck 2014

Alle Drucke dieser Auflage sind inhaltlich unverändert und können im Unterricht nebeneinander verwendet werden.
© 2014 Cornelsen Schulverlag GmbH, Berlin

Das Werk und seine Teile sind urheberrechtlich geschützt. Jede Nutzung in anderen als den gesetzlich zugelassenen Fällen bedarf der vorherigen schriftlichen Einwilligung des Verlages.

Hinweis zu den §§ 46, 52 a UrhG: Weder das Werk noch seine Teile dürfen ohne eine solche Einwilligung eingescannt und in ein Netzwerk eingestellt werden. Dies gilt auch für Intranets von Schulen und sonstigen Bildungseinrichtungen.

Druck: Mohn Media Mohndruck, Gütersloh

ISBN 978-3-06-033071-3 – broschiert

PEFC zertifiziert
Dieses Produkt stammt aus nachhaltig bewirtschafteten Wäldern und kontrollierten Quellen.
www.pefc.de

English G Access 2 enthält folgende Teile:

Units	die sechs Kapitel des Buches
Access story	*Reading for fun* – eine Geschichte in zwei Teilen
(www)	zusätzliche Materalien, die du unter *www.englishg.de/access* finden kannst
Wordbank	Mini-Bildwörterbuch zu verschiedenen Themen
Skills File (SF)	eine Beschreibung wichtiger Lern- und Arbeitstechniken
Grammar File (GF)	eine Zusammenfassung der Grammatik jeder Unit
Vocabulary	das Wörterverzeichnis zum Lernen der neuen Wörter jeder Unit
Dictionary	alphabetisches Wörterverzeichnis zum Nachschlagen (Englisch-Deutsch und Deutsch-Englisch)

In den Units findest du diese Überschriften:

Background file	Informationen über Land und Leute
Everyday English	Englisch in Alltagssituationen
Looking at language	Beispiele sammeln und sprachliche Regeln entdecken
Language help	Hilfe in Form von sprachlichen Regeln
Practice	Aufgaben und Übungen
Reading course	englische Texte besser lesen
The world behind the picture	vom Bild in den Film – Videoclips mit Aufgaben
Text	eine spannende oder lustige Geschichte

Du findest auch diese Symbole:

((☞))	Texte, die du dir anhören kannst: *www.englishg.de/access*
▪▪▫▫▫	Übungssequenz: neue Grammatik intensiv üben und dann anwenden
Early finisher	zusätzliche Aktivitäten und Übungen für Schüler/innen, die früher fertig sind
More help	zusätzliche Hilfen für eine Aufgabe
You choose	eine Aufgabe auswählen
EXTRA	zusätzliche Aktivitäten und Übungen für alle
My Book	schöne und wichtige Arbeiten sammeln
Study skills	Einführung in Lern- und Arbeitstechniken
Your task	Was du gelernt hast, kannst du in der Lernaufgabe am Ende jeder Unit noch mal zeigen und dich auch selbst einschätzen.
🎧 💬 📖 ✎	Hören Sprechen Lesen Schreiben
🇬🇧	Mediation (zwischen zwei Sprachen vermitteln)
👥 👥✓ 👥👥 🧩	Partnerarbeit Partnercheck Gruppenarbeit Kooperative Lernform

Inhalt

	Lerninhalte	**Your task** (Lernaufgabe)	**Texte**
Unit 1 In the holidays	• über die Ferien sprechen • über eine Reise sprechen • telefonieren • neue Nachbarn kennenlernen	Make a poster about a good place for a holiday in Germany. (S. 26) 	**Song** *Song for Weston-super-Mare* (S. 10) **Background file** Boarding schools (S. 21) **Text** *My USA log book* (S. 24)
Unit 2 A school day	• Schulalltag in Großbritannien • Berge und Flüsse Großbritanniens • über Pläne und Vorhaben sprechen • über Musik, Filme und Theateraufführungen sprechen	Write a short article about music for a class magazine. (S. 44)	**Background file** British pop music – old and new (S. 37) **Text** *Disco night* (S. 42)
Unit 3 Out and about	• Stadtpläne lesen • sich in einer Stadt orientieren • einkaufen: Dinge und Mengen benennen • einkaufen: über Preise sprechen	Put together a rally around your town or area for a visitor from Britain. (S. 60) 	**Background file** British money (S. 48) **Song** *Money* (S. 52) **Text** *Master Wu and the magic book* (S. 58)

Access story · *Because of Winn-Dixie*

> Die hier und auf den Folgeseiten aufgeführten Angebote sind nicht obligatorisch abzuarbeiten. Die Auswahl der Übungen und Übungsteile richtet sich nach den Schwerpunkten des schulinternen Curriculums.

Inhalt

Kompetenzen	Sprache	
Methoden Making notes with a crib sheet (S. 13) **MyBook** Make a crib sheet about a day in your summer holidays. (S. 13) **Hör-/Sehverstehen** *A day at the Eden project* (S. 13) *Reading course* Understanding new words (S. 19)	**Wortschatz** *holidays, the weather, getting in touch* **Strukturen** *simple present, simple past, present progressive (Revision); subject/object questions; present progressive with future meaning* *Everyday English* Where's my mobile? (S. 23)	**8** Part A 10 Part B 14 Part C 20
🎧 **Schwerpunkt Listening** **Methoden** A vocabulary picture poster (S. 40) **MyBook** Writing a conversation. (S. 43) **Hör-/Sehverstehen** *Plymkids* (S.41) *Reading course* Reading aloud (S. 35)	**Wortschatz** *school, stage and film, the natural world* **Strukturen** *going to-future; comparison of adjectives; possessive pronouns* *Everyday English* At the cinema (S. 41)	**28** Part A 30 Part B 32 Part C 36
💬 **Schwerpunkt Speaking** **Methoden** Study posters (S. 56) **Hör-/Sehverstehen** *A German tourist in Plymouth* (S. 57) **MyBook** Tell a story with pictures or text (S. 60) *Reading course* Scanning a text (S. 53)	**Wortschatz** *public buildings; giving directions; shopping, buying food; describing things/ people/actions* **Strukturen** *relative clauses; adverbs of manner* *Everyday English* The way to Peter's house (S. 57)	**46** Part A 48 Part B 54
		62

Lucy

Inhalt

	Lerninhalte	**Your task** (Lernaufgabe)	**Texte**
Unit 4 On Dartmoor 	• englische Landschaft kennenlernen • Bilder und Fotos beschreiben • Über Erlebnisse sprechen	Write a poem about a place in the countryside. (S. 82) Maya	**Background file** Dartmoor ponies (S. 68) **Text** *A tulip garden* (S. 80)
Unit 5 Celebrate! 	• Über Feiertage und Feste sprechen • Bräuche in Großbritannien • Voraussagen machen • Zungenbrecher	Plan a class party with a British theme. (S. 100)	**Background file** Britain's favourite dishes (S. 96) **Text** *A day to celebrate* (S. 98)
Unit 6 A class trip 	• Kelten und Römer in Großbritannien • eine Geschichte über King Arthur • Pläne für die Ferien machen • *wh*-Fragen beantworten	Write an article for a class magazine about a school trip that you went on. (S.116)	**Background file** The Roman Baths at Aquae Sulis (S.111) **Text** Theaterstück: *The sword in the stone* (S. 114)

Access story · *Because of Winn-Dixie*

122 More help	140 Wordbank	178 Vocabulary
134 Early finisher	145 Skills File	208 Dictionary English – German
136 Partner pages	156 Grammar File	229 Dictionary German – English

6

Inhalt

Kompetenzen	Sprache	
📖 **Schwerpunkt Reading** **Hör-/Sehverstehen** *Letterboxing* (S. 75) **MyBook** Write a dialogue for a film scene. (S. 75) **Methoden** Describing a picture (S. 79) *Reading course* Marking up a text (S. 74)	**Wortschatz** *the countryside* **Strukturen** *present perfect; some/any and their compounds; verb + adjective after state verbs* *Everyday English* At the information centre (S. 75)	**66** Part A 68 Part B 72 Part C 76
🇬🇧 **Schwerpunkt Mediation** **Methoden** Presenting a photo Peer feedback (S. 93) **Hör-/Sehverstehen** *The sea show* (S. 97) **MyBook** Write about Lord Mayor's Day. (S. 99) *Reading course* Taking notes (S. 89)	**Wortschatz** *celebrations, food, clothes* **Strukturen** *will-future; question tags; conditional sentences I* *Everyday English* Can I go to the concert, please ? (S. 113)	**84** Part A 86 Part B 90 Part C 94
✏️ **Schwerpunkt Writing** **MyBook** Write a report about a class trip. (S. 111) **Hör-/Sehverstehen** *The Romans in Britain* (S. 113) *Reading course* Using skills that you have learned (S. 109)	**Wortschatz** *parts of the body, feeling ill* **Strukturen** *past progressive*: conditional sentences II (Extra); contact clauses (Extra) *Everyday English* At a takeaway (S. 113)	**102** Part A 104 Part B 110 118

Justin

247 List of names	250 True and false friends	255 Classroom English
248 Irregular verbs	252 Early finisher – answers	256 Arbeitsanweisungen
249 English sounds	253 Quellenverzeichnis	

1 Unit

In the holidays

Leistungsmessung Unit 1

Lernfeld S. 8–9: Die S können **Ereignisse und Aktivitäten** in den Sommerferien beschreiben und sich darüber mit jemandem unterhalten. Dazu benutzen sie das **simple past**.

A

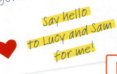

So many different places!

B — Patara Beach, Turkey

Hi Maya!
This is the best beach in the world!!! The water is so warm and it's always sunny. There are mountains too and lots of beautiful birds here. I met a German girl at our hotel. Her name is Antonia, she speaks English and she's really nice. Yesterday we went sailing alone ... without Tim! Maybe next year we can come here together!

Say hello to Lucy and Sam for me!

Hi Sam! I'm in Plymouth, MASSACHUSETTS in the USA!!! This is a picture of Plymouth Rock. It's the place where British people arrived in America in 1620. Plymouth is the first stop on our camping trip. More later ...

D

Hi Spot,
°Greetings from Seal World fun Park!

+wind

+forest, rain (n), rain (v)

E

Hi Abby! I'm on Dartmoor with Lucy's grandparents. It's cold and windy, so we're making scones with Lucy's grandma.

Next week we want to visit the Eden Project! I can't wait to see the rainforest °dome. Here's a photo of the plants and trees.
See you soon!

8

KV 1

Unit 1

Lernfeld S.8–9: Die S können Postkarten und SMS verstehen, die wesentlichen Informationen in einer Tabelle festhalten und sich darüber mit jemandem austauschen.

Patara Beach, Turkey

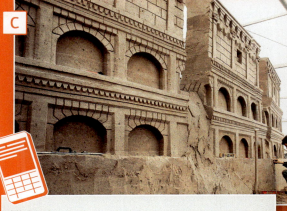

C

Hi Justin,
Guess where I am! London? Rome???
I'm by the sea. These are sand °sculptures!
They're so cool! I went °bodysurfing yesterday.
The waves were big and the weather was warm and sunny. It's cloudy and cold today, so we're in our caravan now. Oh sorry – Dad says I have to stop now!

+cloud

1 Holiday messages

a) Copy the table.
   Read the postcards and text messages.
   Who are they from? Write the letters A – E
   next to the right names in your table.

NAME	MESSAGE	WHERE?	WHAT?
Abby	B	Turkey	Abby: beach, mountains, sunny, met German girl, went sailing, …
Justin	A	Plymouth, Mass.	Justin: camping trip, Plymouth Rock, …
Maya	E	Dartmoor	Maya: visited Lucy's grandparents, cold, windy, Eden Project, …
Sam	C	by the sea	Sam: bodysurfing, big waves, warm and sunny, sand sculptures; …
Silky	D	Seal World Fun Park	

b) Read the holiday messages again.
   Where did the writers go? What did they do?
   Add the information to the table.

c) Compare your table with a partner's.
   Do you have the same information?

2 Your summer holidays

a) Collect words about your summer holidays.
   Use a list, a mind map or a table.
   ➔ Wordbank 1 (p. 140)

b) Make appointments with two other students. At each appointment, talk about a great day in your summer holidays.

KV 1: Appointment partners unterstützt die Durchführung der *Appointment*-Methode.

Your task

At the end of this unit:
Make a poster about a good place for a holiday in Germany.

➔ Workbook 1 (p. 2)

9

Part A

FöFo 1.1 • KV 1 • LAS 1.1, 1.2

Lernfeld S. 10: Die S können einen kurzen Text zum Thema Sommerferien verstehen.

1 Phone calls 1 ⏵ 02

In the last week of the school holidays, Sam **phoned** Justin's home. Mrs Skinner **answered**.

Mrs S: Hello.
5 Sam: Hello, Mrs Skinner. It's Sam here.
Mrs S: Hello, Sam.
Sam: Can I speak to Justin, please?
Mrs S: No, sorry, Sam. He**'s not in**. Do you want to **leave a message**? (+be out)
10 Sam: Er … no, thanks. I can phone his mobile.
Mrs S: OK, Sam. Bye now.
Sam: Bye.

Sam phoned Justin's mobile.

Justin: Hi, Sam.
15 Sam: Hi, Justin.
Justin: Hey, thanks for the cool picture of the sand sculpture. Where did you take it?
Sam: In Weston-super-Mare. We went there on **holiday**.
20 Justin: **What was it like?**

Sam: The weather was really hot **at first**. So we went swimming a lot. But later it was cloudy and cold.
Justin: What did you do then?
25 Sam: We went to the °pier. It's fantastic. I have some great photos of Dad and me on the go-karts. We had a **race** and I won because he crashed - ha!
Justin: I have some great photos too.
30 Sam: Oh, right. You visited your dad in America. When did you get back?
Justin: Two days **ago**.
Sam: What was it like?
Justin Well, it's a really big **country**, and …
35 Sam: Did you see the Empire State **Building**?
Justin: I wasn't in New York, Sam. My dad lives in Boston.
Sam: Oh … So what did you do?
Justin: We went camping and I saw a bear.
40 Hey, do you want to meet? Then I can show you the °logbook of my trip.
Sam: Cool. What about **tomorrow** morning?
45 Justin: All right, see you at my house at ten o'clock. And **bring** your photos **if** you like.

(Box „bringen", Voc, S. 180)

Lernfeld: Die S können einen kurzen Song mit weitgehend bekannten Vokabeln von einer CD verstehen und korrekt mitsingen.

2 The boys' holidays

a) Finish the sentences.
1 Sam told Justin about his holiday in …
2 When it was hot, he …
3 When it was cold, …
4 Justin's holiday was in …
5 He visited …
6 They went …
7 Justin saw …
8 He made a … about his holidays.

1 Weston-super-Mare
2 went swimming a lot
3 he went to the pier
4 America
5 his dad
6 camping
7 a bear
8 logbook

b) 👥 Which do you think is better: a seaside holiday in Britain or camping in the USA? Tell your partner. Give reasons.

More help ➔ p. 122
More help bietet sprachliche Hilfen.

Alternativ Durchführung von b) mit *Appointment*-Methode, unterstützt durch KV 1: **Appointment partners.**

3 Song for Weston-super-Mare

Listen and sing the first verse. 1 ⏵ 03–04
Then sing along with the chorus.
Track 1.04 ist die Instrumentalversion zum Mitsingen.

We have the best pier in the land
°Miles of beach and golden sand
Families come from °far and wide

It's summer, it's summer, it's summer
It's so good.

EXTRA Write another verse for the song.

🌐 See more pictures of seaside towns in Britain. Listen to a traditional seaside song.
(Fakultative Vertiefung online.)

10

Folie 1 • KV 2 A/B

Part A Practice 1

Lernfeld S. 11–12: *Simple past* und *simple past wh-questions* (REVISION).

1 WORDS The weather

a) Match the weather words to the numbers.

> cold · sunny · windy · rainy ·
> warm · cloudy · hot

– Number 1 is "rainy".

b) What can you do when it's rainy/sunny/…?
When it's rainy, I can play computer games / ..
When it's sunny, I can …

EXTRA Copy the table. Add the words from a).

☺ I like … weather. | ☹ I don't like … weather.

👥 Then talk to a partner about your table.

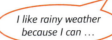

I like rainy weather because I can …   *I don't like rainy weather because ..*

➡ Workbook 2 (p. 3)

2 REVISION Justin went camping (Simple past)

Say what the people did and didn't do in their holidays. You can use words from the box.

Justin went camping. He didn't make scones / go to Turkey / …

> go camping · go sailing · make · play · see · send · take photos · visit · watch · write · …

Justin went camping. He didn't …

Abby went sailing. She didn't …

Sam took photos. He didn't …

Maya and Lucy made scones. They didn't …

➡ GF 1 a/b: The simple past (p. 157)
Abby wrote a letter/postcard. She didn't …

3 EXTRA REVISION Did you go swimming? (Simple past)

a) Write a list of questions like this:

> Did you go swimming in the summer?
> Did you write °postcards?
> Did you …

🧩 Then make a double circle and ask your questions.

Differenzierung: In leistungsschwächeren Klassen überprüfen die S ihre Fragen zunächst im Partnercheck, bevor sie ins Kugellager gehen.

b) Say what you remember about your partners.

Nedim wrote postcards, but Anne didn't write postcards. Emma went …

➡ Workbook 3–8 (pp. 3–5)
➡ GF 1 c: The simple past, Yes/No questions (p. 158)

11

1 Part A Practice

Folie 1 • FöFo 1.2

Lernfeld S. 12: Die S können einfachen Hörtexten über vertraute Themen (hier: kurze Telefonate) konkrete Informationen entnehmen *(listening for details)*.

4 Uncle Amar's questions (Simple past: *wh*-questions)

[ˈæmə, ˈʌmə]

Language help

Simple past:
question word + **did**

Where		you take the photos?
What	did	you do then?
When		you get back?

➡ GF 1 d: The simple past: questions with question words (p. 158)

Maya's uncle phoned. He had lots of questions. Look at Maya's answers. What were the questions?

She never tells me much!

1 What did you do in the holidays?
2 … go there?
3 … get there?
4 … do there?
5 … visit them?
6 … see on the farm?

I went to Dartmoor with Lucy.
Two weeks ago, Uncle.
We went by bus.
We visited Lucy's grandparents.
Because they have a really nice farm.
Animals, Uncle. Lots and lots of animals.

He always asks so many questions.

2 When did you … • 3 How did you … • 4 What did you … •
5 Why did you … • 6 What did you …

➡ Workbook 9–10 (pp. 5–6)

5 On the phone

1 ▶ 05–08

a) Listen to four phone calls. After each call, say who phoned and who answered the phone.
– In the first call, Lucy phoned and … answered the phone.   1 Lucy / Mrs Bennett • 2 Lucy / Mrs Bennett •
3 Sam / Lucy's voicemail • 4 Lucy / Sam

b) Match the English phrases to the German ideas. Then listen again. Who uses phrases 3–8?

1 Hello.
2 It's Lucy here.
3 Can I speak to Sam, please?   Lucy
4 Can you phone back later, please?   Mrs Bennett
5 Hold on a minute.   Mrs Bennett
6 Do you want to leave a message?   Mrs Bennett
7 Can he phone me back?   Lucy
8 I got your message.   Lucy

1g • 2f • 3a • 4c •
5d • 6h • 7b • 8e

a fragen, ob man jemanden sprechen kann
b fragen, ob jemand zurückrufen kann
c jemanden bitten, später zurückzurufen
d jemanden bitten, dranzubleiben
e sagen, dass man die Nachricht erhalten hat
f sagen, wer dran ist
g sich am Telefon melden
h fragen, ob jemand eine Nachricht hinterlassen will

c) 👥 Act out a phone call. Partner A: Go to p. 136. Partner B: Go to p. 138.

➡ Workbook 11 (p. 6)

6 Lucy and Maya's summer 🎧

1 ▶ 09

Listen to Lucy's phone call with Sam. Are these statements right or wrong?

1 In the holidays Lucy and Maya …
   a travelled to another country.   wrong
   b were in Plymouth all the time.   wrong
   c went on day trips in the summer.   right
   d went to Dartmoor together.   right
   e went to the Eden Project.   right
   f went to Disneyland.   wrong

2 The Eden Project is a place …
   a near Plymouth.   right
   b with lots of animals.   wrong
   c with lots of plants.   right

3 At the Eden Project …
   a you can see plants from hot countries.   right
   b all the plants are in domes.   wrong
   c there is no place to have lunch.   wrong

➡ Workbook 12 (p. 6)

FöFo 1.3 | **Part A Practice 1**

Lernfeld S. 13: Die S können zu einem Text und einer eigenen Geschichte Notizen in Form eines **Spickzettels** *(crib sheet)* anfertigen und dabei **Piktogramme, Schlüsselwörter** und **-phrasen** verwenden. Sie sprechen mit Hilfe eines Spickzettels über einen Tag in den Ferien.

7 Study skills: Making notes with a crib sheet

Before you write or talk about a topic, it helps to make notes. One way to do this is with a crib sheet.

a) When you make notes, you can use words.
You can also use pictures or symbols.
What words do these symbols stand for?

b) Look at two crib sheets about Abby's holiday. Find out:
what country she visited, what big city she stayed in, and what she saw there.

Turkey • Istanbul • the beach/hotel/ Patara Beach/the sea/mountains/…

A

B

c) Go to p. 139. Read the text about Abby's holiday.
Then look at the crib sheets again. Is it easy or difficult to understand them?

On crib sheet A, I can see what the weather is like.

Why are there so many suns on crib sheet B?

> **TIP**
> Every crib sheet is different.
> When you make a crib sheet, it's important that you understand all the words, pictures and symbols.

d) Make a crib sheet about a day in your holidays (the first/last day? a funny/hot/… day?).
You can put your crib sheet in your MyBook.
➜ Wordbank 1 (p. 140)

e) Make a double circle. Take turns and tell your partner about the day in your holidays. Use your crib sheet to help you to remember everything you want to say.

On the last day in my summer holidays, I …

Study skills

Making notes with a crib sheet

Ein Spickzettel hilft mir, wenn ich …
Wenn ich einen Spickzettel mache, kann ich:
- Bilder benutzen
- …

Vergleiche deine Ideen mit dem Abschnitt im Skills File.

➜ SF 5: Making notes with a crib sheet (p. 147)

➜ Workbook 13 (p. 7)

Part B

FöFo 1.4 • LAS 1.3

Lernfeld S. 14–15: Die S können kurze Texte verstehen und sich über vertraute Themen aus ihrem Alltag unterhalten.

1 A new neighbour

It was Saturday morning, the last weekend of the summer holidays. Lucy found a note in the living room. She read it and then called her mum's mobile.

*Lucy,
Tea with the Coopers @ 4 pm!
Don't forget!
Love, Mum*

Mum: Hi, Lucy. Did you read my note?
Lucy: Yes, Mum, but I can't be at home at 4. Sam and I want to go to the Hoe together.
Mum: But I told you last week.
Lucy: Who did you tell? Not me! Maybe you told Holly. You always tell her about your plans.
Mum: What?
Lucy: It's true, Mum! For example: who told me about Grandpa's surprise birthday party? Nobody!
Mum: That was last year, Lucy.
Lucy: Yes, but still …
Mum: Lucy, please be at home this afternoon. You really have to meet the Coopers.
Lucy: The Coopers? Who are the Coopers?
Mum: The Coopers are our new neighbours.
Lucy: New neighbours?
Mum: Yes, they moved into number 37 two weeks ago.
Lucy: So?
Mum: And their son (+daughter) is your age. Mrs Cooper says he already knows you.
Lucy: Who knows me?
Mum: Leo Cooper, her son.
Lucy: Oh, what school does he go to?
Mum: He goes to Plymstock, Lucy.
Lucy: He isn't in any of my classes …
Mum: Oh Lucy, I'm sure you know him. Maybe you and Leo can walk to school together.
Lucy: Yes, OK, but there's no school today and I want to meet Sam!
Mum: Well, you can invite Sam to tea too if you like. Maybe Sam already knows Leo.
Lucy: What? I can't hear you, Mum. Who does Sam know? *Box „Who …?", Voc, S. 181*
Mum: Leo! You all go to the same school!
Sorry, Lucy, I have to stop now. See you later!
Lucy: What? Mum? Mum! … That really isn't fair! Nobody ever asks me what *I* want to do.

Lucy

2 That's not fair!

a) How does Lucy feel after the phone call? Give reasons for your answer.

happy   angry   excited

Lucy feels angry. She wants to meet Sam but her mum says she has to meet the new neighbours.

EXTRA Choose one part of the dialogue: lines 12–20 or lines 35–49.
Read it aloud with feeling.

b) Can you always do what you want in your free time? Or do your parents say what you have to do?

I often want to meet my friends, but my mum sometimes says I have to stay at home.

More help *p. 122*   **More help** stellt weitere Redemittel zur Verfügung.

Part B 1

3 At Lucy's house

Look at the photo. You see Leo, Sam and Lucy.
What do you know about Leo?

"I'm still angry with Mum," said Lucy.
"Why?" asked Sam.
"She always makes plans for *my* weekend," said Lucy.
5 "My mum doesn't do that very often."
"Lucky you," said Lucy. +be lucky
"But when I get home from school, Mum usually goes shopping and I have to look after Lily," said Sam.
10 "That's not too bad."
"And I'm not allowed to watch TV in the afternoon," said Sam.
"Really? Oh look, it's already quarter to four, Sam," said Lucy. "Let's have a
15 game of table tennis before those people come for tea."
"Yeah sure, I like ping-pong."
They went outside and started to play.
Lucy hit the ball to Sam, but he missed it and the
20 ball rolled out into the street.
"I have it! I have it!" somebody shouted. Sam and Lucy looked out of the garden. A boy was there. He held up the ball like a prize.
"Here you are," he said.
25 "You're Leo, right?" asked Lucy. "My name is Lucy and this is Sam."
"Hi, Sam. Hi, Lucy," he said.

"My mum says you go to Plymstock School too." said Lucy.
30 "Right!" Leo answered. "I'm in Year 8 this year."
"Cool, we're in Year 8 too," said Sam.
"Hey! Who wants to play ping-ping?" asked Leo suddenly.
"Ping-ping? Oh, table tennis!" said Lucy.
35 "I'd like to play," said Sam.
"Yeah, me too. OK, let's all play. Leo and me against you, Sam, OK?" asked Lucy.
"Sure, why not? I'm good at ping-ping!" said Sam.

4 Tell the story

Read these sentences about the text.
Put them in the right order. 5 · 2 · 4 · 6 · 7 · 1 · 3

1 Lucy, Sam and Leo talked about Plymstock School.
2 Lucy asked Sam to play table tennis with her.
3 Leo asked Lucy and Sam to play table tennis.
4 The ball rolled out of the garden.
5 Lucy and Sam talked about their mums.
6 Leo gave the ball to Sam and Lucy.
7 Leo said hello to Sam and Lucy.

5 EXTRA Neighbours

How often do you meet your neighbours? What do you do together? Tell your group.

I often see my neighbours after school. We play football together.

We never meet our neighbours. They're always out. What about you?

Our neighbours sometimes …

15

1 Part B Practice

Lernfeld S. 16: *Simple present: statements* (REVISION).

1 REVISION That's right, that's wrong (Simple present: statements)

a) Write eight sentences about people in your English book – some right, some wrong.

> 1 Sam goes to Coombe Dean School.
> 2 Abby and Maya like sailing.
> 3 Silky eats …
> 4 …

b) Read your sentences aloud.
Your partner says if they are right or wrong.
1 That's wrong. Sam doesn't go to Coombe Dean School. He goes to Plymstock School.
2 That's right. They like sailing.
3 …

He, she, it – das … muss mit!

➡ GF 2 a–c: The simple present (pp. 158–159); ➡ Workbook 14 (p. 7)

2 REVISION Mr Skinner's questions (Simple present: questions)

Mr Skinner has lots of questions for his son. Look at Justin's answers. Then finish the questions.

1 When does school finish, Justin? — At three o'clock in the afternoon.
2 Do you go home then? — Yes, I do – usually. But not on Thursdays!
3 So … do on Thursdays? — I go to the Film Making Club. You know that, Dad.
4 … go to other clubs too? — No, I don't. Just to Film Making.
5 What about your friends? … go to the Film Making Club with you? — No, they don't. Lucy goes to the Samba Club. And Sam plays basketball.
6 So … meet your friends? — In my free time. And I see them every day at school, of course.

3 So what do you do on Thursdays?
4 Do you go to other clubs too?
5 Do they go to the Film Making Club with you?
6 So when do you meet your friends?

➡ Workbook 15 (p. 8)
➡ GF 2 d–e: The simple present, questions (pp. 159–160)

3 REVISION Who plays basketball? (Simple present: questions)

How much can your partners remember? Ask questions with *Who …?*

Who plays basketball?
That's Sam! Who has a big sister?
That's …

eat crabs
play basketball
make films
live in a flat
go sailing
live in Plymstock library
come from London
do kung fu
live in Wembury
have a big sister
go to a maths and ICT school
skype with his father
visit her grandparents on a farm

➡ Workbook 16 (p. 8)

Differenzierung: In leistungsschwächeren Lerngruppen erarbeiten die S zunächst ihre Fragen und Antworten in EA und stellen und beantworten die Fragen dann im Plenum oder in einer *Milling around activity*.

Folie 2

Part B Practice 1

Lernfeld S. 17: *Subject/object questions* (*simple present* und *simple past*).

> **Language help**
>
> Look at these questions and answers.
> 1 Q: Who skypes with his father?
>   A: Justin.
> 2 Q: Who invited the Coopers to tea?
>   A: Mrs Pascoe.
>
> 3 Q: Who does Justin skype with?
>   A: His father.
> 4 Q: Who did Mrs Pascoe invite to tea?
>   A: The Coopers.
>
> In 1 and 2, who **means** wer in German.
> It's the **subject** of the question.
> When who is the subject, questions
> don't need ~~do/does/did~~.
>
> In 3 and 4, who means wem or wen in
> German. It's the **object** of the question.
> When who is the object, questions
> need do/does/did.
>
> ➡ GF 3: Subject and object questions (pp. 160–161)

Who did Morph see? Lots of children at school. Who saw Morph? Nobody! Hee hee!

4 Lucy, Sam and Leo (Subject/Object questions)

Ask and answer questions. Take turns.
Du willst wissen, …
1 wer am Samstag auf den Hoe gehen will.
   A: Who wants to go to the Hoe on Saturday?
   B: Lucy and Sam.
2 wen Lucy am Samstagmorgen angerufen hat.
   B: Who did …? – A: …
3 wer vor zwei Wochen in Nr. 37 gezogen ist.
   A: Who …? – B: …

4 auf wen Sam am Nachmittag aufpasst.
   B: Who … after in the afternoon? – A: …
5 wen Sam und Lucy vor Lucys Haus getroffen haben.
   A: Who …? – B: …
6 mit wem Leo Tischtennis gespielt hat.
   B: Who … with? – A: …

2 Who did Lucy phone on Saturday morning? – Sam. • 3 Who moved into number 37 two weeks ago? – The Coopers. • 4 Who does Sam look after in the afternoon? – His sister Lily. • 5 Who did Sam and Lucy meet in front of Lucy's house? – Leo. • 6 Who did Leo play table tennis with? – Sam and Lucy.

More help ➡ p. 122   **Early finisher** ➡ p. 134
➡ **Workbook** 17, 18 (p. 9)

More help: Die S ergänzen nur die korrekten Verbformen.
Early finisher: Die S korrigieren einige fehlerhafte Sätze über die *Plymouth kids* und entwickeln eigene.

5 EXTRA A quiz

a) Think of six questions about the story so far in your new English book. Write your questions on a card. Write the answers on the back of the card.

Es bietet sich an, für jeden S eine große Karteikarte bereitzuhalten.

Jan and Ela's QUIZ – Questions
1 Where did Justin go in the holidays?
2 What can you do in Weston-super-Mare?
3 Who did the Coopers visit on Saturday?
4 Who sent a postcard to …?
5 When …?
6 …?

Jan and Ela's QUIZ – Answers
1 To the USA.
2 You can make sand sculptures or you can …
3 …
4 …
5 …
6 …

You can ask questions about me too.

b) Swap quizzes with another pair. Answer the questions and check your answers on the back of the card.

17

1 Part B Practice

FöFo 1.5, 1.6 • KV 3

Lernfeld S. 18: Die S können sich über vertraute Themen aus ihrem Alltag unterhalten.

6 WORDS Getting in touch +(to) stay in touch

make: phone call
read: blog • email • letter • postcard • text (message)
send: email • letter • postcard • text (message)
use: email • mobile • Skype • social networking site
write: blog • email • letter • postcard • text (message)

a) Copy the table. Add more nouns from the box.

make	read	send	use	write
phone call	blog	...	...	...
...	...			

blog • email • letter • mobile • phone • phone call • postcard • Skype • social networking site • text (message) • ...

b) How do you get in touch with your friends and family? How do they get in touch with you? Write two sentences for each heading. You can use your table from a).

my best friend
I send text messages to my best friend all the time.
She often phones me.

my other friends
I text my other friends too.
They ...

my parents/brothers/sisters
I ... my mum or dad.
They ...

my aunts/uncles/cousins/grandparents
...

c) What's your favourite? The phone, social networking, your mobile, ...? Tell your group why.

I love my mobile. I send lots of text messages because they're so easy to write.

I write in my blog every day. Then all my friends can read about me online.

I use Skype a lot because it's free and I can talk to my cousins in Hamburg.

→ Workbook 19 (p. 10)

7 School rules

Lernfeld: Die S können Fragen zu einem deutschen Sachtext auf Englisch beantworten oder diskutieren.

A British student at a German school wants to know the rules for mobile phones. Read the school rules. Then answer the student's questions.

Umgang mit Handys und MP3-Playern

- Die Benutzung persönlicher elektronischer Medien und Kommunikationsmedien (Handys, MP3-Player, Digitalkameras, etc.) ist im Schulgebäude und auf dem Schulgelände untersagt. Handys bleiben während der gesamten Schulzeit ausgeschaltet, jegliches Handyzubehör (auch Kabel und Kopfhörer) bleibt in der Schultasche.
- Sollte das Handy zur Kontaktaufnahme mit den Eltern benötigt werden, so darf dies nur nach Rücksprache mit einem Lehrer erfolgen.
- Schülerinnen und Schüler, die gegen die Bestimmungen der Schulordnung verstoßen, müssen ihr Handy abgeben.
Am Ende des Schultages können sie dieses Gerät im Sekretariat wieder abholen.

1. Can I bring my mobile to school?
2. And am I allowed to use it at school?
3. Sometimes I have to phone my host family. Is that OK?
4. I can check my text messages at break, right?
5. My phone has an MP3 player too. Can I use that?
6. And the camera in my phone?
7. So what if I use my mobile at school?
8. When can I get it back?

More help → p. 123   **More help:** Die S vervollständigen vorgegebene Satzanfänge.

→ SF 12: Mediation (Revision) (p. 151)

→ Workbook 20 (p. 10)

1 Yes, you can bring your mobile to school. • 2 No, you aren't allowed to use it at school. • 3 It's OK, but you must ask a teacher first. • 4 No, you can't check text messages at break. • 5 No, you can't use that. • 6 No, you can't use the camera. • 7 If you use your mobile at school, you must give it to your teacher. • 8 You can get it back at the end of a school day.

Reading course

FöFo 1.7

Lernfeld S. 19: Die S können sich beim Lesen eines Textes **unbekannte Wörter selbst erschließen**.

Understanding new words

a) When you're reading, don't stop at every new word and look it up. You can often understand new words without a dictionary. Try it – read the story below. Are there any words you really can't understand? Write them down in a list.

A *pony* came to tea

Our holiday *cottage* was a dream, a *lovely* little house with a beautiful *view*. The children loved it. We arrived at our holiday home on Dartmoor one afternoon in August – me and my two children, Robbie, 10, and Amber, 13. It was sunny and when we *entered* the cottage for the first time, it was very hot. So we opened all the windows, the *front door* and the *back door*. We *unpacked* our things, put some cakes and *flowers* on the kitchen table and then went and sat outside on the *grass*.

I just looked at the view and felt the wind on my face. Robbie looked for animals on the *moor* through his *binoculars*, and Amber took some photos with her mobile and sent them to her best friend.

After a *while*, I got up to go and make some tea. I walked *towards* the cottage and then stopped because I could hear something.

"I think there's someone in the house," I said. Robbie and Amber got up and then we all walked to the front door together and looked inside. "Wow!" said Robbie. "It's a Dartmoor pony. Isn't it beautiful?"

"Well, yes, but it's eating our cakes."

Amber took a photo and then she shouted at the pony: "Shoo! Get out, go on, get out of here!" Amber's voice *scared* the pony. It suddenly turned around and *knocked over* the kitchen table. The cakes and flowers fell to the floor.

Then it walked through the living room and left black *marks* on the white *carpet*. Before it went out of the back door, it knocked over the sofa in the *lounge*, turned

around and looked at us. Then it ran away *across* the moor.

After the pony came to tea our dream cottage was a bad dream, a real *nightmare*.

b) All the coloured words in the story are new. Are any of them in your list? Here's how you can understand them:

Pink words Can you guess the **meaning** from the **context**?
The cottage was a dream, so lovely **must** *mean something like* nice *or* beautiful.

Green words Can you get the meaning from the pictures? *Robbie is looking through his* binoculars *in the picture, so* binoculars *means …*

Red words Are there other words with the same meaning?
The first two sentences show that cottage *means the same as* little house.

Blue words Do you know parts of the word?
You already know scary, *so it's easy to guess what* scared *means.*

Orange words Do you know **similar** words in German?
Pony is the same in English and German.

Purple words Do you know a similar word in another language, like French or Latin?
Enter is similar to entrer *(French),* intrare *(Latin), so maybe it means the same in English too.*

➡ SF 6: Understanding new words (Revision) (p. 148)
➡ True and false friends (pp. 250–251)
➡ Workbook 21 (p. 11)

Part C

Lernfeld S. 20–21: Die S können einen kurzen Text verstehen und sich über vertraute Themen aus ihrem Alltag unterhalten.

1 🔊 Abby's news

"Skip! What are you doing?" shouted Abby.
"He's barking at something under that rock," said Maya. "A crab, I think."
"Oh, he always does that," said Abby. She pulled
5 her dog away. The two girls walked on in the warm sun.
"Phew," said Maya. "It's so hot. Just like the Eden Project."
"Oh, yes, you went there with Lucy last weekend.
10 What was it like?" Abby asked.
"Well, like I said: it was really hot in those big domes."
"Yes, but I mean what was the Eden Project like," said Abby.
15 "Er … well," said Maya. "The rainforest dome was fantastic, and the other domes looked interesting too. But we didn't see them all."
"Why not?" Abby asked.
"Well, we went with Lucy's grandparents, and
20 they wanted to see all the gardens."
"Gardens?"
"Yes, I was so bored. But Lucy was happy. She loves gardens."
"Me too," said Abby.
25 "Well," Maya smiled, "Lucy is joining Plymstock's Gardening Club next term. You can join too."
Suddenly Abby looked worried.

"What's the matter?" Maya asked.
30 "Er – I have to tell you something, Maya," her friend said. Skip came back to the girls, and Abby sat down and held him.
"What is it, Abby?" Maya asked again.
"Well, it's about school, about Plymstock."
35 "What about it?"
"Er … I'm not going back to Plymstock School. I'm going to a new school next week. A boarding school. Mum went there when she was a girl."
Maya looked at her friend. She was so shocked,
40 she didn't say a word. Abby just looked at Skip.
"It's a great school for outdoor activities," she went on, "you know, climbing, sailing, … I'm really looking forward to that. But …"
"But what about me? What about your friends at
45 Plymstock?" Maya said.
"We can still be friends," Abby said. "We can text every day and write cards and send emails and photos. And I'm coming home in the next holidays. Maybe you can visit me at school one
50 weekend. It's not far away. Maya! Say we can still be friends. Please!"
But Maya couldn't say a word. She just looked at Abby. She could feel the tears in her eyes.

20

FöFo 1.5   **Part C**

Lernfeld S. 21: Die S können sich **unbekannte Wörter selbst erschließen**.

2 New words

Can you understand these new words?

> bored *(l.22)* · boarding school *(l.37)* ·
> shocked *(l.39)* · outdoor activities *(l.41)* ·
> I'm looking forward to *(l.43)* · tears *(l.53)*

3 Abby and Maya

Put the sentences in the right order.   2 · 4 · 1 · 3
1. Abby told Maya her news about school.
2. Abby and Maya went to the beach with Skip.
3. Maya was very unhappy about Abby's news.
4. The two girls talked about the Eden Project.

4 How did they feel?

> angry · bored · excited · happy · lonely · sad · shocked · unhappy · worried

a) Say how they felt. Use a word from the box.
1. Skip: when he found a crab.
   Skip felt … when he found a crab.
2. Maya: in the gardens at the Eden Project.
3. Abby: when Maya talked about the Gardening Club at Plymstock School.
4. Maya: when she heard Abby's news.

1 Skip felt excited … · 2 Maya felt bored … · 3 Abby felt worried … · 4 Maya felt shocked/sad/unhappy …

b) Compare your answers.

EXTRA What about you? Choose an adjective from the box and say when you felt that way.
– I felt bored/excited/sad/shocked/… when …

Das Extra kann auch als **Early finisher**-Aufgabe dienen, in der die schnellen S weitere Beispielsätze formulieren.

EXTRA Background file

Boarding schools

°Probably just like you, °most children in Britain go to school °during the day but live at home with their families. In Britain, °however, there are also °about 70,000 students at boarding schools. They live at their school during the school year and only go home in the holidays.
British parents sometimes send their children to boarding schools because they also went there when they were young. But more and more students at boarding schools come from other countries, °including Germany.
Most boarding schools are °private schools and you have to °pay to go there. Some of them can be very expensive, °especially really °famous schools like *Eton College*.
There are many boarding schools in English °literature too. A good example is *Hogwarts* in the *Harry Potter* stories.

Would you like to go to a boarding school? What about a boarding school in Britain? Talk about your reasons in your group. Then tell the class.

Eton College

Eton College boys

Lernfeld: Die S können einen englischen Text zum Thema Internate verstehen und über das Thema in der Gruppe diskutieren. Sie können über die Ergebnisse der Diskussion sprechen.

➔ Workbook *22 (p. 11)*

1 Part C Practice

Folie 3

Lernfeld S. 22: *Present progressive statements* (REVISION) und *present progressive with future meaning*.

1 REVISION This Saturday is different (Present progressive statements)

Read what everyone usually does on Saturdays.
Then look at the pictures.
Say what's different this Saturday.

> Maya usually gets up early, but this Saturday she's staying in bed.

1. Maya usually gets up early.
2. Abby usually has breakfast with her family.
3. Leo sometimes goes swimming.
4. Justin usually skypes with his father.
5. Sam often goes to kung fu.
6. Mr Bennett usually works in the garden.
7. Lucy often phones her grandma.
8. Mrs Pascoe usually does yoga.

➡ GF 4 a: Simple present and present progressive (p. 161); **More help** ➡ p. 123; ➡ Workbook 23 (p. 12)

..., but this Saturday ...
1 ... she's staying in bed. • 2 ... she's having breakfast alone. • 3 ... he's riding a bike. • 4 ... he's writing an email. •
5 ... he's playing basketball. • 6 ... he's making a salad. • 7 ... she's writing a letter. • 8 ... she's playing tennis.

More help: Die Verben sind in Klammern vorgegeben.

2 Abby's diary (Present progressive with future meaning)

> **Language help**
>
> You can also use the present progressive when you talk about appointments.
> We sometimes call this the *diary future*.
> What are you doing tomorrow?
> – I'm meeting my friends in the park.

a) Look at Abby's diary for next week.
   Say what she is and isn't doing.
   – On Monday Abby is meeting Lucy.
   – She isn't visiting her grandparents.
   – On Tuesday she's ...

b) Write your diary for next week.
   👥 Then talk to your partner like this:
   – What are you doing on Monday?
   – On Monday? I'm going to the cinema.

➡ GF 4 b: The present progressive with future meaning (pp. 161–162)
➡ Workbook 24 (p. 12)

KV 4 | ▶ The world behind the picture | **1**

1 A day at the Eden Project

a) Look at the picture. What do you think you can do at the Eden Project?

b) Watch the film.

c) 👥 Look at pictures A–D and answer the questions about each picture.

What can you see in the picture?
What part of the Eden Project does it show?
Is it inside or outside? Is it very hot, warm or cold?

Länge: 7:21

A B C D

d) 👥 Watch the film again.
Make notes about your favourite part.
Then talk to your partner about it.

c) A This is the ticket office. It's inside and warm. • B There are some trees. This could be the Rainforest Dome. It's inside and very hot. • C You can see a banana plant. It's also inside, in the Rainforest Dome, so it's very hot too. • D This must be the Outdoor Gardens. It's outside and colder than inside.

2 EVERYDAY ENGLISH
Where's my mobile?

a) Watch scene 1.
Where are these things at the beginning of the scene? Where are they at the end?
1 Jack's sandwich   *in the bag / in the jacket*
2 Jack's mobile phone   *in his jacket / in the litter bin*
3 Jack's chocolate   *in his jacket / in the litter bin*
                                    pocket

bag   jacket   litter bin

b) Watch the rest of the film. How does Jack feel at the end?
Jack feels nervous when he phones the Eden Project. At the end he's happy because they find his mobile phone.

Länge: 7:44   Jack

c) 👥 Write a short dialogue for 1, 2 or 3.
Use some of the phrases in the box.
1 The woman at the Eden Project calls Jack back and says that they have his mobile phone.
2 Jack calls Ruby back and tells her the good news. Ruby isn't home, so Jack leaves a message.
3 Jack calls Oliver back and tells him the good news. His mum answers the phone. Oliver is at home.

> Hello. • It's <name> here. •
> Can I speak to <name>, please? •
> How can I help you? • Just a minute, please. •
> Can I leave a message? • Is <name> there?

d) 👥 Act out your dialogue.

1 Text

Lernfeld S. 24–25: Die S können einen Lesetext verstehen und dabei **unbekannte Wörter selbst erschließen**.

🔊 My USA logbook

1 ▶ 14 My first day in Boston. Dad's **apartment** is great! It has a big **screen** in the living room, so Dad can watch films there. In the evening he showed me his first film. He was 15 when he made it! It was about
5 his dog, Sir Charles, and was really funny. After the film, Dad made hamburgers and **fries** for dinner. I helped him to **wash the dishes**.

1 ▶ 15 Saturday, 4th August
There is a Plymouth in the US too! Today we went to
10 Plymouth, Massachusetts, **to** see a big grey rock – Plymouth Rock. It's at the place where British people arrived in America in 1620. But Dad said that's just a story. Their ship **landed** in a different place. But lots of people come to the rock. (+land (n))
15 I bought a postcard of it for Mum.

Dad and me

1 ▶ 16 Sunday, 5th August
We're on the way to Baxter State Park in Maine. We have our camping kit in the car. It's just me and Dad on a road trip in the USA! We're listening to Dad's
20 CDs. He likes old bands like the Rolling Stones, U2, Queen and Talking Heads. **Right now** we're listening to Queen and "We are the champions". (Box „right", Voc, S. 183)

1 ▶ 17 Monday, 6th August
This morning we had breakfast at Rosie's °**Diner** –
25 see the postcard. I **ordered** six **pancakes** with °**maple syrup**. They were good, but six were too many for me. Dad ate the last two.

Outside Rosie's Diner

1 ▶ 18 Tuesday, 7th August
We're here! Our **campsite** is right **next to** a small river. No time to write now ... I have to help Dad with
30 the **tent**!

1 ▶ 19 Wednesday, 8th August
I saw a °**moose** today! First, Dad and I walked to a lake near the campsite. It was very hot, so we went
35 swimming. When I got out of the water, I saw the moose. It was in the water too. I didn't have my video camera with me, so I used Dad's mobile phone and took this photo. Dad was in the water and didn't see the moose right behind him! He laughed when I
40 showed him the photo!

Moose in the water!

1 ▶ 20 Thursday, 9th August
Today we climbed Mount Katahdin. It was very **rocky** and really high. But Dad and I got to the top! And when we looked down, we could see all of the park,
45 with its lakes and rivers and the **shadows** of clouds. I love mountains.

Folie 4 • VAS 1.1, 1.2   Text **1**

Mount Katahdin [ˌmaʊnt kəˈtɑːdɪn]

Dad and I roasted marshmallows over the open fire.
They were big and soft and really good.
Later Dad played a song on his harmonica. I looked
50 up at the night sky.

21 Friday, 10th August
Yesterday I woke up in the middle of the night.
I heard something outside the tent. First I thought it
was Dad, but he was asleep right next to me. I heard
55 the sound again: it was like "crush-crush". I looked
through the door of the tent, but it was so dark that
I saw nothing. I just heard that scary sound: "crush-
crush". I turned on my torch and pointed it outside.
A black bear was on top of the picnic table!
60 Every night before we go to bed, we put all our food
in a bag. We hang up the bag in a tree so wild
animals can't get it. But this bear wanted our food!
He hit the bag again and again. Then Dad woke up.
He saw the bear and turned off my torch. "Quiet!" he
65 said, and we sat in the tent for ten long minutes.
But I had to sneeze … aaah-chooo! The bear came
very near the tent and it was really scary! We heard
the "crush-crush" sound. Then it was suddenly quiet
again. The bear left the campsite. Dad gave me a
70 hug. Phew!

Saturday, 11th August   **22**
Dad and I are ready to go back to Boston. Our
things are already in the car. There are more
mountains to climb, but it's time to go back home.
75 We want to stop at a diner for breakfast. I think I can
eat all six pancakes this time!

Monday, 13th August   **23**
Today Dad worked at home. He helped me to edit a
film. It was so cool! He said I can try with my own film
80 of Plymouth tomorrow. Then we went out for pizza:
one XXL pizza … mmm!

Wednesday, 15th August   **24**
My room looks great! Today we bought a new desk,
lamp and chair for my bedroom. I now also have a
85 place here to work on my films!

Saturday, 18th August   **25**
It's my last night in the USA. I don't want to go back
home! Today, Dad gave me a present: his harmonica.
I can already play one song. It's called "This land is
90 your land".

1 What did Justin do there?

👥 Which activities did Justin do? Where?
Take turns and tell your partner what Justin did.

Activities	Places
went surfing	
saw a moose	at Rosie's Diner
listened to music	in a lake
heard a black bear	of Mount Katahdin
watched films	at the campsite
climbed to the top	at his dad's apartment
had breakfast	in his dad's car
played tennis	

– Justin listened to music in his dad's car.
➔ Workbook 25 (p. 13)

2 New words

What is the German for the words in the box?
How do you know? Think of what you learned in
the Reading course (p.19).

land (l.13) · postcard (l.15) · road trip (l.19) ·
band (l.20) · pancakes (l.25) · rocky (l.42) · fire (l.47)

3 Memories

You choose Do a) or b).   **My Book**

Neigungsdifferenzierung:
Die S wählen zwischen zwei
kreativen Aufgaben: Zeichnen
oder Schreiben.

a) Draw a picture for one of Justin's days.
b) Think back to your summer holidays.
   Write a log entry for two or three days.

1 Unit

Your task

Alle Schritte dieser Lernaufgabe sind für GA ausgelegt, sollten also im Unterricht bearbeitet werden. **Step 5** kann im Rahmen eines *Gallery walk* durchgeführt werden.

The four seasons in Germany

People visit Germany at all times of the year. Put together a poster about a good place for one of the **seasons in Germany** for your partner school in Britain.
Make four groups. Each group gets one season:

spring • summer • autumn • winter

STEP 1
Think of a place for your season.
Pair: Talk about your ideas with a partner and agree on a place.
Share your ideas in your group and agree on a place.

STEP 2
Make notes about your holiday place. You can use a **crib sheet**. Think about:
- **where** the holiday place is and what it is like
- **what** people can do on holiday there
- what the **weather** is like in your group's season
- **why** it's a great place to go to
- other **important** things about your place

STEP 3
Discuss your ideas in your group. Your crib sheet can help you.
Choose the best ideas and **write short texts** for your poster.
Think of good **headings** for your texts.

STEP 4
Find or draw good **illustrations** for your poster. (Maybe you only want one illustration.)
Write **captions** for your illustrations.

STEP 5
Arrange your texts, illustrations and captions on your poster and **hang it up** in class.
Look at the other groups' posters.

Take a winter break in Germany and enjoy Nuremberg's world-famous Christmas Market!

season ['siːzn] Jahreszeit

Unit 1

Das lief nicht gut, ich muss mehr üben.

Das war OK, aber ich könnte besser werden.

Das habe ich gut geschafft.

Diese Seite dient der **Selbsteinschätzung** durch die S und kann individuell zu Hause bearbeitet werden.

Wie gut warst du?

Wie schätzt du dich selber ein? Schreibe *Words*, *Making notes*, *Grammar* und *Putting a page together* in dein Heft und ordne dir für jeden Bereich eine Ampelfarbe zu: rot, gelb oder grün.

Words
Fielen dir die Wörter für Jahreszeiten, Urlaubsaktivitäten, Wetter schnell ein? Oder hattest du bei einem Wortfeld Schwierigkeiten?

Making notes
Welche Rechtschreib- oder Grammatikfehler hat dein/e Partner/in in deinen Texten gefunden?

Grammar
Wie sicher warst du bei den Verbformen in euren Texten für das Poster? Z.B.:
Everybody loves Nuremberg (simple present);
Take a break … (imperative).

Putting a page together
War euer Poster für alle interessant und verständlich? Welche Elemente hat ein gutes Poster? Was könntet ihr besser machen?

Wie kannst du besser werden?

Wenn du dich eher rot oder gelb eingeschätzt hast, helfen dir folgende Tipps beim Wiederholen und Üben.

Words
Die Seiten 8–11 enthalten viele Wörter, die mit Ferien, Urlaub und Wetter zu tun haben.
Wähle ein Thema aus und sammle dazu so viele Wörter, wie du kannst.
➡ *S. 8–11*
➡ *Wordbank 1, S. 140*

Making notes
Vergleiche deine Notizen oder deinen Spickzettel mit anderen aus deiner Gruppe. Haben sie Tipps für dich?

Seite 13 und das Skills File helfen dir auch.
➡ *S. 13*
➡ *Skills File 5: Making notes with a crib sheet, S. 147*

Grammar
Schreibe drei weitere Sätze über deinen Ort.
➡ *S. 16, S. 22*
➡ *Grammar File 2, S. 158*
➡ *Workbook 14, S. 7*

Putting a page together
Sieh dir die Poster der anderen Gruppen an. Findest du dort gute Ideen, die ihr für euer Poster verwenden könntet?

27

2 Unit

A school day

Leistungsmessung Unit 2

Lernfelder S. 28–29: Die S können Bildunterschriften den richtigen Fotos zum Thema Schule **zuordnen**. Sie können kurze Gespräche zum **Thema Schule** verstehen und falsche Sätze verbessern.

1 From morning to evening

Match the captions to photos A–E.

1. Students love the food in the °Galley.
2. Students queue in front of the classroom till the teacher arrives.
3. Ready for school?
4. New clubs for a new school year.
5. At °registration the teacher checks who is at school.

1D · 2B · 3A · 4E · 5C

2 Scenes from a school day 1 ▶ 26–30

Listen to the dialogues for each photo.
Correct the wrong sentences.

A Sam opens the door when the doorbell rings.
B The first lesson is with Mr Willis.
C Miss Nixon is Leo's °personal assistant.
D Sam and Leo have pizza for lunch.
E Justin and Lucy want to sing in this year's musical.

A Wrong. Sam's mother opens the door.
B Wrong. The first lesson is with Miss Bell (but she's late).
C Right.
D Wrong. Sam and Leo have burgers for lunch.
E Right.

Unit 2

Lernfeld S. 29: Die S können kurze Sätze zum Thema **Schule** vervollständigen und ihre eigene Schule mit Plymstock **vergleichen**.

3 At Plymstock

a) Finish the sentences. Use words from the box.

> break · canteen · clubs · lessons · queue · registration · uniform

1 Students have to wear a … *uniform*
2 There are five … every day. *lessons*
3 A teacher calls out students' names at … *registration*
4 The … is called the Galley. *canteen*
5 Students can join lots of … *clubs*

b) Compare your school with Plymstock.

➔ Workbook 1 (p. 14)

Alternative: Die S schreiben ein *Acrostic* über ihre Schule, z.B. mit dem Wort *school* als Ausgangspunkt (oder dem Namen der Schule).

Your task

At the end of this unit:
Write a short article about music for a class magazine.

2 Part A

FöFo 2.1

Lernfeld S. 30–31: Die S können einen kurzen Text zum Thema **Aktivitäten** und **Pläne machen** verstehen und über **zukünftige Pläne** berichten *(going to-future)*.

1 🔊 On the way to school [1 ▶ 31]

Leo trägt im Foto ein Hörgerät *(hearing aid)*. Das wird im Text nicht thematisiert, aber die Vokabel kann bei Bedarf eingeführt werden.

Sam:	Hi, Lucy! Hi, Leo! Sorry, I didn't hear the doorbell.
Lucy:	And you still have your **earphones** in!
Sam:	Well, it's a great song! Here, listen to it.
5 Lucy:	Yes. I like it too.
Leo:	Let me listen!
Lucy:	*We are the champions, my friend!* Hey Sam! Don't pull out the earphones! I'm still listening.
10 Sam:	But Leo wants to hear it too. Here, Leo.
Lucy:	*We are the champions, we are …*
Sam:	Hey, you really like Queen.
Lucy:	Yes, and guess what! I'm **going to** sing a Queen song at the auditions today.
15 Sam:	What auditions?
Lucy:	At the School Show Club. They're going to do a musical this year.
Sam:	A musical?
Lucy:	Yes, *We will rock you*. It's a great show and the music is **by** Queen.
Sam:	And you want to be in it?
Lucy:	Yes, the auditions are after school.
Sam:	Are you **nervous**?
Lucy:	No, I'm not nervous … well, maybe **a bit**.
25	But what about you, Sam? Which club are you going to join?
Sam:	I'm not going to join a new club. I'm going to stay with basketball. And Justin is going to start basketball too.
30 Lucy:	Are you going to play in the school team again this year?
Sam:	Yes, I am … if I'm good enough. Hey, Lucy, look at Leo! He's dancing!
Lucy:	He really likes the song. Hey, Leo! Leo!
35 Leo:	What?
Lucy:	You really can dance! Wow! You **should** come to the auditions with me.
Leo:	*We are the champions, my friend!*

Suddenly, a man calls Leo from the other **side** of 40 the road.

Leo:	Hi John! What are you doing here?
John:	Oh, I'm just looking for **a few** things. And you're on your way to school, eh?
Leo:	Yes, with my friends, Sam and Lucy – I 45 love her.
John:	Hi, nice to meet you. So, Leo, how do you like your new house?
Leo:	It's great. Come and visit us.
John:	Is your mum going to be at home this 50 afternoon?
Leo:	Yes, she is.
John:	OK then, maybe see you later.
Leo:	Bye.

2 Feelings

Listen to the dialogue in 1. Then find lines where somebody feels angry, excited, happy or surprised.

I think Lucy is angry in lines … because …

And Sam is surprised when …

 → p. 124

More help: Ausgewählte Zeilen aus dem Text sind vorgegeben. Jedem Satz sind zwei Gefühle zugeordnet, aus denen die S eines auswählen.

3 Have a go

Lernfeld: Die S sprechen vorbewusst über zukünftige Pläne *(going to-future)*.

a) What are they going to do? Make sentences.

Lucy		sing *at the auditions.*
Sam	**is going to**	stay … *with basketball.*
Leo		dance.
John		visit … *Leo's new house.*

b) 👥 Ask and answer.
   A: What are you going to do after school / this afternoon / this evening?
   B: I'm going to …

Folie 5 • FöFo 2.2 • KV 5 • LAS 2.1

Part A Practice 2

Looking at language

a) Copy the table and finish the sentences.
   The text on p. 30 can help you.

b) Read the sentences in your table.
   Then choose the correct answer.
   In these sentences the kids talk about
   1 the past   2 the present   3 the future.
   In these sentences the kids talk about
   1 problems   2 plans   3 parents.

c) Look at the table. How do you make
   sentences with *going to*?

➡ GF 5: The going to-future (pp. 162–163)

I'm	going to	sing	a Queen song.
Justin …	…	…	basketball too.
They …	…	…	a musical this year.
I'm …	going to	join	a new club.
Are you	going to	play	in the school team?
… your mum	…	…	at home this afternoon?

Justin is going to start basketball too. • They're going to do a musical this year. • I'm going to join a new club. • Are you going to play in the school team? • Is your mum going to be at home this afternoon?

1 Sam and Justin are going to have a pizza (*going to*-future)

 1 ▶ 32–34

a) Say what everyone is / isn't going to do.
   1 Sam and Justin • have a pizza • ~~have fish and chips~~ • after school
      – Sam and Justin are going to have a pizza after school.
      – They aren't going to have fish and chips.
   2 Leo • do his homework • ~~watch TV~~ • after dinner
   3 Sam • ~~play basketball~~ • practise kung fu • at 8 pm
   4 Maya • phone Lucy • ~~phone Abby~~ • this evening
   5 Morph • ~~read a book~~ • watch a film • this evening

b) Listen to three dialogues. Who are the speakers?

1 Sam and Justin
2 Justin and his mum
3 Maya and Lucy

c) Listen to the dialogues again – one at a time.
   Take notes about what the people are/aren't going to do.

Dialogue 1

Who	What
Justin, Sam	aren't going to have more pizza
Justin	is going to … clean his room

Dialogue 2

Who	What
…	…
…	…

2 Justin isn't going to skype with his dad today / is going to skype with his dad tomorrow • Justin and his mum are going to have a cup of tea

Dialogue 3

Who	What
…	…
…	…

➡ Workbook 2 (p. 14)

More help ➡ p. 124
More help: Die S wählen aus einer Box.

3 Lucy is going to watch a film • Maya isn't going to watch a film • Maya is going to do her homework • Lucy and Maya are going to meet tomorrow evening

2 Ela is going to feed her snake (*going to*-future)

a) Make notes about your plans for the weekend.

b) 🧩 Make appointments with two partners. Find out about their plans.
   A: What are you going to do at the weekend?
   B: I'm going to ride my bike on Saturday. And I'm going to feed my snake.
   C: I'm going to buy a birthday present for … And I'm going to …

c) Tell the class something interesting about your partners' plans.
   – Ela is going to feed her snake. And Alex is going to …

➡ Workbook 3–4 (p. 15)

31

Part B

Lernfeld S. 32: Die S können einen kurzen Text zum Thema Geographie(unterricht) verstehen.

1 🔊 A geography lesson

On Monday morning, the students waited outside Mrs Taylor's room. Leo was with his other personal assistant, Mary. When Mrs Taylor arrived, everyone went in and sat down.

Mary: OK Leo, let's **get ready**. Take out your geography book, a pencil and your exercise book.
Leo: Uh-oh …
5 Mary: What's the matter?
Leo: My pencil is at home.
Mary: That's OK, you can use **mine**.

❖

Mrs Taylor gave out **worksheets**, and the class worked in groups.
10 Lucy: So, we have to find out what the three **longest** rivers in Great Britain are.
Leo: And the three **biggest** lakes.
Sam: And then we **label** them on this map on our worksheet. (+label (n))
15 Mary: Let's look for **large** lakes on the map in your geography book, Leo.
Lucy: So what *is* the **largest** lake?
Sam: That's easy! It's Lake Windermere.
Mrs T: How are you four **getting on**?
20 Lucy: We're looking for Lake Windermere, Miss. Sam says it's the **largest** lake.
Mrs T: Not bad, Sam. Lake Windermere is the **largest** lake in England, but I'm asking about all of Great Britain.
25 Justin: You **mean** Scotland and Wales too, Miss?
Mrs T: That's right.
Leo: I know, Miss!
Mrs T: Yes, Leo?
Leo: Loch Ness is big! There's a monster there!
30 Mrs T: Very good, Leo. But look at the map again. Loch Ness isn't **as big as** … well, what?

Justin: I think Loch Lomond is **bigger than** Loch Ness.
Lucy: So Loch Lomond is the **biggest** lake in
35 Britain. Sam, label it on the worksheet.
Sam: Right, Lake Lomond.
Lucy: It's *Loch* Lomond, Sam.
Sam: Well, it's still a lake!
Leo: Here's Loch Ness – in Scotland.
40 Lucy: Right, Leo. That's the second biggest lake. But what's the third biggest lake called?

❖

Justin: Hey, Sam. Guess what?
Sam: What?
Justin: I'm going to **get** new basketball shoes this
45 afternoon. (Box "(to) get", Voc, S. 185)
Sam: Cool. Where are you going to buy them?
Lucy: Hey, you two. We don't have time to talk. All the other groups are **faster than** **ours**.
Sam: And Lucy wants to be the **fastest**, of
50 course.
Justin: Right, what do we still have to find out?
Lucy: How long is the River Severn?
Leo: Three hundred and fifty-four kilometres.
Justin: OK, so it's **longer than** the Thames!

❖

55 Lucy: OK, we have all the information. Are you finished with the labels, Sam?
Sam: No, not yet.
Lucy: This is **awful**, Sam. You're so slow.
Sam: OK then, you finish them.

Folie 6 — Part B 2

Lernfeld S. 33–34: Die S können Dinge miteinander vergleichen *(comparison of adjectives)*.

2 Did you get it?

Write down the missing words in a list.
1. The geography lesson is about Britain's lakes and … rivers
2. There are three countries in Great Britain: England, Scotland and … Wales
3. Lake Windermere is the largest lake in … England
4. Loch Ness isn't in England. It's in … Scotland
5. "Loch" is another word for … lake
6. Great Britain's second largest lake is Loch … Ness

Early finisher → p. 134 Early finisher: Die S lösen ein Rätsel.

3 The big mistake

a) Look at the picture. How does Mrs Taylor look? How do Sam and Lucy look?

39 b) Listen and choose the right answer, a) or b).

1. a) Lucy asks Sam not to listen to music.
   b) Lucy tells Sam that she wants to listen too.
2. a) Mrs Taylor says she is going to take Sam's mobile.
   b) Mrs Taylor says she is going to write to Sam's parents.
3. a) At the end, Sam is angry with Lucy.
   b) At the end, Sam isn't angry with Lucy.

4 Britain's lakes and rivers

Use the information in the table to finish these sentences.

1. Britain's largest lakes are all in … Scotland
2. Loch Lomond and … are larger than Loch Awe. Loch Ness
3. The … is Britain's longest river. Severn
4. The … is almost as long as the Severn. Thames
5. The … isn't as long as the Thames. Trent

Largest lakes in Britain	
Loch Lomond	71 sq km (Scotland)
Loch Ness	56 sq km (Scotland)
Loch Awe	39 sq km (Scotland)
Longest rivers in Britain	
Severn	354 km (England/Wales)
Thames	346 km (England)
Trent	297 km (England)

Early finisher Look at the map on the inside cover of your book. Find the lakes and rivers. What mountains can you see in Britain? How high are they? What are Britain's biggest cities?

5 Have a go

Lernfeld: Die S vergleichen vorbewusst Eigenschaften von Dingen/Tieren *(comparison of adjectives)*.

Which is bigger? Make sentences.

1. a castle or a house
2. a dog or a horse
3. a lake or a pool
4. a rabbit or a rat
5. an ant or a butterfly
6. a mountain or a hill

A castle is bigger than a house!

1 A castle is bigger than a house. • 2 A horse is bigger than a dog. • 3 A lake is bigger than a pool. • 4 A rabbit is bigger than a rat. • 5 A butterfly is bigger than an ant. • 6 A mountain is bigger than a hill.

33

2 Part B Practice

Folie 6 • FöFo 2.3 • KV 6 • LAS 2.2

Looking at language

a) Copy the table on the right.
Finish it with the right forms of the adjectives from 1 on p. 32.

b) Copy these sentences into your exercise book and finish them.
A bear is bigger ... a bird.
(größer als)
A whale is ... big ... a house.
(so groß wie)

➔ GF 6 a, d: The comparison of adjectives (p. 163)

cold	colder	coldest
fast	faster	fastest
long	longer	longest
big	bigger	biggest
large	larger	largest
easy	easier	easiest

KV 6 enthält eine Tabelle, in die die S ihre Ergebnisse direkt eintragen können.

1 A snake is scarier (Comparison of adjectives)

Compare the animals in each group.
Use adjectives from the box.

Box "German „groß"", Voc, S. 185

big · fast · friendly · loud · nice · scary · slow · small · tall

I think a snake is scarier than a rat, but a lion is the scariest.

➔ Workbook 5 (p. 16)

2 As big as (Comparison of adjectives)

What is about the same? What is different?
1 Venus · Mercury · the Earth (big)
   Venus is about as big as the Earth.
   Mercury is smaller.
2 Spain · Greece · England (hot)
3 Luxemburg · Germany · Poland (large)
4 a plane · a bus · a car (fast)
5 March · April · July (cool)
6 Stuttgart · Leipzig · Berlin (big)
7 Carrantuohill · Ben Nevis · Snowdon (high) [ˌkærənˈtuːl]

More help ➔ p. 124
More help: Die wählen die passenden Adjektive/Komparative für die bereits vorgegebenen Sätze.

➔ Workbook 6 (p. 16)

3 Game

On four cards, write one adjective and three things to compare.

hard
maths
French
German

big
hamster
guinea pig
rabbit

Swap cards with another group.
Pick a card and say as many things as you can.

I think maths is as hard as German.   *No, maths is harder than German.*   *French is the hardest subject!*

➔ Workbook 7 (p. 17)

2 Spain is about as hot as Greece. England is colder. • 3 Germany is about as large as Poland. Luxemburg is smaller. • 4 A bus is about as fast as a car. A plane is faster. • 5 March is about as cool as April. July is warmer. • 6 Stuttgart is about as big as Leipzig. Berlin is bigger. • 7 Carrantuohill s about as high as Snowdon. Ben Nevis is higher.

KV 7 | Reading course 2

Lernfeld S. 35: Die S können einen Text laut und betont vorlesen.

Reading aloud

When you read aloud, it's important that people can understand you. Here are three tips:
1. Make sure that you understand what everything means.
2. Think about the feeling in a text and try to show it in your voice.
3. Punctuation helps you to choose the right voice and to pause in the right places.

a) Here is part of Justin's logbook from Unit 1.

> Friday, 10th August
> Yesterday I woke up in the middle of the night. I heard something outside the tent. First I thought it was Dad, but he was asleep right next to me. I heard the sound again: it was like "crush-crush". I looked through the door of the tent, but it was so dark that I saw nothing. I just heard that scary sound: "crush-crush". I turned on my torch and pointed it outside. A black bear was on top of the picnic table!

Read it **quietly** to yourself to make sure that you understand everything.

b) Look at the marked sentences in a).
How does Justin feel here? Choose a feeling from the box for each sentence.
Listen to the text.
Then read the sentences aloud.

> excited · happy · nervous · sad · scared · surprised

c) Read about punctuation marks in the table on the right.
Which of the punctuation marks can you find in the text in a)?
1 ▶ 40 Listen to the text.
Then read it aloud.

? (question mark)	show when you should
! (exclamation mark)	**change** your voice
, (comma)	
. (full stop)	show where you should pause
: (colon)	

Box "Punctuation", Voc, S. 186

d) 👥 Choose one of these texts or another text from Units 1 or 2.

> My first day in Boston. Dad's apartment is great! It has …

p. 24, ll. 1–7

> Today we climbed Mount Katahdin. It was very rocky and really high. But Dad and I …

p. 24, ll. 43–47

- Use all the tips on this page and practise reading your text aloud.
- Read the text to your group.
- Give the reader feedback:
  Was it easy to understand the reader?
  Did he/she read with feeling?
  Did he/she pause in the right places?

KV 7: Reading aloud: Feedback bietet ein vorgefertigtes Raster, mit dem die S das laute Vorlesen kriterienorientiert bewerten und den Mit-S eine strukturierte Rückmeldung geben können.

➡ *Workbook* 8 (p. 18)

www Find other texts to read aloud.
➡ *SF 6: Reading aloud (p. 149)*

Follow the link bietet weitere Texte, mit denen die S das laute Lesen üben können.

2 Part C

LAS 2.3

Lernfeld S. 36–39: Die S können einen kurzen Text zu den Themen **Musik**, **Bühne**, **Shows**, **Theater/Musicals** verstehen und auch über diese Themen sprechen.

1 Auditions for the show

After their last lesson, Lucy and Leo went to the auditions for the school show.

Box "Possessivpronomen", Voc, S. 186

Part C 2

After the singing auditions, the teachers called the dancers onto the stage. The children all danced on their own and in a group to songs from the musical *We will rock you*. The teachers chose five talented boy dancers for the show – and Leo was one of them! Lucy cheered and clapped.

2 Did you get it?

Finish each sentence with one word.
1 Lucy and Leo are at the … for the school show.
2 Lucy wants to be a … in the show.
3 Leo wants to …
4 The teachers … the other girls' voices.
5 One teacher thinks Lucy's voice is the most …
6 The teachers choose … dancers for the show.
7 … is one of these dancers.
8 When Lucy hears that, she is very …

> **More help** ➔ *p. 125*
> **More help:** Die Wörter sind in einer Box vorgegeben.

1 auditions • 2 singer • 3 dance • 4 like • 5 interesting • 6 eight • 7 Leo • happy

3 Lucy's audition

Listen to Lucy's audition for the show.
Are the sentences right or wrong?
Correct the wrong sentences.
1 This is Lucy's second audition for a school show.   *Wrong. It's her first audition.*
2 Lucy tells the teachers that she plays an instrument.   *Right.*
3 Lucy says that she loves singing.   *Right.*
4 Lucy says that she knows all the songs in *We will rock you*.   *Wrong. She knows lots of them, but not all.*
5 The teachers say that Lucy isn't good enough to sing in the show.   *Wrong. The teachers say they can use her in the show.*

EXTRA Background file

British pop music – old and new

The most successful pop band of all time is a 1960s band from Britain: the Beatles, with sales of about 1 billion records and CDs. There are also many other successful British pop artists from the last century, like Elton John, the Rolling Stones, the Spice Girls, or Queen.

Today, newer British artists are still successful, like the band Coldplay, or Adele. She sold more records in 2011 than anyone else and in 2012 she won six Grammy awards. In 2013, she won an Oscar for the best song.

The Beatles
Adele
Queen

> **Lernfeld:** Die S können einen englischen Sachtext über englische Popmusik verstehen.

In two minutes, write down the names of songs – new or old – by British bands or singers.
How many did you get?
What are your favourite songs at the moment?

37

2 Part C Practice   Folie 6

1 WORDS Stage and film

Lernfeld: Wortfeld *stage and film*.

a) Copy the table. Add more nouns from the box.

act in	learn	play	go to
a show	the piano	the drums	the theatre
a film ·	the drums ·	the piano ·	a play
a musical ·	the guitar ·	the guitar ·	a concert · a show ·
a play	an instrument ·	an instrument ·	a film · a musical ·
	the recorder	the recorder	the cinema

the cinema · a **concert** · the drums ·
a film · the guitar · an instrument ·
a musical · the piano · a play ·
the **recorder** · a show · the **theatre**

b) 👥 Do you act or sing or play an instrument? Would you like to be in a show or a group?
What do you like to go to: musicals, plays, films, …?

Do you play an instrument?

*Yes, I do. I play the recorder.
I'm in our school music group.*

*I like to go to musicals.
And I like films too.*

➡ Workbook 9 (p. 19)

2 Have fun on Saturday (Comparison of adjectives)

Language help

You know:	small	smaller	smallest	(for one-**syllable** adjectives)
	happy	happier	happiest	(for two-syllable adjectives with -y at the end)
There is also:	exciting	more exciting	most exciting	(for adjectives with two or more syllables)

➡ GF 6 b–d: The comparison of adjectives (pp. 163–164)

a) Read the adverts and finish them. Use *most* and two adjectives from each box.

awful · brilliant · talented

A MEMORY TO LAST A LIFETIME
CATS
Don't miss it – Andrew Lloyd
Webber's … musical with some of
Britain's … young singers.
Saturday 7.30 pm
Theatre Royal, Plymouth

most brilliant · most talented

TOP MODELS

wear the … new designer clothes in the …
fashion show this year.
Saturday, 8 pm. · At the shopping centre

boring · exciting · important

most exciting · most important

beautiful · dangerous · expensive

Our round-the-world bike tour
Photo show with pictures of the …
mountains and the … wild animals!
Saturday 3 pm at the town hall

most beautiful · most dangerous

b) Finish the sentences with the right form of the adjectives. Use -er, -est, *more* or *most*.

~~big~~ · cold · dangerous · exciting · high · hot · ~~interesting~~ · long · scary

We went to the photo show at the town hall. The speakers showed us the *most interesting* photos of their world tour. They were on the road for four years. That's much … than I imagined. I liked the pictures of the snow in Alaska (the … place on their trip). The sand in Sudan (the … place) was great too. But the … part of their trip was in Asia.

longer · coldest · hottest · most exciting · higher · more dangerous · scariest

The mountains there are much … than here. Lots of wild animals live there, and they are much *bigger* and … than the animals in our country. The … animal of all was the snow leopard!!

More help ➡ p. 125

More help: Die Adjektive sind vorgegeben und müssen nur noch gesteigert werden.

➡ Workbook 10–13 (pp. 19–20)

FöFo 2.4   Part C Practice 2

3 Southwest Superstar

a) Listen and choose the right answer for each question: a), b) or c).

1 *Southwest Superstar* is a
 a) musical.
 (b) TV show.)
 c) school show.

2 In last night's show
 (a) there was one dancer and two singers.)
 b) there were two dancers and one singer.
 c) there were three singers.

3 The winner was
 a) Jade Wing.
 (b) Natasha.)
 c) Ricky.

4 Sam thinks Jade Wing was better than Natasha
 a) because Jade had a better voice.
 b) because Jade could sing and dance.
 (c) because Jade wrote her own song.)

b) Listen again. Who is the biggest fan of the show? Who isn't so interested? Give reasons.

➡ Workbook 14 (p. 21)   Lucy is the biggest fan. It's her favourite TV show and she knows a lot about the people in it. Justin isn't interested. He didn't watch the show and he doesn't know anything about the people in it.

> Die S können die Ergebnisse während des Hörens in einer Tabelle festhalten.

4 Whose cat is that? (Possessive pronouns)   Lernfeld: *Possessive pronouns*.

a) Match the cats to the parts of the rhyme.   1E · 2C · 3B · 4D · 5A · 6F

A   B   C   D   E   F

[1] Whose cat is that, asleep for hours?
   Oh, that cat is … ours

[2] Whose cat is that, so fat and fine?
   Oh, that cat is … mine

[3] Whose cat is that, with °pearls and °furs?
   Oh, that cat is … hers

[4] Whose cat is that – she's doing a quiz?
   Oh, that cat is … his

[5] Whose cat is that – with bright white paws?
   Oh, that cat is … yours

[6] And whose cat runs up and down the stairs?
   Oh, that cat is … theirs

▶45 b) Listen to the rhyme and finish it with the right pronouns: *mine, yours, his, hers, ours, theirs*.

c) Now read the rhyme aloud.

➡ Workbook 15 (p. 21)

5 Let's go to a musical!

👥 Partner B: Go to p. 137.

Partner A: You and your German friend are in London and want to see a musical.
You have an idea: *We will rock you*.

Read the information and make notes.
Tell your friend about your musical, then listen to him/her.
Together, agree on one of them.

➡ SF 12: Mediation (Revision) (p. 151);   ➡ Workbook 16 (p. 22)

> **Zusatz:** Die S schreiben zur Sicherung einen kurzen Text und erklären, warum sie sich für eines der beiden Musicals entschieden haben. Die Argumente werden der Klasse präsentiert.

'MASSIVELY ENTERTAINING' CAPITAL RADIO
WE WILL ROCK YOU
MUSICAL BY QUEEN AND Ben Elton

IN THE FUTURE THE PEOPLE ON PLANET MALL ARE NOT ALLOWED TO PLAY MUSICAL INSTRUMENTS. ONLY COMPUTERS MAKE MUSIC FOR THE PEOPLE TO DOWNLOAD. BUT MAYBE °SOMEWHERE, SOMEONE STILL HAS REAL INSTRUMENTS …

Union Theatre, Mon – Sun 7.30 pm
Underground: Tottenham Court Road
Runs 2 hrs 40 min – Only for children 10 years or older

39

2 | **Part C Practice** | FöFo 2.5

Lernfeld S. 40: Die S können ein bildgestütztes **Vokabelposter** erstellen.

6 Study skills: A vocabulary picture poster

A picture poster can help you to remember vocabulary.

a) **Think**: Choose one of the umbrella words on the right. Find words to go under it.

Pair: Find a partner with the same umbrella word. Compare your lists and add more words if you can.

Share: Find another pair with the same umbrella word and compare lists. Choose six words from your lists. Draw or find a picture for them.

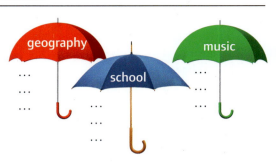

b) Plan your poster. Think of an idea for a "picture frame" for your words – a map for geography words, for example. Then put your poster together.

c) Swap your poster with another group. Make a table for your feedback. Say what you think about the other poster.

What I liked about this poster	What **could** be better about this poster
…	…

I really liked your poster because/…
- it's interesting/**clear** …
- it's the right **size** / easy to read /…
- the drawings/pictures are good/interesting/ **correct** / go with the words /…
- …

You could make your poster better like this:
- Make your writing bigger/smaller/…
- Use brighter/more colours
- Find better pictures to go with your words
- …

Study skills
- Ein Vokabelposter hilft mir …
- Wenn ich ein Vokabelposter mache, sollte ich …

A VOCABULARY PICTURE POSTER

Vergleiche deine Ideen mit dem Abschnitt im Skills File.

→ SF 3: Vocabulary picture posters (p. 146)

→ Workbook 17 (p. 22)

2 The world behind the picture

1 Plymkids

Lernfeld: Die S können einen kurzen **Film verstehen** und beschreiben, was die Personen darin tun. Dafür benutzen sie das *present progressive*.

a) What are the kids in the picture doing?
   Where do you think they are?

b) Watch the film.
   Say what else the children are doing.
   Choose the right activities from the list.

   (dancing)   (running)
   (lying) on the floor   (jumping)
   playing ball   (singing)
   (moving and clapping) (waking up their faces)
   playing the drums sleeping

Länge: 3:09

What sort of club is Plymkids? It's a school club where you learn to act. It's called a drama club.

c) What feelings do the kids show?
   Choose the right feeling for each scene below.

   angry · happy · nervous · sad · **shy**

Scene 1: happy

Scene 2: shy

Scene 3: nervous

2 EVERYDAY ENGLISH At the cinema

Lernfeld: Die S können Gespräche über **Kino und Film** verstehen und selber führen.

a) Copy the table. Watch part 1 of the film.
   Who wants to see which film? Why?

	Miley Cyrus	James Bond	Madagascar
Who?	Ruby	Oliver	Jack
Why?	Miley Cyrus is her favourite actor.	It's the best of all the James Bond films.	The last Madagascar film was very funny and this one is even better.

b) Watch the whole film and check your answers.
   Which film do they watch in the end?
   How do they like it?

c) Which of the films would you like to see?
   Try to agree on a film with your partner.

   What do you want to see? ·
   I'd like to see … · I don't want to see … ·
   Can we choose something different? ·
   Why don't we …? · What about …? ·
   I think it's the funniest / most boring /
   most exciting / … film. ·
   I like action/comedy/… films more. ·
   That is/isn't a good idea.

Länge: 4:13

b)
They decide to watch "The Hobbit".
Ruby and Jack like the movie. Jack says it's a great film. Ruby likes the dragon and thinks the film is scary. Oliver thinks the film isn't bad.

41

2 Text

Lernfeld S. 42–43: Die S können eine Geschichte über eine Schulparty verstehen.

Disco night

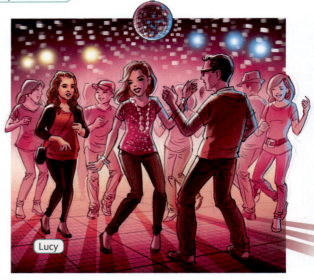
Lucy

1 46 At lunchtime on Friday, Sam, Justin, Lucy and Leo sat together in the canteen.
"It's the disco for years 7 and 8 this evening. Are you going to be there, Sam?" asked Lucy.
5 Sam **stuck** his **fork** into a potato. He didn't look happy. "I'd like to go, but I have to stay at home this week," he said.
+knife, +spoon
"Why?" asked Lucy.
"Mrs Taylor sent Mum and Dad a note about my
10 phone," said Sam. "They were really angry. I have to stay at home every evening this week, so I can't go to the disco." He looked at the potato on his fork and then **dropped** it on the plate.
"Oh, no!" Lucy said. "How can we have fun
15 without you, Sam?"
"Well, I'm going to be there," said Justin. "I'm going to take photos for the school magazine."
"Oh, of course, Justin. That's good," Lucy said and smiled. "What about you, Leo?"
20 "Disco!" said Leo. He jumped up from the table and did a little dance.
"So Leo is going to be there too," said Justin.
"Yes, you can all go and have fun – but I can't," said Sam.
25 "Oh, well," said Justin. "I can send you some pictures of the disco from my mobile, Sam."
"No, thanks, Justin," Sam said and looked down at his plate again. "I don't want to see you there when I have to stay at home."

❖

30 In the afternoon, Lucy chose her best dance
1 47 clothes and got ready.
The disco was in the **drama** studio. When Lucy arrived, the room looked very different. It was dark with red, yellow and blue disco lights. There
35 were lots of kids there, but almost all of them were in Year 7.
"They look funny," thought Lucy. "That girl is wearing too much make-up! And that boy has lots of **gel** in his hair! And how can he see with his
40 **sunglasses** on?"   +glasses
Lucy couldn't see any of her friends. Suddenly she felt a hand on her **arm** and turned around. It was Leo. He looked great. He wore black jeans and a black T-shirt with the words *It's only rock 'n' roll*.
45 He also had gel in his hair.

"Hi Lucy!" he shouted. "Dance?" he asked.
"Yeah, good idea!" Lucy said.
She took Leo's hand and pulled him onto the dance floor. Leo clapped his hands to the music.
50 Lucy knew the song.
"I really like this song!" shouted Lucy. Leo didn't answer. He just danced. He was a really good dancer and knew lots of dance steps. Suddenly there was a **flash**. Lucy looked up and Justin
55 smiled back at her. He held his mobile up with his photo of Leo and Lucy.
"Come and dance, Justin," Lucy shouted, but Justin just laughed and **shook** his head.

❖

Sam's mobile **beeped**. It was a photo from Justin: 1 48
60 Leo and Lucy on the dance floor. He smiled and started to write Justin a text message when he heard somebody outside his room. It was his dad.
"Did I hear your mobile, Sam?" his father asked. "Aren't you doing your homework?"
65 "Er … no, I mean yes, I'm finished. Justin sent me this photo. Look," Sam said and showed it to his dad.
"So, your friends are all at the disco?" Mr Bennett asked.
70 "Yes," said Sam. He sounded very unhappy. "I **wish** I was there too!"
"Well," said his dad, "you know why you're not there."
"Yes, Dad, I know."

❖

Folie 7 • FöFo 2.6 • KV 8 • VAS 2.1, 2.2   Text **2**

75 Justin and Lucy stood and watched Leo and the other kids on the dance floor. Most of them were girls. Suddenly the music stopped in the middle of a song. One by one, all the kids stopped dancing. All the kids except one – Leo. He didn't need the
80 music from the °sound system, he had the music in his head.

Leo

"Look at Leo," Lucy said and pulled Justin's arm. "He's still dancing."
Justin laughed. "Yes, but I hope that's not the end
85 of …"
Before Justin finished, the music started again and all the students cheered.

"Yeah!" shouted Lucy. "Come on, Justin, let's go and dance with Leo. Before the music stops
90 again."
She looked for Leo on the dance floor. "Where is that boy now?"
A voice behind her answered, "You mean that good-looking, blond boy?"
95 "No," Lucy said and turned around, "I don't … Sam! What are you doing here?"
Sam smiled. "Well, I did all my homework. Then I was in my room and Dad came in and saw the photo of you and Leo on my mobile …"
100 "It was a great photo, right?" said Justin.
"Yes, it was funny. Anyway, Dad talked to me about school rules and why Plymstock has the phone rule. Then he said: 'OK, Sam, you're not often in trouble at school. So you *can* go to the
105 disco, but don't use your phone in class again.' So here I am."
"And here's Leo," Justin said.
"Hi everybody!" Leo said. "Let's dance!"
Leo and Lucy ran onto the dance floor.
110 "Sam! Justin!" Lucy shouted. "Come on. You too!"
But the two boys just laughed and shook their heads.

1 Lucy talks to Maya

Lucy tells Maya about the disco.
Finish her sentences.
1 "Sam had to stay at home because …" *Mrs Taylor sent his parents a note about his phone.*
2 "The Year 7 kids …" *looked funny.*
3 "Justin didn't …" *dance.*
4 "Justin took a photo and …" *sent it to Sam.*
5 "When the music stopped, …" *Leo didn't stop dancing.*
6 "When the music started again, …" *all the students cheered.*

2 New words

Work out what these words and phrases mean.

> fork (l. 5) · sunglasses (l. 40) · shake (shook) his head (l. 58) · beep (l. 59) · one by one (l. 78)

Then write a sentence with each of them.
Sam eats a potato with a fork, so *fork* means …
– I put food into my mouth with a fork.

3 Reading aloud   *Falls nötig, wiederholen die S vorher die Tipps für das laute Lesen (S. 35).*

Find lines in the text where somebody is feeling excited, sad, surprised, happy or angry. Read your lines aloud. Can your group say who is speaking and what the feeling is?

4 A part of the story   *Neigungsdifferenzierung: Die S wählen zwischen einer darstellerischen Aufgabe und einer kreativen Schreibaufgabe.*

You choose Do a) or b).

a) Without words, one student acts out part of the story. Then he/she stops the action.
The others guess which part of the story it is.

b) Read lines 101–105 again. Imagine what Sam and his dad said, and write their conversation.

More help ➔ p. 125   **More help:** Sprachliche Hilfen und Redemittel zur Erstellung des Dialogs.

➔ Workbook 18 (p. 23)

2 Unit

Your task

Steps 1–4 können zu Hause bearbeitet werden. *Steps 5–7* sollten im Unterricht durchgeführt werden, wobei *Step 7* sich z.B. auch gut als *Gallery walk* eignet.

Music magazine

Make an English music magazine for the parents and teachers of your class. How?
Put together an A4 page about music. Then put everyone's pages into a folder to make the magazine.

You choose Make a page about *one* of these topics.

STEP 1
- a music group at your school
- a singer/band/musician
- your favourite instrument

STEP 2
Make notes for your page. What could be interesting for your parents and teachers?
- **music group at your school:** Who is in it? – What do the musicians do? – What kind of music do they make? – How often do they practise? – How often do they give concerts? – …
- **singer/band/musician:** age? – hometown? – type of music (rock, hip hop, classical, …)? – best song/album/…? – biggest hit/video/…? – Why do you like him/her/them? – …
- **instrument:** What is it? – Why do you like it? – Is it easy/hard/fun/… to play? – …

➜ Wordbank 2, S. 141.

STEP 3
Find or draw pictures for your page.

STEP 4
Use your notes to write texts for your page. Don't make your texts too long – and don't copy information from the internet!

STEP 5
👥 Swap your texts with a partner and check his/her texts. Look at grammar and spelling.

STEP 6
Arrange your texts and pictures to make an A4 page about your topic.

STEP 7
Collect all the pages from the class in a folder. Give your class music magazine a title.

MY FAVOURITE SINGER

My favourite singer is Taylor Swift. Taylor sings country music and plays the guitar. She comes from Pennsylvania in the USA. She is 23 years old and started singing when she was very young. Her first chart hit was 'Our Song' in 2006. She was the first young person to get a number 1 hit in the country music charts.

People all over the world listen to Taylor Swift. Some of her most famous songs are 'Love Story', 'You Belong With Me' and 'Trouble'. I like Taylor Swift because her music videos are funny and she has a great voice!

44

Unit 2

Das lief nicht gut, ich muss mehr üben.

Das war OK, aber ich könnte besser werden.

Das habe ich gut geschafft.

Wie gut warst du?

Wie schätzt du dich selber ein? Schreibe *Words, Writing, Grammar* und *Putting a page together* in dein Heft und ordne dir für jeden Bereich eine Ampelfarbe zu.

Words
Fielen dir Wörter für Instrumente oder Musikrichtungen ein? Bei welchen Wörtern hattest du Schwierigkeiten?

Writing
Welche Rechtschreib- oder Grammatikfehler hat dein/e Partner/in in deinen Texten gefunden?

Grammar
Brauchtest du Steigerungsformen wie *a more exciting group* oder *the coolest band*, um deine Lieblingsgruppe zu beschreiben? Wusstest du, wie man welches Adjektiv richtig steigert?

Putting a page together
Konntest du dich daran erinnern, wie man eine gute Text- und Bildseite zusammenstellt?

Wie kannst du besser werden?

Dort, wo du dich rot oder gelb eingeschätzt hast, helfen dir folgende Tipps beim Wiederholen und Üben.

Words
Die Seiten 30 und 36–39 sowie der Unit-Text enthalten viele Redewendungen und viel Wortschatz zum Thema Musik und Musikaufführungen.

Schwierige Wörter kannst du mit einem *vocabulary picture poster* gut lernen.
➡ *S. 28, 34–37; S. 40;* ➡ *Wordbank 2, S. 141*
➡ *Skills File 3: Vocabulary picture posters, S. 146*

Writing
Korrigiere deine Rechtschreibfehler. Übe mit deinem Partner / deiner Partnerin die richtige Schreibweise.
Besprich Grammatikfehler mit deinem Partner / deiner Partnerin. Seht euch gemeinsam die Erklärungen im Grammar File an.
➡ *Skills File 13: Writing (Revision), S. 151*

Grammar
Vielleicht gibt es Sätze in deinem Text, die du durch den Gebrauch einer Steigerungsform verbessern könntest. Wenn du nicht mehr sicher bist, wie das geht, dann schau dir Übung 2 auf Seite 38 noch einmal an.
➡ *S. 31–32, S. 38;*
➡ *Workbook 5–6, S. 16; 10–11, S. 19–20*
➡ *Grammar File 6, S. 163*

Putting a page together
Sieh dir die Seiten von anderen in deiner Klasse an. Was findest du gut oder anders daran? Findest du dort Ideen, wie du deine Seite besser machen könntest?
➡ *Skills File 19: Peer feedback, S. 155*

3 Unit

Folie 8 • KV 9 • Leistungsmessung Unit 3

Out and about

Lernfeld S. 46–47: Die S können Wegbeschreibungen geben und verstehen.

1 Morph's map

a) Where can you see Morph on the map? What does he look like?
- A: I can see Morph next to the Big Wheel. He looks like a tree.
- B: Right, and I can see him …

Die fünf Morphs sind in der Karte markiert.

b) Talk about the places in the list.
1. theatre
2. post office
3. shopping centre
4. market
5. bus station
6. museum
7. hotel
8. church
9. roundabout
10. harbour

Use phrases from the box.

> It's in … Street/Road/… ·
> It's near / next to / … · It's opposite
> … · It's in front of / behind … ·
> It's between … and … ·
> It's on the corner of … and …

Where's the theatre?

It's in Royal Parade, opposite Derry's Cross. Where's …?

2 How do you get there?

2 ▶ 01

a) Listen to Morph. Where is he? Where does he go? Follow him with your finger on the map.

Morph is in the library. He goes to the harbour, the bus station and the market. (for way: see below)

b) You are at Plymouth bus station. Your partner asks the way to a place on the map. Use the phrases to explain the way.

> Go along … Street/Road. ·
> Cross … Street/Road. ·
> Turn left/right. · Go straight on. ·
> Go past the church/hotel/…

Box "left – right", Voc, S. 189

Box "Entschuldigung", Voc, S. 189

- A: Excuse me, please. Can you tell me the way to …?
- B: Yes, go along … Street. Then turn right into … Road. The … is on the left/right.

+ask sb. the way

→ Workbook 1–5 (pp. 28–29)

Your task

At the end of this unit:
Put together a rally around your town or area for a visitor from Britain.

way to the harbour: Hoe Approach, Notte St, Vauxhall St, Vauxhall Quay • way to the bus station: Vauxhall Quay, Vauxhall St, Breton Side • way to the market: Exeter St, St. Andrew's Cross, Royal Parade, Derry's Cross, Raleigh St, New George St

46

Unit 3

47

3 Part A

Lernfeld S. 48–49: Die S können einen Text zum Thema *shopping* verstehen.

Folie 10

1 🖐 At the shops

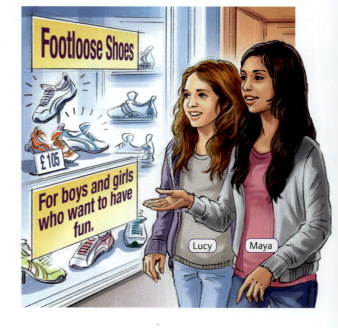

2 ▷ 02 After school on Friday, Lucy and Maya had to do some shopping, so they took a <u>bus which stopped</u> in Royal Parade, near the <mark>pedestrian zone</mark>. <mark>Just after</mark> they got off, Lucy saw a shoe shop.

5 Lucy: Look at those trainers, Maya! They're really cool. *Footloose Shoes – for boys and <u>girls who want to</u> have fun*. I could have fun in those.
Maya: Yes, Lucy, but look at the price! They <mark>cost</mark>
10 £105!
Lucy: Wow! So it really means: *for boys and <u>girls who have</u> lots of money*.
Maya: Right, so come on, Luce. The shops <mark>close</mark> soon. Mum says I have to get a present
15 for your grandparents – for our visit to Dartmoor.
Lucy: What kind of present?
Maya: Maybe <mark>chocolates</mark>? It's your <u>grandma that likes</u> chocolates, right?
20 Lucy: Right. She *loves* chocolates.
Maya: Well, there's the little <u>shop that makes</u> its own chocolates.

Lucy: You don't mean the shop in the Barbican!
Maya: Yes, their chocolates are really yummy.
25 Lucy: But I <mark>need to</mark> get some things for school for next week. And in the Barbican, there aren't any <mark>shops which sell</mark> school things.

EXTRA Background file

Money
Britain doesn't use euros like Germany, but pounds and pence.

Lernfeld: Die S können verstehen, was jemand kauft und wie viel es kostet.

Pounds [paʊndz] **and pence** [pens]

You write:	You say:
1p	one p [piː]
45p	forty-five p
£1	one pound / a pound
£1.25	one (pound) twenty-five (p)
£2	two pounds
£2.50	two (pounds) fifty (p)
£3.79	three (pounds) seventy-nine (p)

°**Euros** [ˈjʊərəʊz] **and** °**cents** [sents]

You write:	You say:
1c	one cent
20c / €0.20	twenty cents
€1	one euro / a euro
€50	fifty euros
€49.55	forty-nine (euros) fifty-five (cents)

2 ▷ 04–08 Listen to the conversations and take notes. What do the people buy? How much do the things cost? How much change do they get?
👥 Did you get the same answers?

1 The boy buys five tomatoes. They cost £2.03. He gets £2.97 change. • 2 The man buys things for £31.79. He pays by card. • 3 The boy buys a cheeseburger and small cola. They cost £3.74. He gets 6p change. • 4 The girl buys a T-shirt. It costs £9.99. She gets 1p change. • 5 The girl buys an ice cream and a bottle of water. They cost £3.20 or €4. She gets 80p change.

Folie 10

Part A 3

Maya:	Oh, OK. We can find another shop.
Lucy:	Grandma likes flowers too.
30 Maya:	Does she? There's a flower stall that mum likes at the City Market. We can go there.
Lucy:	OK, but let's go to Smith's first. I need one of those plastic things for maths.
Maya:	Plastic things?
35 Lucy:	Yes, those plastic things that look like a °triangle. Mine broke last week.
Maya:	Oh, you mean a °set square.
Lucy:	Yes, a set square. And some new felt pens.

40

▶03 **As** they went into Smith's, Lucy's mobile beeped.

Lucy:	It's a text from Sam.
Maya:	What does it say?
Lucy:	*Kung Fu Master Wu in "The old ship". Radford Park. Action!*
45 Maya:	What does it mean?
Lucy:	I'm not sure.
Maya:	But we can't go to Radford Park now. Text Sam and tell
50 | him. |

Sorry, shopping for Dartmoor trip. Are you ready?

In Smith's, Lucy found some felt pens and went to the cash desk.

Lucy :	How much are they?
55 Assistant:	£5.99. But you can get two sets of these pens for £7.99.
Lucy:	No, thanks. I only need one set.
Assistant:	Is that everything then?
Lucy:	Er … have you got set squares?
60 Assistant:	Yes, but only in maths sets with other things in them too. You can't buy set squares on their own. Sorry.
Lucy:	Oh, OK.
Assistant:	So, it's just the pens?
65 Lucy:	Yes, please.
Assistant:	That's £5.99, please.
Lucy:	Here you are.
Assistant:	£10. Thank you. And here's your change, £4.01.
70 Lucy:	Thank you. Bye.
Maya:	OK, Luce, let's go to the market and buy those flowers for your grandma.
Lucy:	You know, Maya, you don't have to buy a present. Grandma just likes to
75	see us.
Maya:	But … well, all right then.
Lucy:	Right, now we can go to Radford Park and see what Sam is doing.

Box "German "haben"", Voc, S. 190

2
Lucy: what: felt pens / why: – / buy: yes · what: a set square / why: needs it for maths / buy: no – you can only buy them in maths sets · what: trainers / why: could have fun in them / buy: no – they cost a lot of money
Maya: what: chocolates / why: present for Lucy's grandparents / buy: no – Lucy doesn't want to go to the Barbican · what: flowers / why: a present for Lucy's grandparents / buy: no – Lucy says her grandma just likes to see them

2 What do they buy?

a) Make notes about these things from 1.

> chocolates · felt pens · flowers ·
> a set square · trainers

- Who wants to buy them: Lucy or Maya?
- Why does she want them?
- Does she buy them? If not, why not?

More help ➡ *p. 126*

More help: Hilfen zur Strukturierung der Aufgabe.

b) 👥 Talk about the things in the box like this:

Maya wants to buy chocolates. She needs a present for …

But she doesn't buy chocolates because …

3 Have a go

Lernfeld: Die S bilden vorbewusst **Relativsätze**.

Choose the right ending for sentences 1–6.

1f · 2d · 3a · 4e · 5b · 6c

1 That's the bus …
2 And there's the shoe shop …
3 *Footloose Shoes* are for people …
4 Maya is the girl …
5 Lucy is the girl …
6 Where's the market …

a) … who want to have fun.
b) … that needs new felt pens.
c) … that sells plants and flowers?
d) … which sells expensive trainers.
e) … who wants to buy a present.
f) … which stops in Royal Parade.

49

3 Part A Practice

Folie 9 • KV 10 • LAS 3.1

Lernfeld S. 50–51: Die S können Personen und Dinge näher beschreiben *(relative clauses, relative pronouns)*.

Looking at language

Relative clauses give information about a thing or a person:
– So they took a **bus** which stopped in Royal Parade.
– Footloose Shoes: for **boys and girls** who want to have fun.

a) Find these sentences on p. 48.
   What is the relative pronoun: who or which?
   – Footloose Shoes: for **boys and girls** ... have lots of money.   who
   – In the Barbican, there aren't any **shops** ... sell school things.   which

b) Find these sentences on p. 48. What is the relative pronoun?
   – It's your **grandma** ... likes chocolates, right?   that
   – Well, there's the little **shop** ... makes its own chocolates.   that

c) When do you use ⟨which⟩ ⟨that⟩ ⟨who⟩ ?
   Copy the diagram and put the words in the right place.

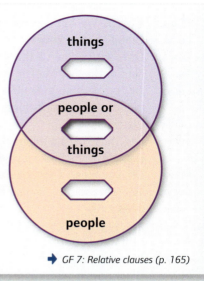

➡ GF 7: Relative clauses (p. 165)

1 I like people who laugh a lot   (Relative pronouns: who or which)

a) Copy the table. Add the words from the box.

"who"-words	"which"-words
parents people · bands · teachers	animals books · clothes · shops

animals · bands · books · clothes · parents ·
people · shops · teachers

b) Say what you like and don't like. Use words from your table.

➡ Workbook 6 (p. 30)

2 Shopping in town   (Relative pronouns: who, which or that)

You're in town. You hear lots of people in the shops.
Finish their sentences with who, which or that. Use each pronoun at least once.

1 Do you have a T-shirt ... isn't too expensive?
2 I'm looking for the assistant ... sold me this pen.
3 How much are cameras ... you can use in water?
4 I need a present for a friend ... likes music.
5 Where are the nice toys ... you had last week?
6 I need somebody ... knows about phones!
7 I bought a torch here ... broke the next day.
8 I'd like some trainers ... are OK for the gym.

1 which/that · 2 who/that · 3 which/that · 4 who/that · 5 which/that · 6 who/that · 7 which/that · 8 which/that

Early finisher   Make three or four sentences that you or your friends could say at a shopping centre.
Let's find a shop which ...
I'm looking for a ... that ...
I know somebody who would like ...

➡ Workbook 7 (p. 30)

FöFo 3.2 | Part A Practice | 3

3 GAME Who is who? (Relative pronouns: *who/that*)

a) Think about four people at your school.
   Write down relative clauses to describe them.
   a girl who does judo
   a boy that is wearing blue trainers today
   a teacher who ...
   More help ➔ p. 126   **More help:** Die S bilden Sätze aus Satzbausteinen.

b) Walk around the class.
   Describe your people to other students.
   Can they say who they are?
   A: I'm thinking of a girl who does judo.
   B: Ah, that's Kristin!
   A: Right, your turn. / No, try again!

4 I don't know the English word

Relative clauses can help you to explain words that you don't know.
Look at a picture and explain what you see. Can your partner guess the picture?

"It's a person who helps ..."
"It's a thing that you use when ..."
"It's an animal that ..."
"That's picture number ..."

More help ➔ p. 126   **More help:** Satzenden sind in einer Box vorgegeben, aus denen die S den jeweils passenden auswählen.

Early finisher Hide something (a pen, a rubber, ...) behind your back.
Explain what it is to your partner. Can your partner guess what it is? Take turns.
➔ Workbook 8–9 (p. 31)

5 Helping tourists in Dresden

Lernfeld: Die S können die wichtigsten Informationen aus einem deutschen Flyer auf Englisch zusammenfassen.

Partner B: go to p. 137.
Partner A:
a) An English family with two children don't understand this flyer.
   Explain what happens on the tour and what it costs.

PEEKABOO-TOUR: DresdenCity Express – Pfiffige und unterhaltsame Schnitzeljagd durch Dresden

Genau richtig für pfiffige Besucher mit wenig Zeit. Mr Peekaboo hat auf seiner Schnitzeljagd-Tour CityExpress seine Hinweise und Rätsel in Schaufenstern, Gebäuden und den wichtigsten Sehenswürdigkeiten gut verpackt.
Die Teilnehmer lösen gemeinsam die Aufgaben aus dem Tourenpaket und erkunden auf diese unterhaltsame Weise die Dresdner Innenstadt zu Fuß. Mr Peekaboo's Hilfehotline steht während der Tour zur Seite.
Mindestteilnehmerzahl für alle Touren: 2 Personen.

Preis: Erw.: 12,50 €; Kinder: 5,50 € **Dauer:** ca.1,5–2 Std. Laufzeit (geeignet für Rollstuhlfahrer und Kinderwagen)
Info und Kauf: Tourist-Information

---

b) Your partner explains another idea for a tour in Dresden.
   Listen. Ask questions if you don't understand something.

➔ *SF 12: Mediation (Revision) (p. 151);* ➔ Workbook 10 (p. 32)

3 Part A Practice

Folie 10 • FöFo 3.1 • KV 11

Lernfeld S. 52: Die S können sich über vertraute Themen aus ihrem Alltag unterhalten und Texte zum Thema Einkaufen verstehen.

6 WORDS A bottle of milk

Lernfeld: Die S können **Mengenangaben** machen.

a) Match the phrases to the things in the pictures. Box "a bottle of …, a packet of …", Voc, S. 190

Es bietet sich an, Realia (verschiedene Packungen etc.) mitzubringen.

200 **grams** of · a bag of · a bottle of · a box of · a kilo of · a **packet** of · a **tin** of

200 grams of cheese · a bag of potatoes · a bottle of milk/orange juice · a box of chocolates · a kilo of tomatoes · a packet of biscuits/cornflakes · a tin of tomato soup

b) Sam and his dad have to go shopping. Finish their dialogue. Then act it out.

Sam: I think we need milk, Dad.
Dad: OK, a bottle of milk.
Sam: Oh, and a … orange **juice**. bottle of
Dad: Right. Then we need … new potatoes. a bag of
Sam: What about a … chocolates for Mum? box of
Dad: Good idea! And some biscuits for us.
Sam: Yeah! A … biscuits. packet of
Dad: Then we need some of the cheese that your mum likes. How much?

Sam: She always buys … cheese. 200 grams of
Dad: OK. Then I want a … cornflakes for breakfast tomorrow. packet of
Sam: I want to make a big **tomato** salad – I need a … tomatoes. kilo of
Dad: And let's get a … vegetable soup too. tin of
Sam: Vegetable soup? But Dad, it's only you who likes vegetable soup.

➔ Workbook 11 (p. 32)

7 Cool presents for kids

Lernfeld: Die S können sagen, was sie jemandem (nicht) schenken würden und warum. Sie können sagen, was ein Geschenk kostet.

a) Talk about how much the presents cost.
   A: How much is/are the …?
   B: Nine pounds. How much do/does the … cost?

b) Choose a present for a classmate.

Let's get … for Jan. It's really funny.

I think it's silly. And it costs …

More help ➔ p. 127   More help bietet Redemittel.

£9.00 · £7.99 · £11.50 · £14.75 · £4.90 · £22.65

ice cream earphones · cool water bottles · snake **socks** · scary watches · zebra sharpener · monster rucksack

KV 11: **British money** bietet ein Einkaufsspiel, mit dem die S den Umgang mit britischem Geld lernen können.

➔ Workbook 12 (p. 33)

8 SONG Money

2 ▶ 09

a) Read the first verse of the song. What does the writer think about money?

Money (that's what I want)
The best things in life are free
But you can **keep** them for the birds and **bees**
Now give me money
That's what I want (that's what I want) …

b) Listen to the song, sing along and clap.

c) **Think:** Think of three great free things.

Pair: Compare ideas. Choose the best three.

Share: Compare your best ideas with another pair. What great things in life are free? When is it sometimes important to have money?

52

Reading course 3

FöFo 3.3

Lernfeld S. 53: Die S können einen Text nach bestimmten Informationen absuchen *(scanning)*.

Scanning a text

When you're looking for specific information in a text, you don't need to read every word. You can scan for **keywords** and just read that part of the text.

a) Read these questions.
1. At how many places can you have a **picnic**?
2. Where can you do **learning activities**?
3. Where can you go if you like **discos**?
4. Where can you buy great **souvenirs**?
5. Where can you ask questions about **animals**?
6. How many things cost **under £5**?

b) Scan the text. Maybe the keywords from a) 'jump' into your eyes.
Morph's tip: maybe it helps if you fly over the page in S-shapes with your finger.

c) Answer the questions when you find the information. Check your answers with a partner.

1 at 2 places (Tinside Lido, Sea life) · 2 Plymouth Pavilions (skating lessons) / Sea life learning centre · 3 Plymouth Pavilions · 4 the aquarium shop · 5 the Monkey Sanctuary · 6 day ticket for children at the Tinside Lido / a skating session at the Plymouth Pavilions / sanctuary garden tickets for children

Out and about in Plymouth

There are lots of great places for kids in Plymouth. Choose a place and °plan a day of fun.

Tinside Lido

The Hoe is a great place on a warm summer day and the Tinside Lido a great place for swimming. The Lido is an outdoor sea-water pool with a big °fountain in the centre. You can bring a picnic or have lunch at the Tinside °restaurant. The big °deck is a great place if you want to lie in the sun or look at the beautiful view of Plymouth Sound.
Children under 15: Day ticket £4.70

Winter sports from January to December

There are also great winter sports centres in Plymouth that you can visit °all year round. The Plymouth Pavilions is °the only ice rink in Devon and Cornwall that opens every month of the year. It has lots of different activities for young and old, °including skating lessons and an Ice Disco with an exciting laser show every Tuesday and Friday evening.
Skating °session: £4.50 (£6 with skate °hire)
Ice Disco: £7   Skating lessons: 30 minutes £20

Sea life

The Aquarium, right next to Sutton Harbour, is the largest in the UK. There you can see sea life from all corners of the earth – °octopuses, sharks and much, much more. The learning centre has activities for children of all ages, and you can also watch films about all kinds of sea life. There are two restaurants and an outdoor picnic area where you can °relax and °enjoy delicious food. You can also visit the aquarium shop which sells great souvenirs for you and your friends.
Children under 15: Day ticket £8.75

°Rescue centres in Plymouth

Plymouth has lots of rescue centres for animals in trouble. Some of them, like the Monkey °Sanctuary, are open to visitors. At the Monkey Sanctuary you can meet 36 monkeys! And there are always animal °keepers who can answer all your questions.
The sanctuary also has a big garden with lots of beautiful plants, all kinds of birds, frogs and °insects.
Tickets for children under 15 cost £5. For children under five, the sanctuary is free.

➡ **Workbook** 13 (p. 33)
➡ SF 9: Scanning (p. 149)

3 Part B

Lernfeld S. 54: Die S können einen kurzen Text verstehen und sich über vertraute Themen aus ihrem Alltag unterhalten.

1 On the way to Radford Park

On Friday afternoon, Sam and Justin walked down Radford Park Road. Sam was very excited. "Here's my idea for the film: Master Wu finds an old boat on Radford Lake. On it, there's a magic
5 book that can make him the greatest kung fu master in the world. But then, another kung fu master arrives and wants the book too. So Master Wu has to fight him."
"That's a nice idea," said Justin. "But who's going
10 to play the other kung fu master?"
"Lucy – I sent her a text."
Just then Sam's mobile beeped.
"Oh no," said Sam. "She's shopping … she can't come."
15 "So how can we make the film then?" asked Justin.
Sam shook his head slowly: "I don't know."
"Hello, Sam! Hello Justin!" said a voice quietly.
"Who said that?" Justin asked.
20 At that moment Leo jumped up from behind a garden wall. He looked at Sam and Justin and laughed loudly. "You didn't see me! You didn't see me!"
Then the door opened and Leo's mum came out.
25 "Hello, Mrs Cooper," Sam said.
"Hello, Sam," said Leo's mum. "Are you going to the park?"
"Yes," Sam said excitedly. "My friend Justin and I want to make a film there."
30 "A film? Like Spiderman! Watch this!" Leo said, and jumped at the wall.
His mother smiled. "You do that Spiderman trick very nicely, Leo."
"Hey, Leo!" Sam said. "Why don't you act in our
35 film? We need a kung fu master."

2 ▶ 10

"Yes! Yes, I can do that!" Leo looked at his mother.
"I'm not sure, Leo," she said. "Maybe it's better if you stay here in the garden."

40 Leo looked at his mother sadly. "Please, Mum."
"Yes, Mrs Cooper," said Sam. "Can't he come?"
"All right, Leo," said Mrs Cooper. "You can go."
"Yay!" Leo shouted in a loud voice and danced happily up and down.
45 Mrs Cooper took her son carefully by the arm. "Leo, you must be good and do everything that Sam and Justin tell you."
"OK, Mum, but I'm not a baby!" he said.
"Of course you aren't," said Mrs Cooper.
50 "And Sam," she said, "you and Justin have to be responsible for Leo, and look after him well."
"Don't worry, Mrs Cooper. We can look after him, right, Justin?" said Sam.
"Sure," said Justin.
55 "Thank you," Mrs Cooper said, and gave Sam her mobile number. "And phone me if there are any problems, OK?"

2 What happens?

a) Answer the questions.
   1 Why are Sam and Justin going to the park?
   2 Who do they meet on the way?
   3 What does Leo do nicely?

b) Write three more questions about the text.

c) Give your questions to your partner. Answer your partner's questions.

a) 1 They go to the park because they want to make a film there. • 2 They meet Leo and his mother. • 3 Leo does the Spiderman trick nicely.

3 You're responsible

Sam and Justin have to be responsible for Leo. When do you have to be responsible for something or someone? Swap ideas.

Sometimes I have to look after my little brother.

I have to …

Hier bietet sich auch eine Kettenübung an.

Folie 11 • FöFo 3.4 • KV 12 • LAS 3.2

Part B Practice 3

Lernfeld S. 55: Die S können Personen und Dinge beschreiben und können eine Handlung näher bestimmen (*adjectives* und *adverbs*).

Looking at language

Adjectives describe a **person** or a **thing**.
Adverbs describe **how somebody does something**.

a) Find the missing words from these sentences from the text on p. 54.
Are they adjectives or adverbs?

1 "That's a … idea, Sam," said Justin.   nice
2 "You do that Spiderman trick very …, Leo."   nicely
3 He looked at Sam and Justin and laughed …   loudly
4 "Yay!" Leo shouted in a … voice.   loud

b) Finish this sentence:
To make an adverb, add … to the adjective.

Scan 1 on p. 54 and find more adverbs.

Careful! Some adverbs are *irregular*!

➡ GF 8: Adverbs of manner (pp. 166–167)

1 a) angrily • badly • dangerously • happily • loudly • madly • nervously • quietly • slowly • wildly

1 Mad – madly (Adjectives and adverbs)

a) Make adverbs from these adjectives.

> angry • bad • dangerous • happy • loud •
> mad • nervous • quiet • slow • wild

b) Make sentences about what you hear.
Use the verbs below and an adverb from a).

2			
♪11	1	bark	A dog is barking madly.
♪12	2	ride a bike	Somebody is riding a bike …
♪13	3	speak	… 2 … dangerously. •
♪14	4	shout	3 A man is speaking quietly. • 4 Somebody is eating loudly. •
♪15	5	eat	5 A woman is shouting angrily. • 6 People are clapping wildly. •
♪16	6	clap	7 A girl is singing badly.
♪17	7	sing	

➡ Workbook 14–15 (p. 34)

Weitere Übungsmöglichkeiten zum Thema bietet **KV 12: Adverbs.**

2 Sam's film (Adjectives and adverbs)

Sam tells Justin and Leo more about his film.
Finish his sentences with the right word.

1 Wu runs (excited / **excitedly**) … to the boat.
2 He's a bit (**nervous** / nervously) …
3 He gets the magic book and puts it (careful / **carefully**) … into his bag.
4 Suddenly the boat starts to move (wild / **wildly**) … – it's Master Wong.
5 "I want that book too!" shouts Wong (loud / **loudly**) …
6 Wong and Wu start to fight. They're (**good** / well) … fighters and they fight (good / **well**) …
7 "There is no winner!" says Wu. So they leave the boat and read the book (happy / **happily**) … together.

➡ Workbook 16–18 (pp. 34–36)

3 GAME Are you playing the drums quietly?

a) 👥 Write 15 activities and 10 adverbs, each on one card.

b) 👥 Mix the activity cards. Put them on a desk, face down. Put the adverb cards around them.

c) 👥 Take a card and act out the activity with one of the adverbs. Can the others say what you are doing?

Are you playing the drums quietly?
Are you drinking a cup of tea slowly?

Part B Practice

Lernfeld S. 56: Die S verstehen den Aufbau von Lernpostern und können selbst eines erstellen *(study posters)*.

4 Study skills: Study posters

Study posters show important things about a **topic** on one big page. They **hang** on the wall, so you can read them from your desk.

a) Here's a study poster about relative clauses. Match Morph's tips to the speech bubbles.

b) Make a draft for a study poster about adverbs.
   1 Collect information about adverbs.
      ➡ *Looking at language (p. 55)*
      ➡ *GF 8 (pp. 166–167)*
   2 Draw a **draft** of your study poster. Remember Morph's tips!
   3 Check your draft for mistakes.

c) 👥 Compare your drafts. Choose the best ideas from each one.

d) 👥 Make one study poster about adverbs on a big piece of paper.

e) Hang up all the posters and say what is good about each poster. Choose the best poster and keep it on the wall.

Study skills

Study posters
Ein Lernplakat hilft mir, wenn ich ...
Wenn ich ein Lernplakat mache, sollte ich:
– groß genug schreiben
– ...

Vergleiche deine Ideen mit dem Abschnitt im Skills File.

➡ *SF 4: Study posters (p. 147)*

➡ **Workbook** 19 (p. 36)

FöFo 3.5 ▶ The world behind the picture **3**

1 A German tourist in Plymouth

> Lernfeld: Die S können einen kurzen Film verstehen.

a) Look at the photo. How does it feel when you are in a place that you don't know?

b) Watch the film.

c) 👥 Describe Sandra's problems in Plymouth.

d) 👥 For each of Sandra's problems, write a tip on a large piece of paper.
Watch the film without sound and hold up the tips at the right moment.

e) **EXTRA** What do visitors to Germany have to be careful about?
Write a list of *dos* and *don'ts*.

Länge: 5:44

2 EVERYDAY ENGLISH The way to Peter's house

> Lernfeld: Die S können beschreiben, wo sich etwas befindet und wie sie dort hinkommen.

a) Watch the film and answer the questions.
1 How does Jack know the way to Peter's house? *He checked the Internet before he left home.*
2 What mistake do the two boys make? *They turned into Woodford Crescent.*
3 How do they find the right way? *A woman tells them the right way.*

b) 👥 Think of a place in your hometown and describe where it is. Can the others tell you what the place is?
A: It's opposite our school, next to the museum.
B: Is it the cinema?
A: That's right.

> behind · between ... and ... · in ·
> in front of · near · next to ·
> on the corner of · opposite

Länge: 3:53

c) 👥 Ask your partner how to get from one place to another in your town. Take turns.
A: Can you tell me the way from our school to the park, please?
B: Yes, walk along Lindenstraße to Maxfeldstraße. Then turn left and walk along Maxfeldstraße to the park.

> Cross the road. · Go along ... Road. ·
> Turn left/right (into ... Street). ·
> Go past the cinema/church/... ·
> It's on your left/right.

3 Text

Lernfeld S. 58–59: Die S können eine Geschichte verstehen und dabei **unbekannte Wörter** erschließen. Außerdem können sie die Geschichte fortführen.

Master Wu and the magic book

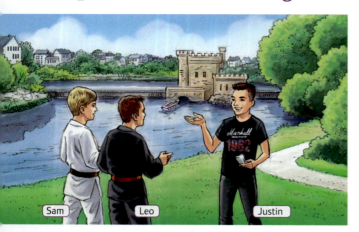

2|18 When the boys arrived at the park, there weren't many people there. Justin pointed to the old gatehouse on the other side of the lake.
"Maybe that's a good place for our film," he said.
5 "OK, but the action scenes have to be at the old boat," Sam said.
"What boat?" asked Justin.
"Can't you see it? It's right in front of the gatehouse," said Sam.
10 "I see it, Sam," said Leo.
"Oh yes, I see it now - but it's so old and broken."
"That's why it's good. It's much more exciting," explained Sam. "Come on, let's go!"
"This is a good place for the first scene," Justin
15 said as they arrived at the °gatehouse.. "Sam, you can walk through the gate on your way to the boat, and then Leo can come out from behind the building and follow you."
"That sounds good," said Sam.
20 Justin filmed the first scene at the gatehouse. Leo hid behind the building and then followed Sam quietly as he walked slowly to the boat.
25 "Cut!" said Justin. "That was great!"
2|19 He looked up at the gatehouse.
"Hey, I have an idea for the next scene."
Then he ran to the gate and
30 disappeared. When Sam and Leo got there, they only found an open door.

"Hey, I'm up here!" shouted Justin from the roof.
"Go in through the door and come up! I have a great view. I can film the scene on the boat from
35 up here!"
Sam and Leo ran up the stairs, and the three boys talked about the next scene of the film. Then Sam and Leo went back down to the boat.
"OK, team, get ready!" shouted Justin from the
40 roof.
Sam jumped onto the deck of the old boat. Leo stayed on the shore.
"OK, Leo," said Sam, "first I'm going to do a few kung fu tricks. Then I'm going to shout: 'The
45 book! I have to find the book!' The second time that you hear the word 'book', you jump onto the boat too, OK?"
"OK, I can do that," said Leo.
"Are you ready?" shouted Justin from the roof.
50 "Ready!" shouted Leo.
"Ready!" shouted Sam.
"ACTION!" Justin shouted and started to film.

Lucy and Maya arrived at the park. 2|20
"There they are!" whispered Lucy. "Let's not tell
55 them that we're here."
"Good idea – we can hide behind the gatehouse," said Maya.

Sam started to do kung fu tricks.
"Sam! The boat is moving," shouted Leo, but Sam
60 didn't hear him. The boat moved further and further away from the shore.
"The book! I have to find the book!" Sam shouted and jumped up again.

58

KV 13 · VAS 3.1, 3.2 📄 Text **3**

This time, when he landed, there was a loud
65 CRACK! and he fell through a **hole** in the boat. Leo
saw everything. He wanted to help, but the boat
was too far from the shore.
"Leo!" shouted Sam. "The water is **up to** my **waist**
and I can't move. Get Justin!"
70 Leo ran to the gatehouse. He was very scared.
Then he saw Lucy. "Lucy! Sam needs help!"

🔊 21 From the roof, Justin also saw that Sam was in
trouble. He left his camera and ran down the stairs
and saw the others.
75 "I can't move!" Sam shouted. "I can't move!"
The only way to help him was to go into the water.
"I'm going in," said Maya.
She ran into the lake and swam out to the boat.
"Are you hurt?" she asked.
80 "I don't know," said Sam. "The water is so cold,
I can't feel my legs."
Maya pulled and pushed the old **wood** away from
Sam's body.
"Can you move now?" Maya asked.
85 "I'm not sure," said Sam. "I can try."
Sam started to swim slowly. "It's OK," he said to
Maya. "I can swim."
So they swam back to the shore. Justin, Lucy and
Leo **hurried** over to them.
90 "Are you all right?" asked Justin.
"Sure, I'm all right," Sam answered. "**Thanks to**
Maya. I'm just a bit wet and very c-c-c-cold," he
laughed nervously. His **lips** were blue.

🔊 22 Leo came over to Sam and gave him a hug.
95 "Don't **hug** me – you don't want to get wet too!
What's your mother going to say?"
"What's *your* mother going to say when she sees
you, Sam?" said Lucy.
Everybody laughed.
100 "You were great, Maya!" said Lucy.
"Maybe, but let's go home now!" said Maya. "I'm
so cold and I don't want to get sick before our trip
tomorrow."
"Wait!" said Justin. "My camera is still in the
105 gatehouse." He went back and ran up the stairs.
Then he came out onto the roof.
"Guess what!" he shouted down to the others,
"I didn't turn my camera off. So we have a scene
with Master Wu on the boat, and a scene where
110 Ninja Maya **rescues** Wu from the water!"

1 At Radford Park

a) Who did what at Radford Park?
   Make as many sentences as you can.

*Justin, Sam and Leo arrived at the park.
Leo followed Sam to …*

> **Differenzierung:**
> Stärkere S können auch eigene Sätze bilden.

Justin	arrive	at the park
Leo	fall	at the gatehouse
Lucy	follow Sam	behind the gatehouse
Maya	film a scene	through a hole …
Sam	jump	to the boat
	hide	onto the deck …
	swim	from the roof …
		back to the shore

b) 👥 Compare your sentences. Use six of them
   to tell the story in a short text.

More help ➔ *p. 127* **More help:** Anleitung zur Auswahl von Sätzen für die Zusammenfassung.

2 New words

Scan the text and find these new words.
How can you work out what they mean?

> gatehouse · gate · roof · view ·
> whispered · hole · hurried · lips

More help ➔ *p. 127* **More help:** Zeilenangaben zu den Wörtern sowie Tipps zur Worterschließung.

3 What next?

> **Neigungsdifferenzierung:**
> Die S wählen zwischen einer künstlerischen Aufgabe und zwei kreativen Schreibaufgaben.

You choose Do a), b) or c).

a) Sam arrives home. His mother sees him.
   Draw a picture with speech bubbles.

b) Maya texts her friend Abby about what
   happened. Write the text.

c) Justin skypes with his father. What does he
   say about the film? Write a short dialogue.

Early finisher ➔ *p. 134* **Early finisher:** Buchstabenrätsel.

➔ **Workbook** 20 (p. 37)

Zusatz: Mit Hilfe von **KV 13: A story to tell** denken sich die S einen eigenen Film aus.

Workbook Checkpoint (pp. 38–41)

3 Unit

Your task

Alle **Steps 1–5** können von den S zu Hause bearbeitet werden. In **Step 6** sollten die S Gelegenheit bekommen, die Rallyes auch tatsächlich zu machen.

Town rally

A rally is a great way to help visitors to learn about your town or area.
The following steps help you to put together a rally.
Maybe you can also learn something new about your town or area.

STEP 1
Choose six places. It's important that people can walk to each place, or go there by bus or tram.
➡ Wordbank 3 (p. 142)

STEP 2
For each place, write down a question that people can only answer when they are there. Maybe you have to go to the place to think of a good question.

STEP 3
Think about the route for your rally. What is the best place to start and the best place to finish? Put your six places in the right order.

STEP 4
How can people get from place to place? Walk along the route or check on a map.

STEP 5
Put your rally together.
- Write down the place where your rally starts.
- Add questions about that place.
- Describe the way to the next place.
- Go on like this until you get to the last place.
- Maybe use pictures of some of the places.
- Write your name and class on your rally.

STEP 6
Give your rally to another student and do his or hers.

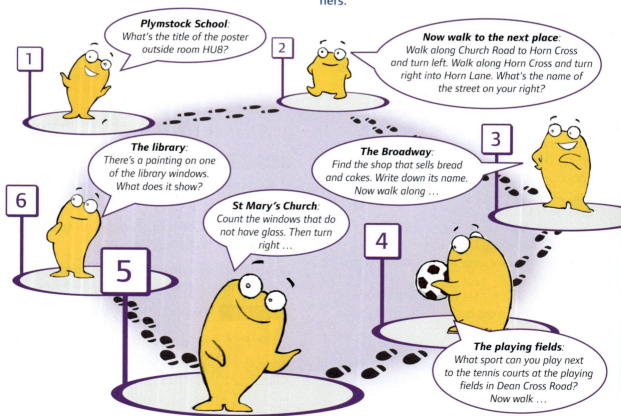

1. **Plymstock School**: What's the title of the poster outside room HU8?
2. **Now walk to the next place**: Walk along Church Road to Horn Cross and turn left. Walk along Horn Cross and turn right into Horn Lane. What's the name of the street on your right?
3. **The Broadway**: Find the shop that sells bread and cakes. Write down its name. Now walk along …
4. **The playing fields**: What sport can you play next to the tennis courts at the playing fields in Dean Cross Road? Now walk …
5. **St Mary's Church**: Count the windows that do not have glass. Then turn right …
6. **The library**: There's a painting on one of the library windows. What does it show?

60

Unit 3

Wie gut warst du?

Wie schätzt du dich selber ein? Schreibe *Words*, *Grammar* und *Writing* in dein Heft und ordne dir für jeden Bereich eine Ampelfarbe zu.

Words
Fielen dir passende Wörter zur Beschreibung deiner Wohngegend ein?

Hattest du Probleme mit Wegbeschreibungen?

Grammar
Hast du Relativsätze verwendet?
Konntest du dich an die Relativpronomen *(who, which, that)* erinnern?

Writing
Hast du dir Notizen zu deinen Ideen gemacht, bevor du deinen Text für die Rallye geschrieben hast?

Konntest du die Wege von Ort zu Ort beschreiben?

Wie kannst du besser werden?

Dort, wo du dich rot oder gelb eingeschätzt hast, helfen dir folgende Tipps beim Wiederholen und Üben.

Words
Druck dir einen Stadtplan von deiner Wohngegend aus und trage die englischen Wörter (*post office, hotel, shop* usw.) an der passenden Stelle ein.

Die wichtigsten Redewendungen und Wörter, die du für eine *town rally* brauchst, findest du hier:
- *S. 46–47, S. 57*
- *Wordbank 3, S. 142*
- *Workbook 1, S. 28*

Grammar
Mach dir ein *study poster* zu Relativsätzen. Trage Beispiele über Läden in deiner Wohngegend ein, z. B. „Bäckerei Müller is the shop that sells great cakes."
- *Grammar File 7: Relative clauses; S. 165*
- *Looking at language S. 50, Übungen S. 50–51*
- *Workbook 6–9, S. 30–31*
- *Skills File 4: Study posters, S. 147*

Writing
Wenn du dir am Anfang Notizen machst, vergisst du beim Schreiben keine deiner guten Ideen.

Wiederhole Übung 2b auf Seite 46. Beschreibe dann deinen Schulweg.

Access story

Because of Winn-Dixie *by Kate DiCamillo*

> Die Auszüge aus *Because of Winn-Dixie* dienen v.a. dem **reading for fun**. Daneben zielen sie auf die zentrale Kompetenz des **extensiven Lesens**. Geübt werden u.a. das **Erschließen unbekannten Wortschatzes** und **eigenständiger Umgang mit Annotationen**. Die Auszüge können auch zum weiteren Üben des **lauten Lesens** verwendet werden.

Chapter One

My name is India Opal Buloni, and last summer my daddy, the preacher, sent me to the store for a box of macaroni-and-cheese, some white rice and two tomatoes, and I came back with a
5 dog. This is what happened: I walked into the produce section of the Winn-Dixie grocery store to pick out my two tomatoes and I almost bumped right into the store manager. He was standing there all red-faced, screaming and
10 waving his arms around.

"Who let a dog in here?" he kept on shouting. "Who let a dirty dog in here?"

At first, I didn't see a dog. There were just a lot of vegetables rolling around on the floor,
15 tomatoes and onions and green peppers. And there was what seemed like a whole army of Winn-Dixie employees running around waving their arms just the same way the store manager was waving his.

20 And then the dog came running around the corner. He was a big dog. And ugly. And he looked like he was having a real good time. His tongue was hanging out and he was wagging his tail. He skidded to a stop and smiled right
25 at me.

I had never before in my life seen a dog smile, but that is what he did. He pulled back his lips and showed me all his teeth. Then he wagged his tail so hard that he knocked some oranges
30 off a display and they went rolling everywhere, mixing in with the tomatoes and onions and green peppers.

The manager screamed, "Somebody grab that dog!"

35 The dog went running over to the manager, wagging his tail and smiling. He stood up on his hind legs. You could tell that all he wanted to do was get face to face with the manager and thank him for the good time he was having in
40 the produce department, but somehow he ended up knocking the manager over. And the manager must have been having a bad day because, lying there on the floor, right in front of everybody, he started to cry. The dog leaned
45 over him, real concerned, and licked his face.

"Please," said the manager, "somebody call the pound."

"Wait a minute!" I hollered. "That's my dog. Don't call the pound."

---

preacher [ˈpriːtʃə] Prediger/in • **produce section** [ˈprɒdjuːs ˌsekʃn] Obst- und Gemüseabteilung • **grocery store** [ˈɡrəʊsəri stɔː] Lebensmittelgeschäft • (to) **bump into sb.** [bʌmp] mit jm. zusammenstoßen • (to) **keep on doing sth., kept** [kiːp, kept] etwas pausenlos tun, etwas immer weiter tun • **employee** [ɪmˈplɔɪiː] Angestellte(r) • **ugly** [ˈʌɡli] hässlich • **tongue** [tʌŋ] Zunge • (to) **wag its tail** [wæɡ, teɪl] mit dem Schwanz wedeln • (to) **skid** [skɪd] schlittern • **display** [dɪˈspleɪ] (Waren-)Auslage • (to) **knock sb. over** [nɒk] jn. umwerfen • (to) **lean** [liːn] sich lehnen, sich beugen • **concerned** [kənˈsɜːnd] besorgt • **pound** *hier*: Tierheim • (to) **holler** [ˈhɒlə] schreien

Access story

50 All the Winn-Dixie employees turned around and looked at me, and I knew I had done something big. And maybe stupid, too. But I couldn't help it. I couldn't let that dog go to the pound.

55 "Here, boy," I said.

The dog stopped licking the manager's face and put his ears up in the air and looked at me, like he was trying to remember where he knew me from.

60 "Here, boy," I said again. And then I figured that the dog was probably just like everybody else in the world, that he would want to get called by a name, only I didn't know what his name was, so I just said the first thing that 65 came into my head. I said, "Here, Winn-Dixie."

And that dog came trotting over to me just like he had been doing it his whole life.

The manager sat up and gave me a hard stare, like maybe I was making fun of him.

70 "It's his name," I said. "Honest."

The manager said, "Don't you know not to bring a dog into a grocery store?"

"Yes sir," I told him. "He got in by mistake. I'm sorry. It won't happen again."

75 "Come on, Winn-Dixie," I said to the dog.

I started walking and he followed along behind me as I went out of the produce department and down the cereal aisle and past all the cashiers and out the door.

80 Once we were safe outside, I checked him over real careful and he didn't look that good. He was big, but skinny; you could see his ribs. And there were bald patches all over him, places where he didn't have any fur at all. Mostly, he 85 looked like a big piece of old brown carpet that had been left out in the rain.

"You're a mess," I told him. "I bet you don't belong to anybody."

He smiled at me. He did that thing again, 90 where he pulled back his lips and showed me his teeth. He smiled so big that it made him sneeze. It was like he was saying, "I know I'm a mess. Isn't it funny?"

It's hard not to immediately fall in love with a 95 dog who has a good sense of humour.

"Come on," I told him. "Let's see what the preacher has to say about you."

And the two of us, me and Winn-Dixie, started walking home.

(to) figure ['fɪgə] sich denken • **a hard stare** [steə] ein strenger Blick • **(to) make fun of sb.** sich über jn. lustig machen • **honest** ['ɒnɪst] ehrlich • **cereal aisle** ['sɪərɪəl ˌaɪl] Gang mit Müsli und Frühstücksflocken • **cashier** [kæ'ʃɪə] Kassierer/in • **safe** [seɪf] sicher, in Sicherheit • **bald patches** [ˌbɔːld 'pætʃɪz] kahle Stellen • **You're a mess.** etwa: Du siehst ja schlimm aus. • **(to) belong to sb.** [bɪ'lɒŋ] jm. gehören • **immediately** [ɪ'miːdɪətli] sofort • **sense of humour** [ˌsens əv 'hjuːmə] (Sinn für) Humor

Access story

Chapter Two

100 That summer I found Winn-Dixie was also the summer me and the preacher moved to Naomi, Florida, so he could be the new preacher at the Open Arms Baptist Church of Naomi. My daddy is a good preacher and a nice man, but 105 sometimes it's hard for me to think about him as my daddy because he spends so much time preaching or thinking about preaching or getting ready to preach. And so, in my mind, I think of him as "the preacher". Before I was 110 born he was a missionary in India and that is how I got my first name. But he calls me by my second name, Opal, because that was his mother's name. And he loved her a lot.

Anyway, while me and Winn-Dixie walked 115 home, I told him how I got my name and I told him how I had just moved to Naomi. I also told him about the preacher and how he was a good man, even if he was too distracted with sermons and prayers and suffering people to go 120 grocery shopping.

"But you know what?" I told Winn-Dixie, "you are a suffering dog, so maybe he will take to you right away. Maybe he'll let me keep you."

Winn-Dixie looked up at me and wagged his 125 tail. He was kind of limping like something was wrong with one of his legs. And I have to admit, he stank. Bad. He was an ugly dog, but already I loved him with all my heart.

When we got to the Friendly Corners Trailer 130 Park, I told Winn-Dixie that he had to behave right and be quiet, because this was an all-adult trailer park and the only reason I got to live in it was because the preacher was a preacher and I was a good, quiet kid. I was 135 what the Friendly Corners Trailer Park manager, Mr Alfred, called "an exception". And I told Winn-Dixie he had to act like an exception, too; specifically, I told him not to pick any fights with Mr Alfred's cats or Mrs Detweiler's 140 little yappy Yorkie dog, Samuel. Winn-Dixie looked up at me while I was telling him everything, and I swear he understood.

"Sit," I told him when we got to my trailer. He sat right down. He had good manners. "Stay 145 here," I told him. "I'll be right back."

The preacher was sitting in the living room, working at the little fold-out table. He had papers spread all around him and he was rubbing his nose, which always meant he was 150 thinking. Hard.

Baptist [ˈbæptɪst] Baptist/in; Baptisten- · (to) **spend, spent** [spend, spent] verbringen · **in my mind** in meinem Kopf · **missionary** [ˈmɪʃənri] Missionar/in · **distracted** [dɪˈstræktɪd] abgelenkt · **sermons and prayers** [ˈsɜːmənz, preəz] Predigten und Gebete · (to) **suffer** [ˈsʌfə] leiden · (to) **take to sb.** an jm. Gefallen finden · (to) **keep, kept** [kiːp, kept] behalten · (to) **limp** [lɪmp] hinken, humpeln · (to) **admit** [ədˈmɪt] zugeben · **trailer park** [ˈtreɪlə pɑːk] Wohnwagensiedlung · (to) **behave** [bɪˈheɪv] sich benehmen · **adult** [ˈædʌlt, əˈdʌlt] Erwachsene(r) · **reason** [ˈriːzn] Grund · **exception** [ɪkˈsepʃn] Ausnahme · **specifically** [spəˈsɪfɪkli] insbesondere · (to) **pick a fight** einen Streit anfangen · **yappy dog** [ˈjæpi] (infml) Kläffer · **fold-out table** Klapptisch · **spread** [spred] ausgebreitet · (to) **rub** [rʌb] reiben ·

64

Access story

"Daddy?" I said.

"Hmmm," he said back.

"Daddy, do you know how you always tell me that we should help those less fortunate than ourselves?"

"Mmmm-hmmm," he said. He rubbed his nose and looked around at his papers.

"Well," I said, "I found a Less Fortunate at the grocery store."

"Is that right?" he said.

"Yes sir," I told him. I stared at the preacher really hard. Sometimes he reminded me of a turtle hiding inside its shell, in there thinking about things and not ever sticking his head out into the world. "Daddy, I was wondering. Could this Less Fortunate, could he stay with us for a while?"

Finally the preacher looked up at me. "Opal," he said, "what are you talking about?"

"I found a dog," I told him. "And I want to keep him."

"No dogs," the preacher said. "We've talked about this before. You don't need a dog."

"I know it," I said. "I know I don't need a dog. But this dog needs me. Look," I said. I went to the trailer door and I hollered, "Winn-Dixie!"

Winn-Dixie's ears shot up in the air and he grinned and sneezed, and then he came limping up the steps and into the trailer and put his head right in the preacher's lap, right on top of a pile of papers.

The preacher looked at Winn-Dixie. He looked at his ribs and his matted-up fur and the places where he was bald. The preacher's nose wrinkled up. Like I said, the dog smelled pretty bad.

Winn-Dixie looked up at the preacher. He pulled back his lips and showed the preacher all of his crooked yellow teeth and wagged his tail and knocked some of the preacher's papers off the table. Then he sneezed and some more papers fluttered to the floor.

"What did you call this dog?" the preacher asked.

"Winn-Dixie," I whispered. I was afraid to say anything too loud. I could see that Winn-Dixie was having a good effect on the preacher. He was making him poke his head out of his shell.

"Well," said the preacher, "he's a stray if ever I've seen one." He put down his pencil and scratched Winn-Dixie behind the ears. "And a Less Fortunate, too. That's for sure. Are you looking for a home?" the preacher asked, real soft, to Winn-Dixie.

Winn-Dixie wagged his tail.

"Well," the preacher said, "I guess you've found one."

Der Roman *Because of Winn-Dixie* steht auch als Lektüre in der *Cornelsen English Library* zur Verfügung (ISBN: 9783060330775).

---

less fortunate [les ˈfɔːtʃnət] weniger glücklich · **(to) remind sb. of sth.** [rɪˈmaɪnd] jn. an etwas erinnern · **turtle** [ˈtɜːtl] Wasserschildkröte · **shell** [ʃel] (Schildkröten-)Panzer · **(to) wonder** [ˈwʌndə] sich fragen · **(to) grin** [ɡrɪn] grinsen · **lap** [læp] Schoß · **pile** [paɪl] Stapel · **matted-up** [ˌmætɪd ˈʌp] verfilzt · **his nose wrinkled up** [ˌrɪŋkld ˈʌp] er rümpfte die Nase · **crooked** [ˈkrʊkɪd] schief · **(to) flutter** [ˈflʌtə] flattern · **(to) poke** [pəʊk] stecken · **stray** [streɪ] streunender Hund · **(to) scratch** [skrætʃ] kratzen, kraulen

4 Unit

Folie 12, 13 • Leistungsmessung Unit 4

Lernfeld S. 66–67: Die S können ein **Bild beschreiben** und verstehen, was in einem Interview über **Dartmoor** gesagt wird.

On Dartmoor

1 Dartmoor countryside

a) 👥 Look at the photos of Dartmoor.
Play *I spy with my little eye*.
A: I spy with my little eye something that **begins** with S.
B: Sky?
A: No.
C: …

b) 👥 Choose a photo. Say what you see and where it is in the picture.
You might need these new words.

| field · footprint · grass · mist · pony · tor · valley |

+foot, *pl* feet

– There's a tor in the background.
– On the left I can see …

➡ Wordbank 4 (pp. 143–144)

Unit **4**

2 A walk on Dartmoor

a) Justin hears a radio interview. The speakers talk about three of the topics in the box.

> (what the countryside looks like) ·
> (farm animals (cows, sheep, goats, etc).) ·
> how many people live on Dartmoor ·
> (what the weather is like) ·
> where tourists can stay

Listen. Which topics do they talk about?

b) Listen again. Take notes on each topic.
   Then compare your notes.

➜ Workbook 1–2 (p. 42)

3 EXTRA A Dartmoor °legend: "The °Devil's footprints"

Listen to the rest of the interview.
What did people find in the snow in 1885?
What did they think about it?
they thought only the devil could do that

footprints in the snow that went up the wall and across the roofs of houses

Your task

At the end of this unit:
Write a poem about a place in the countryside.

Run, river, run,
Into the forest, between the hills, °across the
Valley, °below the °bridge and
°Empty into the sea,
Run, river, run

4 Part A

Lernfeld S. 68–69: Die S können eine Geschichte verstehen.

KV 14

Zusatz: **KV 14: Saturday morning** enthält *right/wrong*-Aufgaben und Lückentexte zum Text.

1 🔊 Saturday morning

8:59, on the bus to Tavistock

Sam: Lucy, your mobile is ringing.
Lucy: Thanks, Sam. Oh hi, Grandma. Yes, we're on the right bus. – I've texted you the time that we arrive: 9:29. – No, Mum hasn't phoned me. Why? – Yes, we've checked the times of the bus back to Plymouth. Don't worry. See you soon, Grandma.
Sam: Wow, she really asks lots of questions!
Lucy: Yes, she has already phoned twice this morning. She always worries so much.

+once

9:29, at Tavistock bus station

Maya: I can't see anybody, Lucy. Where's your grandma?
Lucy: There she is! Over there. Hi, Grandma!
Grandma: Hi, Lucy, hello, Maya. And you must be Sam and Justin. Lucy has told me all about you! Come on, let's get into the car. I've just made some scones – they're still warm. So I hope you're all hungry.
Lucy: I am! I haven't eaten anything today.
Maya: I am too! I haven't had breakfast yet.

Box "Irregular past participles", Voc, S. 193

10:30, after tea and scones

Lucy: Does anybody want to feed the rabbits with me?
Maya: I do!
Grandpa: OK Maya, you go with Lucy, and the boys can look around the farm with me.

Oh, and you must be Sam.

Maya · Lucy · Grandma Tizzard · Sam · Justin

11:45, on the tour of the farm

Justin: Wow, that's a big tractor.
Grandpa: We use it to bring in hay from the fields. Come on, climb up. But don't touch the key.
Sam: I've never been on a tractor before.
Justin: It's really cool in here …
Sam: Yeah! It's so high. I can see the ponies.
Justin: Those are horses, Sam, not ponies.
Sam: But Lucy says that you own lots of ponies, Mr Tizzard.
Grandpa: Yes, we do. But they don't live on the farm. They live out on the moor.
Justin: And they never come back to the farm?
Grandpa: Just once a year. We °round them up in autumn. We use the horses to do that.
Sam: So we can't see the ponies?
Grandpa: Don't worry, Sam. After lunch we can all go out onto the moor.

Box "before" Voc, S. 193

EXTRA **Background file**

Lernfeld: Die S können einen kurzen Text mit Informationen über **Dartmoor ponies** verstehen.

Dartmoor ponies

There are about 3,000 ponies on Dartmoor. Most of the year they live on the open moor. New °foals – baby ponies – °are born in the spring. In autumn, groups of farmers °round up the ponies and take them back to the farms. There they count and check them and then sell some – °mostly as children's ponies. All the others go back to the open moor again and °spend the winter there. The cold winter is too hard for other kinds of ponies, but the Dartmoor pony is a very °strong animal.

a) Find three interesting facts about Dartmoor ponies.

b) 👥 Compare your ideas.

68

Part A 4

2 Saturday afternoon

3 Who says what?

Lernfeld: Personalpronomen *(personal pronouns)*.

Find these sentences in 1 and 2.
Who are the speakers?
Who do the pronouns stand for?

1 Yes, we're on the right bus.
 – Lucy is the speaker, and the we stands for …
2 Wow, she really asks lots of questions!
3 Lucy has told me all about you!
4 But Lucy says that you own lots of ponies.
5 Yes, we do. But they don't live on the farm.
6 After lunch we can all go out onto the moor.
7 He hasn't finished his bath yet.

1 Lucy / we = Lucy, Sam, Justin • 2 Sam / she = Lucy's grandma • 3 Lucy's grandma / you = Sam, Justin • 4 Sam / you = Lucy's grandpa • 5 Lucy's grandpa / they = ponies • 6 Lucy's grandpa / we = Sam, Justin, Maya, Lucy, Lucy's grandparents • 7 Lucy's grandpa / he = Sam

4 Have a go

Lernfeld: Die S verwenden vorbewusst das *present perfect*.

a) 👥 Say what you have already done today:

I've already phoned	my mother/Ben/…
I've already had	a bath / breakfast / a maths lesson/…
I've already eaten	a sandwich/hamburger/… some cheese/fruit/…

b) 👥 Say what you haven't done yet today.

I haven't phoned	my brother / Maria / …	
I haven't had	lunch / a PE lesson /…	yet.
I haven't eaten	any biscuits/chocolate/…	

69

4 Part A Practice

LAS 4.1

Lernfeld S. 70–71: Die S können das **present perfect** bilden und verwenden. Sie lernen einige unregelmäßige Partizipien.

Looking at language [Box "Irregular past participles", Voc, S. 194]

a) Look at these sentences.
   I've <u>texted</u> you the time that we arrive.
   No, Mum <u>hasn't</u> <u>phoned</u> me.

Now look at lines 7 to 36 in 1 on p. 68.
Find more sentences with a form of have.
Write them down and underline the two parts of the verb.

Yes, we<u>'ve</u> <u>checked</u> the times ...

b) Write down the <u>infinitives</u> of the verbs like this:
   Yes, we've checked the times ... (check)

How do you form this new tense?
Which verbs are irregular?

➡ GF 9 a–c, e: The present perfect (pp. 167–169)

➡ List of irregular verbs (p. 248)

I haven't eaten any breakfast yet.

"... haven't eaten"? That must be irregular.

1 8:35 at Plymstock School (Present perfect: statements) ■▫▫▫▫

What has already happened at Plymstock School? What hasn't happened yet?
Add the right forms: has, have (+) or hasn't, haven't (-).

1 Sam and Leo **have** already arrived. (+)
2 But Lucy and Justin ... arrived yet. (-) **haven't**
3 Justin ... finished his breakfast yet! (-) **hasn't**
4 The school library ... already opened. (+) **has**
5 Morph ... already hidden on a shelf. (+) **has**
6 The library cat ... seen him yet. (-) **hasn't**
7 Miss Bell ... already opened her classroom. (+) **has**
8 Some of the students ... already come in. (+) **have**
9 But lessons ... started yet. (-) **haven't**

Early finisher Write more sentences about Morph.
Morph has already made his bed. He hasn't ...

➡ Workbook 3–4 (p. 43)

2 My mobile has fallen into the river (Present perfect: statements) ■■▫▫▫

a) Write down all the infinitives.
   broken – break
   eaten – ...

   broken · eaten · fallen · gone · heard · hidden · left · made · met · seen · taken · written

b) Finish these sentences with a verb from a). Use the present perfect.
   1 My mobile **has fallen** into the river.
   2 We'... ... the wrong bus! **We've taken**
   3 I'... ... my money at home. **I've left**
   4 Grandma ... ... scones for us. **has made**
   5 My parents ... ... away for the weekend. **have gone**
   6 Sorry, but I'... ... a cup. **I've broken**
   7 We'... ... that film before. **We've seen**
   8 Jack ... ... too many chocolates. **has eaten**

More help ➤ p. 128 **More help:** Das passende Verb ist jeweils vorgegeben. Die S bilden nur noch die korrekte *present perfect*-Form.

c) 👥 Make short dialogues. Match sentences from b) to these sentences. Act out the dialogues.
   My mobile has fallen into the river. Oh dear. So you can't phone home now.

   a Yes, but I'd like to see it again.
   b <mark>Oh dear</mark>. So you can't phone home now.
   c OK, let's get off at the next bus stop.
   d Oh, I see. That's why he feels so sick now.

   e Don't worry. We have lots of cups.
   f Great! We can have cream tea today.
   g Let's meet at your house, then.
   h Don't worry. I can buy our drinks.

   1b · 2c · 3h · 4f · 5g · 6e · 7a · 8d

➡ Workbook 5 (p. 44)

Part A Practice 4

3 I've done all my homework (Present perfect: statements)

Jo and Jessie have a list of jobs for this weekend.

Partner B: You're Jo. Go to p. 138.
Partner A: You're Jessie.

JESSIE'S JOBS
1 do all my homework for Monday
2 write a thank-you mail to Uncle Jim
3 buy new felt pens
4 practise the piano
5 help Mum in the kitchen
6 clean my bike
7 make a birthday card for Grandma
8 feed my hamster
9 throw away my old magazines
10 collect pictures for my project

a) Write down your ten jobs in a table like this:

	Me	Jo
homework		
thank-you mail		
...		

b) It's Sunday morning now.
Tick (✓) five jobs that you have done.

c) 👥 Take turns. Say what you have/haven't done. Fill in the table for your partner.
A: I've done all my homework for Monday.
What about you?
B: No, I haven't done my homework, but I've …

d) Write about your partner.
Jo hasn't done all his homework, but he has written …

➡ Workbook 6 (p. 44)

4 They've just seen a ghost (Present perfect: statements)

Alternative: Es können auch eigene Fotos (auf Folie gezogen) als Grundlage verwendet werden.

a) What has just happened? Write down your idea for each picture.

1   2   3   4   5

1 They've just seen a ghost / a lion in the park / a …

More help ➡ p. 128
More help: Textbausteine als Hilfe (Ideen, Lexik, Satzstruktur).

b) 👥 Compare your ideas.

EXTRA 👥 Write one more sentence for your partner. Draw a picture for your partner's sentence.

➡ Workbook 7 (p. 44)

5 This week, this month, this year 💬

a) Write three sentences on a card like this:

> I've played football this week.
> I've bought new trainers this month.
> I've … this year.

Don't write your name on the card.

b) Put all the cards together.
One student takes a card and reads it aloud.
Can the others guess who it is?
A: That must be Florian. He's played football this week.
B: But Florian hasn't bought new trainers this month. So it can't be him.

71

4 Part B

Lernfeld S. 72: Die S können eine Geschichte verstehen.

KV 15 • LAS 4.2

1 The lambs in the barn

Alternative: KV 15: The lambs in the barn enthält Aufgaben zum Text.

Lucy   Maya

Sunday morning on the farm

Grandpa: Well, well, the two °sleeping beauties have woken up at last.
Lucy: Oh Grandpa – stop that!
5 Grandpa: I've made your favourite breakfast, °Princess Lucy: bacon and eggs.
Lucy: Mmm … that smells good.
Grandpa: And what would Princess Maya like to drink?
10 Maya: Me? Er … a glass of milk, please.
Grandma: Have you ever tried sheep's milk, Maya?
Maya: No, I haven't. But …
Grandma: It's really delicious. Come on, try it!
Maya: Hmm, it's very … er … different.
15 Lucy: Grandpa, what can we do today?
Grandpa: Well, we could go on a short trip. Maya, have you ever been to Tavistock °Abbey?
Maya: No, I haven't.
20 Lucy: But I have, Grandpa, and I don't want to go there again. I'd like to do something on the farm.
Grandpa: Have you seen our new lambs yet?
Lucy: No, we haven't.
25 Grandpa: Well, there are seven little lambs in the barn. You can give their mothers some hay and clean water.
Maya: I'd love to do that.
Grandma: Have you brought any other shoes with
30 you, Maya?
Maya: No, I've only brought these trainers.
Grandma: They could easily get dirty. But I'm sure I can find an old pair of boots for you.
Grandpa: And please, princesses: don't forget to
35 close the barn door behind you. I don't want to lose any lambs. They aren't strong enough to live out on the moor.

Box "Verb + Adverb, Verb + Adjektiv", Voc, S. 194

At the barn

Maya: Can you see anything, Lucy? It's so
40 dark in here.
Lucy: Here's the light.
Maya: Oh look! The lambs! They're so sweet!
Lucy: Here's the hay, Maya. Help me. It's heavy.
45 Maya: Time for lunch, sheep! Come and get it!
Lucy: Now, let's check the sheep's water.
Maya: Hey look, Lucy! That lamb is drinking its mother's milk. I've never seen that before. I'm going to get my camera.

❖

50 Lucy: Maya, have you taken enough photos?
Maya: Please, Lucy. Just one more.
Lucy: Maya, you haven't closed the door. Look! It's still open.
Maya: Oh no! Sorry, Lucy.
55 Lucy: Quick, let's count the lambs and make sure that they're all still there.
Maya: Right. Oh, Lucy. There are only six lambs. One is missing. I'm sorry. I …
Lucy: There's no time to talk, Maya. Let's go
60 and find it. Now!

Der Dialog bietet viel Dramatik und bietet sich an, um an ihm das **reading aloud** (Unit 2) zu wiederholen und zu üben.

2 Who does what?

Write sentences that say who does the things: Grandpa, Grandma, Lucy, Maya or the lambs.

- makes breakfast   *Grandpa makes breakfast.*
- drinks sheep's milk   … *Maya drinks …*
- gets boots for Maya   *Grandma gets …*
- calls Maya and Lucy princesses *Grandpa calls …*
- turns on the light in the barn *Lucy turns on …*
- gives the sheep hay   *Maya and Lucy give …*
- wants to take photos   *Maya wants …*
- leaves the barn door open *Maya leaves …*

72

Part B Practice

Folie 14 • FöFo 4.1 • KV 16

Lernfeld S. 73: Die S können **Fragen im** *present perfect* (mit *ever* und *yet*) bilden und verwenden. Sie lernen einige unregelmäßige Partizipien.

Language help
Box "Irregular past participles", Voc, S. 195

a) You already know present perfect statements:

I have brought these trainers.

You make questions like this:

Have you brought any other shoes?

b) In the present perfect, you often ask questions with *ever* and *yet*.

Have you seen our new lambs **yet**?

Have you **ever** been to Tavistock Abbey?

➔ GF 9 d, e: The present perfect: (pp. 168–169)

1 Has the rain stopped yet? (Present perfect: questions with *yet*)

1 2 3 4 5

a) It's 10 o'clock on Saturday morning. Look at the pictures and say what is happening.
1 It's raining. • 2 Grandpa is shopping. • 3 The girls are cycling to Plymouth. • 4 The cats are sleeping. • 5 The teacher is correcting the homework.

b) Now it's 11 o'clock. Write questions about each picture.

| rain · stop? | Grandpa · finish the shopping? | girls · arrive in Plymouth? | cats · wake up? | teacher · correct the homework? |

Has the rain stopped yet? Has … • 2 Has Grandpa finished the shopping yet? • 3 Have the girls arrived in Plymouth yet? • 4 Have the cats woken up yet? • 5 Has the teacher corrected the homework yet?

31–35 c) Listen and find out the answers to your questions.   ➔ Workbook 8 (p. 45)
👥 Then ask and answer the questions. 1 Yes, the rain has stopped. • 2 No, Grandpa hasn't finished the shopping yet. • 3 No, the girls haven't arrived in Plymouth yet. • 4 Yes, the cats have woken up. • 5 No, the teacher hasn't corrected the homework yet.

2 Have you ever tried sheep's milk? (Present perfect: questions with *ever*)

a) Copy the questionnaire.
Add five questions.

Die S verwenden alternativ KV 16: Have you …?.

More help ➔ p. 128

b) Add two columns to your questionnaire.
Answer the questions for yourself.
Use words or phrases from the box below.

Have you ever	tried sheep's milk?
	been on a farm?
	won a prize?
	…?

Me	Partner
No, never.	
Yes, twice.	
…	

never · once · twice · three times · lots of times · often

c) 👥 Ask your partner your questions.
Write down their answers.

Have you ever drunk sheep's milk?
Yes, I have. Three times.

d) What interesting things have you found out?
Write some sentences.

Jan has never drunk sheep's milk, but he has been on a farm once.

➔ Workbook 9 (p. 45)

4 Reading course

Lernfeld S. 74: Die S entnehmen einem Werbeprospekt durch **Markieren** die wichtigsten Informationen.

Marking up a text

When you read a long text, it's a good idea to mark up keywords and phrases in it.
You can use these keywords and phrases to tell other people about the text.

a) Read about Becky Falls. Try to understand new words before you look them up in a dictionary.

→ SF 6: Understanding new words (Revision) (p. 148)

b) Read the marked phrases in the first two paragraphs. Which of these questions do they answer?
Where can you eat? How can you get there? (What can you do at Becky Falls?)

c) Ask your teacher for a copy of the text. Read the rest. Which paragraphs answer the two other questions from b)? Draw two more lines at the side of the page.

d) Read the rest of the text again. Mark up the keywords that answer the two questions.
- First: Underline keywords with a pencil.
- Second: Check the words that you underlined. Do they all answer the questions in b)?
- Third: Highlight only words that answer the questions.

→ SF 11: Marking up a text (p. 150)

Becky Falls Woodland Park

There's lots to see and do at Becky Falls. Meet lots of strange °insects in our °'Ugly Bug' show. Some of them are very large and scary! You can also see, feed and touch wild animals.

We have great river walks, but you need good shoes for them – don't wear flip-flops! We're sorry, but our woodland walks aren't °wheelchair-friendly.

In warm weather, swimming in the river is a great idea.

For °indoor people, the theatre is the place for fun and °creative activities.

Where can you eat?
Becky Falls has a fantastic café, with hot °meals, snacks and ice creams. You can also bring a picnic. We have picnic areas, or you can choose a place on our walks, right at the °waterfall for example!

There is also a shop where you can buy yummy Dartmoor goods, like jams and chocolate, or books on Dartmoor and toys.

How can you get there?
Becky Falls is °half an hour by car from Exeter and about 40 minutes from Torbay or Plymouth. You can also get here on the Haytor Hoppa bus – see the Dartmoor °National Park website for °details.

Did you like your family day out at Becky Falls Woodland Park? Tell us about it, so other people know it's a great place to go. Go to our website and write about your great day: http://www.beckyfalls.com/

Thank you – come again!

e) 👥 Compare your keywords and phrases. Discuss the differences. Make changes if you find better keywords and phrases.

f) Write a short text about why you would/wouldn't like to go to Becky Falls. Your keywords and phrases can help you to give reasons.
I would like to go to Becky Falls. The first reason is that you can …

Early finisher 👥 Find a partner and read your text to him/her.

→ Workbook 10 (p. 46)

FöFo 4.2 • KV 17   ▶ The world behind the picture   **4**

Lernfeld S. 75: Die S können kurze Filmclips verstehen und Aufgaben dazu bearbeiten. Sie können Gesprächen folgen, dazu Fragen beantworten und Äußerungen Personen zuordnen.

1 EVERYDAY ENGLISH
At the information centre

a) Watch the film and find out:
  – What information does Ruby want?
  – Where does she *decide* to go?
  – What does Oliver want to do there?

b) 👥 Check your answers.

c) Who says these things, Ruby or the information officer?
  1 What can I do for you?
  2 I need some information for me and my friends.
  3 What are you *interested in*?
  4 Are there any *waterfalls* on Dartmoor?
  5 How can we get there?
  6 The best way is to take the *train*.
  7 What time does the train leave?
  8 There are trains every hour.
  9 How long do they *take*?
  10 How much does Becky Falls cost?
  11 It's £6.75 for children under 16.
  12 Do you have any more questions?

Ruby: 2, 4, 5, 7, 9, 10
Information officer: 1, 3, 6, 8, 11, 12

Länge: 7:36

d) 👥 Partner A: You want to find out what you can do at Becky Falls.
Partner B: You work in the information centre.

Use the information and language from pp. 74–75 and work out a dialogue together.
Act it out for the class.

2 °Letterboxing

a) Watch part 1 of the film.
In what order do these things happen?
There is one sentence that you don't need.

Alternative Erarbeitung mit **KV 17: Letterboxing**.

3 • 5 • 8 • 2 • 1 • 7 • 4

a stamp

1 They put their stamp in the Scary Tor book.
2 Paul finds the °**letterbox**.
3 Sarah shows the others the stamp.
4 Anna reads a letter.
5 The kids arrive at Scary Tor.
6 The kids feed the ponies.
7 They put the Scary Tor stamp in their book.
8 They look for the letterbox.

b) 👥 Compare your answers.

EXTRA Write down how letterboxing works.
When you go letterboxing, you need …
You look for …

Where could you go letterboxing in your area?

Beim **Letterboxing** geht es darum, im Gelände versteckte Behälter mit Hilfe von Hinweisen, Karte und Kompass zu finden.

Länge: 4:25

c) 👥 Before you watch part 2, discuss these questions:
  – Who do you think is coming?
  – What's going to happen then?

Now watch part 2 without the sound.
Were you right?

d) Write your own dialogue for part 2. Then watch part 2 with the sound and compare.

4 Part C

Lernfeld S. 76: Die S können eine kurze Geschichte verstehen.

FöFo 4.3 • LAS 4.3, 4.4

1 🔊 Out on the high moor

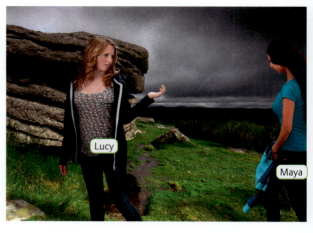

[2 ▶ 36] "Lucy, we've looked **everywhere**," said Maya. "And there's still no sign of the lamb. Let's phone your grandpa."
"Not yet," said Lucy, "let's look a bit more."
5 "But where?" asked Maya. "The moor goes on **for ever** and I can't see any sheep."
"I can," said Lucy. "Over there. Look! Let's go."
"Have you ever gone that way before?"
"Of course. I was there last summer. I went right
10 to the top of that hill. That's King's Tor."
"OK," said Maya, "but that hill is very far away."

[2 ▶ 37] "We've walked **for miles**," Maya said. "And we still aren't there."
"It's not much further," Lucy answered.
15 "Hey, look at those goats!" said Maya. "I've never seen wild goats before."
"Yes, you have," said Lucy. "We saw some yesterday – when we were out on the moor."
"Oh, right."
20 "Come on," Lucy said. "We're almost at the top of the hill."

[2 ▶ 38] "What now?" Maya asked.
"Let's climb this tor," said Lucy. "From the top we can see even more."
25 "These boots are **hurting**," said Maya, "and it's so windy. I can't climb **any more**."
"Come on, Maya. There's a great view **across** the moor up here. Come on, you're almost there."
"How can we find a little lamb in this big place?"
30 asked Maya. "It's **impossible**."

[Box "hurt", Voc, S. 195]

"Don't say that, Maya," said Lucy. "Look at those sheep over there. We haven't checked them yet."
"Yes, we have. We **passed** them an hour ago."
"Are you sure?" asked Lucy.
35 "Yes, of course. There's the **path** that we came on. And look, it's starting to rain now, and we haven't brought our **raincoats**. Let's get down quickly. We can wait under that rock at the bottom of the tor **until** the rain is over."

[+coat]

40 "I've never seen rain like this before," said Maya. [2 ▶ 39]
"The poor little lamb," Lucy whispered. "It must be very wet."
"Lucy, phone your grandpa, pleeease."
"Wait a minute, Maya," said Lucy. "I can hear
45 something. It's **crying**. Maybe it's the lamb."
"I can't hear anything, Lucy ... just the rain."
"No ... listen ... there it is again," said Lucy.

2 Lucy or Maya?

a) Who could say these things? Lucy or Maya? At what part of the story could they say them?

- I don't want to get wet!
- I can't go on.
- Don't worry. We'll be OK.
- What's that sound?
- Let's get help.
- The moor is so big.

b) 👥 Compare your ideas.

Maya could say "I can't go on" in line 21 or in line ...

3 The end of the story

a) Do Lucy and Maya find the missing lamb? Do they get back to the farm? Write your own ending for the story.

More help ➔ p. 129   **More help:** Ideen in Form von Fragen, die die Kreativität der S anregen.

b) 👥 Read your ending to your group. Which ending is the best? Why? Then listen and find out how Lucy and Maya's adventure on the moor ended. [2 ▶ 40]

FöFo 4.4 — Part C 4

Lernfeld S. 77: Die S können ein Gedicht verstehen und mit anderen darüber sprechen.

4 °Jigsaw poem

A — My mother °has gone 〔2 ▶ 41〕
They come in the autumn of every year,
With their horses and °shouts they bring us down,
We run from the moor where the °air is clear
Down to the farms near the °noisy town.
One autumn they took my mother away,
Young and alone, I went back to the moor,
I waited and waited all that day,
I cried in the night, but she came °no more.

B — °Storm on the moor 〔2 ▶ 42〕
The moor is my home and in twenty years
I have never seen a sky so black,
The rain will fall like the coldest tears,
I'm far from the forest and cannot go back.
I remember a storm when I was a foal,
I stood °by my mother and hid from the rain,
The clouds on the tor were as black as °coal,
And the °lightning danced again and again.

C — The face in the storm 〔2 ▶ 43〕
My own young foal watches the sky
And stands by my side as the day gets dark,
I see the lightning in her eye,
Hear the birds that cry and the dogs that bark.
The wind comes fast, the rain hits the tor,
Across the sky the black clouds °race,
I remember my life on the open moor
And in the eye of the storm see my mother's face.

D — The moor and the mother 〔2 ▶ 44〕
I stand by the tor that my mother knew,
The rocks of grey and the grass so green,
I °dream of summer when the sky is blue,
The most beautiful sky that I have seen.
We ran together on the moor so °wide,
We drank from the rivers and stood on the tor,
We watched the moon, played °side by side,
But she has gone and will come no more.

a) Make groups of four students.
Each student chooses one verse of the poem.
Read your verse quietly to yourself.
Try to understand new words before you
check them in a dictionary.
➡ SF 6: Understanding new words (Revision) (p. 148)

b) Read your verse again. Who is the speaker?
What story does the speaker tell?
Take notes about the main points.

c) Use your notes and tell your partners about your verse.

> In my **verse**, the speaker is … She talks about …
> In my verse, the speaker tells us about …

d) Agree on a good order for the four verses. Then think of a title for the poem.

> I think verse C is first because …
> I don't agree. I think the first verse is …

(www) Find out more about Dartmoor animals and see photos of them here.

4 Part C Practice

Folie 14

1 Yes, I went there last summer (Present perfect or simple past?)

> **Lernfeld:** Die S können entscheiden, ob sie das **present perfect** oder das **simple past** verwenden müssen.

a) Finish the short dialogues. Use the present perfect or the simple past forms of the verbs.

1 Lucy, … you ever … to the Eden Project? (be)
   Yes, I … there with Maya last summer. (go)
2 Justin, … … ever … to New York? (be)
   Yes, I … New York with my dad last year. (visit)
3 Sam, … you … your project yet? (finish)
   No, I …
4 Maya, … … ever … sheep's cheese? (eat)
   No, … … But I … sheep's milk at Lucy's
   grandma's two days ago. (drink)
5 Lucy, … the rain … yet? (stop)
   Yes, it … ten minutes ago.
6 Sam, … … ever … Mrs Tizzard's scones? (eat)
   Yes, I …! I … some last weekend. (have)
7 … Silky ever … to Dartmoor? (be)
   No, of course she …

> ### Language help
>
> You use the <u>present perfect</u> with words like *never*, *ever*, *yet*.
>
> You use the <u>simple past</u> with words like *yesterday*, an hour/ten minutes/… *ago*, *last* week/summer/year/…
>
> – I've *never* seen wild goats before.
> – Yes, you have. We saw some *yesterday*.
>
> ➡ *GF 10: Present perfect or simple past? (p. 169)*

b) 👥 Ask and answer questions like these:
A: Have you ever eaten crab meat?
B: Yes, I have. I ate some last summer.
B: Have you ever seen the Loch Ness monster?

➡ **Workbook** 11–12 (p. 47)

1 have … been / went · 2 have you … been / visited · 3 have … finished / haven't · 4 have you … eaten / I haven't
… drank · 5 has … stopped / stopped · 6 have you … eaten / have had · 7 Has … been / hasn't

2 Questions for Lucy (*some* and *any*)

> **Lernfeld:** Die S können unterscheiden, wann sie **some** und wann sie **any** verwenden müssen.

a) Finish the dialogue. Add *some* or *any*.

Lucy: Do you have … questions? *any*
Ruby: Do your grandparents have … ponies? *any*
Lucy: Yes, they have … ponies out on the moor. *some*
Ruby: Have you ever ridden … of their ponies? *any*
Lucy: No, they're too wild. But Grandpa sells … *some*
        ponies to … riding centres. They **train** the *some*
        ponies and then people can ride them.
Oliver: Are there … **otters** near the farm? *any*
Lucy: Well, Grandpa says there are … otters in *some*
        the River Walkham, but I haven't seen … *any*
Oliver: Well, Jack and I saw … otters yesterday! *some*

b) 👥 What wild animals live near you?

> There are some **deer** in the town park.

> Are there any wild ponies there?

> ### TIP
>
> There are *some* ponies over there. (positive)
> There aren't *any* sheep. (negative)
> Are there *any* cows or horses? (question)
>
> ➡ *GF 11 a: some and any (p. 170)*

➡ **Workbook** 13 (p. 48)

3 Leo talks about Dartmoor (*something, somebody, anything, anybody*)

> **Lernfeld:** Die S können **something/somebody** und **anything/anybody** korrekt verwenden.

Mary asks Leo about Dartmoor. Finish the dialogue. Add *something, somebody, anything and anybody*.

Mary: So tell me … about Dartmoor, Leo.
Leo: I don't know … about Dartmoor. I've never been there. I don't know … there.
Mary: But you've just heard Lucy's talk. Do you remember … about it?
Leo: Oh, I remember …! The ponies are wild. You can't ride them.

Mary: Do you know … more about the ponies? Where do they take them?
Leo: To riding centres. … trains the ponies and then you can ride them.
Mary: Do you know … who can ride a pony?
Leo: No, I don't know … But I know … who can ride a bike. Me!

More help ➡ p. 129; **Early finisher** ➡ p. 135; ➡ GF 11 b: somebody/anybody (p. 170); ➡ **Workbook** 14–16 (pp. 48–50)

> **More help:** Die S wählen aus zwei vorgegebenen Optionen.

> **Early finisher:** Wortübung mit *scrambled letters*.

something · anything · anybody · anything · something · anything · Somebody · anybody · anybody · somebody

78

FöFo 4.5   **Part C Practice**   **4**

4 Snakes in the Alps 🇬🇧

Lernfeld: Die S können deutsche Informationen auf Englisch wiedergeben.

You are in a hostel in the Alps. An English roommate asks you about poisonous snakes.
You find some information online. Answer your roommate's questions in English.

Where do they live?
What do adders do when they meet people?
When can they be dangerous?
What should you do if a snake bites you?

Gibt es giftige Schlangen in den Alpen?
Ja, die Kreuzotter. Die findet man vor allem in Wäldern und auf Mooren.
Kreuzottern sind nicht aggressiv und versuchen bei Gefahr immer zu flüchten. So kann es nur zu einem Biss kommen, wenn man ihnen zu nahe kommt und sie dadurch in Angst versetzt. Ihr Gift verursacht zwar Schmerzen, ist aber relativ harmlos – ein Arzt sollte dennoch aufgesucht werden.

adder

More help ➔ p. 129; ➔ SF 12: Mediation (Revision) (p. 151)

More help: Die gesuchten Informationen sind farbig hervorgehoben. ➔ **Workbook** 17 (p. 50)

they live in woods and on moors • they are scared and try to get away • when people get near them • you should see a doctor

5 Study skills: Describing a picture

Lernfeld: Die S können Bilder beschreiben und sagen, was darauf passiert. Sie verwenden dazu das *present progressive*.

a) Describe the photo.
• Say what the picture is about in one or two sentences.
• Say who/what you see, and where they are.
• Give information about the colours, time of day, time of year, …
• Say what is happening and who is doing what.

– This is a photo of a cold day in winter.
– There's / There are … in the foreground.
– I can see … in the background.
– At the top/bottom …
– On the right/left …

– It's night / day / early morning / …
– It's summer/winter / …

– Somebody / A man / A girl is …ing.

b) Partner A: Go to p. 136. Partner B: Go to p. 139.

Study skills   **Describing pictures**

Wenn ich ein Bild beschreibe, muss ich auf folgende Dinge achten:
- was/wer sich wo …
- was passiert und wer …
- …

Vergleiche deine Ideen mit dem Abschnitt im Skills File.
➔ SF 17: Describing pictures (p. 154)
➔ **Workbook** 18 (p. 51)

79

4 Text

Lernfeld S. 80–81: Die S können eine Geschichte verstehen und darin wichtige Informationen markieren und wiedergeben. Sie setzen sich in einer kreative Aufgabe mit dem Text auseinander.

The tulip garden

2 | 45 In the evening, the weather on Dartmoor was even worse. Rain fell from big, dark clouds, and the wind was strong and cold. After their hot baths, Lucy and Maya found warm clothes and
5 went downstairs to the kitchen.
"Good evening, princesses," said Grandpa. "How are you feeling after your adventure?"
"Much better," Lucy said. Maya nodded.
"Come and have a nice cup of tea," said
10 Grandma.
"Yes, and don't wander around the moor tomorrow," Grandpa said. "Now, after dinner, we can have some cocoa and watch a DVD. Or I can tell you an old Dartmoor story. What do you
15 say?"
"Story, story!" both girls shouted.

❖

After dinner, they all sat in armchairs in front of the fireplace with big mugs of hot cocoa.
"You know Merrivale, Lucy?" Grandpa asked.
20 "Yes," Lucy answered. "It's the village near here."
"Right – and have you ever seen that old ruin just outside the village?" Grandpa asked.
"You mean that ruin where the ground is always brown? Where there's never any grass?"
25 "Yes, that's the place. Well, this is an old story about it," said Grandpa.

2 | 46 Many, many years ago, in the village of Merrivale, there was a pretty little cottage with a beautiful garden. An old
30 woman lived there, all alone. But she was never lonely. The village children often came to visit her, and she was friendly to all the animals and birds on the moor. She left food and water for them in her garden and that's how many of
35 the birds got through the winter. The old woman loved her garden and worked in it all the time. It was full of the prettiest flowers. One night, when she was very tired and already in bed, she thought she heard the
40 sound of music in her garden. She got up. When she looked out of the window, she couldn't believe what she saw. There, on the grass, was a group of °pixies!
Pixies are the little magic people of the moor.
45 They're kind to people who are friendly. But make a pixie angry and see what happens!

80

VAS 4.1, 4.2　　　　　　　　　　　　　　　　　　　　　　📖 **Text** **4**

Now, the pixies danced in the old woman's
garden that night because she was friendly and
kind to all the animals and birds. The pixies
50 played music on the grass and the old woman
saw that even her tulips moved with the music.
When she looked more **closely**, she saw that there
was a baby pixie in every tulip. The babies were
all asleep. The old woman was so happy that the
55 pixies liked her garden. 'This is an **honour** for
me!' she thought. 'I must make sure that I always
have lots of tulips in my garden for the pixies and
their babies.'
One night, after many happy years with the pixie
60 dances in her garden, the old woman died.
Then an old man from a **nearby** town moved into
her cottage. He didn't like flowers or grass in the
garden. 'Why do I need flowers and grass?' he
asked. 'I can't eat them!' So he grew vegetables
65 **instead**. He didn't like birds or animals **either**.

'The birds and animals only want to eat my
vegetables,' he said. So he put a **fence around**
the garden.　　　　　　　　　　Box "around", Voc, S. ̄ 97
Life got hard for the birds and animals on the
70 moor. The pixies had no place to dance and no
beds for their babies and they weren't happy.
No, the pixies were very angry with the old man.
'Nothing is ever going to **grow** in this garden
again!' they said.
75 Every year after that, the new vegetables that
the old man **planted** died. Nothing grew in the
garden, **not even** grass. The old man left the
cottage and nobody moved in after him. Now
the cottage is just a ruin on the moor.
80 But the pixies didn't forget their friend, the old
woman. No, at every full moon, they went to her
grave and sang and danced there. And people say
that every year, on the day that the old woman
died, tulips suddenly **appear** on her grave.

1 What's the story?

a) Match the parts of the story to the
sub-headings.
1 *ll. 1–16* — A friendly old woman
2 *ll. 17–26* — After the adventure
3 *ll. 27–37* — Cocoa and stories
4 *ll. 38–43* — The babies in the tulips
5 *ll. 44–51* — Music from the garden
6 *ll. 52–58* — What pixies are like

b) Find sub-headings for these parts of the
story: *ll. 59–68; ll. 69–79; ll. 80–84*

c) 👥 Compare your sub-headings.

d) Choose three words from each part of the
story that best show its atmosphere.
1 rain, dark, …　　　2 …

2 Marking up the text

a) On a copy of the story, highlight keywords
and phrases about one of these topics:
– the old woman
– the cottage and the garden
– the Dartmoor pixies
– the old man

b) When you're satisfied with what you have
highlighted, write down your keywords.

c) 👥 Make groups with other students with
the same topic. Agree on the best keywords.
Use them to tell the class about your topic.

d) What do you think we can learn from this old
legend today?

3 The pixies

You choose　Do a) or b).
a) Imagine you're a Dartmoor pixie. Describe
what you're going to do at the next full moon.

b) Imagine what a Dartmoor pixie looks like.
Then draw a picture and write a caption for it.

Neigungsdifferenzierung: Die S wählen zwischen einer kreativen
Schreibaufgabe und einer kombinierten Zeichen- und Schreibaufgabe.

Early finisher　This Dartmoor legend is about
pixies, the "little magic people of the moor".
What strange people or animals are there in
legends and stories from your area?
➜ **Workbook** *19 (p. 51)*

Workbook Checkpoint (pp. 52–55)

4 Unit

Your task

Steps 1–4 können von den S zu Hause bearbeitet werden. Step 5 kann, wenn sich die Gelegenheit ergibt, bei einem Elternabend durchgeführt werden.

The countryside

Write a poem in English about the countryside – the countryside near you, your favourite place in the countryside, or the countryside of your dreams.

STEP 1
Decide what place you are going to write about.

STEP 2
Think of words about the countryside, nature, the weather, buildings, animals – words that you might need for your poem.
- Look back through the texts in this unit for help, like the poem on p. 77.
- Collect your words in a list or a mind map.

➡ Wordbank 4 (pp. 133–134)

STEP 3
What kind of poem are you going to write?
- You can choose one of Morph's models.
- Or you can just write your own poem.

STEP 4
Write your poem. Make it look nice.
- Highlight or decorate special words.
- Find or draw a picture that goes with your poem.

STEP 5
👥 Together, do a poetry show.
- Read your poems aloud.
- Give the group feedback about their poems.
- Learn your poems by heart.
- Find some music for your poetry show.
- Hang up the poems so that everyone can see them.

You can do your poetry show in class or at a parents' evening.

---

acrostic [əˈkrɒstɪk] Akrostichon • **real** [rɪəl] echt • **snowy** [ˈsnəʊi] schneebedeckt • **shape** [ʃeɪp] Gestalt, Form

*In an **acrostic**, each line starts with the first letter of a word or phrase.*

Look!
Out there on the Lake
Can you see
Her?

Nessie! She has lived here for
Ever and a day
She's real. Believe me!
She's a real monster!

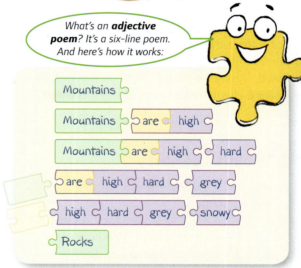

*What's an **adjective poem**? It's a six-line poem. And here's how it works:*

Mountains
Mountains are high
Mountains are high hard
are high hard grey
high hard grey snowy
Rocks

Line 1: noun
Line 2: same noun + is/are + adjective (adj.) 1
Line 3: same noun + is/are + adj. 1, adj. 2
Line 4: is/are + adj. 1, adj. 2, adj. 3
Line 5: adj. 1, adj. 2, adj. 3, adj. 4
Line 6: new (but similar) noun

***Shape poems** have the shape of their topic.*

82

Unit 4

Das lief nicht gut, ich muss mehr üben.

Das war OK, aber ich könnte besser werden.

Das habe ich gut geschafft.

Wie gut warst du?

Wie schätzt du dich selber ein? Schreibe *Words*, *Writing* und *Speaking* in dein Heft und ordne dir für jeden Bereich eine Ampelfarbe zu.

Words
Fielen dir passende Wörter ein, um z.B. über Landschaften oder das Wetter zu schreiben? Bei welchen Wörtern oder Wortfeldern hattest du Schwierigkeiten?

Writing
Bist du mit deinem Gedicht zufrieden?

Hattest du Probleme bei der Rechtschreibung oder der Grammatik?

Speaking
Konntest du dein Gedicht flüssig vorlesen?

Wie kannst du besser werden?

Dort, wo du dich eher rot oder gelb eingeschätzt hast, helfen dir folgende Tipps beim Wiederholen und Üben.

Words
Hattest du dir schon in Unit 2 ein *vocabulary picture poster* zu *geography words* gemacht? Schau es dir noch einmal an. Kannst du es um Wörter aus Unit 4 ergänzen?

Oder mach dir ein neues *vocabulary picture poster* zu den Themen Landschaft, Natur, Wetter usw. Den Wortschatz findest du in den Texten dieser Unit und in der Wordbank.

➡ *S. 66–69, 72, 74, 76–77, 80–81*
➡ *Wordbank 4, S. 143–144*
➡ *Skills File 3: Vocabulary picture posters, S. 146*
➡ *Workbook 1, S. 42*

Writing
Suche jemanden, der dasselbe Beispielsgedicht gewählt hat. Findet gemeinsam Ideen, wie du dein Gedicht besser machen kannst, und schreib es neu.

Korrigiere deine Fehler mit einem Partner/einer Partnerin und schreib dein Gedicht auf ein neues Blatt Papier.
Vielleicht fallen dir dabei auch andere Verbesserungen ein.

Speaking
Sieh dir die Seite 35 (*Reading aloud*) nochmals an. Versuche mit Hilfe der Tipps auf der Seite, dein Gedicht noch besser vorzulesen.

➡ *S. 35; Skills File 8: Reading aloud, S. 149*

5 Unit

Folie 15 • Leistungsmessung Unit 5

Lernfeld S. 84–85: Die S können über **Feiern** und **Feiertage** sprechen.

Celebrate! +celebration

The **parade** on Lord **Mayor**'s Day

A

1 My favourite celebration

What's your favourite celebration?
When is it? What do you do?

- On my birthday, Mum **lights candles**, and I **blow** them **out**.
- Box "Irregular past participles", Voc, S. 198
- On **New Year's Eve**, we watch **fireworks**.
- I **dress up** in a **costume**.
- We watch the parade at **Carnival**.
- We eat **special** food.

➔ Wordbank 5 (p. 144)

More help ➔ p. 130

More help bietet Ideen und Redemittel.

2 British celebrations

a) 👥👥 Work in groups of three. Each student describes one photo. The words and phrases in the box can help you.
Together, write your ideas down.

> **bucket** · **crowd** · **festival** · **flag** · music ·
> **raise money** for **charity** · **take part** in a parade

b) Listen to radio reports about the three celebrations. What do the reporters say about them? Take notes.
Compare your notes with your ideas from a).

3 ▶ 01

c) 👥👥 Choose one of the celebrations. Collect information about it in your group. Describe the celebration to the class.

EXTRA Make a calendar of celebrations that are special for you.

➔ Workbook 1 (p. 56)

Dies kann auch in Form eines Klassenkalenders geschehen, der alle wichtigen Festtage enthält und in der Klasse aufgehängt wird.

84

Unit **5**

B *Red Nose Day*

C °*Diwali*
[diːˈvaːli]

> **Your task**
>
> **At the end of this unit:**
> Plan a class party with a British theme.

85

5 Part A

Lernfeld S. 86: Die S können einen kurzen Text verstehen.

LAS 5.1

1 🔊 The juggler

+(to) juggle

Box "German „einsteigen" – „aussteigen"", Voc, S. 199

Falls die S das Einrad (unicycle) in dem Foto erwähnen wollen, sollte L das Wort einführen.

3 ▶ 04 On Saturday, Sam's dad drove Sam and Justin to the Hoe.
Dad: OK, you two, time to get out. Sam, put your cap on and don't forget your frisbee!

Box "clothes", Voc, S. 199

+(to) take sth. off

5 Sam: Thanks, Dad.
Justin: Come on, Sam! Hurry, or we'll miss the girls.
Sam: But Lucy is °rehearsing with her rock choir today.
10 Justin: Oh, right – for Lord Mayor's Day. When will the °rehearsal be over?
Sam: Not till three.
Justin: What about Maya, then?
Sam: She probably won't come without Lucy.
15 But we can play frisbee on our own, can't we?
Justin: Of course we can. Hey! What's happening over there? Look at that big crowd of people.
20 Sam: Wow! It's a street artist – a juggler.
Justin: And he's juggling with fire! Let's go to the front – the view will be better there.

❖

3 ▶ 05 Juggler: Now I need some helpers for my last trick. Maybe you, °sir? You aren't nervous,
25 are you? Don't worry. Everything will be OK. Just stand here, please. And, yes, the man in the red trousers and the silly hat! Come over here, please. Yes, take the hat off if you like. And now …
30 Leo: Me! Choose me too, John.
Juggler: Thanks, Leo. Not this time. I have enough help with this trick now.
Sam: Look, Justin! That's Leo, isn't it?
Justin: And he knows the juggler.
35 Sam: Yes, now I remember – the juggler's name is John. He's a friend of Leo. We met him once on the way to school.

Leo

Juggler: Now, this won't be easy. I have to climb onto this big ball. Give me the torches,
40 please. Don't try this at home, kids, it's too dangerous. Do it at school!
Crowd: Ha, ha, ha!
Juggler: OK, everybody, clap! Here we go! One … two … three!
45 Sam: Wow … he's juggling five torches!
Justin: He's good, isn't he?
Juggler: OK, everyone, thank you all for watching!
Sam: The show isn't over now, is it?
Justin: Yes it is. He's passing around his hat.
50 Juggler: Thank you, everybody. Thank you.
Crowd: Hooray! Yay! Encore! Encore! Encore!
Juggler: Sorry, people. That's it for today. But I hope you'll all be at Lord Mayor's Day next Saturday. You'll see some tricks that
55 I've never done before. I promise it'll be the best show that you've ever seen!
Justin: That sounds interesting. Let's go and see him on Lord Mayor's Day.
Sam: Yes! And now let's go and talk to Leo.
60 Maybe we can talk to John too.
Justin: OK. Maybe he'll tell us something about his new tricks!

2 Why …

1 … do Sam and Justin go to the Hoe?
2 … does Lucy have a rehearsal?
3 … don't Sam and Justin play frisbee?
4 … doesn't John choose Leo?
5 … does John pass around his hat?
6 … does the crowd shout "Encore!"?
7 … do Sam and Justin want to talk to John?

1 to play frisbee · 2 the rehearsal is for Lord Mayor's Day · 3 they see the juggler and watch his show · 4 he has enough help · 5 to collect money · 6 the people want to see more tricks · 7 they want to talk about his new tricks

Folie 16 • FöFo 5.1 • KV 18

Part A Practice 5

Lernfeld S. 87: Die S können über die **Zukunft** sprechen **(will-future)**.

1 On Lord Mayor's Day
(*will*-future: statements)

What will happen on Lord Mayor's Day?
Finish the sentences. Choose will or won't.
1 The people of Plymouth will meet their new mayor. (meet)
2 The city centre streets … full of people. (be)
3 Cars … to drive in the centre. (be allowed)
4 Lots of people … in the parade. (take part)
5 People … interesting costumes. (wear)
6 Kids … go to school. (have to)
7 Lots of stalls … food and drink. (sell)
8 Everybody hopes it … (rain).
➔ Workbook 2 (p. 56)

2 will be • 3 won't be allowed • 4 will take part • 5 will wear • 6 won't have to • 7 will sell • 8 won't rain

> **Language help**
>
> You make positive statements about the future with …'ll (long form: *will*) + infinitive:
> Hurry, or we'll miss the girls.
>
> You make negative statements with *won't* (long form: *will not*) + infinitive:
> Maya probably won't come without Lucy.
>
> You make questions like this:
> When will the rehearsal be over?
>
> ➔ GF 12: The will-future (p. 171)

2 Abby will sail around the world (*will*-future: statements)

a) Who do you think will do these things?
   Match the names to the activities.
   Then make sentences like this:
   I think Abby will sail around the world.

1	Abby	travel to India.
2	Justin	play basketball for England.
3	Leo	sail around the world.
4	Lucy	dance in musicals.
5	Maya	sing in shows in London.
6	Sam	make films in the USA.

➔ Workbook 3 (p. 57)

2 Justin will make films in the USA. • 3 Leo will dance in musicals. • 4 Lucy will sing in shows in London. • 5 Maya will travel to India. • 6 Sam will play basketball for England.

b) 👥 Do you think the Plymstock kids will do these things in the future? Give reasons.

> buy a farm on Dartmoor · join the navy · move to the USA · climb Mount Everest · learn Chinese · swim across the Atlantic · go on a journey to Mars · meet the Queen

I think Maya will swim across the Atlantic because she's very good at swimming.

I don't think she'll swim across the Atlantic. There are too many sharks!

3 When will the parade start? (*will*-future: questions)

a) A tourist in Plymouth asks about Lord Mayor's Day. Put the words in the right order.
1 will • the parade • start • When • ?
   When will the parade start?
2 be over • When • the parade • will • ?
3 elephants • in the parade • there be • Will • ?
4 the Lord Mayor • Will • see • I • ?
5 fireworks • Will • there be • ?
6 there be • activities for children • Will • ?
7 good weather • have • Will • we • ?

2 When will the parade be over? • 3 Will there be elephants in the parade? • 4 Will I see the Lord Mayor? • 5 Will there be fireworks? • 6 Will there be activities for children? • 7 Will we have good weather?

b) Now listen to the dialogue. Write down the answers to the tourist's questions.

c) 👥 Ask and answer the questions.

When will the parade start?

The parade will start at …

➔ Workbook 4–5 (pp. 57–58)

Alternative: KV 18: A tourist in Plymouth (Mediation) enthält den Dialog als Mediation-Übung.

5 Part A Practice

4 WORDS What are you wearing?

3 ▶07 a) Listen. Which of these boys is Tom? *Tom is the boy on the left.*

b) Say what a student in your class is wearing. The others must guess who it is.

c) 👥 Finish the sentences with *put on, take off* or *wear*.

1 A: It's so hot in here!
 B: Then … your pullover.
2 A: Do they … uniforms at German schools?
 B: No, most students just … everyday clothes.
3 A: It's cold outside. You should … a jacket before you go out.
 B: OK, maybe I should … gloves too.

1 take off • 2 wear / wear • 3 put on / put on

cap
T-shirt
jacket
gloves
pullover
jeans
shoes

Lernfeld: Die S können verstehen und sagen, welche **Kleidung** jemand trägt.

➡ Workbook 6–7 (p. 58)

5 A "Volksfest"

Your host family in England asks about the *Hamburger Dom*.
You find information on the internet. In English, explain what the *Dom* is, how often it takes place, and where.

TIP
Remember: Don't try to **translate** word for word. Just explain the key points.

The Dom is a big festival in Hamburg. It takes place in March, July and November every year.

Lernfeld: Die S können essentielle Informationen über ein Volksfest vom Deutschen ins Englische übertragen.

Der **Hamburger Dom** ist ein Volksfest, das dreimal im Jahr auf dem Heiligengeistfeld in Hamburg stattfindet, jeweils ca. 4 Wochen im November (Winterdom/Dom-Markt), März (Frühlingsdom/Frühlingsfest), Juli (Sommerdom/Hummelfest). Jährlich besuchen mehrere Millionen Menschen die Veranstaltung. Das Riesenrad ist immer wieder aufs Neue das Wahrzeichen des Doms. Die Besucher erwartet eine bunte Mischung aus Kinderkarussells, Losbuden, Imbissbetrieben, Mandelbuden und schnellen Fahrgeschäften.

➡ SF 12: Mediation (Revision) (p. 151); ➡ Workbook 8 (p. 59)

6 EXTRA … isn't it? (Question tags)

Finish each sentence with a question tag.

1 Lord Mayor's Day is in May, *isn't it?*
2 Lots of people take part in it, … they?
3 You see lots of street artists there, … you?
4 John can do tricks with fire, … he?
5 He isn't nervous, …
6 In Germany, we have big parades too, …
7 The biggest parade is at Carnival, …
8 But they don't have Carnival in England, …

➡ Workbook 9 (p. 59)

2 don't they? • 3 don't you? • 4 can't he? • 5 is he? • 6 don't we? • 7 isn't it? • 8 do they?

Language help

Lernfeld: Die S können Frageanhängsel verstehen und verwenden *(question tags)*.

In German, you often use … *nicht wahr?*
… *gell?* or … *oder?* at the end of a sentence.
In English, people use question tags.
You make them like this:

positive statement – negative tag
That's Leo, isn't it?
Justin goes to Plymstock School, doesn't he?

negative statement – positive tag
The show isn't over now, is it?
You don't live in Berlin, do you?

➡ GF 13: Question tags (p. 172)

Reading course 5

Lernfeld S. 89: Die S können Notizen zu Texten anfertigen.

Taking notes

When you want to remember something that you have read, you can use cards to take notes on the most important information.

a) Read the text and compare it with the notes.

> Guy Fawkes Night
> 5.11. celebration: bonfire + "guy", fireworks, food (e.g. potatoes, sweet things)
> 1605: plan to kill King J.
> Soldiers find GF → ~~explosion~~
> Now celeb. - explosions ✓ + fire ✓

TIP
Only use keywords, not full sentences.
Underline important words.
Use symbols, abbreviations and numbers,
e.g. →←, =, ?, !, ☺, ♥, GF, 5.11.
Think of *who, what, when, where* and *why*.

Guy Fawkes Night

Every year on 5th November, people in Britain celebrate the day when nothing happened. They go to a party in their village or town, where a °model of a man – it is called a "guy" – °burns on a big °bonfire. They watch the °explosion of beautiful fireworks in the sky. On the bonfire they °roast food like potatoes in °foil or °marshmallows, and they eat sweet things like °toffee apples and bonfire toffee.
And why do they celebrate like this?
In 1605, a small group of men in Britain wanted to °kill King James. They planned a big explosion for 5th November, the day when the king opened °parliament. But the king's °soldiers found one of the men, Guy Fawkes, in a room under the building. Nothing happened.
But 400 years later people still celebrate – with explosions and fire.

b) Read this text about pancake races.
  1 Try to understand or guess new words.
  2 Take notes.
     More help → *p. 130*
     More help: Der Text ist bereits markiert; die S machen Notizen aufgrund der Vorauswahl.
  3 👥 Compare your notes with the tip and add or cross out notes.

EXTRA Prepare a short talk on pancake races.

Pancake Races

There is a Tuesday every year in February or March when lots of people in Britain take part in a special race. They run with a pancake in a °frying pan and °toss the pancake on the way. °Traditionally, °Christians used up all their °butter and eggs to make pancakes before °Ash Wednesday, when they started to °fast for °Lent. Today on Pancake Day, many people in Britain still eat pancakes with °sugar and °lemon juice. Kids of all ages love them.
And the race? There is a °legend that on one Pancake Day in the 15th century, a woman in the village of Olney still had a pancake in her pan when she heard the church bells. She didn't want to be late for church, so she ran all the way with her frying pan in her hand.
Pancake races are a fun part of an old festival.

➔ *SF 10: Taking notes (Revision) (p. 150)*
➔ **Workbook** 10 *(p. 60)*

89

5 Part B

Lernfeld S. 90: Die S können eine kurze Geschichte verstehen.

FöFo 5.2, 5.3

1 Best friends 　3 ▶ 08

"Look, Lucy and Maya are here," shouted Leo. He dropped the frisbee and ran over and gave Lucy a big hug.

"Lucy!" Sam called. "How was your rehearsal?"

5 "It went really well," Lucy answered. "I sang beautifully. At least that's what the director said. If I practise hard, I'll be better than ever."

"I'm sure you will," Sam said. He looked over at Justin and rolled his eyes. Justin nodded.

10 "Here," Lucy said. "I've brought the programme for Lord Mayor's Day."

"Hey," Sam shouted. "I'm in the programme too – with my kung fu group. If you come at 10:30, you'll see me in a really cool demonstration."

15 "10:30?" Lucy said. "Sorry, but I can't come. I'm in the children's parade too, you see. I have to be there at 11. So if I go to your thing, I'll be late!"

"I can come, Master Wu!" said Leo.

"And if you like, I'll film it all," Justin offered.

20 "Sorry, Sam, but I can't go," Maya said sadly. "And I can't go to the children's parade either."

"Why not?" Lucy asked.

"Dad has an Indian food stall in Armada Way," Maya explained. "I've promised to help from 10
25 o'clock. When Mukesh comes at two, I'll be free."

"You mean *if* Mukesh comes at two, you'll be free," said Lucy. "Anyway, don't forget: *We will rock you* is at 3 pm."

"I know, Lucy," said Maya. "But I don't think I can
30 come to your show. It's Abby's weekend at home. We want to meet in Wembury in the afternoon."

"But Maya, you have to come! You're my best friend!" cried Lucy.

Maya looked at Lucy. "If I don't meet Abby on
35 Saturday, I won't see her till the summer holidays."

"Oh I understand. Abby is more important to you than I am."

"That isn't true, Lucy! I've already seen *We will*
40 *rock you* three times."

"But this time is different!"

"Oh come on, Lucy. It's just one show."

"Yes, but it won't be the same if you don't come!" Sam's mobile beeped. "Oh, Dad's waiting for me,"
45 he said. "If you want a lift, you can come with us."

"No thanks!" said Lucy. "I think I'll take the bus home. Alone!"

Lucy　Maya　Leo　Justin　Sam

2 Which event?

a) Match the event to the times.

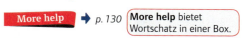

10:30 am — children's parade
11 am — We will rock you
3 pm — kung fu demonstration

b) Why can't Maya go to Lucy's events? How do they feel about this?

More help → *p. 130* **More help** bietet Wortschatz in einer Box.

EXTRA 👥 How can Lucy and Maya be good friends again? Think of ideas.

3 Have a go

Lernfeld: Die S verwenden vorbewusst Bedingungssätze (*conditional sentences 1*).

a) What will you wear? Finish the sentences.
1 If it's very hot tomorrow, I'll wear …
　If it's very hot tomorrow, I'll wear a T-shirt and …
2 If it's warm and sunny tomorrow, I'll wear …
3 If it's cold tomorrow, I'll wear …
4 If it's rainy tomorrow, I'll wear …
5 If it's windy tomorrow, I'll wear …
6 If there's a storm tomorrow, I'll wear …

b) 👥 Now tell your partner.

90

Folie 17 · LAS 5.2

Part B Practice **5**

Lernfeld S. 91–92: Die S können Bedingungssätze bilden und verwenden (*conditional sentences 1*).

Looking at language

a) Copy the table and finish sentences 1–5 from
1 on page 90 (ll. 7–26).
Underline the verbs in both clauses.

What tense is the verb in the *if*-clauses?
What tense is the verb in the main clauses?

	if-clause	main clause
1	If I practise hard,	I'll be better than ever.
2	If you come at 10:30,	you'll see me in a really cool demonstration.
3	So if I go …to your thing,	I'll be late!
4	And if … you like,	I'll film it all.
5	You mean if Mukesh … comes at two,	you'll … be free.

b) Finish sentences 6–8 (ll. 34–45) and answer
these questions:
Which negative verbs can you see?
What's different about sentence 8?

6 If I … Abby on Saturday, I …
7 It … the same if you …
8 If you want a lift, you … with us.

6 don't meet / won't see her till the summer holidays.
7 won't be / don't come.
8 can come

➡ *GF 14: Conditional sentences 1 (pp. 172–173)*

1 If you read the programme, … (Conditional sentences 1) ■ ■ ■ ■ ■

Choose the right ending for sentences 1–8.   2a · 3f · 4g · 5h · 6e · 7c · 8b

1 If you read the programme,
2 If Justin takes his camera,
3 If you go to Mr Sen's stall in Armada Way,
4 If Maya helps her dad at the stall,
5 Maya will be sad
6 If Mr Bennett gives the kids a lift,
7 Everyone will have fun
8 If you aren't in Plymouth at the weekend,

a) he'll film lots of different events.
b) you'll miss all the fun.
c) if it's warm and sunny on Lord Mayor's Day.
d) you'll find out all about Lord Mayor's Day.
e) they'll get home faster.
f) you'll see lots of Indian food.
g) he won't have so much work.
h) if she doesn't see Abby at the weekend.

2 If you come to Plymouth, … (Conditional sentences 1) ■ ■ ■ ■ ■

Finish the sentences with the correct form of the verbs in brackets.

1 If you (come) to Plymouth at the weekend, you (have) a great time.
   If you come to Plymouth at the weekend, you'll have a great time.
2 If you (not arrive) early enough, you (not see) the start of the parade.
   If you don't …
3 If Justin (not film) the kung fu event, Sam (feel) a bit sad.
4 If Maya (see) *We will rock you* again, she (be) bored.
5 If you (dress up) in a costume, your friends (not know) who you are.
6 You (miss) some of the shows if you (take part) in the parade.
7 We (watch) the fireworks if Dad (let) us stay up late.
8 They (not have) the fireworks show if it (rain).
9 I (stay) for the evening concert if my mum (let) me.
10 If we (not leave) at 9:30, we (miss) the bus home.

If we get there early, we'll see the seals' parade.

2 don't arrive / won't see · 3 doesn't film / will feel · 4 sees / will be · 5 dress up / won't know · 6 will miss / take part · 7 will watch / lets · 8 won't have / rains · 9 will stay / lets · 10 don't leave / will miss

More help ➡ *p. 131*   **More help:** Eine der Verbformen pro Satz ist bereits gebildet.

Early finisher Think of other endings for sentences 1 and 2.

➡ **Workbook** *11 (p. 60)*

91

5 Part B Practice

KV 19

3 Chain game
(Conditional sentences 1)

You take part in a TV quiz show.
The first prize is one million pounds.
Play the game with if-sentences, like this:

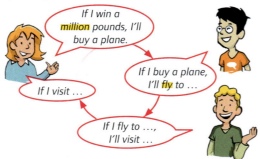

- If I win a million pounds, I'll buy a plane.
- If I buy a plane, I'll fly to …
- If I fly to …, I'll visit …
- If I visit …

Make as many sentences as you can.

4 If you don't …
(Conditional sentences 1)

Make sentences that start with If you don't … and say what will happen. You can use these ideas.

answer your phone · drink enough water · eat a good breakfast · feed your cat · go to school · speak loudly enough

If you don't feed your cat, it will look for a new home.

More help ➔ p. 131   ➔ Workbook 12 (p. 61)
More help: Ideen und Formulierungshilfen.

5 If I don't like it, I can leave

a) Talk about what you can do in these situations.

If you don't …
… like a film at the cinema.
… understand the homework.
… have enough money to buy a snack.
… like the colour of your bedroom walls.

A: What can you do if you don't like a film at the cinema?
B: If I don't like a film, I can leave.
A: Yes, or you can just close your eyes!

Early finisher Think of more difficult situations and talk about them.   ➔ Workbook 13–14 (pp. 61–62)

6 Red Nose Day at a British school

Lernfeld: Die S können Informationen aus einer englischen Email ins Deutsche übertragen.

A British friend told you how his school raised money for charity on Red Nose Day. Read his email.
In German, describe three of the activities. How much money did the school raise?

Every school in Britain tries to raise money on Red Nose Day. The money that our school made is for °homeless people.
So what did we do? Of course, we had a non-uniform day. Most students dressed up. Three of my friends and I wore °banana costumes. So everyone gave £1.30. You °pay £1 if you don't wear a uniform and the red noses cost 30p. We also had a school °talent show. The people who watched had to pay 20p (or more). I played the guitar, but I didn't win a prize. :-(In my year (Year 8) we had a cake °sale. We made lots of funny red cakes and we raised £57.62.

This is the cake that I made. Yummy! In Year 9, the students helped people at a °supermarket to put their shopping into their bags and the people gave them money. Like every Red Nose Day – it's every two years – the teachers did lots of things too. We had a "guess the teacher" °competition. 15 teachers wore costumes and °masks, and the students had to °guess who they were. You paid 10p for five guesses. And our German teacher got £1 from every other teacher because she coloured her hair red! °Altogether we made £2,795.

Early finisher ➔ p. 135   **Early finisher:** Reading challenge.   ➔ Workbook 15 (pp. 63)

Part B Practice 5

Lernfeld S. 93: Die S können ein Foto beschreiben und präsentieren.

7 Study skills: **Presenting** a photo (+presentation)

If you have to present a photo to a group, you can follow these steps.
a) Choose a photo: one that you took, or one from your English book, from a magazine, …
   Make sure that everyone can see the photo. Hand out copies, or use one big copy or a projector.
b) 👥 Give your presentation to your group. Organize it like this and use phrases from the boxes.

1 Introduce your photo.

> I'd like to talk about this photo of …
> I found it in a magazine / on the internet / …

2 Describe your photo.

> In the middle of the photo you can see …
> In the foreground/background there is/are …
>
> ➜ SF 17: Describing pictures (p. 154)

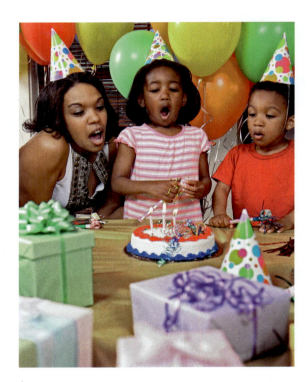

3 Say what you think of the photo.

> I really like this photo because …
> I chose the photo because …
> It's funny/interesting/… because …
> I love the colours/light/background/…
> The colours make it funny/warm/…

4 Finish your presentation.

> Thank you for listening.
> Do you have any questions?

c) Make a table like this with feedback for the others in your group.
   👥 Tell your partners what you thought about their presentations. Listen to their feedback.

What I liked	What you could do better
You chose a great photo. ☺ You spoke clearly and looked at us. …	Next time, say what is happening in the photo. Sometimes you stood in front of the photo. …

> **TIP**
> Practise your presentation with a partner first.
> When you give your presentation:
> • look at your classmates when you speak
> • speak slowly and clearly
> • point to your photo when you talk about it
> • don't stand in front of your photo

Study skills

Presenting a photo
Wenn ich ein Foto präsentiere, sollte ich …
– das Foto kurz vorstellen
– …

Vergleiche deine Ideen mit dem Abschnitt im Skills File.
➜ SF 18: Presenting a photo (p. 155)
➜ SF 19: Peer feedback (p. 155)

➜ **Workbook** 16 (pp. 63)

93

5 Part C

FöFo 5.4, 5.5

Lernfeld S. 94–95: Die S können Bilder mit Texten zu einem **Fest** verstehen und über sie sprechen. Sie können eine **Radiosendung** verstehen und sagen, was sie gerne **tun** und **essen** würden.

1 Lord Mayor's Day

 Work in groups of four. Each student chooses one of the four pictures.

a) Look at your picture and the texts in it. What do they tell you about Lord Mayor's Day? Do they tell you anything else about Britain? Take notes.

b) Tell your partners about your picture. Use your notes. Decide where to go first.

2 On the radio 🎧

3 ▶ 09–11

a) Listen to part 1 of the radio programme. Find the mistakes.
 1 The first pasties came from Cornwall. Plymouth
 2 The recipe is from 1610. 1510
 3 They make their pasties with a new recipe. traditional

b) Listen to part 2 of the programme. Explain …
 1 what this Francis Drake knows about the Spanish °Armada. He doesn't know anything.
 2 what the Queen thinks of Francis and why. He's the best man for the job because he has sailed around the world.
 3 why they aren't waiting on the Hoe. The Armada isn't there yet.

c) Now listen to part 3. Which of these two sentences is the town crier's tongue-twister?
 1 If two °witches watch two watches, which witch will watch which watch?
 2 If two witches watch two watches, which watch will watch which witch?

3 ▶ 12–15 Listen to some more of the town crier's tongue-twisters and try to repeat them.

More help ➔ p. 131   **More help:** Die Zungenbrecher können hier nachgelesen werden.

3 What would you like to do?

👥 Choose three things that you would like to do and one thing that you would like to eat. Explain your choices.
 – I'd like to go to … / see the … / try …
 – The … look yummy! I'd like to try one.

Elizabeth I was Queen of England from 1558 to 1603.

She °made Sir Francis Drake a knight in 1581, after he became the first Englishman who sailed around the world.

Sir Francis Drake was a famous °seaman who defended England.

In 1588, 130 Spanish ships tried to invade England. Drake was on the Hoe when they arrived. People say that he finished his game of °bowls first, before he and the English navy attacked the Spanish °Armada and destroyed it.

5 Part C Practice

Folie 18 • FöFo 5.6, 5.7 • KV 20

1 Pronunciation: [f], [v], [w]

Lernfeld: Die S können zwischen den Lauten [f], [v] und [w] unterscheiden.

a) Listen to the sentences. Which word from each word pair do you hear?
- In sentence 1 I hear *wall*.
- In sentence 2 I hear *fall*.

wall – fall
ferry – very | fair – wear | first – worst | fish – wish
view – few | fight – white | fell – well | walk – fork

3 ferry • 4 very • 5 wear • 6 fair • 7 first • 8 worst • 9 wish • 10 fish
11 view • 12 few • 13 fight • 14 white • 15 well • 16 fell • 17 fork • 18 walk

b) Now try and say the tongue twisters.
1 Will Willy wear white to the kung fu fight?
2 Which fish visited the witches' wicked village?
3 A few views from the ferry in very funny weather.
4 Mr Wood will walk to work with a fork.

Zusatz: KV 20: A tongue-twister ➔ Workbook 17 (p. 64)

2 At the food stalls

Lernfeld: Die S können Einkaufsdialoge verstehen und bilden.

a) Listen to the dialogues at the Lord Mayor's Day food stalls.
What do the Plymstock kids buy?

b) Put together a food stall menu in your group. Write short dialogues for your stall. You can use phrases from the box.

- What would you like?
- What can I get you?
- Would you like … on your …?
- Would you like a drink?
- Here you are.
- Here's your change.

- I'd like …
- Can I have …?
- Yes, please.
- No, thanks.
- The same for me, please.
- No, I don't think so.

c) Act out your dialogues.

➔ Workbook 18–19 (p. 64)

a) Lucy: pasty • Sam and Justin: curry • Abby: jacket potato with cheese • Maya: jacket potato with sour cream

EXTRA Background file

Lernfeld: Die S verstehen einen Text über Lieblingsgerichte der Briten und können auf Deutsch sagen, was sie davon essen möchten und was das ist.

Britain's favourite °dishes

What do °Brits love to eat when they °go out for a °meal? Here are four favourites:

Fish and chips
In Britain, you're never very far from a fish and chip shop. Fish and chips has become °popular around the world. Brits eat it with °salt and °vinegar.

Shepherd's °pie
A delicious °mixture of °mince and vegetables in °gravy with °mashed potatoes on top. Put it in the °oven till the potatoes are °golden brown. Yummy!

Vegetable °stir-fry
Chinese °takeaways are as popular as fish and chip shops. The British favourite is a °spicy stir-fry of vegetables and °noodles – and it's what people most like to °cook at home too.

Curry
It's not from Britain °originally, but everyone in Britain loves a meat, fish or vegetable curry – and curries are easy to find, with Indian °restaurants around every corner.

Imagine you're in Plymouth. Which of these dishes would you like for dinner this evening? Take turns and phone your parents. Explain to them in German what you'd like to eat.

➔ Workbook 20 (p. 65)

96

5 The world behind the picture

Lernfeld S. 97: Die S können kurze Filmclips verstehen.

1 Craig's puppet show

a) 👥 Watch the film. What are Craig's jobs? What can he do well? Write your ideas down. Compare your answers.

b) Watch the film again. Match the description to the correct character.

Länge: 5:00 — Craig — Ruan

– helps Craig to pick up rubbish. Ruan
– is the Captain's friend. Crabby
– loves swimming. Morwenna
– thinks she is very beautiful. Morwenna
– likes to hide. Crabby
– likes to be funny. Crabby/Ruan/The Captain
– is made of an old glove. Crabby
– can't find Crabby. The Captain

c) Craig says that Ruan is his "friend". Watch the scene with Ruan at the end of the film. Would you like to have a friend like this? Give reasons.

2 EVERYDAY ENGLISH Can I go to the concert … please?

a) Watch the film. Say who is allowed to go to the rock concert. Jack, Oliver and Ruby

b) Who says these things?
Are they asking for or giving permission?
1 Is it OK if she sleeps in your room? Ruby's mum / asking
2 Yes, of course, Mum. Ruby / giving
3 Can I go to the concert too, please? Ruby / asking
4 That's true. OK, then, you can go. Ruby's mum / giving
5 Is it OK if I go with them? Oliver / asking
6 No, I don't think so. Oliver's mum / not giving

c) Watch again and check your answers.

d) 👥 You and a boy/girl from your English host family want to go to the cinema / a concert / a party / …
You ask for permission from your host parents. Write a dialogue like the one in the film.
You can use phrases from the box.

Länge: 5:32
"Well, I'm not sure, Ruby."

- Is it OK if …?
- When does it start?
- (I promise) I'll call if I'm late.
- What time will you be back?
- I can pick you up at …
- Yes, you can go. / No, you can't go.

5 Text

Lernfeld S. 98–99: Die S können eine Geschichte verstehen und Falschaussagen dazu korrigieren sowie selber welche schreiben. Sie schreiben einen kreativen Text zur Geschichte.

👆 A day to celebrate

When Lucy woke up, the sky was grey and cloudy. Again, like every morning for the last two weeks, Lucy sang her songs in front of the bathroom **mirror** after she cleaned her **teeth**. But this time
5 she didn't smile. She sang the songs again in her room. She waited for the sound of clapping, but it was quiet. The doorbell rang. Lucy took her bag and ran to the door. It was Leo.
"You look great, Lucy!" he said.
10 "Thanks, Leo, but I don't feel great. Look at that sky!" she said. The sound of **thunder** shook the quiet morning. A °**raindrop** hit Lucy's face. "If it rains today, we can't do our show."
"Yes, we can," said Leo. "Watch this!"
15 He took a few steps onto the path and did a funny dance. Lucy had to laugh.

Leo / Lucy

"Now you," he shouted.
"OK," she said. "I have a song to sing …", she sang softly, and then more loudly. "And **even if**
20 the rain falls, I'll sing it. Even if the sky shakes, I'll sing it. I'll sing it, I'll sing it … All day long!" They sang and danced all the way to the bus stop. Lucy looked almost happy.

❖

"OK, Maya, put the **bowls** there. And the
25 vegetable curry here," said Maya's father. There was loud music in the **air** and small children walked around with red and yellow flags and **painted** faces.
At lunchtime, people queued at their stall. She
30 had to work quickly.
"I **asked for** one vegetable curry and two °**mango** lassis," said one woman in an angry voice. "I'm still waiting for the second lassi."
35 "I'm sorry," said Maya in a soft voice. "It will be ready soon."
She could hear the sounds of the parade from Cornwall Street. She wanted to go and watch, but it was still too early and Mukesh wasn't there yet.
40 She heard the next person: "I'd like a large mango lassi, please."
Maya didn't look up. "I'm sorry, we only have one size …," she said. "But wait! I know that voice. Can it be?" Yes, it was!
45 "Abby!" She was so happy to see her friend and gave her a hug. Then Mukesh arrived, so the two girls ran away to see the end of the parade.

❖

Lucy looked out from the side of the big stage.
Her **heart** raced wildly. There were so many people
50 in the **audience**. She looked at all the faces. She saw Mum and Holly, and Sam and Justin were there too.
"OK, take a **deep breath**," she said quietly.
"And now, welcome to the Plymstock School Rock
55 Choir!"
Lucy heard loud clapping.
"Good luck!" whispered her teacher.
First, the choir sang *We will rock you*. Then Leo did a short solo dance – the audience loved it.
60 Lucy heard the piano with the first part of *We are the champions*. She walked to the front of the stage and sang: "I've **paid** °**my dues** …" She sang loudly and clearly. The guitars °**came in** and she started the **chorus** when she saw **lightning** in the
65 sky. A **second** later she heard loud thunder. The music stopped. Lucy looked out at the audience and saw Maya and Abby. In her loudest voice she sang: "We are the champions, my friends! We'll go on fighting till the end …" Then, "Come on,
70 everybody! Sing!" she shouted. Everybody knew the chorus and sang with her: "No time for losers, 'cause we are the champions … of the world!" At the end of the song the rain was very **heavy** but the audience still clapped and clapped. The choir
75 **bowed** and left the stage.

❖

After the show Lucy and Leo jumped down from
the stage to say hello to their friends. Maya gave Lucy a big hug.

"You were better than ever!" said Maya.
"And I'm so happy I could see the show," said Abby.
Some minutes later, the rain stopped. Abby began to tell her friends all about her boarding school.
"Er …" said Justin, "I don't want to interrupt, but we have to hurry. We can't miss John's show."
"Who is John?" asked Lucy. "And what kind of show will it be?"
"John is my friend!" shouted Leo.
"Just come with us," said Sam. "I'm sure you'll love it."

❖

25 The kids ran to the Barbican. They had to move like snakes through the people to see the action. John wore a clown's costume.
"And now: my newest trick," he shouted. "Can everybody please take a few steps back and look after small children. Fire can be dangerous!"
There was strange music with loud, slow drums. John poured something that looked like water in a big circle. He touched the circle with one of his torches. Suddenly the circle became a big ring of fire.
John jumped into the ring and juggled first four, then five torches. He put the torches down and looked at the audience.
"I need someone who's not too heavy for this trick. Hey, come on, Leo!" he shouted.

"I'm coming, John!" said Leo and jumped into the circle. John now had seven gold rings in his hand. Leo took two, climbed up and sat on John's shoulders. He put his arms into the rings and moved them around and around in big circles. John juggled the other gold rings and the fire lit up the faces of the audience. Everyone went "Oooh!" and "Aaah!". John then threw the rings up one last time and Leo caught them all. Then he jumped down and bowed. The audience clapped, shouted and whistled. It was a great ending to a great day.

Box "Irregular past participles", Voc, S. 202

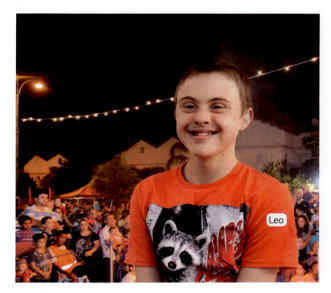
Leo

1 Right or wrong?

a) Correct the wrong sentences.
Find parts of the story that show that the sentences are wrong.
1 Lord Mayor's Day is sunny all day.
2 Lucy sings a song about the weather with the Plymstock School Rock Choir.
3 Maya and Abby watch the whole parade.
4 Maya and Abby see Leo dance but they don't hear Lucy sing *We are the champions*.
5 Leo and John juggle torches.

b) Write more wrong sentences about the story. Can your partner correct them?

1 Wrong: In the morning the sky is grey and cloudy (l. 1) and later there is thunder and lightning (ll. 64–65). • 2 Wrong: Lucy sings *We are the champions* (l. 60ff.). • Wrong: Maya and Abby watch the end of the parade (l. 47). • 4 Wrong: Maya and Abby see Leo dance and hear Lucy sing (l. 67). • 5 Right.

2 A day to remember

Neigungsdifferenzierung: Fünf kreative Schreibaufträge zur Auswahl.

a) Imagine you are one of the kids. Write about what happened on Lord Mayor's Day.
  You choose Choose one:
1 Lucy's diary entry at the end of the day
2 Justin's conversation on Skype with his dad
3 Maya's letter to Uncle Amar
4 Sam's conversation with his dad
5 Leo's conversation with John after the show

b) Read your texts aloud and give feedback to your group.

Early finisher Write about your day to remember.

➡ Workbook 21 (p. 65)

5 Unit

Your task

Alle Schritte für diese Lernaufgabe sind Klassen- oder Gruppenarbeit, sollten also im Unterricht durchgeführt werden. Wenn die Rahmenbedingungen es erlauben, sollte die geplante Party tatsächlich stattfinden.

A British class party

You and your class are going to have a party with a British theme. Plan an activity and some food, then give a short presentation of your ideas. You can invite your family and friends to join the celebration.

STEP 1
What could you do at your British class party? Collect ideas in class. Here are some to choose from. Or think of your own ideas.
- Choose an English song to sing. Plan a dance to go with it.
- Learn some tongue-twisters and teach them to people at the party.
- Write and perform a short puppet show or a poem.
- Have a pancake race.
- …

STEP 2
👥 Choose one activity from the class list and work with other students who want to do the same thing.
Plan and prepare your activity for the party and a British dish to eat.

🌐 Find recipes for British dishes. (Is there a British shop near you for the ingredients?)

STEP 3
👥 Put together a poster with ideas for your activity and your dish.
Then present your poster to the class. Describe your activity and say what you need for it. Talk about the British dish that you've chosen. Tell the class why your part of the party will be fun.

STEP 4
In class, plan the party programme. In what order should things happen? What time should the party start and finish?

EXTRA Invite family and friends to your party. In your groups, prepare your activity and your British dish. And on the day of your British class party: CELEBRATE!

Unit 5

Wie gut warst du?

Wie schätzt du dich selber ein? Schreibe *Words*, *Grammar*, *Presenting a poster* in dein Heft und ordne dir für jeden Bereich eine Ampelfarbe zu.

Words
Fiel es dir leicht, die Vorbereitung für deine Aktivität zu beschreiben?

Wie war es mit dem Wortschatz für dein britisches Gericht?

Grammar
Konntest du die neu gelernte Grammatik in deiner Präsentation anwenden? Z. B.:

Everyone will have fun if there is music and dancing.

Presenting a poster
Lief deine Präsentation gut?
Hast du dich auf das Poster bezogen?

Wie kannst du besser werden?

Dort, wo du dich eher rot oder gelb eingeschätzt hast, helfen dir folgende Tipps beim Wiederholen und Üben.

Words
Zeichne die Dinge, die du für deine Aktivität brauchst, und finde die Wörter dafür.

Sammle mit einem Partner/einer Partnerin *food words* in einer Mindmap.
➡ *Wordbank 5, S. 144*
➡ *Skills File 2: Mind maps (Revision), S. 146*

Grammar
Wie kann eure Klassenparty erfolgreich sein? Schreibe fünf Bedingungssätze dazu auf.
If we have tasty food, everyone will be happy.
If …

Tausche deine Sätze mit einem Partner/einer Partnerin aus und überprüfe sie anhand des Grammar File. Solltest du Fehler finden, korrigiere sie.
➡ *Grammar File 14, S. 172*
➡ *Workbook 11–12, S. 60–61*

Presenting a poster
Sieh dir den Tipp-Kasten auf Seite 93 an. Notiere dir die Punkte, auf die du das nächste Mal achten musst.
➡ *Skills File 16: Giving a presentation (Revision), S. 154*
➡ *Skills File 18: Presenting a photo, S. 155*

101

6 Unit

Leistungsmessung Unit 6

Lernfeld S. 102–103: Die S können **Landschaften beschreiben** und sagen, was sie sehen, hören und fühlen.

A class trip

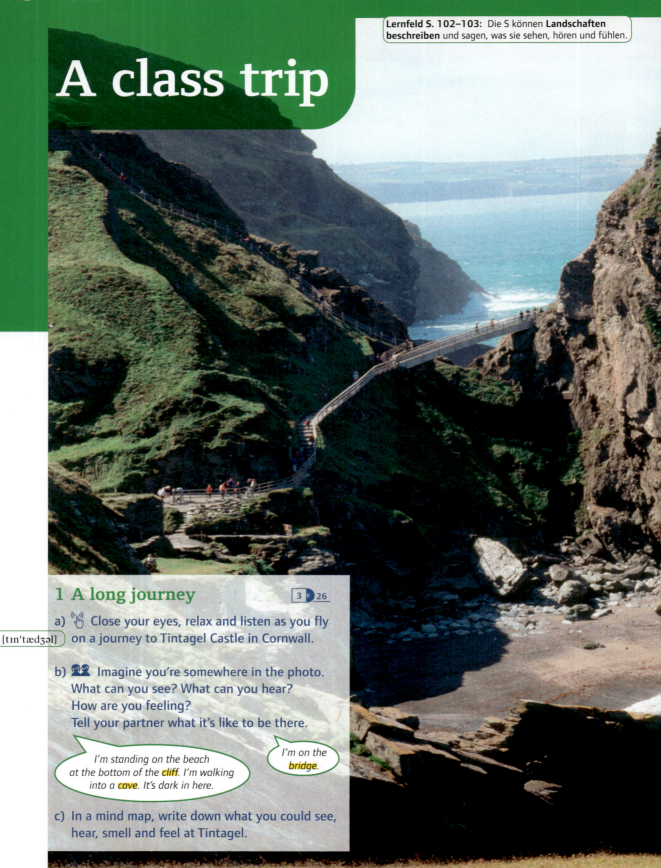

1 A long journey

[tɪnˈtædʒəl]

a) 🔊 Close your eyes, relax and listen as you fly on a journey to Tintagel Castle in Cornwall.

b) 👥 Imagine you're somewhere in the photo.
What can you see? What can you hear?
How are you feeling?
Tell your partner what it's like to be there.

> I'm standing on the beach at the bottom of the **cliff**. I'm walking into a **cave**. It's dark in here.

> I'm on the **bridge**.

c) In a mind map, write down what you could see, hear, smell and feel at Tintagel.

102

Unit 6

Your task

At the end of this unit:
Write an article for a school magazine about a class trip that you went on.

6 Part A

Lernfeld S. 104–105: Die S können kurze Texte und einen Vortrag verstehen.

KV 21

1 A class trip to Tintagel 3 ▶ 27

When class 8EB arrived at Tintagel, they went to the visitor centre, where they saw a short film about the history of the castle.
"I want to see the **real** castle – not a film!" Sam
5 whispered to Lucy.
"Sshh," she whispered back. "It's almost over!"
At the end of the film, a tall man in a °**medieval** costume **entered** the room.
"Hello everybody!" he said. "My name is Conan Petrock.
10 I'm your **guide** today."
Then Miss Bell spoke. "Before we start," she said, "**each** of you take a **copy** of the quiz. You **needn't** write all your answers today, but you **mustn't** forget to **hand** them **in** on Monday."

Box "must – needn't – mustn't", Voc, S. 203

Die Antworten zum Quiz gibt der Hörtext in **2**.

Tintagel Castle Quiz

1. How old is Tintagel Castle?
 almost 800 years
2. Who **built** the castle?
 Prince Richard
3. Why is the castle gate so **narrow**?
 it's easier to defend
4. Which part of the castle did the castle **guards** live in? Why?
 Upper Mainland Courtyard / could see everything
5. What do **legends** say about **King** Arthur? **Write down** two things.
 King of Britain ~450AD · pulled a sword out of a stone · …
6. Why does the castle look so old?
 Prince Richard built a castle that looked older so that people thought it was Arthur's castle

Box "Irregular past participles", Voc, S. 20

➜ Workbook 1 (p. 70)

2 Mr Petrock's tour 🎧 3 ▶ 28

a) Listen to Mr Petrock's tour. Take notes on the people below and the places in the photos.

KV 21: Mr Petrock's **tour** spart hier etwas Zeit.

b) 👥 Use your notes to say what you have learned about the people and places.

c) Listen again. Find answers to the questions in the quiz and write them down. siehe oben

d) 👥 Compare your answers.

1 °Lower °Mainland Courtyard
2 °Upper °Mainland Courtyard

King Henry III
1207 – 1272

Prince Richard
1209 – 1272
+princess

King Arthur

Merlin the °**Wizard**

3 View from the Island Courtyard

FöFo 6.1 — Part A 6

3 What's wrong with Justin?

It was 4 pm. Class 8EB was on the bus back to Plymstock. Lucy and Sam were sitting together. They were reading the King Arthur play. Leo and Justin were behind them, but they weren't
5 listening. Leo was eating sweets. Justin wasn't doing anything.
Suddenly Leo spoke. "Hey, Justin! Let's play *I spy*!"
"No, thanks. I don't want to play," Justin said.

❖

10 "Sam," said Lucy. "I haven't shown you my photos of last weekend."
"No," said Sam, "you haven't."
"Well," said Lucy, "I was staying at Grandma's, and you'll never guess what happened."
15 While Sam and Lucy were talking, Leo called from behind.

"Hey, Sam!"
"Not now, Leo," Sam answered. "Lucy wants to tell me something."
20 "Well," Lucy started, "I was in the barn with Grandma. We were feeding the lambs when we heard a funny sound. It was coming from behind the hay."

Leo tapped Sam on the shoulder. Sam looked
25 back. "Later, Leo," he said. Then he turned back to Lucy. "So what did you do?"
"We looked behind the hay, of course," Lucy said. Leo tapped Sam on the shoulder again.
"Stop it, Leo!" said Sam.
30 "And guess what we saw!" said Lucy excitedly.
"What?"
"A snake," she said. "A great big snake!"
"Weren't you scared?" Sam asked.
"Of course I was scared," Lucy said. "It put its
35 head up and hissed like this: sssssss! I screamed so loud that Grandpa came."
"Did he kill it?" Sam asked.
"No!" said Lucy. "You're not allowed to kill snakes! He opened the door and it went out. It was really
40 fast."
"And did you get a photo of it?" Sam asked.

❖

Suddenly, there was a loud groan from the back of the bus. It was Justin.
"Ooooh! My stomach!"
45 "Sam!" said Leo, "Justin's ill! I tried to tell you!"
Sam turned to Justin. "What's wrong?" he asked.
"I feel sick," said Justin. "Get Miss Bell."
Leo ran to the front of the bus.
"Leo," said Miss Bell. "Why aren't you in your
50 seat?"
"Justin feels sick. Please come."
Miss Bell hurried to the back of the bus. "What's wrong, Justin?" she asked.
"I think I'm going to be sick, Miss," Justin said.
55 The bus stopped. Justin ran out. When he came back a few minutes later, he was smiling a bit.
"That's better," he said, and walked slowly back to his seat.

+(to) groan
Box "ill – sick – well", Voc, S. 204

4 Give reasons why …

1 … Justin doesn't want to play *I spy*.
2 … Leo tries to talk to Sam two or three times.
3 … Sam doesn't want to talk to Leo.
4 … Grandpa doesn't kill the snake.
5 … Leo runs to the front of the bus.
6 … Justin feels better at the end.

5 Have a go

Lernfeld: Die S verwenden vorbewusst das *past progressive*.

Talk about yesterday. One student says a time. The others say what they were doing then.
A: 7 am.
B: At 7 am, I was having breakfast.
C: I was waiting for the bus.
D: I was …

1 … because he feels sick • 2 … because he wants to tell him about Justin • 3 … because he wants to hear Lucy's story • 4 … because you aren't allowed to kill snakes • 5 … to tell Miss Bell about Justin • 6 … because he was sick

6 Part A Practice

Lernfeld S. 106: Die S verstehen Bildung und Gebrauch des *past progressive* und verwenden es, um zu beschreiben, was jemand zu einem bestimmten Zeitpunkt in der Vergangenheit gerade getan hat.

Looking at language

a) Copy the table and add the verbs.
   You can find them in the text on p. 105.

   How do you make this new verb form?

I	was	staying	at Grandma's.
Leo	was	eating	sweets.
It	was	coming	from behind the hay.
We	were	feeding	the lambs.
They	were	reading	the King Arthur play.
Justin	wasn't	doing	anything.

b) Copy the timeline.
   Add the parts of this sentence in the right place.
   – Lucy was talking to Sam when her phone beeped.

I was walking down the street ...   ... when suddenly a dog barked at me.

➡ GF 15: The past progressive (pp. 173–174)

1 Mr Cobb was sleeping (Past progressive: positive statements)

Say what everyone was doing when the bus went into the tunnel.
– When the bus went into the **tunnel**, Mr Cobb was sleeping.

More help ➡ p. 132 (More help: Verben sind in einer Box vorgegeben.)

... Bob and Ben were fighting. • ... Jill was drinking and running. • ... Tiny and Tim were hiding. • ... Anna was throwing sweets at Phil. • ... Mary and Bill were playing cards. • ... Mark was eating yoghurt.

Early finisher

When the bus came out of the tunnel, ...
· Phil had **sticky** sweets in his hair.
· Mary had yoghurt on her jeans.
· Tim had cola on his shirt.

Who was it?   *For Phil, I think it was Anna because she was ...ing ...*

➡ Workbook 2–3 (pp. 70–71)

Folie 19 • FöFo 6.2

Part A Practice 6

Lernfeld S. 107: Die S können über Ereignisse in der Vergangenheit sprechen und dabei *simple past* und *past progressive* verwenden.

2 She was feeding her snake when … (Past progressive and simple past) ■■□

a) Put the verbs into the past progressive. Then choose the best endings for the sentences.

She was feeding her snake when it bit her.

1 She (feed) her snake …
2 They (cross) the ocean …
3 I (wash) the dishes …
4 We (swim) in a lake …
5 He (ride) his bike without a light …
6 She (eat) an apple …

when

a) I broke a plate.
b) a police officer stopped him.
c) she saw a worm in it.
d) their ship hit a rock.
e) somebody took our clothes.
f) it bit her.

2 They were crossing the ocean when their ship hit a rock. • 3 I was washing the dishes when I broke a plate. • 4 We were swimming in a lake when somebody took our clothes. • 5 He was riding his bike without a light when a police officer stopped him. • 6 She was eating an apple when she saw a worm in it.

b) Make correct sentences. Put one verb in the past progressive and one in the simple past.

1 Mr Petrock (wear) a medieval costume when he (meet) Miss Bell's class.
   Mr Petrock was wearing …
2 While Mr Petrock (speak), a student (ask) a question.
3 Justin (film) the castle when a bird suddenly (land) on his shoulder.
4 While Lucy (stand) on the bridge at Tintagel, she (make) a wish.
5 Sam and Leo (stand) near the water when a big wave (hit) them.
6 Lucy's mobile (beep) while she (show) Sam her photos.

1 was wearing / met
2 was speaking / asked
3 was filming / landed
4 was standing / made
5 were standing / hit
6 was beeping / showed

More help ➔ p. 132 More help: Ein Verb pro Satz ist bereits in der richtigen Zeitform vorgegeben. ➔ Workbook 4 (p. 71)

3 GAME °Alibi 💬 ■■■

Someone broke the head teacher's window at 1:30 yesterday.
Today she wants to find out who did it. She interviews two students.

a) Read the head teacher's questions.
   What does she ask?

🔊 32 b) Listen to the interviews. Do the students give the same answers? Are they good alibis?

c) 👥 Make groups of three. Prepare your roles.
   Partner A: You're the head teacher.
   Practise the questions.
   Partners B and C: You're the students.
   Agree on your answers.

d) 👥 Play the game.

HT: What were you doing at 1:30?
Student: I was …
HT: Do you have an alibi?
Student: Yes, … was with me.
HT: What was he wearing?
Student: He was wearing …
HT: And what were you wearing?
Student: I was wearing …
HT: Tell me about something that you saw.
Student: We saw … in the park.
HT: What were they doing?
Student: They were …

➔ Workbook 5–9 (pp. 71–73)

6 Part A Practice

Folie 20, 21 • FöFo 6.3

> **Lernfeld S. 108:** Die S können **Körperteile** benennen und über **Gesundheit und Krankheit** sprechen. Sie können in diesem thematischen Zusammenhang zwischen Englisch und Deutsch vermitteln.

4 WORDS Parts of the body

a) Draw a picture of a king, a queen or a wizard. Label parts of the body in your picture.

More help ➔ p. 132 **More help:** Vier Boxen mit vorgegebenen Wörtern. Die S müssen diese nur noch ihrer Zeichnung zuordnen.

b) Match the body parts to the descriptions. You can add these body parts to your drawing.

> back · chest · fingers · knees · neck · throat · toes · tongue

1 These are on the end of your hands.   *fingers*
2 Food goes through this into your body.   *throat*
3 It's red and inside your mouth.   *tongue*
4 There are five of these on each of your feet.   *toes*
5 Your heart is inside this.   *chest*
6 They're in the middle of your legs.   *knees*
7 This is between your head and your body.   *neck*
8 You can lie on this and look at the sky.   *back*

c) Choose a part of the body. Say what you can do with it. Can your partner guess what it is?

"You can smell through it." — "It's my nose."
"You run with them." — "They're my …"

Early finisher ➔ p. 135 **Early finisher:** Partner A beschreibt, Partner B zeichnet.   ➔ Workbook 10 (p. 73)

5 WORDS What's wrong with you?

Say what's wrong with you.
Your partner says what you can do about it.

What's wrong?		
I don't feel well.	I **have a toothache**.	I've cut my finger.
I'm ill.	I **have a temperature**.	I've hurt my knee.
I feel sick.	I **have a headache**.	I think I've broken my arm.
	I **have a cough**.	
	I have a **sore** throat.	
	I think I **have a cold**.	

Tips and help
I can look for a **plaster**.
We need a **thermometer**.
You need some **fresh** air.
Stop eating sweets.
Sit down and put some ice on it.
You should stay at home.
I think you should see a doctor.
You have to go to the **dentist**.
You have to go to the **hospital**.

6 Susan doesn't feel well   3

Susan, your English visitor, doesn't feel well. You phone your mother and ask what you should do. Finish your part of the conversation below. Then listen to the whole dialogue and go on.

You:	Hallo, Mutti?	**Susan:**	I feel ill. I have a **terrible** headache.	
Mother:	Ja, hallo, was ist denn los?	**You:**	*Sie … Und sie hat …*	fühlt sich krank. • Kopfschmerzen
You:	Susan geht es nicht gut, glaube ich.	**Mother:**	Hat sie auch Fieber?	
Mother:	Was hat sie denn?	**You:**	*Do you have …*	a temperature?
You:	Ich weiß es nicht genau.	**Susan:**	I don't know. But …	
Mother:	Dann frag sie mal, was ihr fehlt.			
You:	*What's … … wrong with you?*			

➔ SF 12: Mediation (Revision) (p. 151);   ➔ Workbook 11 (p. 73)

Sie weiß es nicht, aber sie hat nicht gut geschlafen. • Does anything hurt? Do you have a cough? Is your nose OK? • Sie glaubt, sie hat Halsschmerzen. Es tut beim Trinken und Essen weh. • She thinks you have a cold. If you have a temperature, you must see a doctor. If you don't have a temperature, just keep warm and stay in bed. Drink a lot of water or hot tea and sleep. • Sie bedankt sich.

FöFo 6.4　　　　　　　　　　　　　　📖 **Reading course**　**6**

> **Lernfeld S. 109:** Die S können einen Text überfliegen, um Informationen herauszusuchen *(scanning)*,
> neue **Wörter erschließen**, **Notizen** zum Text machen und den Text **ausdrucksstark vorlesen**.

Using skills that you have learned

Here you can practise some of the reading skills that you've learned this year, all in one text.

SCANNING

You scan a text to find information quickly.
Scan the story for the names of the characters.
Which three names do you find most often? King Uther ·
　　　　　　　　　　　　　　　　　　　Merlin · Arthur

UNDERSTANDING NEW WORDS

a) Read the text. Try to understand it without a
　 dictionary. The tips on p. 19 can help.
　 Write down words that you really can't
　 understand in a list.

b) 👥 Compare your lists. If you can, explain
　 the words on your partner's list.
　 Use a dictionary for the words that you *both*
　 don't understand.

TAKING NOTES

a) Take notes to answer these questions:
　1 **Who** was Uther?　King of Britain, Arthur's father
　2 **When** did he live?　a long, long time ago
　3 **What** did he learn about his future?　disaster; Uther: dies
　4 **Why** did he want to know more?　plan; be ready
　5 **Where** did he learn all this?　Tintagel

b) Organize your notes as keywords in a table.

	who	when	what	why	where
Uther	king				

READING ALOUD

EXTRA 👥 Take turns and read the text aloud.

Uther's °secret son

A long, long time ago, Uther Pendragon °united the different areas of Britain into one country. He had help from a clever man – the °wise wizard Merlin, who told the king about the future.

A few years later, King Uther °fell in love with the beautiful Lady Igraine, from Tintagel in Cornwall. They °married and lived together in Tintagel, in a castle that looked over the sea. They soon had a son and °named the strong and beautiful baby Arthur.

One cold winter's day, Merlin came to Tintagel with a terrible message.

"Your °majesty," he said, "I have seen the future, and there is only °sadness and °disaster. It hurts me so to tell you this."

"Tell me what you see, Merlin," said the king.

"Soon, you will become very ill and die, my Lord."

"Go on! Tell me more!" said the king. "I have to plan and be ready. °What else do you see?"

"I see °war, my Lord – for many, many years. Many men will fight to become the new king," said Merlin, with eyes as bright as °stars. "I come to you, my Lord, because young Arthur is in great °danger. After you die, they will try to kill him! But I have a plan, your Majesty. If you follow my °instructions, Arthur will °be saved!"

"Tell me, °wise one, what is your plan?" asked King Uther. Merlin spoke quietly. "°Tonight, when the moon is °low, you must bring the boy to a cave by the beach. The good Sir Hector will wait for you there. He will take the boy to his home. There, Arthur will grow to be a man. He will be like a °jewel inside a °stone. No one will see him until the time is right."

Soon after, King Uther became very ill and died. Terrible °battles began °all over the country. The people of Britain had to wait 16 long years before Arthur was old enough to bring °peace once again to the great country.

➡ **Workbook** *12 (p. 74)*

109

6 Part B

Lernfeld S. 110: Die S können eine Geschichte verstehen. Sie können Ideen für **Ferienaktivitäten** aufschreiben und darüber sprechen.

1 Ice cream in the Broadway 3 ▷ 34

Sam, Lucy, Leo and Maya were walking to the Broadway when someone suddenly shouted to them from a second-floor window.

"Hey! Justin!" Sam shouted back. "Come down
5 and have an ice cream with us." Justin didn't answer. He disappeared into the room behind the window.

"Did Lucy tell you what happened to Justin on our class trip?" asked Sam.
10 "Of course she did. Poor Justin!" said Maya.

"And how was your trip? You went all the way to Bath, didn't you?" asked Sam.

"Yes, that's right. It was a long trip but it was also very interesting. And look: here's the report I've
15 written – it's for our school magazine."

"That's great, Maya," said Sam.

"Look! Poor Justin is here," shouted Leo.

"Poor Justin?" asked Justin.

"Oh, it's nothing …" said Sam. "Let's go and get
20 some ice cream."

"Here's the shop I like," said Lucy. "It has the best chocolate ice cream."

"I want strawberry," said Leo.

The kids bought their ice creams and went back
25 outside to sit in the sun.

"What are you going to do this summer, Sam?" Maya asked.

"Dad wants to go to Weston-super-Mare again."

"Cool! I want to go to the beach too!" said Maya.
30 "We still have another week of school," said Lucy.

"But the last week will be fun," Sam said.

"Right," said Lucy. "We're going to do a play about King Arthur, Maya. Sam and Justin both want to be Arthur!"

The great wizard Merlin!

Leo Justin Sam Lucy Maya

Box "German „werden"
Voc, S. 206

35 Justin frowned. "No, I don't," he said.

"I don't either," said Sam. "But Lucy really wants to be the beautiful Queen Guinevere."

Lucy went red. "Miss Bell is going to decide the roles tomorrow," she said.
40 "Well," said Maya, "if I was Miss Bell, I'd choose Justin as King Arthur. I wouldn't choose Sam." Maya smiled. "But I *would* choose Sam as Merlin."

"The great wizard Merlin! Yes! He's the character I want to play!" Sam said, and held up his ice
45 cream.

Maya went on. "And of course, if *I* went to Plymstock, *I'd* play Guinevere."

"But you don't go to Plymstock, Maya," said Lucy.

"So I'll have to play Queen Guinevere … *if* Miss
50 Bell chooses me."

"Don't worry, Luce," said Maya. "I'm sure she'll choose you. But be careful, dear Queen Guinevere. Your ice cream is melting and °methinks it will soon fall on your royal shoe!"

2 What are the names?

Add the right names to finish the sentences.

1 When Justin calls down to his friends from the window of his flat, … shouts back. Sam
2 … asks … about her class trip. Sam / Maya
3 … shows … her report about her trip. Maya / Sam
4 … talks about this year's family holiday. Sam
5 … thinks … would be a good Merlin. Maya / Sam
6 … hopes that she can be Queen Guinevere. Lucy

3 EXTRA Plans for the holidays

a) 👥 Sam says he's going to go to Weston-super-Mare again this summer.
What do you think he will do there?
Write down as many ideas as you can.

b) 🧩 Write down three things that you want to do in the summer holidays.
Then find someone else with similar ideas.

110

Part B Practice

FöFo 6.5

Lernfeld S. 111: Die S können einen Bericht über einen Klassenausflug schreiben.

1 Writing a report (the 5 Ws and *how*)

a) Read the questions.
   Then find the answers in Maya's article.
   Which paragraph are the answers in? **1st paragraph**
   1 **Who** went on a class trip? *class 8SW*
   2 **Where** did they go? *they went to Bath*
   3 **When** did they go? *on 7 July*
   4 **Why** did they go there? *they're doing a project on the Romans*
   5 **What** did they visit? *the famous baths*
   6 **How** did they travel? *they went by school bus*

> **TIP**
> A good report answers the 5 Ws:
> **Who? What? Where? When? Why?**
> It also often answers the question **How?**

b) **You choose** Imagine you are Justin, Lucy, or Sam. Write a short report about your class trip to Tintagel.

c) Check your partner's report.
   Does it answer the 5 Ws and *how*?

➡ Workbook 13 (p. 75)

Coombe Dean School News – Vol. 14, no. 7

A class trip to the °Roman Baths
by Maya Sen, 8SW

This year, on 7 July, the school bus took our class, 8SW, on a trip to Bath. We went there because we're doing a project on the Romans. So, of course, we had to visit the famous baths which give the city its name.

Our journey to Bath took over two hours, but it wasn't boring. My friends Lara, Ginny and I did some maths °puzzles that Mrs Wilson gave us. They were fun.

When we arrived, we started our tour of the Roman baths. It was fantastic. I thought the baths were just an old swimming pool. So I was very surprised that they were so big. I didn't know that the Romans had great big °leisure centres °thousands of years ago.

After the tour, we had lunch at a park near the river. Ginny had her frisbee with her, so we all played °for a while. Once, when Lara threw the frisbee, it went °straight towards the back of Mrs Wilson's head. She was sitting on the grass with Mr Doe. "Watch out!" we shouted. In one °movement, Mrs Wilson turned around, put her hand up, caught the frisbee and threw it back to Lara. Then she went on talking to Mr Doe. Cool!

In the afternoon we walked around the city centre for °an hour and a half before the bus took us back to Plymouth.

EXTRA Background file

Lernfeld: Die S verstehen einen kurzen Sachtext über Römische Bäder und vergleichen sie mit modernen Freizeitanlagen.

The Roman Baths at Aquae Sulis

There is a °natural hot °spring in Bath where more than a million °litres of hot water (46 °C) comes out of the ground every day. Over 2,000 years ago, the °Celts °worshipped their °goddess Sulis at the spring. When the Romans came to Britain in the first century °AD, they built a town there and called it *Aquae Sulis*. That means *the waters of Sulis* in °Latin, the Romans' language.
The Romans stayed in Britain for 400 years. °During all that time, the baths at Aquae Sulis were a °huge leisure centre with swimming pools, °changing rooms and toilets. They had hot baths, warm baths and cold baths. There were hot rooms like °saunas. Visitors could have a sauna in a hot room and then jump into a cold bath. At the *Great Bath*, a large swimming pool of hot water from the spring, Romans met friends, swam, had a °massage and a snack or played games.

Compare the Roman leisure centre at Aquae Sulis with a modern leisure centre in your area.
Use a mind map or chart.

6 | **Part B Practice**

2 Pronunciation (Consonants at the end of words) +vowel

Lernfeld: Die S können Laute am Wortende richtig zuordnen und aussprechen.

3 ▶ 35 **a)** You will hear groups of four words like this:

> drink [ŋk] – pink [ŋk] – sing [ŋ] – think [ŋk]

Listen to the sounds at the end of each word.
Which sound do you hear three times?
Which sound do you hear only once?

Groups 1, 2 and 3:	[d] or [t]	1, 3: 1x [d] 3x [t] 2: 3x [d] 1x [t]
Groups 4 and 5:	[b] or [p]	4, 5: 1x [b] 3x [p]
Groups 6, 7 and 8:	[g] or [k]	6, 8: 1x [g] 3x [k] 7: 3x [g] 1x [k]
Group 9:	[ŋ] or [ŋk]	9: 3x [ŋ] 1x [ŋk]

➧ **Workbook** 14 (p. 75)

b) 🖐 **Listen to the poem. Then read it aloud.** 3 ▶ 36

A class trip
I take a big book, and a bag on my back,
In my bag (it is black) is a drink and a snack.
I think of the things that I'll do when I'm there,
I'll sing summer songs and smell the sea air.
I look out of the bus, I see birds, I see sheep.
It is loud, it is <mark>noisy</mark>, *kids shout and phones beep.*
A kid starts to cry, no one knows what is wrong.
Our teacher looks angry, the journey's too long.
I eat a crab sandwich, I look at my map.
We arrive at the° **seaside**, *we cheer and we clap.*

3 EXTRA If you were a guide at Tintagel, ... (Conditional sentences 2)

Lernfeld: Die S können über Dinge sprechen, die unwahrscheinlich oder unmöglich sind *(conditional sentences 2)*.

a) Use the right verb forms in these sentences.

1 If you (be) a guide at Tintagel, you (wear) a medieval costume.
  If you were a guide ..., you would (you'd) ...would wear
2 If tourists (see) your costume, they (love) it. saw / would love
3 If my class (go) to Tintagel, we (want) to go on Mr Petrock's tour. went / would want
4 If I (walk) across the bridge to the island, I (make) a wish too. walked / would make
5 If I (meet) Merlin, I (be) a bit scared. met / would be
6 Merlin (be) a superhero if he (live) today. would be / lived

b) Say what you would do if you had 500 euros.

More help ➧ p. 133   ➧ **Workbook** 15 (p. 76)

More help: Einige Ideen als Anregung.

Language help

You use conditional sentences 2 when something is unlikely or even impossible.

If I went to Plymstock, **I'd play** Guinevere.
(Unlikely: Maya goes to Coombe Dean.)

If I was Miss Bell, **I'd choose** Justin.
(Impossible: Maya cannot be Miss Bell.)

In conditional sentences 2 you use the **simple past** in the if-clause and **would ('d) + infinitive** in the main clause.

➧ *GF 16: Conditional sentences 2 (p. 174)*

4 EXTRA The tickets I bought (Contact clauses)

Lernfeld: Die S können Relativsätze bilden, bei denen das Relativpronomen Objekt des Relativsatzes ist *(contact clauses)*.

a) Write the sentences with the right relative pronoun.

1 Arthur was the king Mr Petrock talked about.
  Arthur was the king who Mr Petrock talked about.
2 This is the play Miss Bell's class wants to do. which/ that
3 Oh no, where are the tickets I bought for my class? which/ that

b) Where can you leave out the relative pronoun?

1 Maya is the girl who went to Bath with her class.
2 Here is the quiz which you have to hand in.
3 This is the path which takes you to the castle.

➧ **Workbook** 16–19 (pp. 76–77)

TIP

If the relative pronoun is the object of the relative clause, you can leave it out.

Here's the report I've written.
Here's the report ~~which~~ I've written.

He's the character I want to play!
He's the character ~~who~~ I want to play!

Here's the shop I like.
Here's the shop ~~that~~ I like.

➧ *GF 17: Relative clauses: contact clauses (p. 175)*

112

FöFo 6.6 • KV 22 The world behind the picture 6

1 The Romans in Britain

Lernfeld: Die S können einen kurzen Film verstehen.

Länge: 3:52

a) Match the captions to the pictures.
   Then watch the film and check.   1B · 2C · 3D · 4A
   1 The Romans heard interesting things about Britain.
   2 When the Romans invaded, there were no good roads or houses.
   3 The Romans had trouble with Scotland.
   4 Britain was rich and peaceful under the Romans.

A B C D

b) Watch the film again. What did the Romans do in these years?

– In 500 BC, the Romans fought their neighbours.

550 BC · 55 BC · 54 BC · 43 AD · 122–128 AD · 450 AD

How did the Romans change Britain? Take notes.
55 BC and 54 BC: The Romans came to Britain but the Britons fought back. · 43 AD: The Romans invaded Britain again and stayed. · 122–128 AD: Emperor Hadrian built a wall (Hadrian's Wall). · 450 AD: The Romans left Britain.

2 EVERYDAY ENGLISH
At the takeaway

Lernfeld: Die S können einen Dialog an einem Imbiss verstehen und vorspielen.

a) Watch the film. Find out:
   What do Ruby, Oliver and Jack eat? burgers and chips / ice cream
   Who is the hungriest of the three? Jack: he wants to eat more
   How do the other two feel about this? they want to do something else, not just eat

Länge: 7:42

b) Read the sentences in the box.
   Match them to the sentences below.

Box "one/ones", Voc, S. 206

   5 Large, please.
   4 No, not that one. The one on the right.
   2 No thanks, just the burger.
   6 That's £3.50, please.
   3 Yes, please. I'll have an iced tea.
   1 Yes, I'm ready.

1 Are you ready to order?
2 Would you like chips with your burger?
3 And would you like a drink with that?
4 This one? The vegetarian burger?
5 What size tea would you like? We have large or small.
6 Here you are.

c) Watch the film again and check your answers.

d) You want to get something to eat at Cap'n Jaspers.
   Write a dialogue and act it out.

113

6 Text

Lernfeld S. 114–115: Die S können ein **Theaterstück** in Textform verstehen und zu einzelnen Szenen Überschriften finden. Sie können über die **Charaktere** des Stückes sprechen und ihnen Adjektive zuweisen.

🔊 PLAY The sword in the stone

Cast
Merlin, a wizard – (Sam)
Sir Hector, a knight – (Ruby, with a beard)
Kay, Hector's first son – (Leo)
Arthur, Hector's adopted son – (Justin)
Guinevere, a beautiful lady – (Lucy) [ˈgwɪnəvɪə]

Scene 1
Merlin's Cave, Tintagel. Merlin holds a baby.
Merlin: *(to the baby)* I see black clouds, Arthur. This is a terrible day for Britain.

Sir Hector enters.
5 Hector: Merlin, it is the day of our worst dreams! We have lost the **battle** and our great king, Uther Pendragon, is dead. Our **enemies** will soon be in Tintagel.
Merlin: Then Arthur is in **danger**, Sir Hector. We
10 must save him from his enemies. Take him with you to live with you and your own son, Kay. We will meet again in 16 years, when all the knights of the land choose a new king in London. Take
15 Arthur, and go quickly.

Merlin gives the baby to Hector. Hector exits.

Scene 2
16 years later. Hector, Kay and Arthur are outside a church in
20 *London.*
Hector: Kay, we must go in with the knights now.
Kay: You're not a knight yet, Arthur. You're too
25 young.
Hector: Arthur, meet us later at our **inn**.

Hector and Kay exit into the church. Guinevere enters and
30 *hides behind a big stone. Merlin enters behind Arthur and touches him with a sword. Arthur falls asleep. Merlin pushes the sword into the stone. He does not*
35 *see Guinevere. Merlin exits.*

Arthur wakes up, gets up and exits. He does not see the sword in the stone. Guinevere looks closely at it.
Hector and Kay enter.
40 Lady G: So tell me, sir, who is our new king?
Hector: We have not yet agreed on a new king, Lady … er …?
Lady G: Guinevere.
Kay: Guinevere. A beautiful name for a
45 beautiful lady.
Lady G: Have you seen this?

Guinevere points to the sword in the stone.
Kay: There's a sword in the old stone. How did it get there?
50 Hector: And there is some **writing** on the stone: Pull this sword out of the stone and you are the true king of Britain.

Merlin enters.
Hector: Merlin, what do you know of this?
55 Merlin: I know only that it is the **truth**. The man who can pull this sword from the stone is our true king. Do you want to try?

Hector and Kay try to pull the sword out, but they cannot. Merlin exits.
60 Hector: We cannot pull the sword out, Merlin. Merlin? Where are you? He has gone. Well, we must have a king. The winner of tomorrow's tournament will also be our new king!
65 Lady G: And that man will also win my heart.

Scene 3
*At the tournament. Guinevere is waiting. Hector, Kay and Arthur enter. Kay walks to Guinevere and **kisses** her hand.*
Kay: Lady Guinevere.
70 Lady G: Sir Kay. Good luck in the tournament.
Kay: I will do my best, my Lady, with this sword … Oh, no. Father, I've left my sword at the inn.
Hector: Quick, Arthur! Go back to the inn and
75 find Kay's sword. Run as fast as you can.

Scene 4
In front of the church. Arthur enters. Guinevere enters behind him. He cannot see her.
Arthur: Our inn is so far away. Kay will have to wait. Oh, look … there's a sword in that

Sam (Merlin)

114

Folie 22 • KV 23, 24 A–C • VAS 6.1, 6.2   Text 6

80   stone. If I take this sword, I won't have to go back to the inn.

Arthur pulls the sword easily from the stone. Guinevere exits quickly. Arthur exits too.

Scene 5

Kay and Hector are at the tournament. Guinevere
85 *enters. Then Arthur enters with the sword.*
Arthur: Here, Kay, here's your sword.
Kay: This isn't my sword, Arthur! How can I fight with this old thing?
Lady G: Wait, I know that sword. Let me see it.
90 Hector: Arthur, this isn't Kay's sword. Where did you get it?
Arthur: I found it in an old stone in front of the church. So I pulled it out and came back.

Merlin enters.
95 Merlin: Yes, Arthur pulled the sword out of the stone. He is Uther Pendragon's son and the true king. He will be the greatest king that Britain has ever known.
Lady G: You have won my heart, King Arthur.
100   Take me as your queen!

*Guinevere **kneels** in front of Arthur.*
Hector: Long live King Arthur!

*Hector kneels. Arthur holds his sword up. Merlin puts a **crown** on Arthur's head.*
105 All: Long live King Arthur!

[Box "Irregular past participles", Voc, S. 207]

1 The best title

a) Choose the best title for scene 1.
   – (A terrible day for Britain)
   – Bad weather in Britain
   – Pendragon is dead

b) Think of titles for scenes 2–5.
   More help ➔ p. 133   **More help:** Vorschläge für Titel zur Auswahl.

2 The characters

a) Make groups of five. Each student chooses a different character from the play.

b) Match your character to one or more of these adjectives. Find reasons in the text.

   angry · beautiful · excited · fast · friendly · **wise** · worried · …

   Guinevere is beautiful. In lines 44–45, Kay says …

c) Tell your partners about your character. Which character would you like to be?

3 Interviews and pictures

Neigungsdifferenzierung: Die S wählen zwischen zwei unterschiedlichen kreativen Aufgaben.

You choose Do a) or b).

a) You're a reporter for the Tintagel Times. Write down three questions for a character in the play. Give them to a partner.

   Read your partner's questions and think of answers. Then act out the interviews.

b) Draw a picture for one scene from the play. Swap pictures with another student. Can you guess the scene?

4 Your play

Mit Hilfe von **KV 23: The sword in the stone: A checklist** planen die S die Umsetzung ihres Theaterstücks.

Make a group of five. Choose and learn your roles.
Think about the props: what can you use for the baby Arthur, a church, a sword, a crown and costumes?
Act out the play for your class.

➔ **Workbook** 20–21 (p. 78)
➔ **Workbook** 22, Quiz (p. 79)

Justin (Arthur)

Zusatz: Die **KV 24A–C: History Time. The Bridge of Swords** bietet einen Auszug aus dem Cornelsen-Comic mit Sprechblasen zum Selbstausfüllen, geeignet als vertiefende Leseaufgabe.

Workbook Checkpoint (pp. 80–83)

6 Unit

Your task

> Alle Schritte dieser Lernaufgabe können als Hausaufgabe durchgeführt werden, wobei es sich je nach Klassensituation anbieten kann, **Step 5** im Unterricht durchzuführen.

A report about a class trip

Write a report for your school magazine about a class trip.

STEP 1
Make a mind map or a table about your trip.
Fill in information for the 5 Ws and *how*.

STEP 2
Use your mind map or table to write about your trip. Organize your information in paragraphs.
For example:

Paragraph 1: Introduction
· Who went on the trip?
· Where did you go? When did you go?
· How did you get there? What did you do there?
· Why did you go on the trip?

Paragraph 2: Activities
· What were the highlights?
· What did you do for lunch?
· Did anything exciting or surprising happen?

Paragraph 3: What I liked / didn't like
· Did you enjoy the trip? Why or why not?
· Would you like to go to a similar place on your next class trip?

STEP 3
Read your text again.
· Check for spelling and grammar mistakes.
· Does your report tell the reader what happened first, next, after that, at the end?

STEP 4
Choose one or two photos for your report.
Write captions to go with the photos.
Put together a page with your text and photos.

STEP 5
👥 Swap reports with your partner.
Read his/her text and give feedback.
I really liked your report because …
– it's interesting/clear/…
– I learned a lot about …
– the picture(s) is/are good / go with …

You could make your report better like this:
– Write more about what you did on your trip.
– Find better pictures to go with your text.
– Say why you went on the trip.

Coombe Dean School News - Vol. 14, no. 7
A class trip to the Roman Baths
by Maya Sen, 8SW

This year, on 7 July, the school bus took our class, 8SW, on a trip to Bath. We went there because ... a project on the Romans. So, of ... d to visit the famous baths which ... s name.

> I ♥ your article – very funny! ☺☺

... Bath took over two hours, but it ... g. My friends Lara, Ginny ... some maths puzzles that Mrs Wilson ga ... were fun.

When we arrived, we started our t ... Roman baths. It was fantastic. I thoug ... were just an old swimming pool. So I was very surprised that they were so big. I didn't know that ... great big leisure centres ... ago.

> Why didn't you put a photo in?

> I wanted to know more about the tour.

... had lunch at a park near the ... er frisbee with her, so we all ... Once, when Lara threw the frisbee, it went straight towards the back of Mrs Wilson's head. She was sitting on the grass with Mr Doe. "Watch out!" we shouted. In one movement, Mrs Wilson turned around, put her hand up, caught the frisbee and threw it back to Lara. Then she went on talking to Mr Doe. Cool!

In the afternoon we walked around the city centre for an hour and a half before the bus took us back to Plymouth.

STEP 6
Read your partner's feedback. Can you use it to make your text better?

---

introduction [ˌɪntrəˈdʌkʃn] Einleitung

Unit 6

Das lief nicht gut, ich muss mehr üben.

Das war OK, aber ich könnte besser werden.

Das habe ich gut geschafft.

Wie gut warst du?

Wie schätzt du dich selber ein? Schreibe *Words*, *Mind map/table*, *Writing* und *Feedback* in dein Heft und ordne dir für jeden Bereich eine Ampelfarbe zu.

Words
Fielen dir die Wörter ein, die du brauchtest, um Orte und Dinge oder Aktivitäten zu beschreiben?

Mind map/table
Wie hat dir deine Mindmap/Tabelle beim Schreiben geholfen?

Writing
Wie haben dir die *wh*-Fragen beim Schreiben geholfen?

Feedback
Hatten die anderen Gruppenmitglieder Vorschläge, um deinen Text zu verbessern? Wusstest du, was sie mit ihrem Feedback gemeint haben?

Wie kannst du besser werden?

Wenn du dich eher rot oder gelb eingeschätzt hast, helfen dir folgende Tipps beim Wiederholen und Üben.

Words
Sieh dir die Abschnitte zum Lernen von Vokabeln im Skills File an und wähle einen der Tipps aus. Du kannst z.B. die Wörter, die dir gefehlt haben, nachschlagen und in dein Vokabelheft schreiben oder in ein *vocabulary picture poster* eintragen.

➡ *Skills File 3: Vocabulary picture posters, S. 146*

Mind map / table
Vergleiche deinen Text mit deiner Mindmap bzw. deiner Tabelle. Hast du alle wichtigen Informationen daraus in deinem Text benutzt?

Finde einen Partner/eine Partnerin und vergleiche eure Mindmaps bzw. eure Tabellen. Sucht dabei Ideen, wie ihr eure Mindmaps bzw. Tabellen verbessern könntet.

➡ *Skills File 2: Mind maps (Revision), S. 146*
➡ *Skills File 19: Peer feedback, S. 155*

Writing
Frage dich, welche *wh*-Fragen deine Freunde zu eurem Ausflug stellen würden, und beantworte sie.

Feedback
Bitte die anderen Gruppenmitglieder, ihr Feedback zu erläutern, wenn du etwas nicht verstanden hast. Vielleicht haben sie auch weitere Vorschläge.

➡ *Skills File 19: Peer feedback, S. 155*

Access story

> Die S können die Romanauszüge sowohl zu Hause als auch im Unterricht lesen. Eine gemeinsame Lesephase im Unterricht ist aber durchaus sinnvoll und hilfreich.

Because of Winn-Dixie by Kate DiCamillo

Chapter Nine

Just about everything that happened to me that summer happened because of Winn-Dixie. For instance, without him I would never have met Gloria Dump. He was the one who introduced us.

What happened was this: I was riding my bike home from Gertrude's Pets and Winn-Dixie was running along beside me. We went past Dunlap and Stevie Dewberry's house, and when Dunlap and Stevie saw me, they got on their bikes and started following me. They wouldn't ride with me; they just rode behind me and whispered things that I couldn't hear. Neither one of them had any hair on his head, because their mama shaved their heads every week during the summer because of the one time Dunlap got fleas in his hair from their cat, Sadie. And now they looked like two identical bald-headed babies, even though they weren't twins. Dunlap was ten years old, like me, and Stevie was nine and tall for his age.

"I can hear you," I hollered back at them. "I can hear what you're saying." But I couldn't.

Winn-Dixie started to race way ahead of me.

"You better watch out," Dunlap hollered. "That dog is headed right for the witch's house."

"Winn-Dixie," I called. But he kept on going faster and hopped over a gate and went into the most overgrown jungle of a yard that I had ever seen.

"You better go get your dog out of there," Dunlap said.

"The witch will eat that dog," Stevie said.

"Shut up," I told them.

I got off my bike and went up to the gate and hollered, "Winn-Dixie, you better come on out of there."

But he didn't.

"She's probably eating him right now," Stevie said. He and Dunlap were standing behind me. "She eats dogs all the time."

"Get lost, you bald-headed babies," I said.

"Hey," said Dunlap, "that ain't a very nice way for a preacher's daughter to talk." He and Stevie backed off a little.

I stood there and thought for a minute. I finally decided that I was more afraid of losing Winn-Dixie than I was of having to deal with a dog-eating witch, so I went through the gate and into the yard.

"That witch is going to eat the dog for dinner and you for dessert," Stevie said.

"We'll tell the preacher what happened to you," Dunlap shouted after me.

---

for instance [fər ˈɪnstəns] zum Beispiel · **(to) introduce** [ˌɪntrəˈdjuːs] bekannt machen (mit) · **pet** Haustier · **neither one of them** [ˈnaɪðə, ˈniːðə] keiner von beiden · **(to) shave** [ʃeɪv] rasieren · **during** [ˈdjʊərɪŋ] während · **flea** [fliː] Floh · **even though** [ˌiːvn ˈðəʊ] obwohl · **(to) be headed for sth.** [ˈhedɪd] auf etwas zugehen, zusteuern · **witch** [wɪtʃ] Hexe · **overgrown** [ˌəʊvəˈɡrəʊn] zugewachsen, überwuchert · **yard** [jɑːd] Hof, Garten · **Shut up.** [ˈʃʌt ˌʌp] (infml) Halt(et) den Mund. · **Get lost.** (infml) Hau(t) ab. · **ain't** [eɪnt] (infml) = am not / is not / are not · **(to) back off** zurückweichen · **(to) be afraid (of)** [əˈfreɪd] Angst haben (vor) · **(to) deal with sb., dealt, dealt** [diːl, delt] mit jm. fertig werden

Access story

55 By then, I was deep in the jungle. There was every kind of thing growing everywhere. There were flowers and vegetables and trees and vines.

"Winn-Dixie?" I said.

60 "Heh-heh-heh," I heard. "This dog sure likes to eat."

I went around a really big tree all covered in moss, and there was Winn-Dixie. He was eating something right out of the witch's hand.
65 She looked up at me. "This dog sure likes peanut butter," she said. "You can always trust a dog that likes peanut butter."

She was old with crinkly brown skin. She had on a big floppy hat with flowers all over it, and
70 she didn't have any teeth, but she didn't look like a witch. She looked nice. And Winn-Dixie liked her, I could tell.

"I'm sorry he got in your garden," I said.

"You ain't got to be sorry," she said. "I enjoy a
75 little company."

"My name's Opal," I told her.

"My name's Gloria Dump," she said. "Ain't that a terrible last name? Dump?"

"My last name is Buloni," I said. "Sometimes
80 the kids at school back home in Watley called me 'Lunch Meat'."

"Hah!" Gloria Dump laughed. "What about this dog? What you call him?"

"Winn-Dixie," I said.

85 Winn-Dixie thumped his tail on the ground. He tried smiling, but it was hard with his mouth all full of peanut butter.

"Winn-Dixie?" Gloria Dump said. "You mean like the grocery store?"

90 "Yes ma'am," I said.

"Whooooeee," she said. "That takes the strange name prize, don't it?"

"Yes ma'am," I said.

"I was just fixing to make myself a peanut
95 butter sandwich," she said. "You want one, too?"

"All right," I said. "Yes, please."

"Go on and sit down," she said, pointing at a lawn chair with the back all busted out of it.
100 "But sit down careful."

I sat down careful and Gloria Dump made me a peanut butter sandwich on white bread.

Then she made one for herself and put her false teeth in to eat it; when she was done, she
105 said to me, "You know, my eyes ain't too good at all. I can't see nothing but the general shape of things, so I got to rely on my heart. Why don't you go on and tell me everything about yourself, so as I can see you with my heart."

110 And because Winn-Dixie was looking up at her like she was the best thing he had ever seen, and because the peanut butter sandwich had been so good, and because I had been waiting for a long time to tell some person everything
115 about me, I did.

---

vine [vaɪn] Kletterpflanze · **moss** [mɒs] Moos · **peanut butter** [ˌpiːnʌt ˈbʌtə] Erdnussbutter · (to) **trust** [trʌst] (ver)trauen · **crinkly** [ˈkrɪŋkli] faltig · **skin** [skɪn] Haut · **floppy hat** [ˈflɒpi] Schlapphut · **you ain't got to** [eɪnt] *(infml)* = you don't have to · **company** [ˈkʌmpəni] Gesellschaft · **dump** [dʌmp] Müllhalde; *(übertragen auch:)* Bruchbude; Kaff · (to) **thump** [θʌmp] heftig schlagen, klopfen · (to) **be busted** [ˈbʌstɪd] kaputt sein · (to) **rely on** [rɪˈlaɪ] sich verlassen auf

Access story

Chapter Eleven

That night there was a real bad thunderstorm. But what woke me up wasn't the thunder and lightning. It was Winn-Dixie, whining and butting his head against my bedroom door.

120 "Winn-Dixie," I said. "What are you doing?"

He didn't pay any attention to me. He just kept beating his head against the door and whining and whimpering. When l got out of bed and went over and put my hand on his head, he
125 was shaking and trembling so hard that it scared me.

I knelt down and wrapped my arms around him, but he didn't turn and look at me or smile or sneeze or wag his tail, or do any normal kind
130 of Winn-Dixie thing; he just kept beating his head against the door and crying and shaking.

"You want the door open?" I said. "Huh? Is that what you want?" I stood up and opened the door and Winn-Dixie flew through it like
135 something big and ugly and mean was chasing him.

"Winn-Dixie," I hissed, "come back here." I didn't want him going and waking the preacher up.

140 But it was too late. Winn-Dixie was already at the other end of the trailer, in the preacher's room. I could tell because there was a *sproi-i-ing* sound that must have come from Winn-Dixie jumping up on the bed, and then there
145 was a sound from the preacher like he was real surprised. But none of it lasted long, because Winn-Dixie came tearing back out of the preacher's room, panting and running like crazy. I tried to grab him, but he was going too
150 fast.

"Opal?" said the preacher. He was standing at the door to his bedroom, and his hair was all kind of wild on top of his head, and he was looking around like he wasn't sure where he
155 was. "Opal, what's going on?"

"I don't know," I told him. But just then there was a huge crack of thunder, one so loud that it shook the whole trailer, and Winn-Dixie came shooting back out of my room and went
160 running right past me and I screamed, "Daddy, watch out!"

But the preacher was still confused. He just stood there, and Winn-Dixie came barrelling right toward him like he was a bowling ball and
165 the preacher was the only pin left standing, and *wham*, they both fell to the ground.

"Uh-oh," I said.

"Opal?" said the preacher. He was lying on his stomach, and Winn-Dixie was sitting on top of
170 him, panting and whining.

"Yes sir," I said.

"Opal," the preacher said again.

"Yes sir," I said louder.

"Do you know what a pathological fear is?"

175 "No sir," I told him.

---

thunderstorm [ˈθʌndəstɔːm] Gewitter · (to) **whine** [waɪn] winseln · (to) **butt** [bʌt] stoßen *(mit dem Kopf)* · (to) **pay attention to sb.** [əˈtenʃn] auf jn. achten, jn. beachten · (to) **beat, beat, beaten** [biːt, ˈbiːtn] schlagen · (to) **whimper** [ˈwɪmpə] wimmern, winseln · (to) **tremble** [ˈtrembl] zittern · **mean** [miːn] gemein, bösartig · (to) **chase sb.** [tʃeɪs] jn. jagen · (to) **hiss** zischen · (to) **last** (an)dauern · (to) **come tearing back** [ˈteərɪŋ] zurückgerast kommen · (to) **pant** [pænt] keuchen · **confused** [kənˈfjuːzd] verwirrt · (to) **barrel** [ˈbærəl] *(infml, American English)* rasen, preschen · **pathological fear** [ˌpæθəˌlɒdʒɪkl ˈfɪə] krankhafte Furcht, Angst

Access story

The preacher raised a hand. He rubbed his nose. "Well," he said, after a minute, "it's a fear that goes way beyond normal fears. It's a fear you can't be talked out of or reasoned out of."

180 Just then there was another crack of thunder and Winn-Dixie rose straight up in the air like somebody had poked him with something hot. When he hit the floor, he started running. He ran back to my bedroom and I didn't even try 185 to catch him; I just got out of his way.

The preacher lay there on the ground, rubbing his nose. Finally he sat up. He said, "Opal, I believe Winn-Dixie has a pathological fear of thunderstorms." And just when he finished his 190 sentence, here came Winn-Dixie again, running to save his life. I got the preacher up off the floor and out of the way just in time.

There didn't seem to be a thing we could do for Winn-Dixie to make him feel better, so we just 195 sat there and watched him run back and forth, all terrorized and panting. And every time there was another crack of thunder, Winn-Dixie acted all over again like it was surely the end of the world.

200 "The storm won't last long," the preacher told me. "And when it's over, the real Winn-Dixie will come back."

After a while the storm did end. The rain stopped. And there wasn't any more lightning, 205 and finally the last rumble of thunder went away and Winn-Dixie quit running back and forth and came over to where me and the preacher were sitting and cocked his head, like he was saying, "What in the world are you two 210 doing out of bed in the middle of the night?"

And then he crept up on the couch with us in this funny way he has, where he gets on the couch an inch at a time, kind of sliding himself onto it, looking off in a different direction, like 215 it's all happening by accident, like he doesn't intend to get on the couch, but all of a sudden, there he is.

And so the three of us sat there. I rubbed Winn-Dixie's head and scratched him behind 220 the ears the way he liked. And the preacher said, "There are an awful lot of thunderstorms in Florida in the summertime."

"Yes sir," I said. I was afraid that maybe he would say we couldn't keep a dog who went 225 crazy with pathological fear every time there was a crack of thunder.

"We'll have to keep an eye on him," the preacher said. He put his arm around Winn-Dixie. "We'll have to make sure he doesn't get 230 out during a storm. He might run away. We have to make sure we keep him safe."

"Yes sir," I said again. All of a sudden it was hard for me to talk. I loved the preacher so much. I loved him because he loved Winn-235 Dixie. I loved him because he was going to forgive Winn-Dixie for being afraid. But most of all I loved him for putting his arm around Winn-Dixie like that, like he was already trying to keep him safe.

(to) **talk sb. out of sth.** jn. von etwas abbringen · (to) **reason sb. out of sth.** [ˈriːzn] jm. etwas ausreden · **just in time** gerade (noch) rechtzeitig · **there didn't seem to be a thing we could do** es schien nichts zu geben, was wir tun konnten · **surely** [ˈʃʊəli] sicherlich · **rumble** [ˈrʌmbl] Grollen · (to) **quit doing sth., quit, quit** [kwɪt] aufhören, etwas zu tun · (to) **cock** [kɒk] schief legen (Kopf) · (to) **creep, crept, crept** [kriːp, krept] kriechen · **inch** [ɪntʃ] = 2,54 cm · (to) **slide, slid, slid** [slaɪd, slɪd] gleiten, (sich) schieben · (to) **look off in a different direction** [dəˈrekʃn] in eine andere Richtung schauen · **by accident** [ˈæksɪdənt] zufällig, durch Zufall · **all of a sudden** [ˈsʌdn] plötzlich · (to) **keep sb. safe, kept, kept** jn. (be)schützen

1 More help

Part A

2 The boys' holidays
← p. 10

b) 👥 **Which do you think is better: a seaside holiday in Britain or camping in the USA?**
Tell your partner. Give reasons.

I think … is better because …   I like swimming/camping/the sea/animals/mountains …
you can see/do/go/play/…
the weather in … is great/warm/rainy/…

Part B

2 That's not fair!
← p. 14

b) 👥 **Can you always do what you want in your free time?**
Or do your parents say what you have to do?

I often want to …   But my mum/dad sometimes says I have to …
read a book.   do my homework.
play a computer game.   visit my grandma.
play with my dog.   look after my brother/sister/…
listen to music.   practise the piano/…
…   clean my room.
…

Part B Practice

4 👥 Lucy, Sam and Leo (Subject/Object questions)
← p. 17

Ask and answer questions. Take turns.

Du willst wissen, …

1 wer am Samstag auf den Hoe gehen will.
   A: Who wants to go to the Hoe on Saturday?
      – (want)
   B: Lucy and Sam.

2 wen Lucy am Samstagmorgen angerufen hat.
   B: Who did Lucy … on Saturday morning?
      – (phone)
   A: …

3 wer vor zwei Wochen in Nr. 37 gezogen ist.
   A: Who … to number 37 two weeks ago?
      – (move)
   B: …

4 auf wen Sam am Nachmittag aufpasst.
   B: Who … Sam … after in the afternoon?
      – (look)
   A: …

5 wen Sam und Lucy vor Lucys Haus getroffen haben.
   A: Who … Sam and Lucy … in front of Lucy's house? – (meet)
   B: …

6 mit wem Leo Tischtennis gespielt hat.
   B: Who … Leo … table tennis with? – (play)
   A: …

More help 1

7 School rules

← p. 18

A British student at a German school wants to know the rules for mobile phones.
Read the school rules. Then answer the student's questions.

1 Can I bring my mobile to school?
   – Yes, you *can bring it to school.*
2 And am I allowed to use it at school?
   – No, you …
3 Sometimes I have to phone my host family.
   Is that OK?
   – Yes, but … first.
4 Can I check my text messages at break?
   – No, you …
5 My phone has an MP3 player. Can I use that?
   – No, you …
6 And the camera in my phone?
   – No, you …
7 So what if I use my mobile at school?
   – You have to …
8 When and where can I get it back?
   – At the …

Umgang mit Handys und MP3-Playern
- Die Benutzung persönlicher elektronischer Medien und Kommunikationsmedien (Handys, MP3-Player, Digitalkameras, etc.) ist im Schulgebäude und auf dem Schulgelände untersagt. Handys bleiben während der gesamten Schulzeit ausgeschaltet, jegliches Handyzubehör (auch Kabel und Kopfhörer) bleibt in der Schultasche.
- Sollte das Handy zur Kontaktaufnahme mit den Eltern benötigt werden, so darf dies nur nach Rücksprache mit einem Lehrer erfolgen.
- Schülerinnen und Schüler, die gegen die Bestimmungen der Schulordnung verstoßen, müssen ihr Handy abgeben.
Am Ende des Schultages können sie dieses Gerät im Sekretariat wieder abholen.

→ *SF 12: Mediation (Revision) (p. 151)*

Part C Practice

1 REVISION This Saturday is different (Present progressive statements)   ← p. 22

Read what everyone usually does on Saturdays. Then look at the pictures.
Say what's different this Saturday.

1 Maya usually gets up early. But this Saturday *she's staying in bed.* (stay)

2 Abby usually has breakfast with her family. But … (have)

3 Leo sometimes goes swimming. (ride)

4 Justin usually skypes with his father. (write)

5 Sam often goes to kung fu. (play)

6 Mr Bennett usually works in the garden. (work)

7 Lucy often phones her grandma. (write)

8 Mrs Pascoe does yoga. (play)

→ Workbook *XX (p. XX)*

123

2   More help

Part A

2 Feelings   ← p. 30

Listen to the dialogue in 1.
How did the speakers sound in these lines?
Choose one of the feelings in brackets.

I think Lucy is angry in line … because …

And Sam is … when …

l.3   Lucy: And you still have your earphones in! (angry/excited)
l.8   Lucy: Don't pull out the earphones! I'm still listening. (angry/excited)
l.13   Lucy: Yes, and guess what! I'm going to sing a Queen song at the auditions today. (excited/surprised)
l.15   Sam: What auditions? (angry/surprised)
l.41   Leo: Hi John! What are you doing here? (happy/surprised)
l.44   Leo: … Lucy – I love her. (happy/surprised)

Part A Practice

1 Sam and Justin are going to have a pizza (*going to*-future)   ← p. 31

c) Listen to the dialogues again – one at a time.
Choose the correct form of the *going to*-future
for each sentence below.

is going to · are going to ·
isn't going to · aren't going to

Dialogue 1

1   Justin and Sam aren't going to have more pizza.
2   Justin … clean his room.

Dialogue 2

1   Justin … skype with his dad today.
2   Justin … skype with his dad tomorrow.
3   Justin and his mum … have a cup of tea.

Dialogue 3

1   Lucy … watch a film this evening.
2   Maya … watch a film this evening.
3   Maya … do her homework this evening.
4   Lucy and Maya … meet tomorrow evening.

Part B Practice

2 As big as (Comparison of adjectives)   ← p. 34

What is about the same? What is different? Finish the sentences. Use the words in brackets.
1   Venus is about … the Earth. Mercury is … (big/small)
    Venus is about as big as the Earth. Mercury is smaller.
2   Spain is about … Greece. England is … (hot/cold)
3   Germany is about … Poland. Luxemburg is … (large/small)
4   A bus is about … a car. A plane is … (fast/fast)
5   March is about … April. July is … (cool/warm)
6   Stuttgart is about … Leipzig. Berlin is … (big/big)
7   Carrantuohill is about … Snowdon. Ben Nevis is … (high/high)

124

More help **2**

Part C

2 Did you get it?
← *p. 37*

Finish each sentence with a word from the box.

auditions · dance · five · happy · interesting · Leo · like · singer

1 Lucy and Leo are at the … for the school show.
2 Lucy wants to be a … in the show.
3 Leo wants to …
4 The teachers … the other girls' voices.

5 One teacher thinks Lucy's voice is the most …
6 The teachers choose … dancers for the show.
7 … is one of these dancers.
8 When Lucy hears that, she is very …

Part C Practice

2 Have fun on Saturday (Comparison of adjectives)
← *p. 38*

b) Finish the sentences with the right form of the adjectives. Use -er, -est, more or most.

We went to the photo show at the town hall. The speakers showed us the … (interesting) photos of their world tour. They were on the road for four years. That's much (long) than I imagined. I liked the pictures of the snow in Alaska – the … (cold) place on their trip. The sand in Sudan – the … (hot) place – was great too. But the … (exciting) part of their trip was in Asia. The mountains there are much … (high) than here. Lots of wild animals live there, and they are … (big) and … (dangerous) than the animals in our country. The … (scary) animal of all was the snow leopard!

Text

4 A part of the story
← *p. 43*

b) 📘 Read lines 101–105 again. Imagine what Sam and his dad said, and write their conversation.

Start like this:
Dad: Well, you know why you're not at the disco.
Sam: Yes, Dad, I know.

What Sam's dad can say:
– You have to follow the school rules, Sam.
– Nobody can learn when kids play music in class.
– It was right for Mrs Taylor to send us a letter.
– We don't want to get a letter like that again.
– Do you understand what you did wrong?
– You aren't often in trouble at school, so you can go to the disco.
– But remember: no more music in class.
– …

What Sam can say:
– Yes, I understand, Dad.
– I don't usually listen to music in class.
– The music wasn't loud.
– I'm not going to do it again – really!
– Please, can I go to the disco?
– Thanks, Dad.
– …

125

3 More help

Part A

2 What do they buy?   ← p. 49

a) Copy the table. Use it to answer the questions.
- Who wants to buy the things: Lucy or Maya?
- Why does she want them?
- Does she buy them? If not, why not?

Who?	What?	Why?	Does she buy it/them?	Why not?
Maya	chocolates	a present for Lucy's grandparents	No	Lucy doesn't want to go to the chocolate shop in the Barbican.
...	felt pens	...	Yes	...
...	flowers	...	...	...
...	a set square	...	...	...
...	trainers	...	...	...

Part A Practice

3 GAME Who is who? (Relative pronouns: who/that)   ← p. 51

a) Think about four people at your school. Write down relative clauses to describe them.

| a girl who does judo | a boy that is wearing blue trainers today | a teacher who ... |

Here are some more ideas:

a boy / a girl / a teacher — who/that — **does** judo / kung fu / gymnastics / ...
is wearing blue trainers / a green T-shirt / black jeans / ...
has a new phone / car / bike / ...
likes sport / horses / reading / maths / English / ...
plays tennis / chess / the piano / the guitar / ...

4 I don't know the English word 💬   ← p. 51

Relative clauses can help you to explain words that you don't know.
👥 Use ideas from the box to finish the explanations. Can your partner guess the picture?

> has eight legs and lives in the sea · when an animal is sick · when you play tennis ·
> when you do maths · when there is a fire in your house · when you run in a gym

It's a person who helps ...
It's a thing that you use when ...
It's an animal that ...
It's a person who helps ...
It's a thing that you use when ...

More help 3

7 Cool presents for kids 💬
← p. 52

b) 👥 Choose a present for a classmate.

£9.00 · £7.99 · £11.50 · £14.75 · £4.90 · £22.65

ice cream earphones · cool water bottles · snake socks · scary watches · zebra sharpener · monster rucksack

Let's get … for Jan. It's really funny.

I think it's silly. And it costs …

Here are some more ideas:

It's / They're	👍 cool / fantastic / interesting / not too expensive	👎 awful / boring / too expensive
Jan / Maria / …	likes animals/monsters · doesn't have a water bottle/…	doesn't like animals/monsters · already has a water bottle/…

Text

1 At Radford Park
← p. 59

b) 👥 Compare your sentences. Use six of them to tell the story in a short text.

TIP
- Du hast 6 Sätze. Du musst also genau auswählen.
- Wo spielt die Geschichte? Wer ist alles dabei? Warum? Schreib dazu 2 bis 3 Sätze.
- Wem passiert etwas Besonderes? Schreib dazu 2 bis 3 Sätze.

2 New words
← p. 59

Scan the text and find these new words.
How can you work out what they mean?

> gatehouse (l. 3) · gate (l. 16) · roof (l. 33) ·
> view (l. 35) · whispered (l. 54) · hole (l. 65) ·
> hurried (l. 89) · lips (l. 93)

Can you understand the words
– from the pictures?
– from the context?
  (= from the other words in the sentence)?
– from other English words?
– because they're like German?

127

4 More help

Part A Practice

2 My mobile has fallen into the river (Present perfect: statements) ← p. 70

b) Finish these sentences. Use the present perfect of the verb in brackets.

1 My mobile has fallen into the river. (fall)
2 We'… … the wrong bus! (take)
3 I'… … my money at home. (leave)
4 Grandma … … scones for us. (make)
5 My parents … … away for the weekend. (go)
6 Sorry, but I'… … a cup. (break)
7 We'… … that film before. (see)
8 Jack … … too many chocolates. (eat)

4 They've just seen a ghost (Present perfect: statements) ← p. 71

a) What has just happened? Write down your idea for each picture. You can use ideas from the table.

1 They've just seen a ghost / a lion in the park / a …

Part B Practice

2 Have you ever tried sheep's milk? (Present perfect: questions with *ever*) ← p. 73

a) Copy the questionnaire. Add five questions.
You can use ideas from the box.

win a prize · be in the paper ·
have a party all night · feed a lamb ·
live in another country · touch a snake ·
eat Indian food · fall asleep in a lesson ·
meet a pop star · …

More help 4

Part C

3 The end of the story ← p. 76

a) Do Maya and Lucy find the missing lamb? Do they get back to the farm?
Write your own ending for the story. Here are some ideas that can help you.
You don't need to use all of them.

1 Lucy hears something: what is it?
2 What does Lucy say?
3 Does Maya hear it too?
4 How long are the girls on the moor?
5 Does the weather get better/worse?

6 Do the girls get back to the farm?
If yes, …
… do they walk?
… does someone help them (farmer/police/…)?
… what do Mr and Mrs Tizzard say?

Part C Practice

3 Leo talks about Dartmoor (something, somebody, anything, anybody) ← p. 78

Mary asks Leo about Dartmoor. Choose the correct word from the brackets.

Mary: So tell me (anything/something) about Dartmoor, Leo.
Leo: I don't know (anything/something) about Dartmoor. I've never been there. I don't know (anybody/somebody) there.
Mary: But you've just heard Lucy's talk. Do you remember (anything/something) about it?
Leo: Oh, I remember (anything/something)! The ponies are wild. You can't ride them.

Mary: Do you know (anything/something) more about the ponies? Where do they take them?
Leo: To riding centres. (Anybody/Somebody) trains the ponies and then you can ride them.
Mary: Do you know (anyone/somebody) who can ride a pony?
Leo: No, I don't know (anyone/somebody). But I know (anyone/somebody) who can ride a bike. Me!

4 Snakes in the Alps ← p. 79

You are in a hostel in the Alps. An English roommate asks you about poisonous snakes.
You find some information online. Answer your roommate's questions in English.

- Where do they live?
- What do adders do when they meet people?
- When can they be dangerous?
- What should you do if a snake bites you?

> **Gibt es giftige Schlangen in den Alpen?**
> Ja, die Kreuzotter. Die findet man vor allem in Wäldern und auf Mooren.
> Kreuzottern sind nicht aggressiv und versuchen bei Gefahr immer zu flüchten. So kann es nur zu einem Biss kommen, wenn man ihnen zu nahe kommt und sie dadurch in Angst versetzt. Ihr Gift verursacht zwar Schmerzen, ist aber relativ harmlos – ein Arzt sollte dennoch aufgesucht werden.

adder

→ SF 12: Mediation (Revision) (p. 151)

129

5 More help

Lead-in

1 My favourite celebration
← p. 84

What's your favourite celebration? When is it? What do you do? Maybe you can use these ideas:

When I celebrate	What I do at the celebrations
• after a football match • after Ramadan • at Carnival/Halloween/Hanukkah • when the new year begins • at the end of the school year • on 3rd October • on my birthday • …	• dance • get/give presents • go to bed late • play music • send cards • sing songs • wake up early • …

Reading Course

Taking notes
← p.89

b) Read this text about pancake races.

1. Try to understand or guess new words.
2. Take notes. Choose the most important highlighted words and take notes.
3. Compare your notes with the tip and add or cross out notes.

EXTRA Prepare a short talk on pancake races.

Pancake Races

There is a Tuesday every year in February or March when lots of people in Britain take part in a special race. They run with a pancake in a frying pan and toss the pancake on the way. Traditionally, Christians used up all their butter and eggs to make pancakes before Ash Wednesday, when they started to fast for Lent. Today on Pancake Day, many people in Britain still eat pancakes with sugar and lemon juice. Kids of all ages love them.
And the race? There is a legend that on one Pancake Day in the 15th century, a woman in the village of Olney still had a pancake in her pan when she heard the church bells. She didn't want to be late for church, so she ran all the way with her frying pan in her hand.
Pancake races are a fun part of an old festival.

Part B

2 Which event?
← p. 90

b) How do they feel about this?
– I think Lucy feels …
– Maya probably feels …
– They must feel …

> angry • awful • bad • excited • good • great • happy •
> hurt • lonely • nervous • sad • scared • shocked •
> strange • surprised • unhappy • worried

More help **5**

Part B Practice

2 If you come to Plymouth, ... (Conditional sentences I)   ← p. 91

Finish the sentences with the correct form of the verbs in brackets.

1 If you come to Plymouth at the weekend, you (have) a great time.
   If you come to Plymouth at the weekend, you'll have a great time.
2 If you don't arrive early enough, you (not see) the start of the parade.
3 If Justin doesn't film the kung fu event, Sam (feel) a bit sad.
4 If Maya sees *We will rock you* again, she (be) bored.
5 If you dress up in a costume, your friends (not know) who you are.
6 You (miss) some of the shows if you take part in the parade.
7 We (watch) the fireworks if Dad lets us stay up late.
8 They (not have) the fireworks show if it rains.
9 I (stay) for the evening concert if my mum lets me.
10 If we (not leave) at 9:30, we 'll miss the bus home.

4 If you don't ... (Conditional sentences I)   ← p. 92

Make sentences that start with If you don't ... and say what will happen. You can use these ideas.

> answer your phone · drink enough water ·
> eat a good breakfast · feed your cat ·
> go to school · speak loudly enough

... it will look for a new home.
... people won't understand you.
... you will be hungry until lunchtime.
... you won't know what the caller wanted.
... you'll be very thirsty.
... your parents will be angry.

Part C

2 On the radio   ← p. 94

Listen to some more of the town crier's tongue-twisters and try to repeat them.

1 She sells sea shells sitting on the sea shore.
2 Will very famous Francis fish fishes from the
   ferry?
3 Red feather, yellow feather.
4 Thirty thousand feathers on a thrush's throat.

shell [ʃel] Muschel(schale) · **seashore** ['siːʃɔː] Meeresufer · **famous** ['feɪməs] berühmt · **feather** ['feðə] Feder ·
thrush [θrʌʃ] Drossel · **throat** [θrəʊt] Hals

131

6 More help

Part A Practice

1 Mr Cobb was sleeping (Past progressive: positive statements) ← p. 106

Say what everyone was doing when the bus went into the tunnel. You can use these words:

> fight · drink cola · eat yoghurt · hide · run ·
> play cards · sleep · throw sweets at

2 She was feeding her snake when … (Past progressive and simple past) ← p. 107

b) Make correct sentences. Put the verb in brackets into the past progressive or the simple past.
1. Mr Petrock (wear) a medieval costume when he met Miss Bell's class.
   Mr Petrock was wearing …
2. While Mr Petrock was speaking, a student (ask) a question.
3. Justin (film) the castle when a bird suddenly landed on his shoulder.
4. While Lucy (stand) on the bridge at Tintagel, she made a wish.
5. Sam and Leo were standing near the water when a big wave (hit) them.
6. Lucy's mobile beeped while she (show) Sam her photos.

4 WORDS Parts of the body ← p. 108

a) Draw a picture of a king, a queen or a wizard. Label parts of the body in your picture.

> body ·
> heart ·
> stomach

> head ·
> hair ·
> face

> ear · eye · nose ·
> mouth · lip ·
> tooth (teeth)

> shoulder · arm · hand ·
> leg · foot (feet)

132

More help **6**

Part B Practice

3 EXTRA If you were a guide at Tintagel ... (Conditional sentences II)   ← p. 112

b) Say what you would do if you had 500 euros.
   Here are some ideas.
   – invite all my friends to a big party
   – give some money to help the poor
   – buy a new pair of jeans / some new CDs / a new MP3 player / a new mobile / ...
   – buy a train ticket and visit ...
   – go shopping with my best friend

Text

1 The best title   ← p. 115

b) Choose the best title for scenes 2–5.

Scene 2: – A message for Guinevere
          – The writing on the stone
          – The day of the tournament
Scene 3: – Where's my sword?
          – Arthur's job
          – Guinevere's wish

Scene 4: – At the inn
          – On the way to the inn
          – A sword for Kay
Scene 5: – The wrong sword
          – A new king for Britain
          – Guinevere's sword

133

Early finisher

Die S können ihre Antworten selbstständig mit den Lösungen auf S. 252 abgleichen.

1 Part C

Lucy, Sam and Leo

← p. 17, exercise 4

a) What do you remember about the Plymouth kids?
   Read the sentences. Find the mistakes and correct the sentences.

1. Justin's parents live in the USA.
2. Abby gave a name to a sailing boat.
3. The Bennetts have only one child: Sam.
4. Lucy and her brother Tim were at their grandparents' farm in the summer.

b) Make two sentences with mistakes about the Plymouth kids. Give them to a partner. Can he/she correct them?

2 Part B

Did you get it?

← p. 33, exercise 2

Look at your six answers from 2.
Take the **first** or **last** letter of each answer.

1 R I V E R S
2 …

Use the letters to spell the name of a country in Europe.

TIP
There's a map of Europe at the back of your book.

3 Text

Master Wu and the magic book

← p. 59, exercise 3

Make as many words as you can from the letters of these words:

Examples:

Master Wu at Radford Park = road
Master Wu at Radford Park = water

Early finisher

4 Part B Practice

Leo talks about Dartmoor
← p. 78, exercise 3

The letters in these countryside words are in the wrong order. Put them in the right order.

5 Part B Practice

Red Nose Day at a British school
← p. 92, exercise 6

This is the first part of the text about Red Nose Day on page 92.
Lots of letters are missing. Can you still read the text?

Ev_ry sch__l in Bri_ain tri_s to ra_se m_n_y on Re_ No_e D_y. T_e mo_ey th_t our s__ool mad_ is for hom_l_ss p__ple.
So w_at d_d we d_? Of co_rs_, we h_d a non-un_f_rm day. Mo_t stu_en_s dr_ssed up. T_ree of my fr__nds and I wo_e b_n_na cost_m_s. So ev__yone g_ve £1.30. You pay £1 if you d__'t we_r a un_f__m a_d the r_d n_ses co_t 30p.
We al_o had a sc__ol t_l_nt show. The p__ple wh_ w_t_hed had to p_y 20p (or more). I pla__d the g_it_r, but I d_d_'t wi_ a pr_z_. :-(In my ye_r (Ye_r 8) we had a cak_ sale. We m_de lots of f__ny red c_kes and we ra_s_d £57.62.

6 Part A Practice

WORDS Parts of the body
← p. 108, exercise 4

Find a partner who is also finished.
Imagine a monster in your head and describe it to your partner.
He/She has to draw it.

My monster has six eyes and green hair. It doesn't have a neck. It has a shoe for a nose and only one leg. There is a wheel at the end of its leg.

Partner pages

1 Part A Practice

5 On the phone

c) Act out a telephone conversation.
   Partner A: Read your role card.
   Then start the conversation.
   – A: Hello.
   – B: …

> **Your role**
> Parent of an English school kid.
> **The situation**
> A friend of your child phones. Your child is out.
> **What you do**
> Explain why the friend can't speak to your child. Ask the friend to leave a message.

4 Part C Practice

5 Study skills: Describing a picture

c) Partner A:
   Write a description of the photo on the right.
   Remember to:
   • say what the picture is about in one or two sentences
   • say who/what you see, and where they are
   • give information about the colours, time of day, time of year, …
   • say what is happening, who is doing what

Go back to p. 79 for help with what to say.

d) Listen to your partner's description and draw his/her picture. Then compare your drawing to the photo.

e) Read your description to your partner.
   ➡ SF 17: Describing pictures (p. 154)

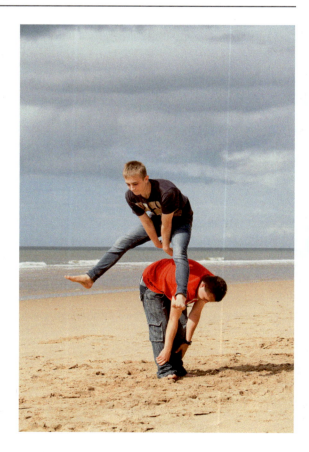

Partner pages

2 Part C Practice

5 Let's go to a musical!

Partner B: You and your German friend are in London and want to see a musical.
You have an idea: *Shrek the musical*.
Read the information and make notes.

Listen to your friend.
Then tell him/her about your musical.

Together, agree on one of them.

→ SF 12: Mediation (Revision) (p. 151)

Shrek the musical
Join your favourite °hero, the green °ogre, and his friend the °donkey, on an °adventure to get his land back and save the beautiful °Princess Fiona from a °terrible dragon … With great new songs and Shrek's °cult *I'm a °believer*.

Theatre Royal, Drury Lane
Underground: Covent Garden

Mon, Thu, Sat 7.30 pm and Wed 7 pm
Cheap family tickets °available
For children age 5+
Runs 2 hrs 15 mins

3 Part A Practice

5 Helping tourists in Dresden

Partner B:
a) Your partner tells you about a tour for families in Dresden.
   Listen and ask questions if you don't understand something.

b) Now you meet a family with two children.
   They don't understand this flyer about a tour.
   Explain how it works and what it costs.

KINDERSTADTPLAN: Dresden zum Aufklappen
Der Kinderstadtplan ist eine gefaltete Karte von Dresden mit handgemalten, bekannten Gebäuden, Zahlen und bunten Symbolen. Durch ein integriertes Suchspiel wird die gemeinsame Planung eines Stadtrundganges für die ganze Familie zum lehrreichen Erlebnis. Interessantes Wissen rund um alle Sehenswürdigkeiten vermittelt zudem ein detailliertes, kindgerechtes Begleitheft.
Preis: Erw.: 9,90 € **Info und Kauf:** Tourist-Information im Kulturpalast und im Hauptbahnhof

→ SF 12: Mediation (Revision) (p. 151)

Partner pages

1 | Part A Practice

5 On the phone

c) Act out a telephone conversation.
   Partner B: Read your role card.
   Your partner starts the conversation.
   Then you speak.
   – A: Hello.
   – B: Hello Mr/Mrs ...

Your role
An English school kid.
The situation
You phone a friend. One of your friend's parents answers the phone.
What you do
Say your name and ask to speak to your friend. Leave a message for your friend.

4 | Part A Practice

3 I've done all my homework (Present perfect: statements)

Partner B: You're Jo.

a) Write down your ten jobs in a table like this:

	Me	Jessie
homework		
thank-you mail		
...		

b) It's Sunday morning now.
   Tick (✓) five jobs that you have done.

c) 👥 Take turns. Say what you have/haven't done. Fill in the table for your partner.
   A: I've done all my homework for Monday. What about you?
   B: No, I haven't done my homework, but I've ...

d) Write about your partner.
   Jessie hasn't done all his homework, but he has written ...

JO'S LIST

1 do all my homework for Monday
2 write a thank-you mail to Uncle Jim
3 buy new felt pens
4 practise the piano
5 help Mum in the kitchen
6 clean my bike
7 make a birthday card for Grandma
8 feed my hamster
9 throw away my old magazines
10 collect pictures for my project

Partner pages

4 Part C Practice

5 Study skills: Describing a picture

c) Partner B: Write a description of the photo below. Remember to:

- say what the picture is about in one or two sentences
- say who/what you see, and where they are
- give information about the colours, time of day, time of year, …
- say what is happening, who is doing what

Go back to p. 79 for help with what to say.

d) Listen to your partner's description and draw his/her picture. Then compare your drawing to the photo.

e) Read your description to your partner.

➡ SF 17: Describing pictures (p. 154)

1 Part A Practice

7 Study skills: Making notes with a crib sheet

c) 👥 Read this text about Abby's holiday. Compare it with the crib sheets on p. 13.

The most beautiful beach in the world
In the summer holidays, we went to Turkey. We stayed in Istanbul for two days and saw lots of interesting buildings. But Tim and I had to sleep in the same room. :(
On the third day, we went to the Turkish Riviera. We stayed in a hotel near Patara Beach for ten beautiful sunny days. It never rained!
We went swimming every day. We also took long walks on the beach and in the mountains. On the last day, we went sailing with my German friend Antonia. We stopped on a small beach for a picnic and to go swimming. I want to go back to Turkey next summer!

Wordbank

Wordbank 1: Holidays ➔ Unit 1 (p. 9 / p. 13 / p. 26)

I/We stayed ...

| in a holiday home | at/in a B & B | at/in a guest house | at/in a youth hostel | at/in a holiday camp | at/on a caravan site |

I/We went ...

surfing   windsurfing   bodyboarding

We spent most days sunbathing and swimming.

snorkelling   diving   waterskiing

sunshine, wetsuit, sunburn, lilo, suncream

hiking   mountaineering   birdwatching

And in winter you can go ...

skiing   sledging   snowboarding   ice skating

And you can build a snowman!

B & B (bed and breakfast) Zimmer mit Frühstück • **diving** [ˈdaɪvɪŋ] • **guest house** [ˈɡest haʊs] Pension • **hiking** [ˈhaɪkɪŋ] • **lilo** [ˈlaɪləʊ] • **mountaineering** [ˌmaʊntəˈnɪərɪŋ] • **skiing** [ˈskiːɪŋ] • **sledging** [ˈsledʒɪŋ] • **snowman** [ˈsnəʊmæn] • **snorkelling** [ˈsnɔːkəlɪŋ] • **sunbathing** [ˈsʌnbeɪðɪŋ] Sonnenbaden • **sunburn** [ˈsʌnbɜːn] • **sunshine** [ˈsʌnʃaɪn] • **wetsuit** [ˈwetsuːt] • **youth hostel** [ˈjuːθ hɒstl]

Wordbank

Wordbank 2: Music ➡ Unit 2 (p. 44)

IN THE PRACTICE ROOM

bass [beɪs] • **cello** [ˈtʃeləʊ] • **choir** [ˈkwaɪə] • **clarinet** [ˌklærəˈnet] • **conductor** [kənˈdʌktə] • **flute** [fluːt] • **member** [ˈmembə] Mitglied • **musician** [mjuˈzɪʃn] • **orchestra** [ˈɔːkɪstrə] • **performance** [pəˈfɔːməns] Vorstellung, Auftritt • **(to) record** [rɪˈkɔːd] aufnehmen, aufzeichnen • **saxophone** [ˈsæksəfəʊn] • **sound engineer** [ˌendʒɪˈnɪə] • **string quartet** [kwɔːˈtet] Streichquartett • **trumpet** [ˈtrʌmpɪt] • **violin** [ˌvaɪəˈlɪn]

141

Wordbank

Wordbank 3: My neighbourhood ➔ Unit 3 (p. 60)

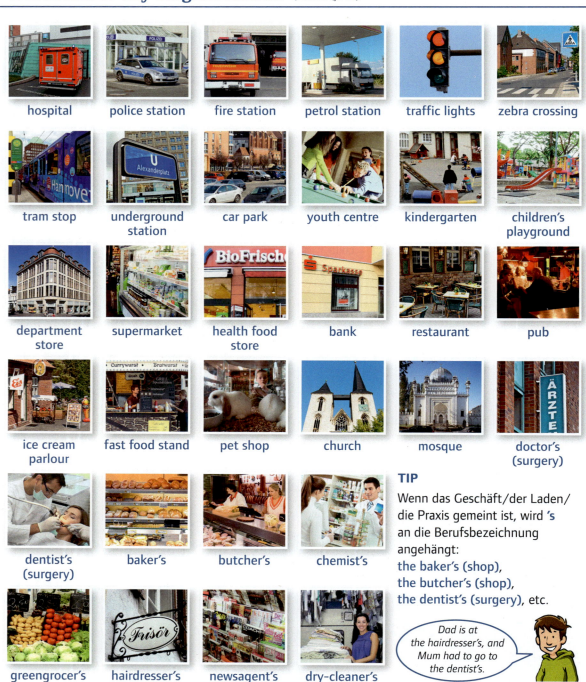

baker's [ˈbeɪkəz] • **butcher's** [ˈbʊtʃəz] • **chemist's** [ˈkemɪsts] Drogerie; Apotheke • **dentist's** [ˈdentɪsts] • **department store** [dɪˈpɑːtmənt stɔː] Kaufhaus • **dry-cleaner's** [ˌdraɪ ˈkliːnəz] chemische Reinigung • **greengrocer's** [ˈgriːnɡrəʊsəz] • **hairdresser's** [ˈheədresəz] • **health-food store** [helθ] Bioladen, Naturkostladen • **hospital** [ˈhɒspɪtl] • **ice-cream parlour** [ˈpɑːlə] • **mosque** [mɒsk] • **neighbourhood** [ˈneɪbəhʊd] Gegend, Viertel • **newsagent's** [ˈnjuːzeɪdʒənts] • **petrol station** [ˈpetrəl] • **pub** [pʌb] • **restaurant** [ˈrestrɒnt] • **surgery** [ˈsɜːdʒəri] • **traffic lights** (pl) [ˈtræfɪk laɪts] • **tram stop** [træm] • **underground station** [ˈʌndəɡraʊnd] • **youth centre** [ˈjuːθ] • **zebra crossing** [ˌzebrə ˈkrɒsɪŋ]

142

Wordbank

Wordbank 4: The countryside (I) → Unit 4 (p. 66 / p. 82)

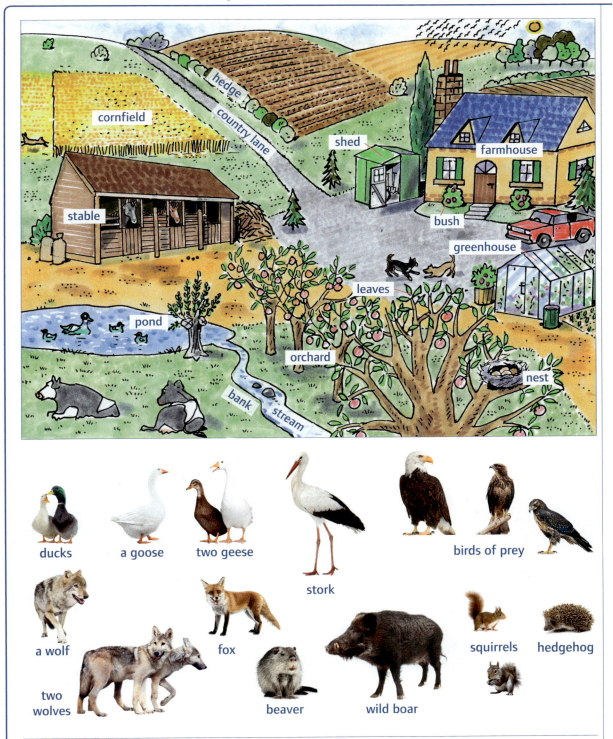

bank [bæŋk] Ufer • beaver ['biːvə] • bird of prey [preɪ] Greifvogel, Raubvogel • bush [bʊʃ] • duck [dʌk] • goose [guːs], pl geese [giːs] • hedge [hedʒ] • hedgehog ['hedʒhɒɡ] • leaf [liːf], pl leaves [liːvz] • orchard ['ɔːtʃəd] Obstgarten • squirrel ['skwɪrəl] • stable ['steɪbl] Stall, Stallung • stream [striːm] Bach • wild boar [bɔː] • wolf [wʊlf], pl wolves [wʊlvz]

Wordbank

Wordbank 4: The countryside (II) ➜ Unit 4 (p. 66 / p. 82)

bright [braɪt] heiter • chilly ['tʃɪli] kühl, kalt, frisch • dry [draɪ] • foggy ['fɒgi] • freezing ['friːzɪŋ] • lightning ['laɪtnɪŋ] • rainbow ['reɪnbəʊ] • shower ['ʃaʊə] • sultry ['sʌltri] schwül • sunshine ['sʌnʃaɪn] • thunder ['θʌndə] Donner • thunderstorm ['θʌndəstɔːm] Gewitter

Wordbank 5: Celebrations ➜ Unit 5 (p. 84)

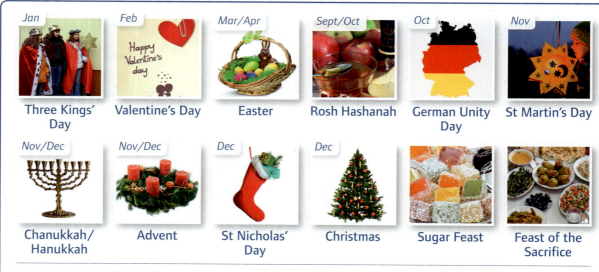

Advent ['ædvent] • Chanukkah/Hanukkah ['hænʊkə] Lichterfest • Christmas ['krɪsməs] • Easter ['iːstə] • Feast of the Sacrifice [ˌfiːst_əv ðə 'sækrɪfaɪs] Opferfest • Rosh Hashanah [ˌrɒʃ hə'ʃɑːnə] jüdisches Neujahrsfest • St Martin [sənt 'mɑːtɪn] • St Nicholas [sənt 'nɪkələs] • Sugar Feast ['ʃʊgə fiːst] Zuckerfest • unity ['juːnəti] • Valentine ['væləntaɪn]

Skills File

Skills File – Inhalt   Seite

STUDY SKILLS
- SF 1   Learning vocabulary (Revision) 145
- SF 2   Mind maps (Revision) 146
- SF 3   Vocabulary picture posters 146
- SF 4   Study posters 147
- SF 5   Making notes with a crib sheet 147

READING SKILLS
- SF 6   Understanding new words (Revision) 148
- SF 7   Working with a dictionary (Revision) 148
- SF 8   Reading aloud 149
- SF 9   Scanning 149
- SF 10 Taking notes (Revision) 150
- SF 11 Marking up a text 150

LANGUAGE SKILLS
- SF 12 Mediation (Revision) 151
- SF 13 Writing (Revision) 151
- SF 14 Listening (Revision) 152
- SF 15 Speaking 153

PRESENTATION SKILLS
- SF 16 Giving a presentation (Revision) 154
- SF 17 Describing pictures 154
- SF 18 Presenting a photo 155
- SF 19 Peer feedback 155

In diesem **Skills File** findest du **Lernhilfen und Methoden,** die dir z.B. den Umgang mit Texten erleichtern, beim Lernen helfen oder Tipps zum Vorbereiten von kleinen Präsentationen geben.

Einige der Einträge wie z.B. **Mindmaps** kennst du schon aus Band 1. Sie sollen dich – kurz zusammengefasst – an das schon Gelernte erinnern. Du erkennst sie am Zusatz **(Revision)**.

STUDY SKILLS

SF 1   Learning vocabulary (Revision)

Worauf sollte ich beim Lernen von Vokabeln achten?

- Führe dein Vokabelheft, dein Vokabelverzeichnis oder deinen Karteikasten aus Klasse 5 weiter.
- Lerne immer 7–10 Vokabeln auf einmal.
- Lerne neue und wiederhole alte Vokabeln regelmäßig.
- Lerne die Vokabeln mit jemandem zusammen. Fragt euch gegenseitig ab.

Skills File

- Gut behalten kannst du Wortschatz besonders mit diesen Techniken:
  - Gegensatzpaare bilden, z.B. *rainy – sunny, happy – sad*
  - Wörter in Wortfamilien zusammenfassen, z.B. *(to) sing – singer – song*
  - Wörter in Wortfeldern sammeln – dabei schreibst du alle Wörter unter Oberbegriffen *(umbrella words)* auf.
- Finde heraus, welcher Lernertyp du bist. Wie kannst du am besten Vokabeln lernen? Durch Hören, durch Bilder, am Computer (z.B. mit deinem e-Workbook) oder indem du dir eine eigene Geschichte um die neuen Vokabeln ausdenkst? Nutze diese Techniken häufig.

rainy   sunny   happy   sad

subjects	sports	animals
English Maths ...	tennis football ...	elephant cat ...

SF 2 Mind maps (Revision)

Wozu dienen Mindmaps?

Mithilfe von Mindmaps kannst du Ideen sammeln und ordnen.

Wie mache ich eine Mindmap?

- Schreibe das Thema in die Mitte eines leeren Blattes.
- Überlege dir Oberbegriffe zu deiner Sammlung von Ideen. Verwende unterschiedliche Farben für diese Hauptäste.
- Ergänze jede Idee, die zu einem Oberbegriff passt, auf einem Nebenast. Nimm dafür nur Schlüsselwörter. Du kannst statt Wörtern auch Symbole verwenden und Bilder ergänzen.

SF 3 Vocabulary picture posters → *p. 40*

Vokabelposter können dir helfen, Wortschatz zu bestimmten Wortfeldern bildhaft zu veranschaulichen, damit du ihn dir besser merken kannst.

Wie mache ich ein Vokabelposter?

- Sammle Vokabeln zu deinem Wortfeld, z.B. in einer Mindmap, einer Tabelle oder in einer Liste.
- Überlege, welches Bild dir zu einem Wortfeld einfällt, z.B. ein Instrument zum Thema *music* oder der Umriss einer Landkarte für geografische Begriffe. Dieses Bild kann den Rahmen für dein Poster bilden.
- Zeichne dein Bild groß auf ein Poster und schreibe alle Wörter, die dir zu dem Wortfeld einfallen, in das Bild. Schreibe groß und gut leserlich.
- Hänge dein Poster an die Wand in deinem Zimmer oder präsentiere es in deiner Klasse.

Skills File

SF 4 Study posters
➜ p. 56

Lernplakate sind ein gutes Hilfsmittel, um dir wichtige Dinge wie etwa Grammatikregeln darzustellen und sie sich so besser zu merken.

Was muss ich beachten, wenn ich ein Lernposter erstelle?

- Schreibe wichtige Informationen zu deinem Thema auf.
- Suche alle Informationen heraus, die du auf dem Poster darstellen willst.
- Überlege, wie du das, was du dir merken willst, am besten darstellen kannst. Du kannst z.B. Kästen oder Tabellen verwenden.
- Finde einen guten Titel für dein Plakat.
- Gestalte dein Plakat. Schreibe groß und gut leserlich.
- Hebe wichtige Punkte hervor, z.B. durch Unterstreichen oder durch unterschiedliche Farben. Verwende aber nicht zu viele verschiedene Farben – sonst wird dein Lernposter unübersichtlich.
- Wenn du ein Lernposter zu einer Grammatikregel machst, kannst du auch ein paar Beispielsätze aufschreiben.
- Häng dein Poster zu Hause oder in der Schule an einer Stelle auf, an der du es häufig siehst.

SF 5 Making notes with a crib sheet
➜ p. 13

Ein Spickzettel hilft dir, wenn du

- jemandem von einem Erlebnis oder über ein Thema berichten möchtest.
- einen kleinen Vortrag halten oder möglichst frei vor Zuhörern sprechen möchtest.

Was muss ich beachten, wenn ich einen Spickzettel erstelle?

Sei ruhig kreativ. Dein Spickzettel ist nur für dich – wichtig ist, dass **du** verstehst, was du notiert hast. Diese Tipps können dir dabei helfen:

- Verwende nur ein kleines Blatt Papier.
- Schreibe keine ganzen Sätze, sondern verwende immer nur Stichwörter.
- Du kannst Symbole und kleine Zeichnungen verwenden, um den Text so knapp wie möglich zu gestalten. Verwende zum Beispiel:
  - "+" für "and"
  - Smileys für Gefühle, Flaggen für Länder, Strichzeichnungen für Dinge und Personen, über die du schreiben oder sprechen möchtest,
  - Pfeile für Richtungen oder Ortsangaben, eine Sonne für Tag/gutes Wetter usw.
- Arrangiere alles so auf deinem Spickzettel, dass die Reihenfolge der Ereignisse, über die du berichtest, deutlich erkennbar ist.

Skills File

READING SKILLS

SF 6 Understanding new words (Revision) → p. 19

Immer gleich im Wörterbuch nachschlagen?

Unbekannte Wörter im Wörterbuch nachzuschlagen kostet Zeit und mindert auf Dauer die Freude am Lesen. Du kannst unbekannte Wörter oft auch ohne Wörterbuch verstehen, wenn du diese Hinweise beachtest:

- Viele englische Wörter werden ähnlich wie im Deutschen geschrieben oder klingen ähnlich, z.B. *discussion, statue, insect*. Ihre Bedeutung kannst du leicht erschließen.
- Du kannst englische Wörter auch verstehen, weil sie einem Wort aus einer anderen Sprache ähnlich sind, z.B. *voice (French: voix; Latin: vox)*.
- In manchen unbekannten Wörtern stecken bekannte Teile, z.B. **sun**shine, **bottle open**er.
- Bilder zum Text zeigen oft Dinge, die du im Text vielleicht nicht verstehst. Schau dir deshalb vor dem Lesen alle Bilder genau an.
- Wörter im Umfeld des unbekannten Wortes können dir helfen, die Bedeutung zu erschließen, z.B. *Let's hurry. The train **departs** in ten minutes*.
- Manchmal gibt es in einem der nächsten Sätze ein Wort mit der gleichen Bedeutung wie das, was du nicht verstehst, z.B. *He picked up a **pebble**. The small stone was red and black.*

Hmm, „insect" heißt dann vielleicht „Insekt", oder?

SF 7 Working with a dictionary (Revision)

Du verstehst ein Wort nicht und kannst es auch nicht erschließen? Du brauchst ein englisches Wort, das dir nicht einfällt? Dann helfen dir die *Dictionaries* im Anhang weiter. Du findest das *English-German Dictionary* auf den Seiten 208–228 und das *German-English Dictionary* auf den Seiten 229–246.

Wie benutze ich das *Dictionary*?

Denk daran:

- Stichwörter sind alphabetisch geordnet: **n** vor **p**, **ph** vor **pl** usw.
- Die Ziffern 1., 2. usw. zeigen, dass ein Stichwort mehrere Bedeutungen hat.
- In eckigen Klammern steht, wie das Wort ausgesprochen und betont wird.
- Die Zahlen hinter der deutschen Übersetzung geben an, wann eine Vokabel zuerst vorgekommen ist: **I** – Band 1; **II 5 (84)** – Band 2, Unit 5, Seite 84
- Zusammengesetzte Wörter und längere Ausdrücke findest du oft unter mehr als einem Stichwort, z.B. *get on a plane* unter **get** und unter **plane** und *in einen Klub eintreten* unter **eintreten** und unter **Klub**.
- Der Pfeil ▶ verweist auf Kästen im *Vocabulary*, in denen du weitere Informationen zu dem Wort findest.

Dictionary	English – German
phrase [freɪz] Ausdruck, (Rede-)Wendung I
plan [plæn]:
1. Plan I
2. planen II 5 (84)
plane [pleɪn] Flugzeug II 2 (34) **get on a plane** in ein Flugzeug einsteigen II 5 (86) **on the plane** im Flugzeug II 2 (34)
▶ S. 185 get
pocket [ˈpɒkɪt] Tasche (Mantel-

Dictionary	German – English
eintreffen arrive [əˈraɪv]
eintreten *(in Zimmer usw.)* enter [ˈentə
in einen Klub eintreten join a club [dʒɒɪn]
Eintrittskarte ticket [ˈtɪkɪt]
einziehen move in **in ein Haus einziehen** move into a house
▶ S. 197 (to) move

148 one hundred and forty-eight

Skills File

SF 8 Reading aloud
➡ p. 35

Warum laut lesen?

Lautes Lesen hilft dir, Texte flüssig und mit Ausdruck zu lesen. Damit das auch gelingt, solltest du den Text gut kennen.

Was sollte ich beim lauten Lesen beachten?

- Stelle sicher, dass du den Inhalt des Textes gut verstanden hast. Kannst du Fragen dazu beantworten? Was passiert wem, wann, wo und warum?

- Überlege, was die Personen im Text fühlen. Sind sie fröhlich? Traurig? Ängstlich? Aufgeregt? Wenn du einen Text gut laut vorlesen willst, solltest du versuchen, diese Gefühle mit deiner Stimme und deiner Körpersprache wiederzugeben.

- Sieh dir die Satzzeichen gut an – sie zeigen dir, wo du Pausen machen oder deine Stimme verändern solltest. Bei einer Frage z.B. geht deine Stimme am Ende nach oben, und Kommas und Punkte zeigen dir, wo du eine sinnvolle Pause machen kannst. Es kann hilfreich sein, diese Stellen im Text zu markieren.

- Bevor du einen Text laut vorliest, übe das Lesen leise für dich, bis du ihn möglichst flüssig lesen kannst.

SF 9 Scanning
➡ p. 53

Wozu ist Scanning gut?

Wenn du in einem Text nach Informationen zu einem bestimmten Thema oder Antworten auf eine Frage suchen sollst, reicht es oft, wenn du den Text nach Schlüsselwörtern *(keywords)* absuchst und nur dort genauer liest, wo du sie findest.

Wie scanne ich einen Text?

- Bevor du auf den Text schaust, überlege dir mögliche *keywords*, nach denen du suchen könntest. Es kann helfen, wenn du sie aufschreibst.

- Stell dir dann die *keywords* gut vor und geh mit deinen Augen sehr schnell durch den Text. Die gesuchten Wörter werden dir sofort „ins Auge springen".

- Du kannst auch mit dem Finger in breiten Bewegungen wie bei einem „S" von oben bis unten durch den Text gehen. Wenn du deine *keywords* gefunden hast, lies dort weiter, um Näheres zu erfahren.

Skills File

SF 10 Taking notes (Revision) → p. 89

Worum geht es beim Notizen machen?

Wenn du beim Lesen oder Zuhören Notizen machst, kannst du dich später besser daran erinnern, wenn du etwas vortragen, nacherzählen oder einen Bericht schreiben sollst.

Wie mache ich Notizen?

In Texten oder Gesprächen gibt es immer wichtige und unwichtige Wörter. Die wichtigen Wörter sind sogenannte Schlüsselwörter *(keywords)*, und nur die solltest du notieren. Meist sind das Substantive und Verben, manchmal auch Adjektive oder Zahlen.

Folgende Punkte können dir auch helfen:

- Verwende Ziffern (z.B. „7" statt „seven").
- Verwende Symbole und Abkürzungen, z.B. ✓ („yes") und + („and"). Am besten erfindest du eigene Symbole.
- Bei Verneinungen verwende „not" oder streiche Wörter durch.

Da hab ich wohl ein paar Symbole zu viel benutzt ...

SF 11 Marking up a text → p. 74

Wann sollte ich einen Text markieren?

Manchmal sollst du einen Sachtext lesen und hinterher zu einem Thema daraus etwas sagen oder bestimmte Fragen dazu beantworten. Dann kann es dir helfen, wichtige Informationen für deine Aufgabenstellung im Text zu markieren.

Wie gehe ich am besten vor?

- Lies dir die Aufgabe genau durch.
- Lies den Text und markiere nur Informationen, die für deine Aufgabe wichtig sind. Nicht jeder Satz enthält Wichtiges, und oft reicht es aus, nur ein oder zwei Wörter in einem Satz zu markieren.
- Hebe wichtige Informationen hervor, z.B. durch Unterstreichen, Einkreisen oder Markieren mit einem Textmarker.
- Wichtig: Markiere nur auf Fotokopien von Texten oder in deinen eigenen Büchern.

Dartmoor ponies
There are about 3,000 ponies on Dartmoor. Most of the year they live on the open moor. New foals – baby ponies – are born in the spring. In autumn, groups of farmers round up the ponies and take them back to the farms. There they count and check them and then sell some – mostly as children's ponies. All the others go back to the open moor again and spend the winter there. The cold winter is too hard for other kinds of ponies, but the Dartmoor pony is a very strong animal.

LANGUAGE SKILLS

SF 12 Mediation (Revision)

Wann brauche ich Mediation?

Hier sind einige Situationen, in denen es sein kann, dass du zwischen Deutsch und Englisch vermitteln musst:

- Du fährst z.B. mit deiner Familie nach Großbritannien, und deine Großeltern, Eltern oder Geschwister wollen wissen, was jemand in einem Café gesagt hat oder was an einer Informationstafel steht.
- Wenn du eine/n Austauschschüler/in aus England (oder einem anderen Land) bei dir zu Hause zu Gast hast, kann es sein, dass er/sie wenig Deutsch spricht und deine Hilfe braucht.
- In Klassenarbeiten musst du manchmal in einem englischen Text gezielt nach Informationen suchen und diese auf Deutsch wiedergeben. Oder du sollst Informationen aus einem deutschen Text auf Englisch wiedergeben.

Worauf muss ich bei Mediation achten?

Übersetze nicht alles wörtlich und gib nur das Wesentliche wieder. Du kannst Unwichtiges weglassen und Sätze umformulieren.

SF 13 Writing (Revision)

Worauf muss ich beim Schreiben von Texten achten?

- Wenn du einen Text schreibst, in dem du eigene Gedanken darstellst, dann kann es hilfreich sein, wenn du dir vorher ein paar Notizen machst.
- Dein Text sollte aus drei Teilen bestehen: einer Einleitung, einem Hauptteil und einem Schluss. Diese drei Teile sollten klar erkennbar sein. Den Hauptteil kannst du unterteilen: jeder Abschnitt enthält eine neue Idee oder einen neuen Aspekt des Themas, über das du schreibst.
- Schreibe nie aus Vorlagen ab, sondern verwende immer deine eigenen Worte.

- Dein Text wird interessanter, wenn du Adjektive oder Adverbien verwendest, um Dinge, Handlungen oder Personen näher zu beschreiben.
- Wenn du fertig bist, dann lies deinen Text noch einmal gründlich durch und kontrolliere ihn auf Fehler. Oder lass deinen Text von einem Partner/einer Partnerin checken.

SF 14 Listening (Revision)

Im Unterricht kann es schwer sein, einem Hörtext zu folgen, weil du die Sprecher nicht sehen kannst und du dich auch noch auf die Aufgaben zum Hörtext konzentrieren musst. Die folgenden Tipps können dir helfen.

Was mache ich vor dem Hören?

- Schau dir die Aufgabenstellung genau an. Was sollst du heraushören?
- Oft findest du zum Text Überschriften und Bilder, die schon einige Fragen beantworten: Wer spricht mit wem, wo sind sie, worüber reden sie?
- Überlege, was du selbst zum Thema schon weißt und welche englischen Begriffe im Gespräch fallen könnten.

Worauf sollte ich während des Hörens achten?

- Lass dich nicht verwirren, wenn es mehrere Sprecher gibt. Versuche dann, die jeweiligen Stimmen einer Person zuzuordnen.
- Wie reden die Menschen miteinander? Gibt es einen, der den Ton angibt, oder einen, der besonders ärgerlich oder traurig klingt?
- Höre gezielt auf die Hintergrundgeräusche – findet das Gespräch z.B. am Strand, auf der Straße oder in der Schule statt?
- Einiges wirst du nicht verstehen – keine Sorge, das ist nicht schlimm. Wichtiger ist, was du alles verstanden hast. Oft ergibt sich dann der Rest

Und nach dem Hören?

- Wenn möglich, vergleiche mit einem Partner/einer Partnerin, was ihr verstanden habt.
- Wenn du einen Text ein zweites Mal hören darfst, notiere dir nach dem ersten Hören kurz, worauf du beim zweiten Hören besonders achten willst.
- Wenn dir die eine oder andere Frage bei der Beantwortung noch Schwierigkeiten macht, dann hilft oft schlaues Raten und Kombinieren.

Skills File

SF 15 Speaking

Worauf kommt es in Gesprächen an?

Lies die beiden Dialoge. Welche Unterschiede erkennst du? Wodurch entstehen sie?

Jen: Hi.
Ben: Hi.
Jen: It's a great parade.
Ben: Yeah.
Jen: Do you like the bands?
Ben: No.
Jen: The food smells good.
Ben: Yeah.
Jen: Do you want some too?
Ben: All right.
Jen: Do you live in Plymouth?
Ben: No.
Jen: …

Ed: Hi there, great parade, isn't it?
Jo: Yeah, I didn't know it was this big.
Ed: Is it your first time here, then?
Jo: That's right, I'm new in Plymouth.
Ed: Okay, so did you come here for the day?
Jo: Yeah, we arrived early this morning … Wow, that food smells good.
Ed: Are you hungry? Look, my friends have this pasties stall over there. Do you want to try one?
Jo: Okay, yes please.
Ed: My name's Ed, by the way.
Jo: Hello Ed, I'm Jo.

Was sage ich denn in so einem Gespräch?

Wenn du dich freundlich auf Englisch unterhalten willst, können dir diese Hinweise helfen:

1 Eröffne das Gespräch mit einer freundlichen Anrede oder Frage.

2 Wenn du etwas gefragt wirst, antworte nicht nur mit einem Wort.

3 Stelle deinem Gesprächspartner/deiner Gesprächspartnerin ein paar freundliche/interessierte Fragen.

4 Erzähle auch etwas von dir. Das hält das Gespräch am Laufen.

5 Verabschiede dich am Ende freundlich.

1 *Hi, can I sit here?*
Hello, how are you?
Hi there, are you from Plymouth?

2 *Fine, thanks. / Yeah, sure.*
Yes, I am. / No, not really.

3 *What about you?*
I'm Nick and you are …?
Do you like …?
So what do you think …?

4 *I'm new here in …*
I'm with my friends over there.
I love these …
And I really like …

5 *Bye then.*
See you.
Have a good time!

one hundred and fifty-three **153**

Skills File

PRESENTATION SKILLS

SF 16 Giving a presentation (Revision)

Wie halte ich eine gute Präsentation?

Vorbereitung
- Sammle Informationen zu deinem Thema.
- Wähle eine Form der Präsentation aus, die das Thema gut veranschaulicht (Poster, Folie, Tafel, …).
- Mach dir Notizen, z.B. auf nummerierten Karteikarten.
- Bereite deine Medien vor (Poster, Folie, Tafelanschrieb, …). Schreibe groß und für alle gut lesbar.
- Übe deine Präsentation zu Hause vor einem Spiegel oder vor einem kleinen Publikum (Eltern, Großeltern, Freunde).
- Sprich laut, deutlich und langsam.

Durchführung
- Warte, bis es ruhig ist. Schau die Zuhörer/innen an.
- Erkläre, worüber du sprechen wirst und wie deine Präsentation aufgebaut ist.
- Lies nicht von deinen Karten ab, sondern sprich möglichst frei.

Schluss
- Sage, dass du zum Ende kommst und bedanke dich fürs Zuhören.
- Frag die Zuhörer/innen, ob sie Fragen haben.

SF 17 Describing pictures   ➔ p. 79

Wenn du ein Bild beschreibst, kann es helfen, wenn du die folgenden Hinweise beachtest.

Was?
- Sage zuerst, was du beschreiben willst:
  a photo · a poster · a drawing

Wo?
- Um zu sagen, wo etwas abgebildet ist, benutze:
  at the top/bottom · in the foreground/background · in the middle · on the left/right
- Du kannst die Redemittel auch kombinieren:
  at the bottom on the left · at the top on the right
- Diese Präpositionen sind auch hilfreich:
  behind · between · in front of · next to · under · over

Wie?
- Geh bei der Beschreibung in einer bestimmten Reihenfolge vor, z.B. von links nach rechts, von oben nach unten oder vom Vordergrund zum Hintergrund.

Skills File

SF 18 Presenting a photo → p. 93

Manchmal sollst du ein Foto vor der Klasse vorstellen. Folgende Hinweise können dir dabei helfen.

Wie stelle ich ein Foto vor?

Wenn du vor anderen über ein Foto sprechen und es vorstellen sollst, dann reicht es nicht, wenn du es nur beschreibst. Am besten gehst du so vor:

1 Stelle das Foto vor und sage, woher es kommt.
2 Beschreibe das Foto *(SF 17: Describing pictures)*.
3 Sage, was dir an dem Foto gefällt oder nicht. Wenn es eine Geschichte zu dem Foto gibt, erzähle sie.
4 Wenn du mit der Vorstellung des Fotos fertig bist, bedanke dich für die Aufmerksamkeit und frage, ob noch jemand Fragen hat.

1. *I'd like to talk about this photo of … I found it on the internet/in a magazine/…*

2. *In the foreground you can see … I think the people in the photo are talking about …/having fun/celebrating/…*

3. *I really like/don't like the photo because … It's interesting/boring/exciting/ … because …*

4. *Thank you for listening. Do you have any questions?*

SF 19 Peer feedback → p. 93

Manchmal sollst du im Unterricht Partnern/Partnerinnen eine Rückmeldung zu einer Aufgabe geben. Das nennt man *peer feedback*.

Wozu ist *peer feedback* gut?

Gegenseitige Rückmeldungen sind für dich und deine Partner *(peers)* wichtig, denn
- du kannst jemanden loben für etwas, das er/sie gut gemacht hat,
- du kannst Hinweise geben, wo deine Partner noch Probleme haben,
- du kannst durch die Rückmeldungen selbst lernen, was du schon gut kannst und was du anders machen solltest.

Was muss ich beachten?

Bei deiner Rückmeldung solltest du drei Dinge beachten:

- Halte dich an die Punkte, zu denen du Rückmeldung geben sollst, z.B. die Aussprache, Betonung und Verständlichkeit bei einem Dialog, die Rechtschreibfehler in einem Text, das Einhalten eines roten Fadens in einer Geschichte usw. Begründe deine Einschätzungen.

- Gib deine Rückmeldung mit Respekt – niemand soll sich angegriffen fühlen. Nenne zuerst Gelungenes und mache dann Verbesserungsvorschläge zu Punkten, die noch nicht so gelungen sind.

- Wenn du eine Rückmeldung bekommst, überdenke die Vorschläge gut. Korrigiere die Fehler, die andere gefunden haben, und arbeite an den Stellen nach, wo du eventuell Probleme hattest.

What I liked	What you could do better
You chose a great photo. ☺ You spoke clearly and looked at us. …	Next time, say what is happening in the photo. Sometimes you stood in front of the photo. …

one hundred and fifty-five **155**

Grammar File

Grammar File – Inhalt   Seite

Unit 1
- GF 1 **REVISION The simple past** Die einfache Form der Vergangenheit 157
- GF 2 **REVISION The simple present** Die einfache Form der Gegenwart 158
- GF 3 **Subject and object questions** Subjekt- und Objektfragen 160
- GF 4 **The present progressive** Die Verlaufsform der Gegenwart 161

Unit 2
- GF 5 **The *going to*-future** Das Futur mit *going to* 162
- GF 6 **The comparison of adjectives** Die Steigerung der Adjektive 163

Unit 3
- GF 7 **Relative clauses** Relativsätze 165
- GF 8 **Adverbs of manner** Adverbien der Art und Weise 166

Unit 4
- GF 9 **The present perfect** Das *present perfect* 167
- GF 10 **Present perfect or simple past?** *Present perfect* oder *simple past*? 169
- GF 11 ***some* and *any* and their compounds** *some* und *any* und ihre Zusammensetzungen 170

Unit 5
- GF 12 **The *will*-future** Das Futur mit *will* 171
- GF 13 **EXTRA Question tags** Frageanhängsel 172
- GF 14 **Conditional sentences (type 1)** Bedingungssätze (Typ 1) 172

Unit 6
- GF 15 **The past progressive** Die Verlaufsform der Vergangenheit 173
- GF 16 **EXTRA Conditional sentences (type 2)** Bedingungssätze (Typ 2) 174
- GF 17 **EXTRA Contact clauses** Relativsätze ohne Relativpronomen 175

Grammatical terms (Grammatische Fachbegriffe) 175

Lösungen der Grammar-File-Aufgaben 176

Das **Grammar File** (S. 156–177) fasst zusammen, was du in den sechs Units deines Englischbuches über die **englische Sprache** lernst.
Hier kannst du nachsehen, wenn du
– selbstständig etwas lernen oder etwas wiederholen möchtest,
– wenn du Übungen aus dem *Practice*-Teil deines Englischbuches oder aus dem *Workbook* bearbeitest,
– wenn du dich auf einen Test vorbereiten willst.

In der **linken Spalte** findest du **Beispielsätze** und **Übersichten**, z. B.

In der **rechten Spalte** stehen **Erklärungen** und nützliche Hinweise (auf Deutsch).

Besonders wichtig sind die Stellen mit den **roten Ausrufezeichen** (!). Sie zeigen, was im Deutschen anders ist, und machen dich auf besondere Fehlerquellen aufmerksam.

Verweise wie ➔ p. 31, exercises 1–2 zeigen dir, wo du Übungen zum gerade behandelten grammatischen Thema findest.

Die grammatischen Fachbegriffe *(grammatical terms)* kannst du auf den Seiten 175–176 nachschlagen.

Am Ende der *Grammar-File*-Abschnitte stehen wieder kleine **Aufgaben** zur **Selbstkontrolle**. Hier kannst du überprüfen, ob du das gerade behandelte Thema verstanden hast.
Auf den Seiten 176–177 kannst du dann nachsehen, ob deine Lösungen richtig sind.

156 one hundred and fifty-six

Unit 1   Grammar File

Unit 1

GF 1   REVISION   The simple past   Die einfache Form der Vergangenheit

a) Positive statements

*We **went** to Spain last year. We **stayed** in a nice hotel in Madrid and **visited** lots of museums.*

stay → stay**ed** [steɪd]	film → film**ed** [fɪlmd]
talk → talk**ed** [tɔːkt]	watch → watch**ed** [wɒtʃt]

1 *It was rainy when we **arrived**.*
2 *Later the rain **stopped**, and it was warm and sunny.*
3 *We **tried** to do some sport, but it was too hot.*
4 *So we **visited** lots of museums. I really **needed** that holiday.*

*Justin **went** to the USA last summer.*	Infinitiv: **go**
*He **got** back two days ago.*	**get**
*Sam and his dad **had** a race.*	**have**
*Abby **met** a German girl at her hotel.*	**meet**
*Sam **took** photos of sand sculptures.*	**take**

➡ *p. 11, exercise 2*

Bejahte Aussagesätze

Mit dem *simple past* kannst du über **Vergangenes** berichten. Das *simple past* steht häufig mit Zeitangaben wie *last year, yesterday, two days ago, in 2010*.

◀ Bei **regelmäßigen** Verben hängst du **-ed** an den Infinitiv, um das *simple past* zu bilden.
Es gibt für alle Personen nur eine Form.

❗ Beachte folgende Besonderheiten:

1 Ein stummes *e* fällt weg: *arrive* → *arrived*
2 Nach einem einzelnen, betonten Vokal wird der Konsonant verdoppelt: *stop* → *stopped*
3 Ein *y* nach Konsonant wird zu **-ied**: *try* → *tried*
4 Nach *t* und *d* wird die *ed*-Endung [ɪd] ausgesprochen: *visited* ['vɪzɪtɪd], *needed* ['niːdɪd]

◀ **Unregelmäßige** Verben haben eine eigene Form für das *simple past*, die du einzeln lernen musst.

Links findest du einige Beispiele.

➡ *Liste der unregelmäßigen Verben, S. 248–249*

b) Negative statements

*Abby **didn't** go sailing with Tim – she went alone.*
*Sam's dad **didn't** win the race because he crashed.*
*Sam **didn't** want to leave a message for Justin.*

➡ *p. 11, exercise 2*

Verneinte Aussagesätze

Eine Aussage im *simple past* **verneinst** du immer mit **didn't** + **Infinitiv** (Langform: *did not*).

Vergleiche: *Abby **went** sailing alone.*
                      *She **didn't** go with Tim.*
   (nicht: *She didn't went with Tim.*)

Dies gilt für regelmäßige und für unregelmäßige Verben.

Alles verstanden? Dann vervollständige diese Sätze in deinem Übungsheft.
(Auf S. 176 kannst du nachschauen, ob deine Antworten richtig sind.)

1 *Justin … (go) to Boston in the school holidays. He … (go) to New York.*
2 *He … (see) an elephant – he … (see) a bear.*
3 *Sam … (stay) in a hotel – he … (stay) in a caravan.*
4 *Maya and Lucy … (make) a cake with Lucy's grandma – they … (make) scones.*

Yesterday evening Morph worked on his computer. He didn't play cards.

one hundred and fifty-seven   **157**

Grammar File Unit 1

c) Yes/No questions and short answers

Did Maya **visit** Lucy's grandparents? – Yes, she **did**.

Did you **go** on holiday in the summer?
– Yes, I **did**. / No, I **didn't**.

Sam: Justin, **did** you **see** the Empire State Building?
Justin: No, I **didn't**.

➔ p. 11, exercise 3

Entscheidungsfragen und Kurzantworten

Fragen im *simple past* bildest du immer mit *did*.

Vergleiche: Maya **visited** Lucy's grandparents.
 Did Abby **visit** Lucy's grandparents?
 (nicht: Did Abby visit~~ed~~ Lucy's grandparents?)

Dies gilt für regelmäßige und für unregelmäßige Verben.

---

d) Questions with question words

What did Sam **do** when it was cloudy and cold?
– He went to the pier.

Where did Sam **take** the photo of the sand sculptures?
– In Weston-super-Mare.

When did Justin **get** back? – Two days ago.

➔ p. 12, exercise 4

Fragen mit Fragewörtern

Fragen mit Fragewörtern (*What, Where, When, Why, How*) bildest du wie Entscheidungsfragen.
Das Fragewort steht am Anfang der Frage, vor *did*.

Vergleiche:
 Abby **went** sailing.
Entscheidungsfrage: **Did** Abby **go** sailing?
Frage mit Fragewort: **When did** Abby **go** sailing?

Die einfache Form der Vergangenheit

Bejahte Aussagen	Verneinte Aussagen	Fragen
I/You/He/She/It visit**ed** …	I/You/He/She/It **didn't** visit …	**Did** I/you/he/she/it visit …?
We/You/They visit**ed** …	We/You/They **didn't** visit …	**Did** we/you/they visit …?

Sieh dir die **Antworten** an und bilde die Fragen.
(Achtung – es ist eine Mischung aus Entscheidungsfragen und Fragewort-Fragen!)

1 (Abby – go in the summer holidays?)   To Turkey.   Where did Abby go …?
2 (Abby – go sailing with Tim?)   No, she didn't.   Did …?
3 (Sam – do in Weston-super-Mare?)   He went swimming.
4 (Sam – phone Justin's home?)   In the last week of the school holidays.
5 (Sam – phone Justin's mobile?)   Yes, he did.

GF 2 REVISION The simple present Die einfache Form der Gegenwart

a) Positive statements

I **get up** at 6:30 every morning. Then I **have** breakfast. After breakfast, I **go** to school. I usually **take** the bus.

Maya **lives** in Plymouth. She **goes** to Coombe Dean School. She often **goes** sailing at weekends.

Lots of children **like** ice cream.
Dogs **eat** meat.

**He, she, it –
das s muss mit!**

 I/You/We/They **like** dogs.
 He/She/It **likes** dogs.

➔ p. 16, exercise 1

Bejahte Aussagesätze

◂ Wenn du darüber redest, was **regelmäßig** (jeden Tag, immer, oft, meistens) oder **nie** geschieht, dann verwendest du das *simple present*.

In *simple present*-Sätzen stehen daher häufig
– die Wörter **always, usually, often, sometimes, never**
– Zeitangaben wie **every day, on Sundays, at weekends**.

◂ Man verwendet das *simple present* auch, um allgemeine Aussagen zu machen.

◂ Verben im *simple present* haben bei **I**, **you**, **we** und **they** keine Endung.
Nur bei **he**, **she** und **it** (der 3. Person Singular) wird ein **s** angefügt.

---

158 one hundred and fifty-eight

Unit 1   Grammar File

b) 3rd person singular: pronunciation and spelling

1 [s] My dog **eats** lots of meat.   [-ts]
        And she **barks** a lot.   [-ks]

2 [z] Morph often **hides** in the library. [-dz]
        Dad always **comes** home late.   [-mz]
        Leo **knows** Lucy.   [-əʊz]

3 [ɪz] Sue often **misses** the bus.   [-sɪz]
        Paul **watches** TV at weekends.   [-tʃɪz]
        Our teacher **uses** red pens.   [-zɪz]

(to) **hurry up** – He's late for school, so he **hurries** up.
(to) **try**   – Sam always **tries** to help his sister.
to) **play**   – John **plays** football every Saturday.

➡ p. 16, exercise 1

3. Person Singular: Aussprache und Schreibung

Der Laut **vor** dem **s** bestimmt die Aussprache.

◀ 1 Nach **stimmlosen Konsonanten**: [s]
     Stimmlose Konsonanten sind z.B. [t], [k], [p], [f].

◀ 2 Nach **stimmhaften Konsonanten** und **Vokalen**: [z]
     Stimmhafte Konsonanten sind z.B. [d], [b], [g], [v], [m].

◀ 3 Nach **Zischlauten**: [ɪz]
     Zischlaute sind z.B. [s], [z], [ʃ], [tʃ], [dʒ].
     Nach Zischlauten wird es oder s angehängt, je nach
     Schreibung des Infinitivs: miss – misses · use – uses.

◀ Bei Verben, die auf **Konsonant + y** enden, gibt es eine
  Besonderheit in der 3. Person Singular: **y + s** ➝ **ies**.

  Aber **Vokal + y** bleibt unverändert: **pla**y **+ s** ➝ **plays**.

---

c) Negative statements

I/You/We/They **don't**   **live** in Britain.

         He/She/It **doesn't live** in Britain.

➡ p. 16, exercise 1

Verneinte Aussagesätze

Eine Aussage im simple present **verneinst** du

• bei I, you, we, they mit **don't** + Infinitiv

• bei he, she, it mit **doesn't** + Infinitiv.

❗ Das **s** der 3. Person Singular steckt im Wort **doesn't**:
        He/She/It **doesn't live** in Britain.
    (nicht: He/She/It doesn't lives̶ …)

Verneinte Aussagen		
Vergleiche:	**Simple present**	**Simple past**
	I **don't** like the Big Wheel.	I **didn't** like the Big Wheel.
	Sam **doesn't** like the Big Wheel.	Sam **didn't** like the Big Wheel.

d) Yes/No questions and short answers

Do you **like** sport? – Yes, I **do**. / No, I **don't**.
Do the Coopers **have** a son? – Yes, they **do**.

Does Sam **like** the Big Wheel? – No, he **doesn't**.
Does Lucy **have** new neighbours? – Yes, she **does**.

➡ p. 16, exercise 2

Entscheidungsfragen und Kurzantworten

Fragen im simple present bildest du

• bei I, you, we, they mit **Do** …

• bei he, she, it mit **Does** …

❗ Das **s** der 3. Person Singular steckt im Wort **does**:
        Does Sam **like** the Big Wheel?
    (nicht: Does Sam likes̶ …)

Fragen		
Vergleiche:	**Simple present**	**Simple past**
	Do you **like** the Big Wheel?	**Did** you **like** the Big Wheel?
	Does Sam **like** the Big Wheel?	**Did** Sam **like** the Big Wheel?

Grammar File Unit 1

e) Questions with question words

When **does** Abby **go** sailing? – On Sundays.

Why **does** Sam **have to** look after Lily in the afternoons?
– Because his mum goes shopping then.

When **do** lessons **finish** at your school?

➡ p. 16, exercise 2

Fragen mit Fragewörtern

Fragen mit Fragewörtern (When, Where, What, Why, How) bildest du wie Entscheidungsfragen.
Das Fragewort steht am Anfang der Frage, vor *do* bzw. *does*. Vergleiche:

	She **goes** sailing.
Entscheidungsfrage:	**Does** she **go** sailing?
Frage mit Fragewort:	**When does** she **go** sailing?

Vervollständige diese Sätze in deinem Übungsheft.
1 Maya … (go) to Plymstock School, she … (go) to Coombe Dean.
  Maya doesn't …
2 And Maya's brother Mukesh? … he (go) to Coombe Dean too? – No, he …
3 Mukesh and Maya's cousins … (live) in Britain. Where … they (live)?
4 Morph … (live) in a hotel. He … (live) in the school library.
5 Morph … (like) the cat. He … (hide) between the books when the cat is in the library.
6 The Blackwells … (have) a nice house in Wembury. – How many children … they (have)?

GF 3 Subject and object questions Subjekt- und Objektfragen

What **happened** on Saturday morning?
Was geschah am Samstagmorgen?

Who **found** a note on the kitchen table? – Lucy.
Wer fand eine Notiz auf dem Küchentisch? – …

Who **invited** the Coopers to tea? – Mrs Pascoe.
Wer hat die Coopers zum Tee eingeladen? – …

What **did** Lucy **find** on the kitchen table? – A note.
Was fand Lucy auf dem Küchentisch? – …

Who **did** Lucy **call** on Saturday morning? – Her mum.
Wen hat Lucy am Samstagmorgen angerufen? – …

Who **did** Mrs Pascoe **invite** to tea? – The Coopers.
Wen hat Mrs Pascoe zum Tee eingeladen? – …

Who does Justin skype *with*? – His father.
Mit wem skypt Justin? – …

What school does Leo go *to*? – Plymstock School.
Auf welche Schule geht Leo? – …

➡ pp. 16–17, exercises 3–5

Mit *who* und *what* kann man nach dem **Subjekt** oder nach dem **Objekt** eines Satzes fragen.

◂ **Subjekt**fragen sind „**Wer** oder **was**?"-Fragen.
Subjektfragen werden **ohne** *do/does/did* gebildet.
Die Wortstellung ist wie in Aussagesätzen,
das Fragewort ist Subjekt des Fragesatzes.
Vergleiche:

	Subjekt	Objekt
Aussage:	Mrs Pascoe	invited the Coopers to tea.
Subjektfrage:	Who	invited the Coopers to tea?
	Wer …?	Antwort: Mrs Pascoe

◂ **Objekt**fragen sind „**Wen/Wem** oder **was**?"-Fragen.
Objektfragen werden im *simple present* **mit** *do/does* und im *simple past* **mit** *did* gebildet.
Das Fragewort ist Objekt des Fragesatzes.

	Objekt	Subjekt
Objektfrage:	Who	did Mrs Pascoe invite to tea?
	Wen …?	Antwort: The Coopers

Sieh dir die Beispielsätze und die Übersetzungen gut an.

❗ Anders als im Deutschen steht die **Präposition** (*with, to*) in englischen Objektfragen am Ende der Frage.

Unit 1   Grammar File

Kannst du zu jedem Satz zwei Fragen bilden? (Achtung – *simple present* oder *simple past*?)

1 Leo knows Lucy.
   A *(Wer kennt Lucy?)* Who … Lucy?
   B *(Wen kennt Leo?)*   Who … Leo know?

2 Mrs Pascoe tells Holly about her plans.
   A *(Wer erzählt Holly …?)* Who … about her plans?
   B *(Wem erzählt Mrs Pascoe …?)* Who … about her plans?

3 Lucy wanted to meet Sam.
   A *(Wer wollte Sam treffen?)* Who …?
   B *(Wen wollte Lucy treffen?)* Who …?

4 In the afternoon, Lucy talked to Sam.
   A *(Wer redete mit Sam …?)* Who … in the afternoon?
   B *(Mit wem redete Lucy…?)* Who … in the afternoon?

GF 4 The present progressive Die Verlaufsform der Gegenwart

a) REVISION Simple present and present progressive

Simple present
*Morph often **plays** cards in the library.*
Morph spielt oft Karten in der Bibliothek.

Present progressive
*Look, Morph **is playing** cards now.*
Sieh mal, Morph spielt gerade Karten.

1 *Maya and Lucy are on Dartmoor. They**'re making** scones with Lucy's grandma.*

2 *Abby and Maya are by the sea. Skip **is running** along the beach.*

➡ p. 22, exercise 1

Einfache Form und Verlaufsform der Gegenwart

Mit dem *simple present* drückt man aus, dass etwas **wiederholt, regelmäßig, immer** oder **nie** geschieht (vgl. GF 2 auf den Seiten 158–160).

Mit dem *present progressive* drückt man aus, dass jemand **gerade dabei** ist, etwas zu tun, oder dass etwas **gerade im Gange** ist. (Daher der Name „Verlaufsform": Man spricht damit über etwas, das gerade im Verlauf ist.)

Das *present progressive* wird mit **am/are/is** + **-ing-Form** des Verbs gebildet:
*I**'m playing** … / He**'s playing** … / They**'re playing** …*

❗ Beachte folgende Besonderheiten:

1 Ein stummes **e** fällt weg: **mak**e → **mak**ing, **com**e → **com**ing, **danc**e → **danc**ing

2 Nach einem einzelnen, betonten Vokal wird der Konsonant verdoppelt: **run** → **run**ning, **get** → **get**ting, **stop** → **stop**ping

b) The present progressive with future meaning

Maya: *Lucy **is joining** Plymstock's Gardening Club **next term**.*

Abby: *I**'m not going** back to Plymstock School. I**'m going** to a new school **next week**.*

Abby: *I**'m coming** home **in the next holidays**.*

➡ p. 22, exercise 2

Das *present progressive* mit futurischer Bedeutung

Das *present progressive* wird auch verwendet, um über **feste Verabredungen** zu sprechen.
Es muss aber deutlich sein, dass es sich um etwas Zukünftiges handelt, z. B. durch eine Zeitangabe *(tomorrow, next term, on Monday)* oder aus dem Zusammenhang.

(Manchmal wird diese Verwendung des *present progressive* als **diary future** bezeichnet, weil es dabei um Verabredungen geht, die man schon in seinen Terminkalender eingetragen hat.)

Grammar File   Unit 2

Regelmäßig? Oder **gerade im Gange?** Oder **fest verabredet?**
Wo brauchst du das *simple present*, wo das *present progressive*?

1 I … (go) to volleyball training two evenings every week.
2 I usually … (go) by bike, but today it … (rain), so Dad … (take) me to the gym in our car.
3 Next Saturday, we … (play) against last year's best team. I'm excited already.
4 My brother … (do) any sport. But he … (play) the guitar in a band. They … (meet) every Friday.
5 Right now, my brother … (practise) in his room. But he … (play) too loud.
6 Next month he and his band … (give) a concert in the gym.
7 Everybody … (look) forward to that.

Unit 2

GF 5 The *going to*-future   Das Futur mit *going to*

*Lucy **is going to** sing a Queen song at the audition today.*
Lucy wird beim heutigen Vorsingen einen *Queen*-Song singen.

*Leo's mum and dad **are going to** be at home this afternoon.*
Leos Mutter und Vater werden heute Nachmittag zu Hause sein.

*The students **are going to** do a musical this year.*
Die Schülerinnen und Schüler werden dieses Jahr ein Musical aufführen / haben vor, dieses Jahr ein Musical aufzuführen.

Wenn du über **Absichten** und **Pläne** für die Zukunft sprechen willst, verwendest du das Futur mit **going to**.

Es wird mit **am/are/is going to** + **Infinitiv** gebildet.
Die Kurzformen kennst du vom Verb **be**:
I'm going to, **you're** going to, **he's** going to usw.

❗ **going to** hat hier nichts mit „gehen" zu tun.
I'm going to … bedeutet „Ich werde …" oder „Ich habe vor …".

I'm not going to join a new club. I want to stay with hockey.

Ich habe nicht vor, in einen neuen Klub einzutreten. …

◀ Die verneinten Formen kennst du ebenfalls schon:
I'm not going to, **you aren't** going to, **he isn't** going to usw.

Are you going to play in the school team again this year?

Yes, I am … if I'm good enough.

◀ Und auch Fragen und Kurzantworten sind wie beim Verb **be**.

  p. 31, exercises 1–2

Das Futur mit *going to*		
Bejahte Aussagen	**Verneinte Aussagen**	**Fragen und Kurzantworten**
I'm going to …	I'm not going to …	Are you going to watch the show?
You're going to …	You aren't going to …	– Yes, I am. / No, I'm not.
He's/She's/It's going to …	He/She/It isn't going to …	Is he/she going to watch the show?
We're/You're/They're going to …	We/You/They aren't going to …	– Yes, he/she is. / No, he/she isn't.

Unit 2   Grammar File

Vervollständige die folgenden Sätze.

1 Sam … (play) in the school team again this year.
2 And Justin? … he … (join) the basketball team?
3 Leo … (join) the Basketball Club.
4 A man … (visit) Leo's parents later this afternoon.
5 And the girls? What … they … (do) this year?

Sam is going to play …
And Justin? Is he g…?

GF 6 The comparison of adjectives Die Steigerung der Adjektive

a) Comparison with -er / -est

Julie is 13. Her brother Jake is **younger** – he's ten. Baby Jodie is the **youngest**, and James is the **oldest**.

1 James thinks that Jake is **nicer** than Julie.
2 The Millers' dog is **bigger** than Jodie.
3 The Millers' dog is the **happiest** dog in Britain.

➡ p. 34, exercises 1–3

Steigerung mit -er / -est

Die **Steigerungsformen** der Adjektive werden verwendet, um Dinge oder Personen miteinander zu vergleichen, z.B.:

young	**young**er	(the) **young**est
jung	jünger	am jüngsten; der/die/das jüngste …

Komparativ   **Superlativ**
(comparative)   *(superlative)*

Die Steigerung mit **-er/-est** verwendet du für
– **einsilbige** Adjektive (young, long, nice, big, …)
– **zweisilbige** Adjektive mit der **Endung -y** (busy, easy, funny, happy, sunny, …).

❗ Beachte folgende Besonderheiten:

1 Ein stummes **e** fällt weg: **nic**e – **nic**er – **nic**est
2 Nach einem einzelnen Vokal wird der Konsonant verdoppelt: **big** – **big**ger – **big**gest
3 **-y** + **-er / -est** wird zu **-ier / -iest**: happ**y** – happ**ier** – happ**iest**

b) Comparison with more / most

*I think sport is **boring**. Football is **boring**, tennis is even **more boring**, and Dad's yoga is **the most boring** sport of all.*

➡ p. 38, exercise 2

The library is the most exciting place in the world.

Steigerung mit *more / most*

Die meisten anderen Adjektive werden mit **more / most** gesteigert:

boring	langweilig
more boring	langweiliger
(the) **most** boring	am langweiligsten; der/die/das langweiligste …

Weitere Beispiele:
beautiful – **more** beautiful – (the) **most** beautiful
careful – **more** careful – (the) **most** careful
expensive – **more** expensive – (the) **most** expensive
interesting – **more** interesting – (the) **most** interesting

Grammar File   Unit 2

c) Irregular comparison

Sam is a **good** swimmer, but Leo is **better**.
And Maya is the **best** swimmer of them all.

The food at our canteen is **bad**, but the food at 'Burger Brothers' is **worse**. And the food at 'Chippy' is the **worst** in town.

How **many** DVDs do you have? – Not **many**. My sister has a lot **more** DVDs, and my brother has the **most**.

Unregelmäßige Steigerung

Wie im Deutschen gibt es einige wenige Adjektive mit unregelmäßigen Steigerungsformen:

good   – better – (the) best
bad   – worse – (the) worst
much/many – more   – (the) most

Die Steigerung der Adjektive		
-er / -est	**more / most**	**unregelmäßig**
• Einsilbige Adjektive: old – older – oldest	Andere zweisilbige sowie mehrsilbige Adjektive: exciting – more exciting – (the) most exciting	good – better – best bad – worse – worst much/many – more – most
• Adjektive auf **-y**: happy – happier – happiest		

d) bigger than – as big as

The Millers' dog is **bigger than** Jodie.
Der Hund der Millers ist größer als Jodie.

Do you think that English is **harder than** French?
Findest du, dass Englisch schwieriger als Französisch ist?

I'm almost **as tall as** my mother now,
but I'm **not as tall as** my father yet.
Ich bin jetzt fast so groß wie meine Mutter,
aber ich bin noch nicht so groß wie mein Vater.

My sister is 10. I'm **older than her**.
Meine Schwester ist 10. Ich bin älter als sie.

Is Holly as old as Maya and Abby?
– No, she isn't **as old as them**.
… Nein, sie ist nicht so alt wie sie.

➡ p. 34, exercises 1–3 • p. 38, exercise 2

„größer als" – „so groß wie"

◂ Wenn Personen oder Dinge **unterschiedlich** groß/alt/schnell/… sind, vergleichst du sie mit dem **Komparativ + than** (deutsch: „als"):

My sister is **older than** your brother.

◂ Wenn Personen oder Dinge **gleich** groß/alt/schnell/… sind, vergleichst du sie mit **as** big/old/fast/… **as**:

My cat is **as fast as** your rabbit.

❗ In Vergleichen mit **than** und **as … as** stehen die Personalpronomen **me/him/her/us** usw. Das ist anders als im Deutschen:

older **than me/him/her/us/them**
älter **als ich/er/sie/wir/sie**

Sieh dir die Zeichnungen an und vervollständige die Vergleiche:

1 (old)   Monty is … … … Sandy.
              Rex is … … Monty and Sandy.
              Rex is the …

2 (fast)   The cat is … … the hamster.
              The horse is … …

3 (expensive) The mobile is … … …
              the MP3 player.
              The TV is … … … the MP3 player.
              The computer is the … …

Unit 3   Grammar File

Unit 3

GF 7 Relative clauses Relativsätze

a) Use

*Shoes for **boys and girls** **who want to have fun**!*
Schuhe für Jungen und Mädchen, die Spaß haben wollen.

*There's **the little shop** **that makes its own chocolates**.*
… der kleine Laden, der seine eigenen Pralinen herstellt.

*It's **a thing that tells you how warm it is**.*
– *Oh, I think you mean a thermometer.*   [θəˈmɒmɪtə]

Gebrauch

Mit **Relativsätzen** beschreibt man genauer, über wen oder was man spricht:

◂ Welche Jungen und Mädchen sind gemeint? – Jungen und Mädchen, die Spaß haben wollen.

◂ Welcher Laden ist gemeint? – Der Laden, der seine eigenen Pralinen herstellt.

◂ Relativsätze sind sehr nützlich, wenn du etwas beschreiben möchtest, wofür du das englische Wort nicht kennst.

b) The relative pronouns *who*, *which* and *that*

1 *I like **teachers who** laugh a lot.*
Ich mag Lehrer und Lehrerinnen, die viel lachen.

2 *The **shop which** sells expensive trainers is near the pedestrian zone.*
Der Laden, der teure Turnschuhe verkauft, …

3 *Lucy is the **girl that** wants to buy a set square.*
Lucy ist das Mädchen, das ein Geodreieck kaufen will.

*"Here are the **felt pens that** you need," said Maya.*
„Hier sind die Filzstifte, die du brauchst", sagte Maya.

*I need a present for a boy **who likes music**.*

… für einen Jungen, **der Musik mag**.

➡ pp. 50–51, exercises 1–4

Die Relativpronomen *who*, *which* und *that*

1 Das **Relativpronomen** *who* steht nur in Relativsätzen, die Personen beschreiben:
The **girl/boy/people/dancer** *who* …

2 Das **Relativpronomen** *which* steht nur in Relativsätzen, die Dinge (und Tiere) beschreiben:
The **shop/bag/things/horses** *which* …

3 Das **Relativpronomen** *that* kannst du für Personen und Dinge verwenden.
Für Personen wird häufiger *who* benutzt.

❗ Beachte die unterschiedliche **Wortstellung** in englischen und deutschen Relativsätzen.

Wo brauchst du *who* oder *that*? Wo brauchst du *which* oder *that*?

1 *Let's go to the stall … sells those nice T-shirts and tops.*
2 *"Look, Lucy, there's the assistant … sold you the felt pens at Smith's."*
3 *We should ask somebody … lives here and knows the place.*
4 *What do you call that maths thing … looks like a triangle?*
5 *You don't know what a satnav is? It's the thing in the car … tells you the way.*

I don't like cats that eat Morphs.

one hundred and sixty-five   **165**

Grammar File   Unit 3

GF 8 Adverbs of manner — Adverbien der Art und Weise

a) Use

Adjectives
That's a **nice** idea.
Sam was very **excited**.

Adverbs
"You do that Spiderman trick very **nicely**."
"Yes," Sam said **excitedly**.
„Ja", sagte Sam aufgeregt / mit aufgeregter Stimme.

Sam schüttelte langsam den Kopf.
Sam **shook** his head **slowly**.

Gebrauch

◄ **Adjektive** beziehen sich auf ein **Nomen**. Man verwendet sie, um Personen oder Dinge näher zu beschreiben – sie drücken aus, wie etwas oder jemand **ist**.

◄ **Adverbien der Art und Weise** (adverbs of manner) beziehen sich auf ein **Verb**. Man verwendet sie, um Handlungen oder Vorgänge näher zu beschreiben – sie drücken aus, wie jemand etwas **tut** oder wie etwas **geschieht**.

❗ Im Deutschen können Adverbien der Art und Weise zwischen Verb und Objekt stehen.
Englische *adverbs of manner* dürfen **nicht** zwischen Verb und Objekt stehen!

b) Regular forms

Adjective		Adverb
excited	→	excited**ly**
nice	→	nice**ly**
loud	→	loud**ly**

Leo smiled **happily**.

It's not good to have a bath every day. We have to use water **responsibly**.   (verantwortungsvoll, -bewusst)

Thank you very much. You did that job **fantastically**.

Adverb   We ride our bikes **carefully**.
Wir fahren **vorsichtig**.
Adjective   We're always **careful**.
Wir sind immer **vorsichtig**.

Regelmäßige Formen

Die meisten Adverbien der Art und Weise werden gebildet, indem **-ly** an das Adjektiv angehängt wird.

❗ Beachte folgende Besonderheiten:

1 **-y** + **-ly** wird zu **-ily**:
   happ**y** → happ**ily**

2 **-le** wird zu **-ly**:
   responsib**le** → responsib**ly**

3 Nach **-ic** wird **-ally** angehängt:
   fantast**ic** → fantast**ically**

◄ Im Deutschen haben Adverbien der Art und Weise und Adjektive dieselbe Form, im Englischen in der Regel nicht.

c) Irregular forms

Sam is a **good** kung fu fighter. He fights **well**.

Rabbits are very **fast** animals. They can run very **fast**.

A job in a TV studio can be **hard** sometimes. Justin's father often has to work very **hard**.

➡ p. 55, exercises 1–3

Unregelmäßige Formen

Einige Adverbien der Art und Weise haben eine unregelmäßige Form, die du einzeln lernen musst:

◄ Das Adverb zu **good** heißt **well**.

◄ Bei **fast** und **hard** haben Adjektiv und Adverb dieselbe Form.

Morph waited nervously on the shelf till the cat walked away.

Unit 4 Grammar File

Welches Wort ist richtig, das Adjektiv oder das Adverb?
Vervollständige die Sätze in deinem Übungsheft.

1 We sailed … down the river.   (**slow / slowly**)
2 The football match got more interesting after a very … start.   (**slow / slowly**)
3 Suddenly there was a … BANG and the lights went out.   (**loud / loudly**)
4 Suddenly somebody sneezed … .   (**loud / loudly**)
5 She looked … at her watch. It was almost too late now.   (**nervous / nervously**)
6 She always plays with her hair when she's … .   (**nervous / nervously**)
7 I slept very … last night.   (**bad / badly**)
8 I always take an umbrella in … weather.   (**bad / badly**)

Unit 4

GF 9 The present perfect Das *present perfect*

a) Use

Grandma: **I've made** some scones. I hope you're hungry.
Ich habe Scones gemacht. …

Maya: Yes, I am. I **haven't had** breakfast yet.
… Ich habe noch nicht gefrühstückt.

Lucy: Yes, Grandma, **we've checked** the times of the bus back to Plymouth. Don't worry.
Ja, Oma, wir haben die Abfahrtszeiten des Busses … gecheckt. Mach dir keine Sorgen.

Gebrauch

Mit dem *present perfect* drückt man aus, dass jemand irgendwann etwas getan hat oder dass irgendwann etwas geschehen ist. Es ist nicht wichtig, wann das war – deshalb wird auch kein genauer Zeitpunkt genannt.

◂ Oft hat die Handlung **Auswirkungen** auf die Gegenwart oder die Zukunft:
Lucy hat die Abfahrtszeiten des Busses nachgesehen, sodass ihre Oma sich nun keine Sorgen machen muss.

(Zum Unterschied zwischen *present perfect* und *simple past* vgl. GF 10 auf S. 169).

b) Form: the past participle

1 We**'ve check**ed the times of the bus.
I**'ve text**ed you the time that we arrive.
Sam **hasn't finish**ed his bath yet.

No, Mum **hasn't phon**ed me.
Don't open the door. The bus **hasn't stop**ped yet.
Maya, **have** you **tri**ed Grandma's scones?

2 I **haven't eaten** anything today.
Oh no, Sam **has fallen** in the mud.
I've never **been** on a tractor before.

Form: das Partizip Perfekt

Das *present perfect* wird mit **have/has** und der 3. Form des Verbs gebildet.
Die 3. Form heißt **Partizip Perfekt** (*past participle*).

1 Bei **regelmäßigen Verben** hängst du **-ed** an den Infinitiv, um das *past participle* zu bilden:
check + **ed** → **check**ed • **text** + **ed** → **text**ed

◂ Beachte die Besonderheiten der Schreibung und der Aussprache. (Vgl. GF 1a auf S. 157)

2 **Unregelmäßige Verben** haben eigene Formen.
Im Vokabelverzeichnis werden unregelmäßige Verben immer so angegeben: *(to) eat, ate, eaten*
Die 2. Form ist die *simple past*-Form (ate).
Die 3. Form ist das *past participle* (eaten).

➡ Liste der unregelmäßigen Verben, S. 248–249

Welche dieser Formen sind *past participles*?
1 *been* • 2 *was* • 3 *were* • 4 *ate* • 5 *eaten* • 6 *done* • 7 *did* • 8 *fell* • 9 *fallen*

Grammar File   Unit 4

c) Positive and negative statements

1 Thanks, Mr Tizzard. We**'ve had** a great time.
  Sam **has done** it again! He**'s fallen** in the mud.

2 I **haven't had** breakfast yet.
  Sam **hasn't finished** his bath yet.

Sam **has fallen** in the mud.
Sam **ist** in den Matsch **gefallen**.

➡ pp. 70–71, exercises 1–5

Bejahte und verneinte Aussagesätze

1 Bejahte Aussagesätze im *present perfect*:
  have/has + **past participle**
  (Kurzform: **'ve/'s** + **past participle**)

2 Verneinte Aussagesätze im *present perfect*:
  haven't/hasn't + **past participle**

❗ Das *present perfect* wird immer mit **have/has** gebildet, egal ob im Deutschen „haben" oder „sein" steht.

Das *present perfect*		
Bejahte Aussagen	**Verneinte Aussagen**	**Langformen**
I've fallen …	I haven't finished …	I/You/We/They have (not) fallen …
You've fallen …	You haven't finished …	
He's/She's/It's fallen …	He/She/It hasn't finished …	He/She/It has (not) fallen …
We've/You've/They've fallen …	We/You/They haven't finished …	

d) Questions and short answers

Have you ever **tried** sheep's milk?
– Yes, I **have**. / No, I **haven't**.

Has the rain **stopped** yet?
– Yes, it **has**. / No, it **hasn't**.

Has Maya **brought** any other shoes with her?
– Yes, she **has**. / No, she **hasn't**.

What **have** you **done**, Maya?
Why **haven't** you **closed** the door?

➡ p. 73, exercises 1–2

Fragen und Kurzantworten

In Fragen im *present perfect* sind **Subjekt** und **have/has** vertauscht.

◀ Fragewörter stehen wie immer am Satzanfang.

❗ Im *present perfect* gibt es **keine Fragen mit when**. When fragt nach einem Zeitpunkt – und dafür musst du das *simple past* verwenden.
(Zu *present perfect* und *simple past* vgl. GF 10 auf S. 169).

Unit 4   Grammar File

e) The present perfect with adverbs of indefinite time

*I'm not hungry. I've **already** eaten.*
Ich habe schon gegessen.

*I've seen the film **before**. I don't want to watch it again.*
Ich habe den Film schon mal gesehen. ...

*Have you **ever** been to Paris? – No, I've **never** been to Paris. But I've **always** wanted to go there.*
Bist du jemals in Paris gewesen? – Nein, ich war noch nie in Paris. Aber ich wollte da schon immer mal hinfahren.

*Have you done your homework **yet**?*
Hast du deine Hausaufgaben schon gemacht?

*Where are Emily and Olivia? – I've **just** seen Emily in the garden. But Olivia **hasn't** arrived **yet**.*
... – Ich habe Emily gerade im Garten gesehen. Aber Olivia ist noch nicht eingetroffen.

➡ p. 70, exercise 1 · p. 71, exercise 4 · p. 73, exercises 1–2

Das *present perfect* mit Adverbien der unbestimmten Zeit

Das *present perfect* drückt aus, dass etwas **irgendwann** geschehen ist. Daher stehen keine genauen Zeitangaben in *present perfect*-Sätzen. Aber das *present perfect* wird oft mit **unbestimmten Zeitangaben** verwendet:

already	schon, bereits
always	(schon) immer
before	(vorher) schon mal
just	gerade (eben), soeben
never	(noch) nie
not … yet	noch nicht
often	(schon) oft

Und in Fragen findest du oft:
ever?	jemals? / schon mal?
yet?	schon?

Diese Adverbien stehen direkt vor dem Verb.
❗ Ausnahmen: **before** und **yet** stehen am Satzende.

Hier zwei kleine Aufgaben zum *present perfect*:

a) Bring die Wörter in die richtige Reihenfolge.

1 Grandpa – has – just – the car – washed
2 We're hungry. We – haven't – yet – breakfast – had
3 Mum, Jenny – has – again – my T-shirt – taken
4 I've – Indian food – often – had. I like it a lot.

b) Vervollständige die Fragen.

1 Ryan's mum has just come back from New York. – And his dad? (he – come – back – yet?)
   Has he come back yet?
2 I've never eaten shark. What about you? (you – ever – eat – shark?)
3 Is this your first visit to London or (you – be – here – before?)
4 Hey, my mobile is missing. (Who – take – it?)
5 Why are you looking at me like that? (you – never – see – a boy with long hair – before?)

GF 10 Present perfect or simple past? *Present perfect oder simple past?*

Son: *I've checked your computer, Mum. It's OK now.*

Mum: *Thank you. **When did** you **do** it?*

Son: *I **checked** it **last night** when you were in bed.*

Has Grandma **phoned** yet?
– Yes, she **phoned** ten minutes ago. Everything's fine.

➡ p. 78, exercise 1

• **Present perfect:**
– wenn du sagen willst, **dass etwas (irgendwann) geschehen ist**
– wenn du fragen willst, **ob etwas geschehen ist**
Ein Zeitpunkt wird nicht genannt (er ist nicht wichtig oder nicht bekannt). Aber in *present perfect*-Sätzen stehen oft unbestimmte Zeitangaben wie *already, before, ever, just, never, not … yet, often, yet.*

• *Simple past:*
– wenn du sagen oder fragen willst, **wann etwas geschehen ist**
In *simple past*-Sätzen stehen oft genaue Zeitangaben wie *yesterday, last year, an hour ago, in 2012.*

Grammar File   Unit 4

GF 11 *some* and *any* and their compounds *some* und *any* und ihre Zusammensetzungen

a) some/any

+ I've made **some** biscuits. And there's **some** milk too.
  … ein paar Kekse …   … etwas Milch …

− I can't see **any** sheep. And there aren't **any** cows.
  … keine Schafe …   … keine Kühe …

? Are there **any** scones?
  Gibt es Scones?
  Do you have **any** questions?
  Habt ihr (irgendwelche) Fragen?

➡ p. 78, exercise 2

some/any

◂ **some** steht vor allem in **bejahten** Aussagesätzen (+). Es bedeutet „einige, ein paar" (*some scones/CDs/boys/…*) oder „etwas" (*some milk/money/music/…*).

◂ **any** steht vor allem in **verneinten** Aussagesätzen (−) und in **Fragen** (?).

❗ Im Deutschen kann man fragen „Gibt es Scones?", aber im Englischen steht meist *any*: *Are there any scones?*

b) somebody/anybody – something/anything

+ I think there's **someone** at the door.   jemand
− No, there isn't **anybody** there.   niemand
? Can you see **anyone**?   (irgend)jemand

+ Let's go and get **something** to eat.   etwas
− I'm too nervous. I can't eat **anything**.   nichts
? Is there **anything** I can do for you?   (irgend)etwas

➡ p. 78, exercise 3

somebody/anybody – something/anything

◂ Für die **Zusammensetzungen** mit *some* (*somebody/someone, something*) und *any* (*anybody/anyone, anything*) gelten dieselben Regeln.

Have you ever read anything about science?

c) Offers and requests

Would you like **something** to eat? **Some** chips perhaps?

No, thanks. But can I have **something** to drink? **Some** lemonade?

Angebote und Bitten

❗ In Fragen, mit denen man etwas **anbietet** oder um etwas **bittet**, verwendet man *some, somebody/someone, something*.

Hmmm, that soup smells delicious. Would you like some?

170 one hundred and seventy

Unit 5

GF 12 The *will*-future Das Futur mit *will*

a) Use

Next Saturday, you**'ll see** some tricks that I've never done before.
Nächsten Samstag werden Sie Kunststücke sehen, ...

When **will** the rehearsal **be** over? – Not till three.
Wann wird die Probe vorbei sein? – Nicht vor drei.

Maya probably **won't come** without Lucy.
Maya wird wahrscheinlich nicht ohne Lucy kommen.

It **will be** warm and sunny tomorrow.
Morgen wird es warm und sonnig (sein/werden).

Hurry, or we**'ll miss** the girls.
Beeil dich, sonst **verpassen** wir die Mädchen.

This evening I'm going to read a book about Dartmoor.

Gebrauch

Du verwendest das **Futur mit will**, um zu sagen, was in der Zukunft geschehen wird.
Das *will-future* steht oft mit Zeitangaben wie *tomorrow, next Saturday, soon, in a few weeks*.

◂ Wenn **Vermutungen** geäußert werden, steht häufig *I (don't) think, I'm (not) sure, maybe* oder *probably*.

◂ Oft geht es um Dinge, die man nicht beeinflussen kann, z.B. **Vorhersagen** über das Wetter.

◂ Im Deutschen benutzen wir oft das Präsens, wenn wir Vermutungen äußern oder Vorhersagen machen. Im Englischen steht das *will-future*.

❗ **Vorsicht** – wenn du über **Pläne** für die Zukunft sprichst, verwendest du *going to*, nicht *will*.
(Zum *going to*-future vgl. GF 5 auf den Seiten 162–163.)

b) Form

Spain **will be** warm and sunny in June.
I'm sure you**'ll like** it.

They're a very good team. I think they**'ll win**.

Will I **meet** Stella at your party on Friday?
– No, you **won't**. She **won't be** in Plymouth on Friday.

What **will** the weather **be** like at the weekend?

My sister **wants to** help us.   ... möchte/will uns helfen.
My sister **will** help us.   ... wird uns helfen.

➡ p. 87, exercises 1–3

Form

Das *will-future* besteht aus **will + Infinitiv**.
Es gibt für alle Personen nur eine Form.

Die **Kurzform** von *will* ist *'ll*: *I'll, you'll, he'll, she'll* usw.

Die **verneinte Form** von *will* heißt **won't** (Langform: *will not*).

❗ **Nicht verwechseln:**
• *I want to do* heißt „ich will tun", „ich möchte tun".
• *I will do* heißt „ich werde tun".

Das Futur mit *will*

Bejahte Aussagen	Verneinte Aussagen	Fragen
I'll/You'll/He'll/She'll/It'll go We'll/You'll/They'll go	I/You/He/She/It won't stay We/You/They won't stay	Will you/he/she/it/they go? – Yes, I/he/she/it/they will. / No, I/he/she/it/they won't.

Vervollständige diese Sätze mit *'ll* oder *will* sowie dem richtigen Verb aus dem Kasten.

1 Why don't you come and visit us! I'm sure you ... Berlin.
2 My brother ... 16 next month.
3 You don't know Ryan? Well, you ... him at my party next Friday.
4 I don't think you ... much money for your old computer.
5 There ... strong winds tomorrow, and we ... some rain in the afternoon.

be • be • get • have • like • meet

Grammar File   Unit 5

GF 13 EXTRA Question tags Frageanhängsel

a) Use

It's a lovely day, **isn't it?**
Schöner Tag, nicht wahr?

But we can play frisbee on our own, **can't we?**
Aber wir können ja allein Frisbee spielen, nicht?

You aren't nervous, **are you?**
Sie sind doch nicht nervös, oder?

Maya doesn't go to Plymstock School, **does she?**
Maya geht nicht auf die Plymstock School, nicht?

Gebrauch

Du kennst bereits das englische Frageanhängsel *right?*:
You're Amy, right?   „Du bist Amy, nicht wahr?"

◀ In den Beispielen links findest du weitere Frageanhängsel. Frageanhängsel werden häufig in der gesprochenen Sprache verwendet.

"…, **right?**" is a question tag too, **isn't it?**

It's a lovely day, **right?**

b) Form

	bejaht	verneint
	The bus stop **is** near here,	**isn't it?**
	I **can** go by bike,	**can't I?**
	The show **was** great,	**wasn't it?**
	We **saw** lots of street artists,	**didn't we?**

	verneint	bejaht
	The show **isn't** over now,	**is it?**
	He **can't** speak Chinese,	**can he?**
	The tickets **weren't** too expensive,	**were they?**
	They **don't** have Carnival in England,	**do they?**

➡ p. 88, exercise 6

Form

Diese Frageanhängsel bestehen aus **Hilfsverb** *(is, are, can, do, …)* + **Personalpronomen** *(I, you, she, we, …)*.

◀ Wenn der Aussagesatz bejaht ist, ist das Frageanhängsel verneint.

◀ Wenn der Aussagesatz verneint ist, ist das Frageanhängsel bejaht.

Ordne den Aussagen das richtige Frageanhängsel zu.

1 The juggler is really good, …
2 Stella sings really well, …
3 You're Olivia, …
4 You aren't from Plymouth, …
5 It can't be 4 o'clock already, …

A are you?
B aren't you?
C can it?
D doesn't she?
E isn't he?

GF 14 Conditional sentences (type 1) Bedingungssätze (Typ 1)

Sam: **If** you come at 10:30, you**'ll see** me in a really cool demonstration.
Wenn ihr um 10 Uhr 30 kommt, seht ihr mich … / werdet ihr mich … sehen.

Maya: **If** I don't meet Abby on Saturday, I **won't see** her till the summer holidays.
Wenn ich Abby nicht am Samstag treffe, dann sehe ich sie bis zu den Sommerferien nicht mehr.

Bedingungssätze bestehen aus zwei Teilen: einem **Nebensatz mit** *if* („wenn", „falls") und einem **Hauptsatz**.

Bedingungssätze (Typ 1) sind „**Was ist, wenn …**"-Sätze: Sie beschreiben, was unter bestimmten Bedingungen geschieht oder nicht geschieht.

Die Bedingung steht im *if*-Satz; der Hauptsatz sagt aus, was passiert, wenn die Bedingung erfüllt wird:

Bedingung	Folge für die Zukunft
If I practise hard,	I'll be better than ever.

Unit 6 Grammar File

if-Satz: simple present	Hauptsatz: *will*-future
If I **practise** hard,	I**'ll be** better than ever.

◀ Im *if*-Satz steht das *simple present*.
Im Hauptsatz steht meist das *will-future*.

Sam: *If you want a lift, you **can** come with us.*

*If you want to see Sam's kung fu group, you **should** be there at 10:30 / you **must** be there at 10:30.*

Come *at 10:30 if you want to see Sam's kung fu group.*

◀ Im Hauptsatz können auch *can, must, should* oder ein Imperativ stehen.

*Please ask Sam to phone me **when** you see him.*
... **wenn** *du ihn siehst.*
(Es steht schon fest, dass du ihn sehen wirst.)

*Please ask Sam to phone me **if** you see him.*
... **falls** *du ihn siehst.*
(Es ist noch nicht sicher, dass du ihn sehen wirst.)

❗ **Nicht verwechseln:**

- *when* heißt „sobald", „dann wenn".

- *if* heißt „wenn", „falls".

I'll be late if I don't hurry up now.

➡ pp. 91–92, exercises 1–5

Schreib die Sätze mit der richtigen Verbform in dein Übungsheft.
1 (**Do you help / Will you help**) me in the garden if you're free tomorrow?
2 If you (**don't have / won't have**) time, I (**ask / will ask**) Gavin.
3 If the weather (**is / will be**) good, we (**have / will have**) a party in the garden.
4 The party (**isn't / won't be**) the same if you (**don't come / won't come**).

Unit 6

GF 15 **The past progressive** Die Verlaufsform der Vergangenheit

It was 4 o'clock in the afternoon. The Plymstock kids were on their way back to Plymstock ...

*Lucy and Sam **were sitting** together. They **were reading** the King Arthur play.*

*Leo and Justin were behind them, but they **weren't listening**. What **were** they **doing**?*

***Were** they **playing** "I spy"? – No, they **weren't**.*

*Lucy **was feeding** the lambs when she **heard** a funny sound.*
Lucy war gerade dabei, die Lämmer zu füttern, als sie einen komischen Laut hörte.

Mit dem *past progressive* drückt man aus, dass jemand zu einem **bestimmten Zeitpunkt in der Vergangenheit gerade dabei** war, etwas zu tun, oder dass etwas **gerade im Gange** war.

Das *past progressive* wird mit **was/were + -ing-Form** des Verbs gebildet:

I **was playing** ... / You **were playing** ... /
He **was playing** ... / They **were playing** ...

Das *past progressive* wird oft verwendet, um zu beschreiben, was gerade vor sich ging, als etwas anderes passierte:

past progressive was gerade vor sich ging,	**simple past** als ...
I **was waiting** for the bus Ich wartete auf den Bus,	when my mobile **rang**. als mein Handy klingelte.

➡ pp. 106–107, exercises 1–3

Grammar File Unit 6

Welche Sätze drücken aus, dass jemand **gerade dabei** war, etwas zu tun?

1 At 7:30 yesterday evening Gavin was reading an adventure story.
2 Last weekend he read two detective stories.
3 Yesterday Stella played tennis with Olivia all afternoon.
4 Gavin and Ryan were playing football in the park when it suddenly started to rain.
5 My brother was watching a DVD when I came home.
6 On Saturday afternoon we stayed at home and watched the sports programme on TV.

GF 16 EXTRA Conditional sentences (type 2) Bedingungssätze (Typ 2)

Maya: **If** I **was** Miss Bell, I**'d choose** Justin as King Arthur. I **wouldn't choose** Sam.
Wenn ich Miss Bell wäre, würde ich Justin als König Arthur wählen. Ich würde nicht Sam wählen.

And **if** I **went** to Plymstock School, I**'d play** Guinevere.
Und wenn ich auf die Plymstock School ginge, würde ich Guinevere spielen.

if-Satz:	Hauptsatz:
simple past	would + infinitive
If I **met** a wizard,	I**'d be** scared.

If we went into town, we **could go** to the cinema.
Wenn wir in die Stadt fahren würden, könnten wir ins Kino gehen.

➡ p. 112, exercise 3

Bedingungssätze (Typ 2) sind „**Was wäre, wenn …**"-Sätze: Sie drücken aus, dass etwas nicht sehr wahrscheinlich oder sogar unmöglich ist:

1 **If** we **met** Sam in Plymouth, we**'d be** very excited.
2 **If** Britain **wasn't** an island, it **would be** easier to get there.

Es ist unwahrscheinlich, dass wir Sam treffen (Satz 1), und Großbritannien ist nun einmal eine Insel (Satz 2). Die Sprecher/innen drücken nur aus, was geschehen würde oder der Fall wäre, wenn …

◀ Im *if*-Satz steht das *simple past*.
Im Hauptsatz steht meist *would* + Infinitiv (Kurzform: 'd).

◀ Im Hauptsatz kann auch *could* („könnte") + Infinitiv stehen.

Welche Wörter gehören in welche Lücke?

1 If I went to Cornwall, I … Merlin's cave.
2 If we … more time, we could look at some more sights.
3 If you … a guide at Tintagel, you would have to wear a costume.
4 If I … his phone number, I could send him a text message.
5 If you … Plymouth, what would you do there?
6 If I was in Miss Bell's class, I … Sam and Justin.

A had
B knew
C would know
D would visit
E visited
F were

If it wasn't so noisy in the library, I wouldn't be so tired.

174 one hundred and seventy-four

Unit 6 Grammar File

GF 17 EXTRA Contact clauses Relativsätze ohne Relativpronomen

subject

1 Justin is the boy **who** **didn't feel** well.
  Justin ist der Junge, **der** sich nicht gut fühlte.

  Is that the bus **which** **goes** to Tintagel?
  Ist das der Bus, **der** nach Tintagel fährt?

object subject

2 Arthur is the boy **[who]** **Merlin** **wanted** to help.
  Arthur ist der Junge, **dem** **Merlin** helfen wollte.

  Is that the bus **[which]** **we** **have to** take?
  Ist das der Bus, **den** **wir** nehmen müssen?

Merlin is the character **Sam wants to play**.
(= … the character **who/that Sam wants to play**.)
Merlin ist die Figur, **die** Sam spielen möchte.

Merlin is the wizard **who** wants to save Arthur.
Merlin ist der Zauberer, **der** Arthur retten möchte.

➡ p. 112, exercise 4

Die Relativpronomen **who, which** und **that** sind entweder **Subjekt** oder **Objekt** des Relativsatzes:

1 In diesen Sätzen sind die Relativpronomen **Subjekt** des Relativsatzes. Sie stehen **direkt vor dem Verb**.

2 Hier sind die Relativpronomen **Objekt** des Relativsatzes. Danach folgt das Subjekt des Relativsatzes, und dann das Verb.

◀ Wenn das Relativpronomen **Objekt** des Relativsatzes ist, dann wird es oft weggelassen. (Im Deutschen ist das nicht möglich.) Relativsätze ohne Relativpronomen werden **contact clauses** genannt.

❗ **Vorsicht:**
Wenn das **Relativpronomen direkt vor dem Verb** steht, dann ist es Subjekt und **darf nicht weggelassen werden**.

In welchen Sätzen kannst du das **Relativpronomen** weglassen? Schreibe die Sätze als *contact clauses* in dein Heft.

1 I'd like to stay in touch with the girl **who** I met on the campsite.
2 Here are the DVDs **that** you wanted.
3 Are these the magazines **that** were on my desk?
4 Where's that book **which** John sent from England?
5 Mum, the woman **who** called this morning is on the phone again.

Grammatical terms (Grammatische Fachbegriffe)

adjective ['ædʒɪktɪv]	Adjektiv (Eigenschaftswort)	good, new, green, interesting, …
adverb ['ædvɜːb]	Adverb	today, there, outside, very, …
adverb of frequency ['friːkwənsi]	Häufigkeitsadverb	always, usually, often, sometimes, never
adverb of indefinite time [ɪn'defɪnət]	Adverb der unbestimmten Zeit	already, ever, just, never, before, yet, …
adverb of manner ['mænə]	Adverb der Art und Weise	nicely, happily, quietly, slowly, well, fast, …
article ['ɑːtɪkl]	Artikel	the, a, an
comparative [kəm'pærətɪv]	Komparativ (1. Steigerungsform)	older; more expensive
comparison [kəm'pærɪsn]	Steigerung	old – older – oldest; expensive – more expensive – most expensive
compound ['kɒmpaʊnd]	Zusammensetzung	somebody, anyone, something, …
conditional sentence [kən'dɪʃənl]	Bedingungssatz	If I see Sam, I'll tell him.
conjunction [kən'dʒʌŋkʃn]	Konjunktion	and, but, …; because, when, …
contact clause ['kɒntækt klɔːz]	Relativsatz ohne Relativpronomen	Here's the report **I've written**.

one hundred and seventy-five **175**

Grammar File

going to-future [ˈfjuːtʃə]	Futur mit *going to*	**I'm going to watch** TV tonight.
imperative [ɪmˈperətɪv]	Imperativ (Befehlsform)	Open your books. Don't talk.
infinitive [ɪnˈfɪnətɪv]	Infinitiv (Grundform des Verbs)	(to) open, (to) go, …
irregular verb [ɪˈreɡjələ]	unregelmäßiges Verb	(to) go – went – gone,
		(to) see – saw – seen, …
negative statement [ˈneɡətɪv]	verneinter Aussagesatz	I don't like oranges.
noun [naʊn]	Nomen, Substantiv	Justin, girl, man, time, name, …
object [ˈɒbdʒɪkt]	Objekt	Justin has **a new camera**.
object question	Objektfrage,	**Who did** Mrs Pascoe **invite** to tea?
	Frage nach dem Objekt	
past participle [ˌpɑːst ˈpɑːtɪsɪpl]	Partizip Perfekt	checked, phoned, tried, gone, eaten, …
past progressive [ˌpɑːst prəˈɡresɪv]	Verlaufsform der Vergangenheit	Olivia **was playing** cards.
personal pronoun [ˌpɜːsənl ˈprəʊnaʊn]	Personalpronomen (persönliches Fürwort)	I, you, he, she, it, we, they; me, you, him, her, it, us, them
plural [ˈplʊərəl]	Plural, Mehrzahl	
positive statement [ˈpɒzətɪv]	bejahter Aussagesatz	I like oranges.
possessive determiner [pəˌzesɪv dɪˈtɜːmɪnə]	Possessivbegleiter (besitzanzeigender Begleiter)	my, your, his, her, its, our, their
possessive form [pəˌzesɪv ˈfɔːm]	s-Genitiv	Sam's sister, the Blackwells' house, …
preposition [ˌprepəˈzɪʃn]	Präposition	after, at, in, into, near, next to, …
present perfect [ˌpreznt ˈpɜːfɪkt]	*present perfect*	We**'ve made** some scones for you.
present progressive [ˌpreznt prəˈɡresɪv]	Verlaufsform der Gegenwart	Olivia **is playing** cards.
pronoun [ˈprəʊnaʊn]	Pronomen (Fürwort)	
question tag [ˈkwestʃn tæɡ]	Frageanhängsel	isn't he?, are you?, can't we?, …
question word [ˈkwestʃn wɜːd]	Fragewort	who?, what?, when?, where?, how?, …
regular verb [ˈreɡjələ]	regelmäßiges Verb	(to) help – helped, (to) look – looked, …
relative clause [ˌrelətɪv ˈklɔːz]	Relativsatz	I like teachers **who laugh a lot**.
relative pronoun [ˌrelətɪv ˈprəʊnaʊn]	Relativpronomen	who – which – that
short answer [ˌʃɔːt ˈɑːnsə]	Kurzantwort	Yes, I am. / No, we don't. / …
simple past [ˌsɪmpl ˈpɑːst]	einfache Form der Vergangenheit	Olivia **played** cards last Friday.
simple present [ˌsɪmpl ˈpreznt]	einfache Form der Gegenwart	Olivia **plays** cards every Friday evening.
singular [ˈsɪŋɡjələ]	Singular, Einzahl	
statement [ˈsteɪtmənt]	Aussage(satz)	
sub-clause [ˈsʌbklɔːz]	Nebensatz	I like Plymouth **because I like the sea**.
subject [ˈsʌbdʒɪkt]	Subjekt	**Justin/He** has a new camera.
subject question	Subjektfrage, Frage nach dem Subjekt	**Who invited** the Coopers to tea?
superlative [suˈpɜːlətɪv]	Superlativ (2. Steigerungsform)	(the) oldest; (the) most expensive
verb [vɜːb]	1. Verb;	go, help, look, see, …
	2. Prädikat	Reading **can be** fun.
will-future [ˈfjuːtʃə]	Futur mit *will*	I'm sure you**'ll like** the new maths teacher.
yes/no question	Entscheidungsfrage	Are you 14? Do you like oranges?

Lösungen der Grammar-File-Aufgaben

p.157
1 Justin **went** to Boston in the school holidays. He **didn't go** to New York.
2 He **didn't see** an elephant – he **saw** a bear.
3 Sam **didn't stay** in a hotel – he **stayed** in a caravan.
4 Maya and Lucy **didn't make** a cake with Lucy's grandma – they **made** scones.

p.158
1 **Where did** Abby go in the summer holidays?
2 **Did** Abby go sailing with Tim?
3 **What did** Sam do in Weston-super-Mare?
4 **When did** Sam phone Justin's home?
5 **Did** Sam phone Justin's mobile?

p.160
1 Maya **doesn't go** to Plymstock School, she **goes** to Coombe Dean.
2 And Maya's brother Mukesh? **Does** he **go** to Coombe Dean too? – No, he **doesn't**.
3 Mukesh and Maya's cousins **don't live** in Britain. Where **do** they **live**?
4 Morph **doesn't live** in a hotel. He **lives** in the school library.
5 Morph **doesn't like** the cat. He **hides** between the books when the cat is in the library.
6 The Blackwells **have** a nice house in Wembury. – How many children **do** they **have**?

176   one hundred and seventy-six

Grammar File

p. 161
1 Leo knows Lucy. –
   A Who knows Lucy?
   B Who does Leo know?
2 Mrs Pascoe tells Holly about her plans. –
   A Who tells Holly about her plans?
   B Who does Mrs Pascoe tell about her plans?
3 Lucy wanted to meet Sam. –
   A Who wanted to meet Sam.
   B Who did Lucy want to meet?
4 In the afternoon, Lucy talked to Sam. –
   A Who talked to Sam in the afternoon?
   B Who did Lucy talk to in the afternoon?

p. 162
1 I **go** to volleyball training two evenings every week.
2 I usually **go** by bike, but today it**'s raining**, so Dad **is taking** me to the gym in our car.
3 Next Saturday, we**'re playing** against last year's best team. I'm excited already.
4 My brother **doesn't do** any sport. But he **plays** the guitar in a band. They **meet** every Friday.
5 Right now, my brother **is practising** in his room. But he**'s playing** too loud.
6 Next month he and his band **are giving** a concert in the gym.
7 Everybody **is looking** forward to that.

p. 163
1 Sam **is going to play** in the school team again this year.
2 And Justin? **Is** he **going to join** the basketball team?
3 Leo **is not going to join** the Basketball Club.
4 A man **is going to visit** Leo's parents later this afternoon.
5 And the girls? What **are** they **going to do** this year?

p. 164
1 Monty is **as old as** Sandy. Rex is **older than** Monty and Sandy. Rex is **the oldest**.
2 The cat is **faster than** the hamster. The horse is **the fastest**.
3 The mobile is **as expensive as** the MP3 player. The TV is **more expensive than** the MP3 player. The computer is **the most expensive**.

p. 165
1 Let's go to the stall **which/that** sells those nice T-shirts and tops.
2 "Look, Lucy, there's the assistant **who/that** sold you the felt pens at Smith's."
3 We should ask somebody **who/that** lives here and knows the place.
4 What do you call that maths thing **which/that** looks like a triangle?
5 You don't know what a satnav is? It's the thing in the car **which/that** tells you the way.

p. 167/1
1 We sailed **slowly** down the river.
2 The football match got more interesting after a very **slow** start.
3 Suddenly there was a **loud** BANG and the lights went out.
4 Suddenly somebody sneezed **loudly**.
5 She looked **nervously** at her watch. It was almost too late now.
6 She always plays with her hair when she's **nervous**.
7 I slept very **badly** last night.
8 I always take an umbrella in **bad** weather.

p. 167/2 **1 been, 5 eaten, 6 done, 9 fallen**

p. 169 a)
1 Grandpa has just washed the car.
2 … We haven't had breakfast yet.
3 Mum, Jenny has taken my T-shirt again.
4 I've often had Indian food. …

p. 169 b)
1 … And his dad? **Has he come back yet?**
2 … **Have you ever eaten shark?**
3 Is this your first visit to London or **have you been here before?**
4 … **Who's (Who has) taken it?**
5 … **Have you never seen a boy with long hair before?**

p. 171
1 Why don't you come and visit us! I'm sure you**'ll like** Berlin.
2 My brother **will be** 16 next month.
3 You don't know Ryan? Well, you**'ll meet** him at my party next Friday.
4 I don't think you**'ll get** much money for your old computer.
5 There **will be** strong winds tomorrow, and we **will have** some rain in the afternoon.

p. 172 **1E, 2D, 3B, 4A, 5C**

p. 173
1 **Will** you **help** me in the garden if you're free tomorrow?
2 If you **don't have** time, I'll ask Gavin.
3 If the weather **is** good, we**'ll have** a party in the garden.
4 The party **won't be** the same if you **don't come**.

p. 174/1 **Sätze 1, 4, 5**

p. 174/2 **1D, 2A, 3F, 4B, 5E, 6C**

p. 175 **Sätze 1, 2, 4:**
1 I'd like to stay in touch with the girl I met on the campsite.
2 Here are the DVDs you wanted.
4 Where's that book John sent from England?

one hundred and seventy-seven **177**

Vocabulary

Das **Vocabulary** (S. 178 – 207) enthält alle Wörter und Wendungen deines Englischbuches, die du lernen musst. Sie stehen in der Reihenfolge, in der sie im Buch zum ersten Mal vorkommen.

Hier siehst du, wie das **Vocabulary** aufgebaut ist:

Diese Zahl gibt die **Seite** an, auf der die Wörter zum ersten Mal vorkommen.
p. 14 = Seite 14

Die **Lautschrift** zeigt dir, wie ein Wort ausgesprochen wird. Eine Übersicht über alle **Lautschriftzeichen** findest du auf S. 249. Die Lautschriftzeichen stehen auch unten auf den **Vocabulary**-Seiten.

Eingerückte Wörter lernst du am besten zusammen mit dem vorausgehenden Wort, weil die beiden zusammengehören.

Diese **Kästen** solltest du dir immer besonders gut ansehen: Hier sind Vokabeln zu einem bestimmten Thema zusammengestellt. Oder du erfährst mehr über ein Wort und wie es verwendet wird.

Das **rote Ausrufezeichen** bedeutet: Vorsicht, hier macht man leicht Fehler!

Dies ist das „Gegenteil"-Zeichen: **happy** ist das Gegenteil von **unhappy**.

Tipps zum Wörterlernen findest du im **Skills File** auf den Seiten 145 und 146.

Im **Vocabulary** werden folgende **Abkürzungen** verwendet:

p. = page (Seite)   pp. = pages (Seiten)
sth. = something (etwas)   sb. = somebody (jemand)
jn. = jemanden   jm. = jemandem
pl = plural (Mehrzahl)
infml = informal (umgangssprachlich)
(F) = verwandtes Wort im Französischen
(L) = verwandtes Wort im Lateinischen

Wenn du **nachschlagen** möchtest, was ein englisches Wort bedeutet oder wie man es ausspricht, dann verwende das **English – German Dictionary** auf den Seiten 208 – 228. Und wenn du vergessen hast, wie etwas auf Englisch heißt, dann kann dir das **German – English Dictionary** auf den Seiten 229 – 246 eine erste Hilfe sein.

178   one hundred and seventy-eight

[iː] green · [i] happy · [ɪ] big · [e] red · [æ] cat · [ɑː] class · [ɒ] song ·
[ɔː] door · [uː] blue · [ʊ] book · [ʌ] mum · [ɜː] girl · [ə] a partner

Unit 1 Vocabulary

Unit 1   In the holidays

pp. 8/9 **stop** [stɒp]	Halt; Station, Haltestelle	The first **stop** on our walk was after 15 kilometres. Get off the bus at the fifth **stop**.
camping [ˈkæmpɪŋ]	Camping, Zelten	We went **camping** in France last summer.
world [wɜːld]	Welt	*English:* the best beach **in the world** *German:* der beste Strand **der Welt** / **auf** der Welt
sunny [ˈsʌni]	sonnig	
mountain [ˈmaʊntən]	Berg	(F) la montagne (L) *mons, montis*
beautiful [ˈbjuːtɪfl]	schön	Her face isn't just nice – it's **beautiful**.
alone [əˈləʊn]	allein	Did you go camping **alone**? – No, I went with Dad.
Say hello to … for me.	Grüß … von mir.	*… And say hello to your brother for me.*
wave [weɪv]	Welle	
weather [ˈweðə]	Wetter	
cloudy [ˈklaʊdi]	bewölkt	**clouds**
cloud [klaʊd]	Wolke	It's **cloudy**.
caravan [ˈkærəvæn]	Wohnwagen	(F) la caravane
fun park	Vergnügungspark	
windy [ˈwɪndi]	windig	It's **windy**. **wind**
wind [wɪnd]	Wind	
project [ˈprɒdʒekt]	Projekt	❗ Betonung: **project** [ˈprɒdʒekt] (F) le projet
I can't wait to see …	Ich kann es kaum erwarten, … zu sehen.	James Bond is great. **I can't wait** to see the next film.
rainforest [ˈreɪnfɒrɪst]	Regenwald	
forest [ˈfɒrɪst]	Wald	(F) la forêt
rain [reɪn]	Regen	
(to) rain [reɪn]	regnen	It's **raining**. **rain**
plant [plɑːnt]	Pflanze	(F) la plante
message [ˈmesɪdʒ]	Nachricht	(F) le message

Part A

p. 10 **phone call** [ˈfəʊn kɔːl] (*kurz auch:* **call**)	Anruf; Telefongespräch	*Hello.*
(to) phone sb. [fəʊn]	jn. anrufen	*Hello Mrs Palmer. It's Tim here. Can I speak to Ryan, please?*
(to) answer the phone	ans Telefon gehen	
(to) be in	zu Hause sein	
(to) be out	nicht zu Hause sein, nicht da sein	
(to) leave a message [ˌliːv‿ə ˈmesɪdʒ], *simple past:* **left** [left]	eine Nachricht hinterlassen	*Sorry, Tim. He's not in. Do you want to leave a message?*

[eɪ] **name** · [aɪ] **time** · [ɔɪ] **boy** · [əʊ] **old** ·
[aʊ] **town** · [ɪə] **here** · [eə] **where** · [ʊə] **tour**

one hundred and seventy-nine   **179**

Vocabulary   Unit 1

holiday ['hɒlədeɪ]	Urlaub	*English:* (to) be **on holiday** / (to) go **on holiday** *German:* **in Urlaub** sein / **in Urlaub** fahren
What was it like?	Wie war es?	We went to Spain this summer. – **What was it like?**
at first [ət 'fɜːst]	zuerst, anfangs, am Anfang	What was the weather like? – It was very cold and windy **at first**. Then later it was hot and sunny.
race [reɪs]	Rennen	a bike race
two days **ago** [ə'gəʊ]	vor zwei Tagen	*English:* **two days / five minutes / a year ago** *German:* **vor** zwei Tagen / fünf Minuten / einem Jahr
country ['kʌntri]	Land *(Staat)*	Germany is a big **country** in the middle of Europe.
building ['bɪldɪŋ]	Gebäude	buildings
tomorrow [tə'mɒrəʊ]	morgen	Can you call me back **tomorrow** morning? *English:* **tomorrow morning** *German:* **morgen früh**
(to) **bring** [brɪŋ], *simple past:* **brought** [brɔːt]	(mit-, her)bringen	

> **German "bringen"**
> (to) **bring** = **mitbringen, herbringen**
> **Bring** me the paper, Max.
> (to) **take** = **wegbringen, hinbringen**
> And now **take** it to Dad.

if [ɪf]	wenn, falls	❗ **if** you see them **wenn/falls** du sie siehst **when** you see them **wenn/sobald** du sie siehst
p. 11 **revision** [rɪ'vɪʒn]	Wiederholung *(des Lernstoffs)*	
p. 12 **Hold on a minute.** [ˌhəʊld ˈ'ɒn] **(**oft auch kurz: **Hold on.)**	Bleib / Bleiben Sie am Apparat. *(am Telefon)*	
p. 13 (to) **make notes (on** sth.) [nəʊts]	(sich) Notizen machen (über/zu etwas) *(zur Vorbereitung)*	
crib sheet ['krɪb ʃiːt] *(infml)*	Spickzettel, Merkzettel	

Part B

p. 14 **neighbour** ['neɪbə]	Nachbar/in	
tea [tiː]	*leichte Nachmittags- oder Abendmahlzeit*	❗ Das Wort **tea** bedeutet nicht nur „Tee". In Großbritannien wird es auch für eine leichte Nachmittags- oder Abendmahlzeit verwendet, die meist aus Sandwiches oder Keksen oder Kuchen und Tee besteht.
Love, ...	Alles Liebe, ... / Liebe Grüße, ... *(Briefschluss)*	

180   one hundred and eighty

[b] **b**oat · [p] **p**ool · [d] **d**ad · [t] **t**en · [g] **g**ood · [k] **c**at · [m] **m**um · [n] **n**o · [ŋ] so**ng** · [l] **h**ello · [r] **r**ed · [w] **w**e · [j] **y**ou

Unit 1   Vocabulary

Who did you tell?	Wem hast du es erzählt?	
Who does Sam know?	Wen kennt Sam?	

> **Who …?**
> 1. **Wer** …?   **Who** likes Abby?   – Maya.
> 2. **Wen** …?   **Who does** Maya like? – Abby.
> 3. **Wem** …?   **Who did** Maya help? – Abby.

for example [fər_ɪgˈzɑːmpl]	zum Beispiel	I like ball games … basketball, **for example**. Ⓕ l'exemple *(m)* Ⓛ exemplum, i
surprise [səˈpraɪz]	Überraschung	A present? For me? That's a nice **surprise**! Ⓕ la surprise
still [stɪl]	trotzdem, dennoch	It wasn't very warm, but we **still** went swimming. ❗ **still** = 1. (immer) noch; 2. trotzdem
this afternoon/evening/…	heute Nachmittag/Abend/…	Can we meet at 4 o'clock **this afternoon**?
(to) move (to) [muːv]	umziehen (nach)	The Bennetts **moved to** Plymouth last year. Ⓛ movere
son [sʌn]	Sohn	
daughter [ˈdɔːtə]	Tochter	
already [ɔːlˈredi]	schon, bereits	Are you going **already**? Can't you stay?
sure [ʃʊə], [ʃɔː]	sicher	She's so clever. I'm **sure** she knows the answer. Can I have your pen? – Yes, **sure**.
(to) invite sb. **(to)** [ɪnˈvaɪt]	jn. einladen (zu)	Can I **invite** all my friends **to** my birthday party? Ⓕ inviter Ⓛ invitare
ever [ˈevə]	jemals	Do you **ever** go to museums? – Yes, sometimes.
p. 15 **Lucky you.** [ˈlʌki]	Du Glückspilz.	
(to) be lucky	Glück haben	❗ Sie **hatte Glück**. = She was **lucky**. Sie **war glücklich**. = She was **happy**.
(to) look after sb.	auf jn. aufpassen; sich um jn. kümmern	Sam often has to **look after** his little sister after school.
(to) be allowed to do sth. [əˈlaʊd]	etwas tun dürfen	**Are** you **allowed to** watch TV on Sunday mornings? I **wasn't allowed to** go to Sue's party last Friday.
(to) hit [hɪt], *simple past:* **hit**	schlagen	A big boy **hit** me on the nose.
(to) roll [rəʊl]	rollen	The ball **rolled** down the hill.
out [aʊt]	heraus, hinaus, nach draußen	The weather is nice. Let's go **out** and play football.
prize [praɪz]	Preis, Gewinn	❗ **prize** [praɪz] = Preis *(den man gewinnt)* **price** [praɪs] = (Kauf-)Preis *(den man bezahlt)* Ⓕ le prix
Here you are.	Bitte sehr. / Hier bitte.	Can you give me that pen, please? – **Here you are**.
…, right?	…, nicht wahr?	You're Amy, **right**? My name is Tim, and this is Ryan.
p. 17 **(to) mean** [miːn], *simple past:* **meant** [ment]	bedeuten	I don't know this word. What does it **mean**?
subject [ˈsʌbdʒekt]	Subjekt	In the sentence *Lucy phoned her mum*, "Lucy" is the **subject** and "her mum" is the **object**. Ⓕ le sujet, l'objet *(m)*
object [ˈɒbdʒekt]	Objekt	
p. 18 **(to) get in touch (with** sb.**)** [tʌtʃ]	(mit jm.) Kontakt aufnehmen; sich (mit jm.) in Verbindung setzen	If you come to Plymouth, **get in touch with** me.

[f] **f**ather · [v] ri**v**er · [s] **s**ister · [z] plea**s**e · [ʃ] **sh**op · [ʒ] televi**s**ion ·
[tʃ] **t**eacher · [dʒ] **G**ermany · [θ] **th**anks · [ð] **th**is · [h] **h**ere

one hundred and eighty-one   **181**

Vocabulary   Unit 1

(to) **stay in touch (with** sb.**)**	(mit jm.) Kontakt halten; (mit jm.) in Verbindung bleiben	My grandpa and his best friend **stayed in touch** for over 50 years.
text message ['tekst mesɪdʒ] (*kurz auch:* **text**)	SMS	
free	kostenlos	We don't have to buy tickets. The show is **free**. ❗ **free** = **1.** frei; **2.** kostenlos
rule [ruːl]	Regel, Vorschrift	Football is fun because its **rules** are so easy.
host family ['həʊst fæməli]	Gastfamilie	
p.19 **meaning** ['miːnɪŋ]	Bedeutung	
context ['kɒntekst]	(Text-, Satz-)Zusammenhang, Kontext	What does 'get' mean? – It has lots of meanings. Show me the word in **context**.
must [mʌst]	müssen	There's somebody at the door. – That **must** be Uncle Bob.
similar (to sth./sb.**)** ['sɪmələ]	(etwas/jm.) ähnlich	Their eyes are **similar** but their noses are different. Ⓕsimilaire Ⓛsimilis, e

Part C

p.20 (to) **walk/run/sail/… on**	weitergehen/-laufen/-segeln/…	He saw me but he didn't stop and just walked **on**.
just like … ['dʒʌst laɪk]	genau wie …	*You look just like your father.*
(to) **be/feel bored** [bɔːd]	gelangweilt sein, sich langweilen	❗ The film was **boring**. **langweilig** I was **bored**. **gelangweilt**
term [tɜːm]	Trimester	The school year in Britain has three **terms**.
boarding school ['bɔːdɪŋ skuːl]	Internat	
shocked [ʃɒkt]	schockiert, entsetzt	
outdoor ['aʊtdɔː]	Außen-, im Freien	**outdoor** activities; an **outdoor** swimming pool
(to) **climb** [klaɪm]	klettern; hinaufklettern (auf)	❗ Aussprache – das „b" wird nicht gesprochen: **climb** [klaɪm] *English:* (to) **climb** a tree *German:* **auf** einen Baum **klettern**
(to) **look forward to** sth. ['fɔːwəd]	sich auf etwas freuen	I'm really **looking forward to** the summer holidays.
tear [tɪə]	Träne	❗ Aussprache: **tear** [tɪə] **tears**
p.21 **unhappy** [ʌn'hæpi]	unglücklich	🙂 **happy** ◄► **unhappy** 🙁
p.22 **future** ['fjuːtʃə]	Zukunft; zukünftige(r, s)	❗ Betonung: <u>future</u> ['fjuːtʃə] Ⓕle futur Ⓛfuturus
p.23 **jacket** ['dʒækɪt]	Jacke, Jackett	
pocket ['pɒkɪt]	Tasche (*Manteltasche, Hosentasche usw.*)	
litter bin ['lɪtə bɪn]	Abfalleimer	

[iː] green · [i] happy · [ɪ] big · [e] red · [æ] cat · [ɑː] class · [ɒ] song · [ɔː] door · [uː] blue · [ʊ] book · [ʌ] mum · [ɜː] girl · [ə] a partner

182   one hundred and eighty-two

Unit 1   Vocabulary

My USA logbook

p. 24	**apartment** [əˈpɑːtmənt]	Wohnung	❗ In den USA verwendet man nur **apartment**. In GB werden **flat** und **apartment** benutzt. Ⓕ l'appartement (m)
	screen [skriːn]	Bildschirm	
	fries (pl) [fraɪz] (American English)	Pommes frites	❗ American English (AE): **fries** British English (BE): **chips** [tʃɪps]
	(to) wash the dishes (pl) [ˌwɒʃ ðə ˈdɪʃɪz]	das Geschirr abwaschen, spülen	They're **washing the dishes**.
	to [tu], [tə]	um zu	We went out **to** play football.
	(to) land [lænd]	landen; an Land gehen	
	land [lænd]	Land	
	right now [raɪt ˈnaʊ]	jetzt gerade	I can't help you **right now**, I have to wash the dishes.

> **right**
> | 1. Three points for the **right** answer. | richtig | 2. **Right now** I'm in the library. | jetzt gerade |
> |---|---|---|---|
> | I think you**'re right**. | … du hast Recht. | Where's Sue? – **Right behind** you. | direkt hinter …, |
> | It's really big, **right**? | …, nicht wahr? | | genau hinter … |
> | **All right**, I'm wrong. You win. | OK / In Ordnung, … | He arrived **right after** the teacher. | gleich nach … |

	(to) order [ˈɔːdə]	bestellen	We went into the café and **ordered** sandwiches.
	pancake [ˈpænkeɪk]	Pfannkuchen, Eierkuchen	
	outside Rosie's Diner [ˌaʊtˈsaɪd]	vor *Rosie's Diner*; außerhalb von *Rosie's Diner*	❗ outside = 1. draußen; nach draußen 2. vor …; außerhalb von …
	campsite [ˈkæmpsaɪt]	Zeltplatz	a campsite right next to a river
	next to [ˈnekst tʊ]	neben	
	tent [tent]	Zelt	
	rocky [ˈrɒki]	felsig, steinig	
	shadow [ˈʃædəʊ]	Schatten	shadow
p. 25	**fire** [ˈfaɪə]	Feuer	
	(to) look up [lʊk_ˈʌp]	hochsehen, aufschauen	
	sky [skaɪ]	Himmel	
	(to) be asleep [əˈsliːp]	schlafen	❗ Wenn man mit **schlafen** meint, dass jemand **nicht wach ist**, benutzt man **be asleep**. Vergleiche: • It was 11 o'clock, but Emma **was** still **asleep**. • My dog Max usually **sleeps** next to my bed.
	torch [tɔːtʃ]	Taschenlampe	a torch
	so that … (*oft auch kurz:* **so …**)	sodass, damit	Dad gave me some money **so (that)** I could go to the cinema.
	wild [waɪld]	wild	❗ Aussprache: **wild** [waɪld]
	again and again	immer wieder	

[eɪ] **name** · [aɪ] **time** · [ɔɪ] **boy** · [əʊ] **old** ·
[aʊ] **town** · [ɪə] **here** · [eə] **where** · [ʊə] **tour**

one hundred and eighty-three   **183**

Vocabulary   Unit 2

(to) **turn** sth. **off** [ˌtɜːn_ˈɒf]	etwas ausschalten	(to) **turn** sth. **on** ◄► (to) **turn** sth. **off**
(to) **give** sb. **a hug** [hʌg]	jn. umarmen	
this time	dieses Mal	❗ **time** = **1.** Zeit; Uhrzeit; **2.** Mal
my **own** film/room/… [əʊn]	mein eigener Film / mein eigenes Zimmer / …	❗ Do you have **your own room**? (*nicht:* ~~an own room~~)
memory [ˈmeməri]	Erinnerung	My dad lived in Berlin twenty years ago. He says he has very nice **memories** of the city. Ⓕ la mémoire Ⓛ memoria, ae

Unit 2   A school day

pp. 28/29

this year's musical	das diesjährige Musical	**last year's** musical – **this year's** musical – **next year's** musical
audition [ɔːˈdɪʃn]	Vorsprechen, Vorsingen, Vorspielen	

call – caller, dance – dancer, …

(to) **call**	anrufen	**caller**	Anrufer/in	(to) **run**	laufen	**runner**	Läufer/in
(to) **dance**	tanzen	**dancer**	Tänzer/in	(to) **shop**	einkaufen	**shopper**	(Ein-)Käufer/in
(to) **fight**	kämpfen	**fighter**	Kämpfer/in	(to) **sing**	singen	**singer**	Sänger/in
(to) **help**	helfen	**helper**	Helfer/in	(to) **speak**	sprechen, reden	**speaker**	Sprecher/in, Redner/in
(to) **listen**	zuhören	**listener**	Zuhörer/in				
(to) **read**	lesen	**reader**	Leser/in	(to) **work**	arbeiten	**worker**	Arbeiter/in

(to) **queue** [kjuː]	Schlange stehen, sich anstellen	They're **queuing** in front of the cinema.
(to) **ring** [rɪŋ], *simple past:* **rang** [ræŋ]	klingeln, läuten	Listen. I think the phone is **ringing**.
(to) **call out the names**	die Namen aufrufen	
article [ˈɑːtɪkl]	Artikel	There's an **article** about Plymstock in the paper. ❗ Betonung: **article** [ˈɑːtɪkl] Ⓕ l'article (m)

Part A

p. 30

earphones (pl) [ˈɪəfəʊnz]	Ohrhörer, Kopfhörer	**earphones**
I'**m going to** sing a song.	Ich werde ein Lied singen. / Ich habe vor ein Lied zu singen.	
by … [baɪ]	von …	*We are the champions* is a song **by** Queen.
nervous [ˈnɜːvəs]	nervös, aufgeregt	❗ Betonung: **nervous** [ˈnɜːvəs] Ⓕ nerveux, se
a bit [ə ˈbɪt]	ein bisschen, etwas	Can you turn on the light? It's **a bit** dark.
You **should** … [ʃʊd], [ʃəd]	Du solltest … / Ihr solltet …	You have a great voice. You **should** sing in a band.
side [saɪd]	Seite	How can we get to the other **side** of the river?
a few [ə ˈfjuː]	ein paar, einige	We didn't have much money, just **a few** pounds.
present [ˈpreznt]	Gegenwart	the **past** – the **present** – the **future** Ⓕ le présent Ⓛ praesens, sentis
dialogue [ˈdaɪəlɒg]	Dialog	❗ Betonung: **dialogue** [ˈdaɪəlɒg] Ⓕ le dialogue

p. 31

184   one hundred and eighty-four

[b] **b**oat · [p] **p**ool · [d] **d**ad · [t] **t**en · [g] **g**ood · [k] **c**at ·
[m] **m**um · [n] **n**o · [ŋ] so**ng** · [l] **h**ello · [r] **r**ed · [w] **w**e · [j] **y**ou

Unit 2 Vocabulary

Part B

p. 32	(to) **get ready (for)** [ˈredi]	sich fertig machen (für); sich vorbereiten (auf)	It's 6:30. Get up and **get ready for** school.
	mine [maɪn]	meiner, meine, meins	Is that Ryan's pencil? – No, it isn't. It's **mine**.
	worksheet [ˈwɜːkʃiːt]	Arbeitsblatt	
	(the) longest ... [ˈlɒŋgɪst]	der/die/das längste ...; am längsten	Grandma wears the **longest** dresses in our family. **long** – **longer** – **longest**
	(to) **label** [ˈleɪbl]	beschriften; etikettieren	
	label	Beschriftung; Schild, Etikett	
	large [lɑːdʒ]	groß	
	(to) **get on** [ˌget ˈɒn]	vorankommen, zurechtkommen	How are you **getting on** with your task? – OK, but it's a bit hard.
	(to) **mean** [miːn], simple past: **meant** [ment]	meinen, sagen wollen	❗ (to) **mean** = 1. bedeuten – What does 'tent' **mean**? 2. meinen, sagen wollen – I don't understand. What do you **mean**?
	(not) as big **as** [æz], [əz]	(nicht) so groß wie	
	bigger **than** [ðæn], [ðən]	größer als	
	(to) **get** sth.	(sich) etwas besorgen, (sich) etwas holen	Can you go to the market and **get** some oranges?

> **(to) get,** *simple past:* **got**
> 1. **bekommen** Did you **get** nice birthday presents?
> 2. **besorgen, holen** Can you **get** the tickets for the match?
> 3. **gelangen, (hin)kommen** How can we **get** to the other side?
> 4. **werden** My parents **get** angry when I'm late.
>
> **Remember:**
> (to) **get on** — vorankommen, zurechtkommen
> (to) **get on/off (the bus)** — ein-/aussteigen
> (to) **get ready** — sich fertig machen
> (to) **get up** — aufstehen

	ours [ˈaʊəz]	unserer, unsere, unseres	Dad, that's not our car! **Ours** is green.
	awful [ˈɔːfl]	schrecklich, fürchterlich	
p. 33	**mistake** [mɪˈsteɪk]	Fehler	
	square kilometre (sq km) [skweə]	Quadratkilometer (km²)	
p. 34	**tall** [tɔːl]	groß (Person); hoch (Gebäude, Baum)	

> **German "groß"**
>
> **big, large** **big** und **large** sind oft austauschbar: a **big**/**large** family; a **big**/**large** lake
>
> **large** wird in der Regel nicht verwendet, um Menschen zu beschreiben. a very **big** man
>
> **tall** **tall** benutzt man, wenn es um die Größe von Personen (und Tieren) oder die Höhe von Gebäuden, Bäumen u.Ä. geht.

a **tall** man

[f] father · [v] river · [s] sister · [z] please · [ʃ] shop · [ʒ] television ·
[tʃ] teacher · [dʒ] Germany · [θ] thanks · [ð] this · [h] here

Vocabulary   Unit 2

(the) earth [ɜːθ] (oft auch: **Earth**)	(die) Erde (der Planet)	*English:* **on earth** *German:* **auf der** Erde
about [əˈbaʊt]	ungefähr	There were **about** 300 people in the park.
plane [pleɪn]	Flugzeug	*English:* **on the plane** *German:* **im** Flugzeug
p.35 (to) **read aloud** [əˈlaʊd]	laut (vor)lesen	
(to) **make sure that** …	sich vergewissern, dass …; darauf achten, dass …; dafür sorgen, dass …	Please **make sure that** you turn off the light when you leave the room.
everything [ˈevriθɪŋ]	alles	**everything ◄► nothing**
(to) **pause** [pɔːz]	innehalten, pausieren; eine Pause einlegen	She **paused** a moment before she answered my question.
scared [skeəd]	verängstigt	❗ The film **was scary**. … **war unheimlich, gruselig.** I was **scared**. Ich **war verängstigt.** / Ich **hatte Angst.**

Punctuation [ˌpʌŋktʃuˈeɪʃn] (Zeichensetzung)

.	**full stop** [ˌfʊl ˈstɒp]	Punkt	?	**question mark** [ˈkwestʃən mɑːk]		Fragezeichen
,	**comma** [ˈkɒmə]	Komma	!	**exclamation mark** [ˌekskləˈmeɪʃn mɑːk]		Ausrufezeichen
:	**colon** [ˈkəʊlən]	Doppelpunkt	-	**hyphen** [ˈhaɪfən]		Bindestrich

(to) **change** [tʃeɪndʒ]	(ver)ändern; sich (ver)ändern	She **changes** her hair colour all the time. Ⓕ changer

Part C

pp. 36/37 **brilliant** [ˈbrɪliənt]	großartig, genial, glänzend	He's only 16 and he's already a **brilliant** footballer.
yours [jɔːz]	deiner, deine, deins; eurer, eure, eures	*Are these yours?* *No, they're hers.*
hers [hɜːz]	ihrer, ihre, ihrs	

Possessivpronomen (Possessive pronouns)

I	**my** dog	**mine**	meiner, meine, meins		we	**our** cat	**ours**	unserer, unsere, unseres
you	**your** dog	**yours**	deiner, deine, deins		you	**your** cat	**yours**	eurer, eure, eures
he	**his** dog	**his**	seiner, seine, seins		they	**their** cat	**theirs**	ihrer, ihre, ihrs
she	**her** dog	**hers**	ihrer, ihre, ihrs					

lovely [ˈlʌvli]	schön, hübsch, herrlich	We had **lovely** weather last week. It was warm and sunny every day.
even [ˈiːvn]	sogar	Everybody tried to help, **even** the children. The River Thames is very long, but the River Severn is **even** longer. (= … sogar noch länger)
more beautiful **(than)** [mɔː]	schöner (als)	Do you think Olivia is **more beautiful than** Stella?
(the) most beautiful [məʊst]	der/die/das schönste …; am schönsten	I think this village is **the most beautiful** place in Britain.
so far	bis jetzt; bis hierher	What's the book like? – **So far** it's really interesting.
stage [steɪdʒ]	Bühne	The band went on **stage** and started to play.

186   one hundred and eighty-six

[iː] green · [i] happy · [ɪ] big · [e] red · [æ] cat · [ɑː] class · [ɒ] song · [ɔː] door · [uː] blue · [ʊ] book · [ʌ] mum · [ɜː] girl · [ə] a partner

Unit 2   Vocabulary

on my/your/their/… own [əʊn]	allein	Ryan didn't want to dance, so I danced **on my own**. The cake looks great. Did you make it **on your own**?
talented [ˈtæləntɪd]	begabt, talentiert	❗ Betonung: **ta**lented [ˈtæləntɪd]
(to) **cheer** [tʃɪə]	jubeln	
(to) **clap** [klæp]	(Beifall) klatschen	*English:* **Clap your hands** if you like it. *German:* **Klatscht in die Hände** …
p.38 **theatre** [ˈθɪətə]	Theater	❗ Betonung: **the**atre [ˈθɪətə] Ⓕ le théâtre Ⓛ theatrum, i
concert [ˈkɒnsət]	Konzert	❗ Betonung: **con**cert [ˈkɒnsət] Ⓕ le concert
recorder [rɪˈkɔːdə]	Blockflöte	a **recorder**
syllable [ˈsɪləbl]	Silbe	Ⓕ la syllabe Ⓛ syllaba, ae
fashion [ˈfæʃn]	Mode	
round the world [raʊnd]	um die Welt	
town hall [ˌtaʊn ˈhɔːl]	Rathaus	
snow [snəʊ]	Schnee	
p.39 **whose?** [huːz]	wessen?	**Whose** shoe is this? – It's mine.
paw [pɔː]	Pfote, Tatze	
stairs *(pl)* [steəz]	Treppe; Treppenstufen	upstairs stairs *Come upstairs, please.* upstairs downstairs
p.40 What **could** be better? [kʊd], [kəd]	Was könnte besser sein?	What can we do this evening? – Well, we **could** watch a DVD or go to the cinema. ❗ **could** = 1. konnte(n); 2. könnte(n)
clear [klɪə]	klar, deutlich	Ⓕ clair, e Ⓛ clarus
size [saɪz]	Größe	It's a nice dress, but it's not the right **size**. It's too big.
correct [kəˈrekt]	richtig, korrekt	Ⓕ correct, e Ⓛ rectus
like this	so	Do it **like this**: take a pencil and a ruler, then …
p.41 (to) **lie** [laɪ], *simple past:* **lay** [leɪ]	liegen	❗ -ing form: **lying** Why are you **lying** on the road?
(to) **wake** sb. **up** [ˌweɪk ˈʌp], *simple past:* **woke up** [ˌwəʊk ˈʌp]	jn. (auf)wecken	Can you **wake** me **up** at 6 tomorrow morning?
shy [ʃaɪ]	schüchtern, scheu	Come on, don't be **shy**. Go and ask them.

Disco night

42/43 (to) **stick** sth. **into** sth. [stɪk], *simple past:* **stuck** [stʌk]	etwas in etwas stechen, stecken	He **stuck** his hand into the box and took out some biscuits.
fork [fɔːk]	Gabel	spoon teaspoon
knife [naɪf], *pl* **knives** [naɪvz]	Messer	knife
spoon [spuːn]	Löffel	fork

[eɪ] name · [aɪ] time · [ɔɪ] boy · [əʊ] old ·
[aʊ] town · [ɪə] here · [eə] where · [ʊə] tour

one hundred and eighty-seven   **187**

Vocabulary   Unit 3

(to) **drop** sth. [drɒp]	etwas fallen lassen	Be careful. Don't **drop** that bottle.
drama ['drɑːmə]	Schauspiel; darstellende Kunst	
gel [dʒel]	Gel	❗ Aussprache: **gel** [dʒel]
sunglasses (pl) ['sʌnglɑːsɪz]	(eine) Sonnenbrille	❗ **glasses** und **sunglasses** sind Pluralwörter!
glasses (pl) ['glɑːsɪz]	(eine) Brille	English: I need my **glasses**. Where **are they**? German: I brauche meine **Brille**. Wo **ist sie**?
arm [ɑːm]	Arm	
flash [flæʃ]	Lichtblitz	
(to) **shake** [ʃeɪk], simple past: **shook** [ʃʊk]	schütteln	English: "No," he said and **shook his** head. German: „Nein", sagte er und **schüttelte den** Kopf.
(to) **beep** [biːp]	piepen	
(to) **wish** [wɪʃ]	wünschen	English: I **wish** it **was** warmer. German: Ich **wünschte**, es **wäre** wärmer.
(to) **stand** [stænd], simple past: **stood** [stʊd]	stehen; sich (hin)stellen	*Stand on the chair, Tom.* Now Tom is standing on the chair.
most people / **most of them** [məʊst]	die meisten Menschen / die meisten von ihnen	**Most** children like hamsters and rabbits.
one by one	einer nach dem anderen	She ate all the biscuits, **one by one**.
except [ɪk'sept]	außer, bis auf	Open daily except Sundays
good-looking [ˌgʊd'lʊkɪŋ]	gutaussehend	
Anyway, ... ['eniweɪ]	Jedenfalls, ... / Wie dem auch sei, ... / Aber egal, ...	Is Justin's dad American? – I'm not sure. **Anyway**, he lives in the United States now. Sorry, I still don't agree with you. **Anyway**, let's stop talking about it.

Unit 3   Out and about

pp. 46/47	**out and about**	unterwegs	post office roundabout
	opposite ['ɒpəzɪt]	gegenüber (von)	
	post office ['pəʊst ˌɒfɪs]	Postamt	
	station ['steɪʃn]	Bahnhof	church
	church [tʃɜːtʃ]	Kirche	
	roundabout ['raʊndəbaʊt]	Kreisverkehr	station
	on the corner of Church Road **and** London Road	Church Road, Ecke London Road	**The post office is opposite the church.**
	(to) **cross** [krɒs]	überqueren, kreuzen; sich kreuzen	Don't **cross** the road here. It's too dangerous. The two roads **cross** in the town centre.

188   one hundred and eighty-eight

[b] **b**oat · [p] **p**ool · [d] **d**ad · [t] **t**en · [g] **g**ood · [k] **c**at ·
[m] **m**um · [n] **n**o · [ŋ] so**ng** · [l] **h**ello · [r] **r**ed · [w] **w**e · [j] **y**ou

Unit 3 Vocabulary

(to) **turn left/right** [left], [raɪt]	(nach) links/rechts abbiegen	(F) tourner à gauche / à droite

> **left – right**
> Do you write with your **left** hand or your **right** hand?
> I think we have to turn **left/right** here.
> I looked **left** and **right** but I couldn't see my friends.
>
> **On the left**, you can see Morris, my cat.
> My dog Alice is **on the right**.
>
> Schreibst du mit der **linken** oder mit der **rechten** Hand?
> Ich glaube, wir müssen hier **(nach) links/rechts** abbiegen.
> Ich sah **nach links** und **nach rechts**, aber …
>
> **Links/Auf der linken Seite** …
> **Rechts/Auf der rechten Seite** …

straight on [streɪt ˈɒn]	geradeaus weiter	The station? Turn left here, and then go **straight on**.
past [pɑːst]	vorbei (an), vorüber (an)	Walk **past** the post office and turn right.
Excuse me, … [ɪkˈskjuːz miː]	Entschuldigung, … / Entschuldigen Sie, …	(F) Excusez-moi, … (L) excusare

> **"Entschuldigung"**
> • **Excuse me, …** sagt man, wenn man jemanden anspricht,
>   z. B. wenn man um eine Auskunft bittet.
>
> • **Sorry, …** sagt man, wenn man sich für etwas
>   entschuldigen möchte.
>
> **Excuse me,** what's the time, please?
> **Excuse me,** does this bus go to Plymouth?
>
> You're late, Stella. — **I'm sorry.** I missed the bus.
> Can you come at three o'clock? — **Sorry,** I can't.

(to) **tell** sb. **the way (to …)**	jm. den Weg (nach …) beschreiben	Excuse me, can you **tell me the way to** the station?
(to) **ask** sb. **the way**	jn. nach dem Weg fragen	I don't know where we are. Let's **ask somebody the way**.
visitor [ˈvɪzɪtə]	Besucher/in, Gast	(F) le visiteur, la visiteuse

Part A

48/49 **pedestrian zone** [pəˈdestrɪən zəʊn]	Fußgängerzone	
after [ˈɑːftə]	nachdem	❗ **after** = 1. nach – **after** school 2. nachdem – **after** I came home **before** ◄► **after**
just after …	gleich nachdem …; kurz nachdem …	It started to rain **just after** we came home.
(to) **cost** [kɒst], *simple past:* **cost**	kosten	How much did your new computer **cost**?
(to) **close** [kləʊz]	schließen, zumachen	(to) **close** ◄► (to) **open**
chocolate [ˈtʃɒklət]	Praline	❗ **chocolate** = 1. Schokolade; 2. Praline
(to) **need to do** sth. [niːd]	etwas tun müssen	You don't **need to** feed the cats. I fed them this morning. (= You don't have to feed the cats.)
flower [ˈflaʊə]	Blume; Blüte	(F) la fleur
stall [stɔːl]	(Markt-)Stand	I bought some T-shirts at a **stall** at the market.
city [ˈsɪti]	Stadt, Großstadt	
plastic [ˈplæstɪk]	Plastik, Kunststoff	
felt pen [ˌfelt ˈpen]	Filzstift	
as [æz], [əz]	als, während	Everybody cheered **as** the band went on stage.

[f] father · [v] river · [s] sister · [z] please · [ʃ] shop · [ʒ] television ·
[tʃ] teacher · [dʒ] Germany · [θ] thanks · [ð] this · [h] here

one hundred and eighty-nine **189**

Vocabulary   Unit 3

cash desk [ˈkæʃ desk]	Kasse *(in Geschäften)*	
shop assistant [ˈʃɒp_əˌsɪstənt] (*kurz auch:* **assistant**)	Verkäufer/in	shop assistant cash desk
set [set]	Satz, Set	
Have you got …? [gɒt]	Haben Sie …? / Hast du …? / Habt ihr …?	

> **German "haben"**
> Im *simple present* wird oft **have got** für das deutsche „haben" verwendet:
> Kurzformen: I**'ve got**, you**'ve got**, we**'ve got**, they**'ve got**
>   he**'s got**, she**'s got**, it**'s got**
>
> My grandparents **have got** a dog.
> We **haven't got** a dog.
> **Have** you **got** a dog?
> – Yes, I **have**. / No, I **haven't**.
>
> ❗ Vorsicht im *simple past*! Nicht ~~had got~~:
>
> When I was little I **had** a hamster.
> **Did** you **have** a hamster when you were little?
> – Yes, I **did**. / No, I **didn't**.

	change [tʃeɪndʒ]	Wechselgeld	
p. 50	(to) **know about** sth.	sich mit etwas auskennen; über etwas Bescheid wissen	Now we **know about** relative clauses.
p. 52	**gram** [græm]	Gramm	
	packet [ˈpækɪt]	Packung, Päckchen	
	tin [tɪn]	Dose	

a bottle of …, a packet of …

a bottle of milk · a packet of biscuits · a plate of chips · a tin of soup · a basket of fruit · a kilo of oranges · 200 grams of cheese

	juice [dju:s]	Saft	(F) le jus
	tomato [təˈmɑːtəʊ], *pl* **tomatoes**	Tomate	(F) la tomate
	sock [sɒk]	Socke	
p. 53	(to) **scan a text** [skæn]	einen Text schnell nach bestimmten Wörtern/Informationen absuchen	
	souvenir [ˌsuːvəˈnɪə]	Andenken, Souvenir	(F) le souvenir

Part B

p. 54	**magic** [ˈmædʒɪk]	magisch, Zauber-	Do you know the story of Aladdin and his **magic** lamp? (F) magique
	(to) **make** sb. sth.	jn. zu etwas machen	"We're going to **make** you a star," the people at the film studio said.
	(to) **fight** sb. [faɪt], *simple past:* **fought** [fɔːt]	jn. bekämpfen; gegen jn. kämpfen	The farmer had to **fight** the rats on his farm.
	just then	genau in dem Moment; gerade dann	At three o'clock we wanted to go swimming, and **just then** it started to rain.

190   one hundred and ninety

[iː] green · [i] happy · [ɪ] big · [e] red · [æ] cat · [ɑː] class · [ɒ] song · [ɔː] door · [uː] blue · [ʊ] book · [ʌ] mum · [ɜː] girl · [ə] a partner

Unit 3   Vocabulary

he shook his head **slowly** ['sləʊli]	er schüttelte langsam den Kopf	❗ • adjective: **slow** – We took a **slow** bus through the mountains. • adverb: **slowly** – The bus travelled **slowly** through the mountains.
wall [wɔːl]	Mauer; Wand	That **wall** is too high. We can't climb it. Every room has four **walls**. Ⓛ vallum
in a loud voice	mit lauter Stimme	*English:* He always speaks **in a loud voice**. *German:* Er spricht immer **mit lauter Stimme**.
good	brav	If you're a **good** boy, you can have an ice cream. ❗ **good** = **1.** gut – a **good** book/film/story **2.** brav – a **good** boy/girl/dog
responsible [rɪ'spɒnsəbl]	verantwortlich	Ⓕ responsable
well [wel]	gut	❗ • adjective: **good** – She has a **good** voice. • adverb: **well** – She sings **well**.
(to) **worry (about)** ['wʌri]	sich Sorgen machen (wegen, um)	My dad **worries about** me if I come home late.
(to) **happen (to)** ['hæpən]	geschehen, passieren (mit)	Your face is black. What **happened to** you?
p.55 (to) **describe** sth. **(to** sb.**)** [dɪ'skraɪb]	(jm.) etwas beschreiben	*English:* **Describe** the picture **to your group**. *German:* **Beschreibe** das Bild **deiner Gruppe**. Ⓕ décrire qc. (à qn.) Ⓛ describere
irregular [ɪ'regjələ]	unregelmäßig	**regular ◄► irregular** Ⓕ (ir)régulier, ère
p.56 **topic** ['tɒpɪk]	Thema, Themengebiet	This is a great article on an interesting **topic**.
(to) **hang** [hæŋ], *simple past:* **hung** [hʌŋ]	hängen	**Hang** the best posters on your classroom wall.
(to) **highlight** ['haɪlaɪt]	hervorheben, markieren *(mit Textmarker)*	
(to) **underline** [ˌʌndə'laɪn]	unterstreichen	
draft [drɑːft]	Entwurf	

Master Wu and the magic book

p.58 **broken** ['brəʊkən]	zerbrochen, kaputt; gebrochen	a **broken** plate a **broken** arm
that's why	deshalb, darum	Oliver was sick. **That's why** he didn't come to school.
gate [geɪt]	Tor, Pforte, Gatter	*I have to cut my hair.*
Cut! [kʌt]	Schnitt! *(beim Filmen)*	
(to) **cut** [kʌt], *simple past:* **cut**	schneiden	
(to) **disappear** [ˌdɪsə'pɪə]	verschwinden	Ⓕ disparaître
up here	hier oben; nach hier oben	"I'm **up here**, on the wall," she shouted. **up here ◄► down there**
roof [ruːf]	Dach	
view (of) [vjuː]	Aussicht, Blick (auf)	We had a great **view of** the area from the roof of the building. Ⓕ la vue
shore [ʃɔː]	Ufer *(eines Sees)*, Strand	
(to) **whisper** ['wɪspə]	flüstern	"I think there's a ghost in the house," he **whispered**.

[eɪ] name · [aɪ] time · [ɔɪ] boy · [əʊ] old ·
[aʊ] town · [ɪə] here · [eə] where · [ʊə] tour

one hundred and ninety-one   **191**

Vocabulary   Unit 4

further [ˈfɜːðə]	weiter	Berlin is **further** from London than Essen. **far** – **further** – **furthest** weit – weiter – am weitesten
p.59 **hole** [həʊl]	Loch	a **hole** in my shoe
up to	bis (zu)	Read **up to** the third paragraph, please. After three days of rain, the water came **up to** the windows of their house.
waist [weɪst]	Taille	
the only … [ˈəʊnli]	der/die/das einzige …; die einzigen…	Jennifer and Julie are **the only** twins in our class.
wood [wʊd]	Holz	
(to) **hurry** [ˈhʌri]	eilen; sich beeilen	It was cold and windy so we **hurried** to the car. **Hurry (up)**, we haven't got much time.
thanks to Maya	dank Maya	We had a great holiday **thanks to** the sunny weather.
lip [lɪp]	Lippe	
(to) **hug** sb. [hʌg]	jn. umarmen	She **hugged** me when I told her the good news.
(to) **rescue** [ˈreskjuː]	retten	I fell into the river, but a dog came and **rescued** me.

Unit 4   On Dartmoor

p.66 **background** [ˈbækgraʊnd]	Hintergrund	There are two boys in the **foreground**. In the **background**, you can see a lake.
foreground [ˈfɔːgraʊnd]	Vordergrund	
at the bottom (of) [ˈbɒtəm]	unten, am unteren Ende (von)	Now do the exercises **at the bottom of** the page. **at the top (of)** ◄► **at the bottom (of)**
countryside [ˈkʌntrisaɪd]	Landschaft, ländliche Gegend	The **countryside** in Devon and Cornwall is beautiful.
(to) **begin** [bɪˈgɪn], *simple past:* **began** [bɪˈgæn]	beginnen, anfangen	(to) start
field [fiːld]	Feld, Acker, Weide	*English:* **in** the field – *German:* **auf** dem Feld
footprint [ˈfʊtprɪnt]	Fußabdruck	
foot [fʊt], *pl* **feet** [fiːt]	Fuß	**two feet** **footprints in the sand**
grass [grɑːs]	Gras; Rasen	
mist [mɪst]	(leichter) Nebel, Dunst(schleier)	
pony [ˈpəʊni]	Pony	❗ Aussprache: **pony** [ˈpəʊni]
valley [ˈvæli]	Tal	Ⓕ la vallée Ⓛ valles
p.67 **cow** [kaʊ]	Kuh	
sheep, *pl* **sheep** [ʃiːp]	Schaf	**cow** **goat** **three sheep**
goat [gəʊt]	Ziege	
etc. (et cetera) [etˈsetərə]	usw. (und so weiter)	We need a lot of things for the sandwiches: bread, cheese, tomatoes, **etc.**
poem [ˈpəʊɪm]	Gedicht	Ⓕ le poème

192   one hundred and ninety-two

[b] **boat** · [p] **pool** · [d] **dad** · [t] **ten** · [g] **good** · [k] **cat** ·
[m] **mum** · [n] **no** · [ŋ] **song** · [l] **hello** · [r] **red** · [w] **we** · [j] **you**

Unit 4   Vocabulary

Part A

p.68	**twice** [twaɪs]	zweimal	
	once [wʌns]	einmal	**once** (1x) – **twice** (2x) – **three times** (3x)
	not ... anybody/anyone ['enɪbɒdi, 'eniwʌn]	niemand	I think there's somebody in the garden. – It's too dark. I ca**n't** see **anybody**.
	over there	da drüben, dort drüben	
	told [təʊld]	3. Form (Partizip Perfekt) von „tell"	❗ Die dritte Form des Verbs nennt man **Partizip Perfekt** (Englisch: *past participle*).
	just [dʒʌst]	gerade (eben), soeben	I'm new in Hamburg. I've **just** moved here.
	made [meɪd]	Partizip Perfekt von „make"	

Irregular past participles

(to) **be**	was/were	**been** [biːn]	sein		(to) **eat**	ate	**eaten** ['iːtn]	essen
(to) **break**	broke	**broken** ['brəʊkən]	(zer)brechen; kaputt machen/gehen		(to) **fall**	fell	**fallen** ['fɔːlən]	(hin)fallen, stürzen
					(to) **go**	went	**gone** [gɒn]	gehen; fahren
(to) **come**	came	**come** [kʌm]	kommen		(to) **have**	had	**had** [hæd]	haben
(to) **do**	did	**done** [dʌn]	machen, tun		(to) **hide**	hid	**hidden** ['hɪdn]	(sich) verstecken
					(to) **see**	saw	**seen** [siːn]	sehen

➡ List of irregular verbs, pp. 248–249

	not ... anything ['eniθɪŋ]	nichts	You should eat something. – I'm too nervous. I ca**n't** eat **anything** right now.
	anybody? / anyone?	(irgend)jemand?	Do you know **anybody** who can help me with this?
	(to) look around (the farm)	sich (auf der Farm) umsehen	
	hay [heɪ]	Heu	
	key [kiː]	Schlüssel	

before

1. vor	Wash your hands **before** lunch.
2. bevor	Wash your hands **before** we eat.
3. (vorher) schon mal	I've seen the film **before**. I don't want to watch it again.
	Have you been to England **before**, or is this your first visit?
4. (vorher) noch nie	I've never eaten crab meat **before**. It's nice.

	(to) own [əʊn]	besitzen	❗ She **owns** (*besitzt*) her **own** (*eigenes*) home.
	moor [mɔː], [mʊə]	Hochmoor	
	once/twice **a week/year**	einmal/zweimal pro Woche/Jahr	We love Indian food. We have it about twice **a month**.
p.69	**that way** [weɪ]	dort entlang; in die Richtung	We have to go **this way** (*hier entlang*), not **that way** (*dort entlang*).
	mud [mʌd]	Schlamm, Matsch	
	(to) leave sth. [liːv]**, left, left**	etwas übrig lassen	Don't eat all the biscuits. **Leave** some for me, please.

(to) leave, left, left

1. lassen	Don't **leave** the windows open when you go.	4. verlassen	It's sad: Mike's mum wants to **leave** his dad.
2. übrig lassen	Don't you think we should **leave** some scones for Mum and Dad?		I took my bag and **left** the room.
3. zurücklassen	You shouldn't **leave** your dog in the car when you go shopping.	5. (weg)gehen; abfahren	Get your jacket. We're **leaving**. When does the bus to Plymouth **leave**?

---

[f] **f**ather · [v] ri**v**er · [s] **s**ister · [z] plea**s**e · [ʃ] **sh**op · [ʒ] televi**s**ion ·
[tʃ] **t**eacher · [dʒ] **G**ermany · [θ] **th**anks · [ð] **th**is · [h] **h**ere

one hundred and ninety-three   **193**

Vocabulary   Unit 4

bath [bɑːθ]	Bad	*English:* (to) **have a bath** / (to) **take a bath** *German:* **baden, ein Bad nehmen**

p.70

Irregular past participles

(to) **bring**	brought	**brought** [brɔːt]	(mit-, her)bringen	(to) **take**	took	**taken** ['teɪkən]	(mit)nehmen; (weg-, hin)bringen
(to) **buy**	bought	**bought** [bɔːt]	kaufen				
(to) **feed**	fed	**fed** [fed]	füttern	(to) **throw**	threw	**thrown** [θrəʊn]	werfen
(to) **hear**	heard	**heard** [hɜːd]	hören	(to) **wake up**	woke up	**woken up** ['wəʊkən]	aufwachen
(to) **meet**	met	**met** [met]	(sich) treffen				
(to) **run**	ran	**run** [rʌn]	rennen, laufen	(to) **win**	won	**won** [wʌn]	gewinnen
➡ *List of irregular verbs, pp. 248–249*				(to) **write**	wrote	**written** ['rɪtn]	schreiben

Oh dear! [dɪə]	Oje!	**Oh dear**, English has lots of irregular past participles.

Part B

p.72

lamb [læm]	Lamm	❗ Aussprache – das „b" wird nicht gesprochen: **lamb** [læm]

barn [bɑːn]	Scheune	
bacon ['beɪkən]	Schinkenspeck	
egg [eg]	Ei	
a glass (of) [glɑːs]	ein Glas	On Sundays, I always have **bacon** and **eggs** and a **glass of** orange juice for breakfast.

Verb + Adverb	Verb + Adjektiv
Wie du weißt, verwendet man **Adverbien der Art und Weise**, um zu sagen, **wie jemand etwas tut**:	Nach Verben wie **feel, sound, look, smell, taste** stehen **Adjektive**, denn hier geht es nicht darum, wie jemand etwas tut, sondern darum, **wie jemand oder etwas ist**:
She shouted **angrily** at me. *Sie schrie mich wütend an.* He looked around **nervously**. *Er sah sich nervös um.* Messi plays **fantastically**. *Messi spielt fantastisch.*	She felt **angry** and a bit **sad**. *Sie fühlte sich wütend und ein bisschen traurig.* He sounded/looked **nervous**. *Er klang nervös / sah nervös aus.* The soup smelled/tasted **fantastic**. *Die Suppe roch/schmeckte fantastisch.*

delicious [dɪ'lɪʃəs]	köstlich, lecker	The pizza looked **delicious**, but it tasted very funny. (F) délicieux, se (L) deliciae
Have you ever **been to** …?	Bist du jemals in … gewesen?	❗ • Has she ever **been to** Italy? – Oh yes, many times. *War sie schon mal in Italien?* … • Has she **gone to** Italy? – Yes, she has. She's in Rome right now. *Ist sie nach Italien gefahren?* …
Have you … **yet?** [jet]	Hast du schon …?	❗ **yet** = 1. *(in Fragen)* **schon**: Have you done your homework **yet**? 2. *(in Verneinungen)* **noch nicht**: I'm hungry. I have**n't** had breakfast **yet**.
I'd love to …	Ich würde sehr gern …	**I'd love to** look at the lambs now.
dirty ['dɜːti]	schmutzig	**dirty** ◄► **clean**
a pair (of) [peə]	ein Paar	a pair of trainers a pair of walking boots
boot [buːt]	Stiefel	

---

194   one hundred and ninety-four

[iː] green · [i] happy · [ɪ] big · [e] red · [æ] cat · [ɑː] class · [ɒ] song ·
[ɔː] door · [uː] blue · [ʊ] book · [ʌ] mum · [ɜː] girl · [ə] a partner

Unit 4   Vocabulary

(to) **lose** [luːz], **lost, lost** [lɒst]	verlieren	(to) **lose money / a job** ◄► (to) **find money / a job** (to) **lose a match** ◄► (to) **win a match**
strong [strɒŋ]	stark, kräftig	
anything?	(irgend)etwas?	Do you know **anything** about sheep farming?
sweet [swiːt]	süß	
heavy [ˈhevi]	schwer *(von Gewicht)*	❗ • a **heavy** box – eine **schwere** Kiste • a **hard** exercise – eine **schwere** Übung
one more photo [mɔː]	noch ein Foto; ein weiteres Foto	We need **two more** photos and **one more** article for our school magazine.
quick [kwɪk]	schnell	I had a **quick** bath after football.
(to) **be missing** [ˈmɪsɪŋ]	fehlen	Almost all my friends were at the party. Only Olivia **was missing**.

---

p. 73

Irregular past participles

(to) **choose**	**chose**	**chosen** [ˈtʃəʊzn]	(aus)wählen	(to) **ride**	**rode**	**ridden** [ˈrɪdn]	reiten; *(Rad)* fahren
(to) **drink**	**drank**	**drunk** [drʌŋk]	trinken				
(to) **find**	**found**	**found** [faʊnd]	finden	(to) **sell**	**sold**	**sold** [səʊld]	verkaufen
(to) **hit**	**hit**	**hit** [hɪt]	schlagen	(to) **show**	**showed**	**shown** [ʃəʊn]	zeigen
(to) **read** [riːd]	**read**	**read** [red]	lesen	(to) **sleep**	**slept**	**slept** [slept]	schlafen

➡ *List of irregular verbs, pp. 248–249*

---

p. 74 (to) **mark** sth. **up** [ˌmɑːk ˈʌp]	etwas markieren, kennzeichnen	
p. 75 (to) **decide** [dɪˈsaɪd]	beschließen, sich entscheiden	We **decided** to do a project about Dartmoor. Ⓕ décider Ⓛ decidere
(to) **be interested (in)** [ˈɪntrəstɪd]	interessiert sein (an), sich interessieren (für)	❗ an **interesting** book **interessant** I'm **interested** in history. **interessiert an**
waterfall [ˈwɔːtəfɔːl]	Wasserfall	
train [treɪn]	Zug	I met two boys from Italy **on the train** to Berlin. (… **im** Zug nach Berlin)
(to) **take** [teɪk], **took** [tʊk], **taken** [ˈteɪkən]	*(Zeit)* brauchen; dauern	The bus to the station only **takes** ten minutes. It **takes** about 15 minutes to get to school.
stamp [stæmp]	Stempel	

Part C

p. 76 **everywhere** [ˈevriweə]	überall	Oh no, look what you've done! Now there's water **everywhere**!
for ever [fər ˈevə]	(für) immer; ewig	I hope Simon arrives soon. We can't wait **for ever**.
for miles [maɪlz]	meilenweit	1 **mile** = 1.6 kilometres
(to) **hurt, hurt, hurt** [hɜːt]	schmerzen, wehtun; verletzen	**hurt** 1. **schmerzen** My feet/These shoes **hurt**. I need a break. 2. **verletzen** I **hurt my foot** in a tennis match. 3. **verletzt** Look, that man is **hurt**. We have to help him.
not … any more	nicht mehr	The Greens don't live here **any more**. They're in London now.

[eɪ] n**a**me · [aɪ] t**i**me · [ɔɪ] b**oy** · [əʊ] **o**ld ·
[aʊ] t**ow**n · [ɪə] h**ere** · [eə] wh**ere** · [ʊə] t**our**

one hundred and ninety-five   **195**

Vocabulary   Unit 4

across the moor/the street [əˈkrɒs]	(quer) über das Moor/die Straße	He ran **across** the road in front of a very fast car.
impossible [ɪmˈpɒsəbl]	unmöglich	It's **impossible** to run a mile in two minutes.
(to) **pass** sth./sb. [pɑːs]	an etwas/jm. vorbeigehen/ vorbeifahren	I **pass** 14 shops every morning on my way to school.
path [pɑːθ]	Pfad, Weg	
raincoat [ˈreɪnkəʊt]	Regenmantel	
coat [kəʊt]	Mantel	
until [ənˈtɪl]	bis	We watched TV **until** 11 pm last night. Let's go inside **until** the rain is over.
(to) **cry** [kraɪ]	schreien; weinen	Someone **cried** "Help!" from an upstairs window. "Oh dear, are you hurt? Don't **cry**, I can help you."
p. 77 **jigsaw** [ˈdʒɪgsɔː]	Puzzle	
verse [vɜːs]	Vers, Strophe	(L) versus, us
p. 78 **otter** [ˈɒtə]	Otter	
(to) **train** [treɪn]	trainieren	
deer, pl **deer** [dɪə]	Reh, Hirsch	
p. 79 **adder** [ˈædə]	Kreuzotter	

an **otter**
an **adder**
deer

The tulip garden

p. 80 **tulip** [ˈtjuːlɪp]	Tulpe	(F) la tulipe
adventure [ədˈventʃə]	Abenteuer	(F) l'aventure (f)
(to) **nod** [nɒd]	nicken	English: "Yes," she said and **nodded her** head. German: „Ja", sagte sie und **nickte mit dem** Kopf. (to) **nod** your head ◄► (to) shake your head
(to) **wander** [ˈwɒndə]	herumlaufen; herumirren	We **wandered** through the town and looked at the old buildings.
cocoa [ˈkəʊkəʊ]	Kakao	
both [bəʊθ]	beide	Do you want to buy **both** T-shirts?
fireplace [ˈfaɪəpleɪs]	Kamin	
a mug (of) [mʌg]	ein Becher	I love a **mug of** hot cocoa when it's cold outside.
ruin [ˈruːɪn]	Ruine	(F) la ruine
ground [graʊnd]	(Erd-)Boden	❗ **ground** = Erdboden − **floor** = Fußboden

196   one hundred and ninety-six

[b] **b**oat · [p] **p**ool · [d] **d**ad · [t] **t**en · [g] **g**ood · [k] **c**at ·
[m] **m**um · [n] **n**o · [ŋ] so**ng** · [l] **h**ello · [r] **r**ed · [w] **w**e · [j] **y**ou

Unit 4 Vocabulary

pretty [ˈprɪti]	hübsch	
cottage [ˈkɒtɪdʒ]	Häuschen, Cottage	a pretty **English cottage**

full (of) [fʊl]	voll	Parts of Devon are **full of** tourists in the summer.
one night/day	eines Nachts/Tages	**One night** our cat went out and never came back.
(to) **believe** [bɪˈliːv]	glauben	That can't be true! I don't **believe** it!
kind [kaɪnd]	freundlich, nett	
p. 81 (to) look **closely** [ˈkləʊsli]	genau hinschauen	"Is there really a bird in that tree? I can't see it." – "Yes, just look more **closely**."
honour [ˈɒnə]	Ehre	Ⓕ l'honneur (m) Ⓛ honor, is
a **nearby** town [ˈnɪəbaɪ]	eine nahegelegene Stadt	

> **(to) move**
> The Greens have **moved to** London.
> And the Browns want to **move** too.
> The Greens **moved into** a nice house in Richmond.
> When did they **move in**?
>
> Die Greens sind **nach** London **(um)gezogen**.
> Und die Browns wollen auch **umziehen**.
> Die Greens sind **in** ein schönes Haus in Richmond **(ein)gezogen**.
> Wann sind sie **eingezogen**?

instead [ɪnˈsted]	stattdessen	I don't want to go swimming. Can't we go sailing **instead**?
not … either [ˈaɪðə], [ˈiːðə]	auch nicht	I'm not going to Sue's party. – I'm **not** going **either**. My sister doesn't like zoos, and I do**n't either**.
fence [fens]	Zaun	
around … [əˈraʊnd]	um … (herum)	

> **around**
> 1. herum…/ umher… — We <u>walked</u> **around** until we found a nice café. The kids <u>ran</u> **around** in the park. — herumlaufen, umherspazieren / herumrennen, umherrennen
> 2. in … umher, durch — Morph walked **around** <u>the library</u> and looked at the books. They rode their bikes **around** <u>the village</u>. — in der Bücherei umher, durch die Bücherei / im Dorf umher, durch das Dorf
> 3. um … (herum) — We're going to put a new fence **around** <u>the garden</u>. Let's run **around** <u>the lake</u> and see who is fastest. — um den Garten (herum) / um den See (herum)
> ❗ *(auch zeitlich:)* Can we meet **around** <u>6 pm</u>? — um 18 Uhr herum, gegen 18 Uhr

(to) **grow** [grəʊ], **grew** [gruː], **grown** [grəʊn]	wachsen	Orange trees don't **grow** in cold countries. ❗ (to) **grow** = 1. wachsen; 2. anbauen, anpflanzen
(to) **plant** [plɑːnt]	pflanzen	The Gardening Club is going to **plant** some trees. Ⓕ planter
not even	(noch) nicht einmal	I don't like desserts. – What? **Not even** ice cream? ❗ • He **even** opened the letter! Er hat den Brief **sogar** geöffnet! • He did**n't even** open the letter! Er hat den Brief **noch nicht einmal** geöffnet!
grave [greɪv]	Grab	
(to) **appear** [əˈpɪə]	erscheinen, auftauchen	(to) **appear** ◄► (to) **disappear** Ⓕ apparaître ◄► disparaître

[f] **f**ather · [v] ri**v**er · [s] **s**ister · [z] plea**s**e · [ʃ] **sh**op · [ʒ] televi**s**ion ·
[tʃ] **t**eacher · [dʒ] **G**ermany · [θ] **th**anks · [ð] **th**is · [h] **h**ere

Vocabulary   Unit 5

Unit 5   Celebrate!

pp. 84/85

(to) **celebrate** [ˈselɪbreɪt]	feiern	My grandmother **celebrated** her 80th birthday last week.	(F) célébrer (L) celebrare
celebration [ˌselɪˈbreɪʃn]	Feier		(F) la célébration (L) celebratio, onis
parade [pəˈreɪd]	Parade, Umzug		
mayor [meə]	Bürgermeister/in	❗ Aussprache: **mayor** [meə]	(F) le/la maire
(to) **light** [laɪt], **lit, lit** [lɪt]	anzünden		
candle [ˈkændl]	Kerze		
(to) **blow** sth. **out** [ˌbləʊ ˈaʊt], **blew** [bluː], **blown** [bləʊn]	etwas auspusten, ausblasen		

(to) **light** a candle

(to) **blow out** a candle

Irregular past participles

(to) **begin**	**began**	**begun** [bɪˈɡʌn]	beginnen, anfangen	(to) **cost**	**cost**	**cost** [kɒst]	kosten
(to) **bite**	**bit**	**bitten** [ˈbɪtn]	beißen	(to) **cut**	**cut**	**cut** [kʌt]	schneiden
(to) **catch**	**caught**	**caught** [kɔːt]	fangen	(to) **draw**	**drew**	**drawn** [drɔːn]	zeichnen

➡ List of irregular verbs, pp. 248–249

New Year's Eve [ˌnjuː jɪəz ˈiːv]	Silvester		
fireworks (pl) [ˈfaɪəwɜːks]	Feuerwerk		
firework [ˈfaɪəwɜːk]	Feuerwerkskörper		

Fireworks!   a firework

(to) **dress up** [ˌdres ˈʌp]	sich verkleiden; sich schick anziehen	I **dressed up** as a monster for Julian's party. We have to **dress up** for Grandpa's 80th birthday.	
costume [ˈkɒstjuːm]	Kostüm, Verkleidung	❗ Betonung: **costume** [ˈkɒstjuːm]	
special [ˈspeʃl]	besondere(r, s)	❗ Betonung: **special** [ˈspeʃl]	(F) spécial, e
bucket [ˈbʌkɪt]	Eimer		
crowd [kraʊd]	(Menschen-)Menge		
festival [ˈfestɪvl]	Fest, Festival		(F) le festival
flag [flæɡ]	Fahne, Flagge	The German **flag** is black, red and gold.	
(to) **raise money (for** sth.**)** [reɪz]	Geld sammeln (für etwas)		
charity [ˈtʃærəti]	Wohlfahrtsorganisation; Wohltätigkeit, wohltätige Zwecke	You could give the money to a **charity** like Oxfam. All the money will go to **charity**. (= … wird für wohltätige Zwecke verwendet.)	
(to) **take part in** sth. [ˌteɪk ˈpɑːt]	an etwas teilnehmen	More than 50 singers **took part in** the concert.	
(to) **plan** [plæn]	planen		
theme [θiːm]	Thema		(L) thema, atis

Unit 5 Vocabulary

Part A

p.86	**juggler** [ˈdʒʌglə]	Jongleur/in	
	(to) **juggle** sth. [ˈdʒʌgl]	mit etwas jonglieren	
	(to) **drive** [draɪv], **drove** [drəʊv], **driven** [ˈdrɪvn]	(mit dem Auto) fahren	Does your mother **drive** to work? – No, she usually goes by bus.
	(to) **get out (of a car)** [ˌget ˈaʊt]	(aus einem Auto) aussteigen	German "einsteigen" – "aussteigen" • (to) **get on** a bus/plane/train • (to) **get off** a bus/plane/train • (to) **get in(to)** a car/taxi • (to) **get out of** a car/taxi
	(to) **put** sth. **on** [ˌpʊt ˈɒn]	etwas anziehen (Kleidung); etwas aufsetzen (Hut, Helm)	
	(to) **take** sth. **off** [ˌteɪk ˈɒf]	etwas ausziehen (Kleidung); etwas absetzen (Hut, Helm)	

(to) put on a pullover ◄► (to) take off a pullover

Clothes

- **caps** [kæps]
- **a hat** [hæt]
- **a pair of gloves** [ˈglʌvz]
- **a pullover** [ˈpʊləʊvə]
- **a shirt** [ʃɜːt]
- **a skirt** [skɜːt]
- **a pair of trousers** [ˈtraʊzəz]

❗ **trousers** ist ein Plural-Wort: **Are** your **trousers** new? **They're** cool. | **Ist** deine **Hose** neu? **Sie ist** cool.
I need **a** new **pair of** trousers / **some** new **trousers**. | Ich brauche **eine** neue **Hose**.

	choir [ˈkwaɪə]	Chor	❗ Aussprache: **choir** [ˈkwaɪə]
	not till three	erst um drei, nicht vor drei	When did he come home last night? – **Not till** ten. I asked her to come at 2, but she did**n't** come **till** 3.
	probably [ˈprɒbəbli]	wahrscheinlich	(F) probablement (L) probabiliter
	artist [ˈɑːtɪst]	Künstler/in	English: **artist** ❗ Betonung: **artist** [ˈɑːtɪst] German: **Künstler/in** (nicht: ~~Artist/in~~) (F) l'artiste (m/f)
	torch [tɔːtʃ]	Fackel	❗ **torch** = 1. Fackel; 2. Taschenlampe
	(to) **pass** sth. **around** [ˌpɑːs əˈraʊnd]	etwas herumgeben, herumreichen	After the concert, the singer **passed around** a hat.
	encore [ˈɒŋkɔː]	Zugabe	
	(to) **promise** [ˈprɒmɪs]	versprechen	I'll come and visit you. I **promise**. (F) promettre (L) promittere
p.87	**journey** [ˈdʒɜːni]	Reise, Fahrt	
	queen [kwiːn]	Königin	
p.88	(to) **translate** [trænsˈleɪt]	übersetzen	Can you **translate** this letter into German for me?

[eɪ] n**a**me · [aɪ] t**i**me · [ɔɪ] b**oy** · [əʊ] **o**ld ·
[aʊ] t**ow**n · [ɪə] h**ere** · [eə] wh**ere** · [ʊə] t**our**

one hundred and ninety-nine **199**

Vocabulary Unit 5

p. 89	(to) **take notes**	(sich) Notizen machen (beim Lesen oder Zuhören)	❗ **take notes** verwendet man, wenn man sich beim Lesen oder Zuhören Notizen macht. **make notes** sagt man, wenn man sich eigene Notizen macht als Vorbereitung auf etwas, z.B. einen Vortrag oder eine Präsentation.
	symbol ['sɪmbl]	Symbol	❗ Betonung: **symbol** ['sɪmbl] Ⓕ le symbole
	abbreviation [ə,briːviˈeɪʃn]	Abkürzung	Ⓕ l'abréviation (f) Ⓛ abbreviatio, onis
	e.g. [ˌiː ˈdʒiː]	z.B. (zum Beispiel)	Ⓛ exempli gratia

Part B

p. 90	**at least** [ət ˈliːst]	zumindest, wenigstens	It was cold but **at least** it didn't rain.
	director [dəˈrektə]	Regisseur/in	
	better **than ever**	besser als je zuvor	The crowds at the concert were bigger **than ever**.
	demonstration [ˌdemənˈstreɪʃn]	Demonstration, Vorführung	
	…, you see.	…, weißt du.	Sue doesn't speak German. She's English, **you see**.
	(to) **offer** ['ɒfə]	anbieten	She looked hungry so I **offered** her something to eat. Ⓕ offrir Ⓛ offerre
	Indian ['ɪndiən]	Inder/in; indisch	
	lift [lɪft]	Mitfahrgelegenheit	English: Can you **give me a lift** to the station? German: Kannst du mich zum Bahnhof bringen / mitnehmen?
	event [ɪˈvent]	Ereignis	The first day at school is a big **event** in a child's life. Ⓕ l'événement (m) Ⓛ eventus, us
	storm [stɔːm]	Sturm, Unwetter, Gewitter	
p. 92	**million** ['mɪljən]	Million	❗ **one million** cars — eine **Million** Autos **two million** cars — zwei **Millionen** Autos But: **million**s of cars — **Millionen** von Autos Ⓕ le million
	(to) **fly** [flaɪ], **flew** [fluː], **flown** [fləʊn]	fliegen	You can **fly** from Berlin to New York in about 8 hours.
p. 93	(to) **present** sth. **(to sb.)** [prɪˈzent]	(jm.) etwas präsentieren, vorstellen	Now **present** your ideas **to** the class. Ⓕ présenter ❗ Betonung: (to) **present** [prɪˈzent] Ⓛ praesentare
	presentation [ˌpreznˈteɪʃn]	Präsentation, Vorstellung	Ⓕ la présentation
	(to) **introduce** sth./sb. **(to sb.)** [ˌɪntrəˈdjuːs]	etwas/jn. (jm.) vorstellen	Mr Brown didn't know me so Dad **introduced** me **to** him. Ⓛ introducere

Part C

pp. 94/95	**speech** [spiːtʃ]	(offizielle) Rede	
	competition [ˌkɒmpəˈtɪʃn]	Wettbewerb	English: (to) **take part in a competition** German: **an** einem Wettbewerb teilnehmen
	workshop ['wɜːkʃɒp]	Workshop, Lehrgang	
	(to) **paint** [peɪnt]	(an)streichen; (an)malen	
	Spanish ['spænɪʃ]	spanisch	

200 two hundred

[b] **boat** · [p] **pool** · [d] **dad** · [t] **ten** · [g] **good** · [k] **cat** ·
[m] **mum** · [n] **no** · [ŋ] **song** · [l] **hello** · [r] **red** · [w] **we** · [j] **you**

Unit 5   Vocabulary

main [meɪn]	Haupt-	the **main** question/road/thing/… = the **most important** question/road/thing/…
tasty [ˈteɪsti]	lecker	
traditional [trəˈdɪʃənl]	traditionell	❗ Betonung: **traditional** [trəˈdɪʃənl] Ⓕ traditionel, le
(to) repeat [rɪˈpiːt]	wiederholen	Can you **repeat** your question, please? Ⓕ répéter
tongue-twister [ˈtʌŋˌtwɪstə]	Zungenbrecher	
puppet [ˈpʌpɪt]	Marionette, Handpuppe	

a puppet

May I have a word with you?	Kann ich Sie kurz sprechen?	
may [meɪ]	dürfen	**May** I come in? (*höflicher für: Can I come in?*)
famous (for) [ˈfeɪməs]	berühmt (für, wegen)	Liverpool is **famous for** the Beatles. Ⓛ famosus
(to) defend sb./sth. **(against sb./sth.)** [dɪˈfend]	jn./etwas verteidigen (gegen jn./etwas)	It's easier to **defend** a country if it is an island like Britain. Ⓕ défendre Ⓛ defendere
(to) invade (a country) [ɪnˈveɪd]	(in ein Land) einmarschieren	Ⓛ invadere
(to) attack [əˈtæk]	angreifen	**(to) attack** ◄► **(to) defend** Ⓕ attaquer
(to) destroy [dɪˈstrɔɪ]	zerstören	Ⓛ destruere
knight [naɪt]	Ritter	❗ Aussprache – das „k" wird nicht gesprochen: **knight** [naɪt]
(to) become [bɪˈkʌm], **became** [bɪˈkeɪm], **become** [bɪˈkʌm]	werden	It **became** warmer when the sun came out.

Irregular past participles

(to) **feel**	felt	felt [felt]	(sich) fühlen	(to) **get**	got	got [gɒt]	bekommen; besorgen;
(to) **fight**	fought	fought [fɔːt]	(be)kämpfen				(hin)kommen; werden
(to) **forget**	forgot	forgotten [fəˈgɒtn]	vergessen	(to) **give**	gave	given [ˈgɪvn]	geben

➡ *List of irregular verbs*, pp. 248–249

---

recipe [ˈresəpi]	(Koch-)Rezept	The cake is delicious! Can I have the **recipe**? ❗ Betonung: **recipe** [ˈresəpi]
p.97 **(to) pick** sth. **up** [ˌpɪk_ˈʌp]	etwas aufheben (*vom Boden*), etwas hochheben	They're **picking up** rubbish.
rubbish [ˈrʌbɪʃ]	Müll, Abfall	
(to) be made of sth.	aus etwas (gemacht) sein	You can't break this bottle. It**'s made of** plastic.
(to) pick sb. **up** [ˌpɪk_ˈʌp]	jn. abholen	He's **picking up** Mr Brown.

---

[f] **f**ather · [v] ri**v**er · [s] **s**i**s**ter · [z] plea**s**e · [ʃ] **sh**op · [ʒ] televi**s**ion ·
[tʃ] **t**ea**ch**er · [dʒ] **G**ermany · [θ] **th**anks · [ð] **th**is · [h] **h**ere

two hundred and one   **201**

Vocabulary   Unit 5

A day to celebrate

p. 98	**mirror** [ˈmɪrə]	Spiegel	a **mirror**
			(F) le miroir
	tooth [tuːθ], *pl* **teeth** [tiːθ]	Zahn	one tooth lots of teeth
	thunder [ˈθʌndə]	Donner	
	even if [ˈiːvn‿ɪf]	selbst wenn	You should go to his party **even if** you don't know many people there.
	bowl [bəʊl]	Schüssel	a **bowl** of cornflakes
	air [eə]	Luft	*(F)* l'air *(m)* *(L)* aer, aeris
	painted [ˈpeɪntɪd]	bemalt, angemalt	
	(to) **ask for** sth.	um etwas bitten	I was thirsty so I **asked for** a glass of water.
	heart [hɑːt]	Herz	
	audience [ˈɔːdiəns]	Publikum, Zuschauer/innen, Zuhörer/innen	At the end of the concert, the **audience** stood up and clapped for five minutes.
	deep [diːp]	tief	Be careful, the water is very **deep** here.
	breath [breθ]	Atem, Atemzug	She took a deep **breath** and jumped into the cold water.
	(to) **pay (for** sth.) [peɪ], **paid, paid** [peɪd]	(etwas) bezahlen	*English:* Let me **pay for** the pizzas. *German:* Lass mich **die Pizzas bezahlen**.
	chorus [ˈkɔːrəs]	Refrain	
	lightning *(no pl)* [ˈlaɪtnɪŋ]	Blitz(e)	*German:* **ein Blitz** – *English:* **a flash of lightning**
	second [ˈsekənd]	Sekunde	❗ Betonung: **second** [ˈsekənd] *(F)* la seconde
	heavy rain [ˈhevi]	starker Regen, heftiger Regen	
	(to) **bow** [baʊ]	sich verbeugen, sich verneigen	
p. 99	(to) **interrupt** [ˌɪntəˈrʌpt]	unterbrechen	Please don't **interrupt** me when I'm talking. Wait until I'm finished. *(F)* interrompre *(L)* interrumpere
	(to) **pour** [pɔː]	gießen	She **poured** the water into the glasses.
	circle [ˈsɜːkl]	Kreis	*(F)* le cercle *(L)* circulus, i
	ring [rɪŋ]	Ring	
	shoulder [ˈʃəʊldə]	Schulter	
	(to) **light** sth. **up** [ˌlaɪt‿ˈʌp], **lit, lit** [lɪt]	etwas erhellen *(aufleuchten lassen)*	The sun came out and **lit up** their faces.

Irregular past participles

(to) **hang**	**hung**	**hung** [hʌŋ]	hängen		(to) **lie**	**lay**	**lain** [leɪn]	liegen
(to) **hold**	**held**	**held** [held]	halten		(to) **mean**	**meant**	**meant** [ment]	bedeuten; meinen
(to) **know**	**knew**	**known** [nəʊn]	wissen; kennen		(to) **put**	**put**	**put** [pʊt]	legen, stellen

➡ *List of irregular verbs, pp. 248–249*

(to) **whistle** [ˈwɪsl]	pfeifen

[iː] green · [i] happy · [ɪ] big · [e] red · [æ] cat · [ɑː] class · [ɒ] song ·
[ɔː] door · [uː] blue · [ʊ] book · [ʌ] mum · [ɜː] girl · [ə] a partner

Unit 6   Vocabulary

whole [həʊl]	ganze(r, s), gesamte(r, s)	Yesterday we played cards the **whole** evening.
entry ['entri]	Eintrag, Eintragung *(im Tagebuch, Wörterbuch)*	There's no **entry** in Jane's diary for 12th June. My new English dictionary has 200,000 **entries**.
conversation [ˌkɒnvə'seɪʃn]	Gespräch, Unterhaltung	(to) have a **conversation** with sb. = (to) talk to sb. about sth. (F) la conversation

Unit 6   A class trip

p. 102 **cliff** [klɪf]	Klippe	
cave [keɪv]	Höhle	(F) la caverne (L) cavus, i
bridge [brɪdʒ]	Brücke	

Part A

p. 104 **real** ['riːəl]	echt, wirklich	That plant isn't **real**. It's made of plastic.
(to) **enter** ['entə]	betreten, hineingehen in; eintreten	Everyone stood up when the Queen **entered** the room. (F) entrer (L) intrare
guide [gaɪd]	Fremdenführer/in; Reiseleiter/in	(F) le/la guide
each [iːtʃ]	jeder, jede, jedes (einzelne)	There were six children at Jamie's birthday party, and **each** of them got a little present.
copy ['kɒpi]	Kopie; Exemplar	Can I make a **copy** of your CD? Here's a **copy** of the new school magazine. ❗ Betonung: **copy** ['kɒpi] (F) la copie
you **needn't** do it ['niːdnt]	du musst es nicht tun, du brauchst es nicht zu tun	I can do the exercise. You **needn't** help me.
you **mustn't** do it ['mʌsnt]	du darfst es nicht tun	You **mustn't** touch the plates. They're hot. ❗ Nicht verwechseln: • **you mustn't** = du <u>darfst</u> nicht • **you needn't / you don't have to** = du <u>musst</u> nicht

---

must – needn't – mustn't

must (müssen)	**needn't** (nicht müssen)	**mustn't** (nicht dürfen)
Mit **must** drückt man aus, dass jemand etwas tun muss:	Mit **needn't** drückt man aus, dass jemand etwas nicht zu tun braucht:	Mit **mustn't** drückt man aus, dass jemand etwas nicht tun darf:
I **must** clean the hamster's cage today. It's dirty. *Ich muss … sauber machen.*	I **needn't** clean the rabbit's cage. It isn't dirty. *Ich muss … nicht sauber machen.*	I **mustn't** forget to feed the lambs. *Ich darf nicht vergessen, …*

(to) **hand** sth. **in**	etwas abgeben; etwas einreichen	If you find money you should **hand** it **in** to the police.
(to) **build** [bɪld], **built**, **built** [bɪlt]	bauen	Dad is going to **build** a tree house for us in the garden.

Irregular past participles

(to) **ring**	**rang**	**rung** [rʌŋ]	klingeln, läuten	(to) **shake**	**shook**	**shaken** ['ʃeɪkən]	schütteln
(to) **say**	**said**	**said** [sed]	sagen	(to) **sing**	**sang**	**sung** [sʌŋ]	singen
(to) **send**	**sent**	**sent** [sent]	schicken, senden	(to) **sit**	**sat**	**sat** [sæt]	sitzen; sich setzen

➡ *List of irregular verbs, pp. 248–249*

[eɪ] **name** · [aɪ] **time** · [ɔɪ] **boy** · [əʊ] **old** ·
[aʊ] **town** · [ɪə] **here** · [eə] **where** · [ʊə] **tour**

two hundred and three   **203**

Vocabulary   Unit 6

narrow [ˈnærəʊ]	schmal, eng	The road was too **narrow** for the big bus.
guard [gɑːd]	Wachposten, Wache	
legend [ˈledʒənd]	Legende, Sage	
king [kɪŋ]	König	

queen   king

(to) **write** sth. **down**	etwas aufschreiben	There are some new words on the board. **Write** them **down** in your exercise books, please.
courtyard [ˈkɔːtjɑːd]	Hof, Innenhof; Vorplatz	
prince [prɪns]	Prinz	(F) le prince
princess [ˌprɪnˈses], [ˈprɪnses]	Prinzessin	
p.105 **What's wrong with** Justin/you?	Was fehlt Justin/dir? Was ist los mit Justin/dir?	He looks awful. **What's wrong with him?**
sweets (pl) [swiːts]	Süßigkeiten	
at Grandma's	bei Oma	Let's meet **at Grandma's**. (= at Grandma's house/flat)
while [waɪl]	während	We met Mr Petrock **while** we were in Cornwall.
(to) **tap** [tæp]	tippen, (vorsichtig) klopfen	I was waiting for the bus when someone **tapped** me on the shoulder from behind.
(to) **turn to** sb. [tɜːn]	sich jm. zuwenden; sich an jn. wenden	Leo **turned to** Justin and said, "Let's play I spy."
Stop it! (infml)	Hör auf (damit)! / Lass das!	
(to) **hiss** [hɪs]	zischen	The cat **hissed** and showed its teeth.
(to) **scream** [skriːm]	schreien	My brother **screamed** when he saw a rat in the kitchen.
(to) **kill** [kɪl]	töten	
groan [grəʊn]	Stöhnen	
(to) **groan** [grəʊn]	stöhnen	
stomach [ˈstʌmək]	Magen	❗ Aussprache: **stomach** [ˈstʌmək] (F) l'estomac (m) (L) stomachus, i
ill [ɪl]	krank	

---

ill – sick – well

• Nach <u>Verben</u> kann **sick** oder **ill** stehen:	(to) <u>be/look</u> **ill/sick**	**krank** sein/aussehen
• Vor <u>Nomen</u> kann nur **sick** stehen:	a **sick** <u>child</u>	ein **krankes** Kind
• Das Adjektiv **sick** bedeutet auch „schlecht, übel": (to) **be sick** heißt „sich übergeben":	I feel **sick**. I'm going to **be sick**.	Mir ist **schlecht**. Ich muss **mich übergeben**.
• Das Adjektiv **well** bedeutet „gesund, gut":	I don't feel **well**. I was ill, but now I'm **well** again.	Mir geht's nicht **gut**. / Ich fühle mich nicht **gut**. … wieder **gesund**.

[b] **b**oat · [p] **p**ool · [d] **d**ad · [t] **t**en · [g] **g**ood · [k] **c**at · [m] **m**um · [n] **n**o · [ŋ] so**ng** · [l] **h**ello · [r] **r**ed · [w] **w**e · [j] **y**ou

Unit 6 Vocabulary

seat [siːt]	Sitz, Platz	When I fly, I always try to get a window **seat**.	
reason ['riːzn]	Grund, Begründung		(F) la raison (L) ratio, onis
p.106 **tunnel** ['tʌnl]	Tunnel	❗ Aussprache: **tunnel** ['tʌnl]	
			(F) le tunnel
sticky ['stɪki]	klebrig		
p.107 **apple** ['æpl]	Apfel		
p.108 **back** [bæk]	Rücken		
chest [tʃest]	Brust, Brustkorb		
finger ['fɪŋgə]	Finger		
knee [niː]	Knie		
neck [nek]	Hals		
throat [θrəʊt]	Hals, Kehle		
toe [təʊ]	Zeh		
tongue [tʌŋ]	Zunge		
(to) **have a toothache / a headache** ['tuːθeɪk], ['hedeɪk]	Zahnschmerzen/Kopfschmerzen haben	I **have a headache**. – Do you often get **headaches**?	
(to) **have a temperature** ['temprətʃə]	Fieber haben	I feel very hot. I think I **have a temperature**. ❗ **temperature** = 1. Temperatur; 2. Fieber Betonung: **temperature** ['temprətʃə]	
			(F) la température
(to) **have a cough** [kɒf]	Husten haben	❗ Aussprache: **cough** [kɒf]	
sore [sɔː]	wund	Your eyes are very red. Are they **sore**? She has a **sore** throat. (Sie hat Halsschmerzen.)	
(to) **have a cold** [kəʊld]	eine Erkältung haben, erkältet sein		
plaster ['plɑːstə]	(Heft-)Pflaster		
thermometer [θə'mɒmɪtə]	Thermometer	❗ Betonung: **thermometer** [θə'mɒmɪtə]	
			(F) le thermomètre
fresh [freʃ]	frisch	Can you open the window? I need some **fresh** air. Is this milk **fresh**? – No, it's four days old.	
dentist ['dentɪst]	Zahnarzt/-ärztin		(F) le/la dentiste
hospital ['hɒspɪtl]	Krankenhaus		(F) l'hôpital (m)
terrible ['terəbl]	schrecklich, furchtbar	another word for "awful"	(F) terrible (L) terribilis, e

Part B

p.110 **floor** [flɔː]	Stock(werk)	You can buy children's clothes on the second **floor**.	
report [rɪ'pɔːt]	Bericht, Reportage		(F) le reportage
strawberry ['strɔːbəri]	Erdbeere		

[f] **f**ather · [v] ri**v**er · [s] **s**ister · [z] plea**s**e · [ʃ] **sh**op · [ʒ] televi**s**ion ·
[tʃ] **t**eacher · [dʒ] **G**ermany · [θ] **th**anks · [ð] **th**is · [h] **h**ere

two hundred and five **205**

Vocabulary   Unit 6

| (to) **frown** [fraʊn] | die Stirn runzeln |
| (to) **go red** | rot werden, erröten |

German "werden"

- Die häufigsten englischen Entsprechungen von „werden" sind (to) **become** und (to) **get**. In der Umgangssprache wir eher (to) **get** verwendet.

  (to) **become/get**   angry/tired/nervous/old/ill/...
  cold/windy/dark/...
  exciting/boring/funny/more interesting/...

  ❗ Vor <u>Nomen</u> kann nur (to) **become** stehen:

  She **became** <u>a doctor</u>/<u>a football fan</u>/<u>a singer</u>/...

- (to) **go** wird oft verwendet
  – bei Farbveränderungen:
  – wenn es um Verschlechterungen geht:

  (to) **go** red/brown/green/...   rot/braun/grün/... werden
  (to) **go** hard *(bread)*   hart werden
  (to) **go** bad *(fish, cheese, eggs)*   schlecht werden
  (to) **go** mad   verrückt werden

| **role** [rəʊl] | Rolle *(in einem Theaterstück, Film)* | Ⓕ le rôle |
| **as** King Arthur [æz], [əz] | als König Arthur | |

as ...
- I would choose Justin **as King Arthur**.
  Ich würde Justin **als King Arthur** wählen.
- **As a child**, I was often scared at night.
  Als Kind hatte ich nachts oft Angst.
- She works **as a teacher**.
  Sie arbeitet **als Lehrerin**.

dear [dɪə]	liebe(r, s)	Elena is one of my **dearest** friends.
(to) **melt** [melt]	schmelzen	Ice **melts** in the sun.
royal [ˈrɔɪəl]	königlich	Tourists love the British **royal** family. Ⓕ royal, e Ⓛ regalis
p.112 **consonant** [ˈkɒnsənənt]	Konsonant, Mitlaut	Ⓕ la consonne
vowel [ˈvaʊəl]	Vokal, Selbstlaut	Ⓕ la voyelle
noisy [ˈnɔɪzi]	laut, lärmend, voller Lärm	**quiet ◄► noisy**
p.113 **peaceful** [ˈpiːsfl]	friedlich	
takeaway [ˈteɪkəweɪ]	*Restaurant/Imbissgeschäft, das auch Essen zum Mitnehmen verkauft; Essen zum Mitnehmen*	

---

one/ones

Wenn du ein schon einmal genanntes <u>Nomen</u> nicht wiederholen willst, kannst du **one** (Singular) bzw. **ones** (Plural) verwenden:

This <u>café</u> is not as good as the **one** in King Street. (= ... not as good as the <u>café</u> in King Street.)
Dieses Café ist nicht so gut wie das in der King Street.

I have three <u>cats</u>, two black **ones** and a white **one**.
Ich habe drei Katzen, zwei schwarze und eine weiße.

Could you give me a <u>felt pen</u>, please? – Which **one**? This **one**? – No, the blue **one**, please.
Kannst du mir bitte einen Filzstift geben? – Welchen? Diesen? – Nein, den blauen, bitte.

I'll have a tea/burger/...	Ich nehme einen Tee/Hamburger/ ... *(beim Essen, im Restaurant)*	
vegetarian [ˌvedʒəˈteəriən]	Vegetarier/in; vegetarisch	Ⓕ le végétarien, la végétarienne
What size tea would you like?	Wie groß soll der/dein Tee sein?	

---

206   two hundred and six

[iː] green · [i] happy · [ɪ] big · [e] red · [æ] cat · [ɑː] class · [ɒ] song ·
[ɔː] door · [uː] blue · [ʊ] book · [ʌ] mum · [ɜː] girl · [ə] a partner

Unit 6 Vocabulary

The sword in the stone

p.114 **stone** [stəʊn] Stein

cast [kɑːst] Besetzung; Mitwirkende *(Theaterstück, Film)*

beard [bɪəd] Bart

adopted [əˈdɒptɪd] adoptiert, Adoptiv- Ⓛ adoptare

battle [ˈbætl] Schlacht; Kampf At the end of the **battle**, hundreds of men were dead.

enemy [ˈenəmi] Feind/in friend ◄► **enemy**
Ⓕ l'ennemi (*m*), l'ennemie (*f*) Ⓛ inimicus, i

danger [ˈdeɪndʒə] Gefahr **danger** (Gefahr) – **dangerous** (gefährlich)
Ⓕ le danger

truth [truːθ] Wahrheit **truth** (Wahrheit) – **true** (wahr)

(to) kiss [kɪs] küssen; sich küssen He's **kissing** her.

p.115 **(to) kneel** [niːl], **knelt, knelt** [nelt] knien Why are you **kneeling** on the floor?
– I'm looking for my key.

Irregular past participles

(to) **speak**	spoke	**spoken** [ˈspəʊkən]	sprechen, reden	(to) **think**	**thought**	**thought** [θɔːt]	denken, glauben
(to) **stand**	stood	**stood** [stʊd]	stehen	(to) **under-stand**	**under-stood**	**understood** [ˌʌndəˈstʊd]	verstehen
(to) **stick**	stuck	**stuck** [stʌk]	stechen, stecken				
(to) **swim**	swam	**swum** [swʌm]	schwimmen	(to) **wear**	**wore**	**worn** [wɔːn]	tragen (*Kleidung*)

➡ *List of irregular verbs*, pp. 248–249

---

crown [kraʊn] Krone **crowns**
Ⓕ la couronne

wise [waɪz] weise

[eɪ] **name** · [aɪ] **time** · [ɔɪ] **boy** · [əʊ] **old** ·
[aʊ] **town** · [ɪə] **here** · [eə] **where** · [ʊə] **tour**

two hundred and seven **207**

Dictionary

Das **Dictionary** besteht aus **zwei alphabetischen Wörterlisten**:
English – German (S. 208 – 228)   und   **German – English** (S. 229 – 246)

Im **English – German Dictionary** kannst du nachschlagen, wenn du wissen möchtest, was ein englisches Wort bedeutet, wie man es ausspricht oder wie es geschrieben wird.

Im **Dictionary** werden folgende **Abkürzungen und Symbole** verwendet:

sth. = something (etwas)   sb. = somebody (jemand)   jn. = jemanden   jm. = jemandem
pl = *plural* (Mehrzahl)   *infml* = *informal* (umgangssprachlich)
° Mit diesem Kringel sind Wörter markiert, die nicht zum Lernwortschatz gehören.

▶ Der Pfeil weist auf Kästen im **Vocabulary** (S. 178 – 207) hin, in denen du weitere Informationen zu diesem Wort findest.

Die **Fundstellenangaben** zeigen, wo ein Wort zum ersten Mal vorkommt.
I = Band 1; II 1 (15) = Band 2, Unit 1, Seite 19

Tipps zur Arbeit mit einem Wörterbuch findest du im Skills File auf Seite 148.

1

°**1960s** [ˌnaɪntiːn ˈsɪkstiːz]: **a 1960s band** eine Band aus den Sechziger-jahren *(des 20. Jahrhunderts)*

A

a [ə] ein, eine I   **once a week/ year** einmal pro Woche/Jahr II 4 (68)
°**abbey** [ˈæbi] Abtei, Kloster
abbreviation [əˌbriːviˈeɪʃn] Abkür-zung II 5 (89)
about [əˈbaʊt]:
  1. **about me/you/…** über mich/dich/… I   **about yourself** über dich selbst I   **It's about a seagull.** Es geht um eine Möwe. / Es handelt von einer Möwe   **know about sth.** sich mit etwas auskennen; über etwas Bescheid wissen II 3 (50)   **What about you?** Und du? / Und was ist mit dir?; Und ihr? / Und was ist mit euch? I   **What is the story about?** Wovon handelt die Geschichte? / Worum geht es in der Geschichte? I
  2. **about 300** ungefähr 300 II 2 (34)
access [ˈækses] Zugang, Zutritt I
across [əˈkrɒs]: **across the moor/ the street** (quer) über das Moor / die Straße II 4 (76)
°**acrostic** [əˈkrɒstɪk] Akrostichon *(Ge-dicht, in dem die Anfangsbuchstaben ein Wort oder einen Spruch ergeben)*
act [ækt] schauspielern II 2 (36)
act out [ˌækt ˈaʊt] vorspielen I
action [ˈækʃn] Action; Handlung, Tat I
activity [ækˈtɪvəti] Aktivität I   **free-time activities** Freizeitaktivitäten I

actor [ˈæktə] Schauspieler/in I
°**AD** *(anno Domini)* [ˌeɪ ˈdiː] n. Chr. *(nach Christus)*
°**add (to)** [æd] hinzufügen, ergänzen, addieren (zu) I
adder [ˈædə] Kreuzotter II 4 (79)
address [əˈdres] Adresse, Anschrift I
adjective [ˈædʒɪktɪv] Adjektiv II 2 (38)
adopted [əˈdɒptɪd] adoptiert, Adoptiv- II 6 (114)
adventure [ədˈventʃə] Abenteuer II 4 (80)
adverb [ˈædvɜːb] Adverb II 3 (55)
°**advert** [ˈædvɜːt] (Werbe-)Anzeige I
after [ˈɑːftə]:
  1. **after breakfast** nach dem Früh-stück I   **right after you** gleich nach dir II 1 (24)
  ▶ S. 183 right
  2. nachdem II 3 (48/49)   **just after …** gleich nachdem …; kurz nachdem … II 3 (48/49)
  3. **run after sb.** hinter jm. herrennen I
afternoon [ˌɑːftəˈnuːn] Nachmittag I   **in the afternoon** nachmittags, am Nachmittag I   **on Saturday after-noon** am Samstagnachmittag I   **this afternoon** heute Nachmittag II 1 (14)
again [əˈgen] wieder; noch einmal I   **again and again** immer wieder II 1 (25)   °**once again** nochmals
against [əˈgenst] gegen I
age [eɪdʒ] Alter I   **… is your age** … ist in deinem Alter; … ist so alt wie du II 1 (14)
ago [əˈgəʊ]: **two days ago** vor zwei Tagen II 1 (10)
agree [əˈgriː]: **agree with sb.** jm. zustimmen   **agree on sth.** sich auf etwas einigen I

air [eə] Luft II 5 (98)
°**album** [ˈælbəm] Album
°**alibi** [ˈæləbaɪ] Alibi
all [ɔːl] alles; alle I   **all of Plymouth** ganz Plymouth, das ganze Plymouth I   **all alone** ganz allein II 4 (80)   **all day** den ganzen Tag II 5 (98)   °**all over the country** im ganzen Land   **all the time** die ganze Zeit II 1 (12)   °**all year round** das ganze Jahr
allowed [əˈlaʊd]: **be allowed to do sth.** etwas tun dürfen II 1 (15)
all right [ɔːl ˈraɪt] okay; in Ordnung I
  ▶ S. 183 right
almost [ˈɔːlməʊst] fast, beinahe I
alone [əˈləʊn] allein II 1 (8)   **all alone** ganz allein II 4 (80)
along [əˈlɒŋ]: **along the street / the river / …** die Straße / den Fluss / … entlang I   °**sing along** mitsingen
aloud [əˈlaʊd]: **read aloud** laut (vor)lesen II 2 (35)
already [ɔːlˈredi] schon, bereits II 1 (14)
also [ˈɔːlsəʊ] auch I
°**altogether** [ˌɔːltəˈgeðə] insgesamt
always [ˈɔːlweɪz] immer I
am: 4 am [ˌeɪ ˈem] 4 Uhr morgens I
an [æn, ən] ein, eine I
and [ænd, ənd] und I
angry [ˈæŋgri] wütend I   **angry with sb.** wütend, böse auf jn. II 1 (15)
animal [ˈænɪml] Tier I   **my favour-ite animal** mein Lieblingstier I   °**animal keeper** Tierwärter/in
another [əˈnʌðə]:
  1. ein(e) andere(r, s) I
  2. noch ein(e) I
answer [ˈɑːnsə]:
  1. antworten; beantworten I

English – German

answer the phone ans Telefon gehen II 1 (10)
2. Antwort I
ant [ænt] Ameise I
any ['eni]: **Are there any ...?** Gibt es (irgendwelche) ...? I **not ... any more** nicht mehr II 4 (76) **There aren't any ...** Es gibt keine / Es sind keine ... I
anybody ['enibɒdi]: anybody? (irgend)jemand? II 4 (68) **not ... anybody** niemand II 4 (68)
anyone ['eniwʌn]: anyone? (irgend)jemand? II 4 (68) **not ... anyone** niemand II 4 (68) °**anyone else** sonst jemand
anything ['eniθɪŋ]: anything? (irgend)etwas? II 4 (72) **not ... anything** nichts II 4 (68)
Anyway, ... ['eniweɪ] Jedenfalls, ... / Aber egal, ... II 2 (42)
apartment [ə'pɑːtmənt] Wohnung II 1 (24)
appear [ə'pɪə] erscheinen, auftauchen II 4 (81)
apple ['æpl] Apfel II 6 (107)
appointment [ə'pɔɪntmənt] Verabredung, Termin I
April ['eɪprəl] April I
aquarium [ə'kweəriəm] Aquarium; Aquarienhaus I
are ['ɑː] bist; sind; seid I **Are you ...?** Bist du ...? I **The DVDs are ...** Die DVDs kosten ... I
area ['eəriə] Bereich; Gebiet, Gegend I
aren't [ɑːnt]: **you aren't** du bist nicht ...; du bist kein/e ...; ihr seid nicht ...; ihr seid kein/e ... I
arm [ɑːm] Arm II 2 (42) **take sb. by the arm** jn. am Arm nehmen II 3 (54)
°**armada** [ɑː'mɑːdə] Armada, Kriegsflotte
armchair ['ɑːmtʃeə] Sessel I
around [ə'raʊnd]:
1. around the library / the beach in der Bücherei / auf dem Strand umher I **look around (the farm)** sich (auf der Farm) umsehen II 4 (68) **walk/run/... around** herumlaufen, umherspazieren / herumrennen, umherrennen II 4 (81)
2. um ... herum II 4 (81) **around 6 pm** um 18 Uhr herum, gegen 18 Uhr II 4 (81)
▶ S. 197 around
arrange [ə'reɪndʒ] anordnen I
arrive [ə'raɪv] ankommen, eintreffen I

art [ɑːt] Kunst I
article ['ɑːtɪkl] Artikel II 2 (28)
artist ['ɑːtɪst] Künstler/in II 5 (86) **street artist** Straßenkünstler/in II 5 (86)
as [æz, əz]:
1. als, während II 3 (48/49)
2. (not) as big as (nicht) so groß wie II 2 (32)
3. as a child als Kind II 6 (110) **She works as a teacher.** Sie arbeitet als Lehrerin. II 6 (110)
▶ S. 206 as ...
°**Ash** [æʃ]: **Ash Wednesday** Aschermittwoch
ask [ɑːsk] fragen I **ask a question** eine Frage stellen I **ask for sth.** um etwas bitten II 5 (98) **ask sb. the way** jn. nach dem Weg fragen II 3 (46) **ask sb. to do sth.** jemanden bitten, etwas zu tun I
asleep [ə'sliːp] **be asleep** schlafen II 1 (25)
assistant [ə'sɪstənt]:
1. (auch **shop assistant**) Verkäufer/in II 3 (48/49):
°**2. personal assistant** persönliche(r) Assistent/in
at [æt, ət] an, bei, in I **at 14 Dean Street** in der Deanstraße 14 I **at first** zuerst, anfangs, am Anfang II 1 (10) **at Grandma's (house/flat)** bei Oma II 6 (105) **at home** daheim, zu Hause I **at last** endlich, schließlich I **at least** zumindest, wenigstens II 5 (90) **at lunchtime** mittags I **at the moment** gerade, im Moment I **at night** nachts, in der Nacht I **at school** in der Schule I **at the top (of)** oben, am oberen Ende, an der Spitze (von) II 4 (66) **at the weekend** am Wochenende I
ate [et, eɪt] siehe eat
°**atmosphere** ['ætməsfɪə] Stimmung I
attack [ə'tæk] angreifen II 5 (94)
attic ['ætɪk] Dachboden I **in the attic** auf dem Dachboden I
audience ['ɔːdiəns] Publikum, Zuschauer/innen, Zuhörer/innen II 5 (98)
audition [ɔː'dɪʃn] Vorsprechen, Vorsingen, Vorspielen II 2 (28)
August ['ɔːgəst] August I
aunt [ɑːnt] Tante I
author ['ɔːθə] Autor/in I
autumn ['ɔːtəm] Herbst I
°**available** [ə'veɪləbl] erhältlich I
°**award** [ə'wɔːd]: **Grammy award** Grammy Award (US-Musikpreis)
away [ə'weɪ] weg, fort I

awful ['ɔːfl] schrecklich, fürchterlich II 2 (32)

B

back [bæk]
1. zurück I
2. Rücken II 6 (108)
3. from the back of the bus aus dem hinteren Teil des Buses II 6 (105)
°**4.** Rückseite **back door** Hintertür
background ['bækgraʊnd] Hintergrund II 4 (66) **background file** Hintergrundinformation(en) I
bacon ['beɪkən] Schinkenspeck II 4 (72)
bad [bæd] schlecht, schlimm I **go bad** (fish, cheese, eggs) schlecht werden II 6 (110)
▶ S. 206 German „werden"
bag [bæg] Tasche, Beutel, Tüte I **school bag** Schultasche I
ball [bɔːl] Ball I
°**banana** [bə'nɑːnə] Banane I
band [bænd] Band, (Musik-)Gruppe II 1 (24)
bark [bɑːk] bellen I
barn [bɑːn] Scheune II 4 (72)
basket ['bɑːskɪt] Korb I
basketball ['bɑːskɪtbɔːl] Basketball I
bath [bɑːθ] Bad II 4 (69)
bathroom ['bɑːθruːm] Badezimmer I
battle ['bætl] Schlacht; Kampf II 6 (114)
°**BC** (before Christ) [ˌbiː 'siː] v. Chr. (vor Christus)
be [bi], **was/were, been:** sein I
beach [biːtʃ] Strand I
bear [beə] Bär I
beard [bɪəd] Bart II 6 (114)
beautiful ['bjuːtɪfl] schön II 1 (8)
°**beauty** ['bjuːti]: **sleeping beauty** Dornröschen („schlafende Schöne")
became [bɪ'keɪm] siehe become
because [bɪ'kɒz] weil I
become [bɪ'kʌm], **became, become** werden II 5 (94)
bed [bed] Bett I
bedroom ['bedruːm] Schlafzimmer I
°**bee** [biː] Biene I
beef [biːf]: **roast beef** Rinderbraten I
been [biːn]:
1. siehe be
2. Have you ever been to ...? ... Bist du schon in ... gewesen? II 4 (72)
beep [biːp] piepen II 2 (42)

two hundred and nine **209**

Dictionary

before [bɪˈfɔː]:
1. bevor ı
2. vor ı **before school/lessons** vor der Schule (vor Schulbeginn) / vorm Unterricht ı
3. (vorher) schon mal II 4 (68) **not/ never before** (vorher) noch nie II 4 (68)
▶ S. 193 before
began [bɪˈgæn] siehe **begin**
begin [bɪˈgɪn], **began, begun** beginnen, anfangen II 4 (66)
begun [bɪˈgʌn] siehe **begun**
behind [bɪˈhaɪnd] hinter ı **from behind** von hinten II 6 (105) **right behind you** direkt hinter dir, genau hinter dir II 1 (24)
▶ S. 183 right
believe [bɪˈliːv] glauben II 4 (80)
°**believer** [bɪˈliːvə] Gläubige(r)
bell [bel] Klingel, Glocke ı
°**below** [bɪˈləʊ] unterhalb (von)
best [best]: **the best** der/die/das beste; die besten; am besten ı
better [ˈbetə] besser ı **better than ever** besser als je zuvor II 5 (90)
between [bɪˈtwiːn] zwischen ı
big [bɪg] groß ı **big wheel** Riesenrad ı **the biggest** der/die/das größte; am größten ı
▶ S. 185 German „groß"
bike [baɪk] Fahrrad ı **ride a bike** Fahrrad fahren ı
°**billion** [ˈbɪljən] Milliarde ı
°**binoculars** (pl) [bɪˈnɒkjələz] Fernglas ı
bird [bɜːd] Vogel ı
birthday [ˈbɜːθdeɪ] Geburtstag ı **My birthday is in May.** Ich habe im Mai Geburtstag. ı **My birthday is on 5th May.** Ich habe am 5. May Geburtstag. ı **When's your birthday?** Wann hast du Geburtstag? ı
biscuit [ˈbɪskɪt] Keks, Plätzchen ı
bit [bɪt]:
1. siehe **bite**
2. **a bit** ein bisschen, etwas II 2 (30)
bite [baɪt], **bit, bitten** beißen ı
bitten [ˈbɪtn] siehe **bite**
black [blæk] schwarz ı
blew [bluː] siehe **blow**
blog [blɒg] Blog (Weblog, digitales Tagebuch) II 1 (18)
blond (bei Frauen oft: **blonde**) [blɒnd] blond ı
blow [bləʊ], **blew, blown: blow sth. out** etwas auspusten, ausblasen II 5 (84)
blown [bləʊn] siehe **blow**

blue [bluː] blau ı
board [bɔːd] (Wand-)Tafel ı
boarding school [ˈbɔːdɪŋ skuːl] Internat II 1 (20)
boat [bəʊt] Boot, Schiff ı
body [ˈbɒdi] Körper ı **part of the body** Körperteil II 6 (108)
°**bodysurfing** [ˈbɒdi ˌsɜːfɪŋ] Bodysurfing (Wellenreiten ohne Brett)
°**bonfire** [ˈbɒnfaɪə] Lagerfeuer
book [bʊk] Buch ı
bookshop [ˈbʊkʃɒp] Buchladen, Buchhandlung ı
boot [buːt] Stiefel II 4 (72)
bored [bɔːd]: **be/feel bored** gelangweilt sein, sich langweilen II 1 (20)
boring [ˈbɔːrɪŋ] langweilig ı
°**born** [bɔːn]: **be born** geboren sein/ werden
both [bəʊθ] beide II 4 (80)
bottle [ˈbɒtl] Flasche ı
bottom [ˈbɒtəm]: **at the bottom** unten, am unteren Ende (von) II 4 (66)
bought [bɔːt] siehe **buy**
bow [baʊ] sich verneigen, sich verbeugen II 5 (98)
bowl [bəʊl]:
1. Schüssel II 5 (98)
°2. **bowls** (pl) [bəʊlz] Bowls (Kugelspiel)
box [bɒks] Kasten, Kiste, Kästchen ı
boy [bɔɪ] Junge ı
°**bracket** [ˈbrækɪt] Klammer (in Texten)
bread [bred] Brot ı
break [breɪk]:
1. Pause ı
2. **(broke, broken)** zerbrechen, kaputt machen ı; brechen, kaputt gehen ı
breakfast [ˈbrekfəst] Frühstück ı **have breakfast** frühstücken ı
breath [breθ] Atem, Atemzug II 5 (98)
bridge [brɪdʒ] Brücke II 6 (102)
bright [braɪt] strahlend, leuchtend, hell ı
brilliant [ˈbrɪliənt] glänzend, großartig, genial II 2 (36)
bring [brɪŋ], **brought, brought** (mit-, her)bringen II 1 (10) **bring in** (hay) einbringen (Heu) II 4 (68)
▶ S. 180 German „bringen"
°**Brit** [brɪt] (infml) Brite/Britin
British [ˈbrɪtɪʃ] britisch ı
broke [brəʊk] siehe **break**
broken [ˈbrəʊkən]:
1. siehe **break**
2. zerbrochen, kaputt; gebrochen II 3 (58)

brother [ˈbrʌðə] Bruder ı
brought [brɔːt] siehe **bring**
brown [braʊn] braun ı
°**bubble** [ˈbʌbl]: **speech bubble** Sprechblase
bucket [ˈbʌkɪt] Eimer II 5 (84)
°**bug** [bʌg] Käfer
build [bɪld], **built, built** bauen II 6 (104)
building [ˈbɪldɪŋ] Gebäude II 1 (10)
built [bɪlt] siehe **build**
burger [ˈbɜːgə] Hamburger II 6 (113)
°**burn** [bɜːn] brennen
bus [bʌs] Bus ı **go by bus** mit dem Bus fahren ı **get on a bus** (in einen Bus) einsteigen II 5 (86)
▶ S. 185 get
busy [ˈbɪzi]: **be busy** beschäftigt sein; viel zu tun haben ı
but [bʌt, bət] aber ı
°**butter** [ˈbʌtə] Butter
butterfly [ˈbʌtəflaɪ] Schmetterling ı
buy [baɪ], **bought, bought** kaufen ı
by [baɪ]:
1. **by the sea** am Meer ı
2. **go by car/bus/…** mit dem Auto/Bus/… fahren ı
3. **by …** von … II 2 (30)
4. **take sb. by the arm** jn. am Arm nehmen II 3 (54)
°5. neben
Bye. [baɪ] Tschüs. ı

C

café [ˈkæfeɪ] Café ı
cage [keɪdʒ] Käfig ı
cake [keɪk] Kuchen ı
call [kɔːl]:
1. rufen; anrufen; nennen ı **call out the names** die Namen aufrufen II 2 (28)
2. (auch: **phone call**) Anruf, Telefonat II 1 (10)
called [kɔːld]: **be called** heißen, genannt werden ı
caller [ˈkɔːlə] Anrufer/in II 2 (28)
came [keɪm] siehe **come**
camera [ˈkæmərə] Kamera, Fotoapparat ı
cameraman [ˈkæmrəmæn], pl **cameramen** [ˈkæmrəmen] Kameramann ı
camping [ˈkæmpɪŋ] Camping, Zelten II 1 (8) **go camping** zelten gehen II 1 (8)
campsite [ˈkæmpsaɪt] Zeltplatz II 1 (24)

210   two hundred and ten

English – German

can [kæn, kən] können ı **we cannot** ['kænɒt], **we can't** [kɑːnt] … wir können nicht … ı

candle ['kændl] Kerze ıı 5 (84)

canteen [kæn'tiːn] Kantine, (Schul-) Mensa ı

cap [kæp] Mütze, Kappe ıı 5 (86)

captain ['kæptɪn] Kapitän/in ı

caption ['kæpʃn] Bildunterschrift ı

car [kɑː] Auto ı **go by car** mit dem Auto fahren ı **get in(to) a car** (in ein Auto) einsteigen ıı 5 (86)
► S. 185 get

caravan ['kærəvæn] Wohnwagen ıı 1 (8)

card (to) [kɑːd] Karte (an) ı

careful ['keəfl] vorsichtig ı

°**carnival** ['kɑːnɪvl] Fasching, Karneval ı

°**carpet** ['kɑːpɪt] Teppich ı

cart [kɑːt] Karren ı

cash desk ['kæʃ desk] Kasse (in Geschäften) ıı 3 (48/49)

cast [kɑːst] Besetzung; Mitwirkende (Theaterstück, Film) ıı 6 (114)

castle ['kɑːsl] Burg, Schloss ı

cat [kæt] Katze ı

catch [kætʃ], **caught, caught** fangen ı

caught [kɔːt] siehe **catch**

cave [keɪv] Höhle ıı 6 (102)

celebrate ['selɪbreɪt] feiern ıı 5 (84)

celebration [ˌselɪ'breɪʃn] Feier ıı 5 (84)

°**Celsius (C)** ['selsɪəs] Celsius ı

°**Celt** [kelt] Kelte/Keltin ı

°**cent** [sent] Cent ı

centre ['sentə] Zentrum; Mitte ı **shopping centre** Einkaufszentrum ıı 3 (46)

century ['sentʃəri] Jahrhundert ı

chain [tʃeɪn] Kette ı

chair [tʃeə] Stuhl ı

champion ['tʃæmpɪən] Meister/in, Champion ıı 1 (24)

change [tʃeɪndʒ]:
1. (ver)ändern; sich (ver)ändern ıı 2 (35)
2. Wechselgeld ıı 3 (48/49)

°**changing room** ['tʃeɪndʒɪŋ ruːm] Umkleideraum ı

chaos ['keɪɒs] Chaos ı

character ['kærəktə] Figur, Person (in Roman, Film, Theaterstück) ı

charity ['tʃærəti] Wohlfahrtsorganisation; Wohltätigkeit, wohltätige Zwecke ıı 5 (84)

cheap [tʃiːp] billig, preiswert ı

check [tʃek]:
1. Überprüfung, Kontrolle ı
2. (über)prüfen, kontrollieren ı

cheer [tʃɪə] jubeln ıı 2 (36)

cheese [tʃiːz] Käse ı

chess [tʃes] Schach ı

chest [tʃest] Brust, Brustkorb ıı 6 (108)

child [tʃaɪld], pl **children** ['tʃɪldrən] Kind ı

°**Chinese** [ˌtʃaɪ'niːz] chinesisch ı

chips (pl) [tʃɪps] Pommes frites ıı 1 (24)

chocolate ['tʃɒklət]:
1. Schokolade ı
2. Praline ıı 3 (48/49)

choir ['kwaɪə] Chor ıı 5 (86)

choose [tʃuːz], **chose, chosen** aussuchen, (aus)wählen; sich aussuchen ı

chorus ['kɔːrəs] Refrain ıı 5 (98)

chose [tʃəʊz] siehe **choose**

chosen [tʃəʊzn] siehe **choose**

°**Christian** ['krɪstʃən] Christ/in ı

church [tʃɜːtʃ] Kirche ıı 3 (46)

cinema ['sɪnəmə] Kino ı

circle ['sɜːkl] Kreis ıı 5 (99)

city ['sɪti] Stadt, Großstadt ıı 3 (48/49)

clap [klæp] (Beifall) klatschen ıı 2 (36) **Clap your hands.** Klatscht in die Hände. ıı 2 (36)

class [klɑːs] (Schul-)Klasse ı °**in class** im Unterricht ı

°**classical music** ['klæsɪkl] klassische Musik ı

classmate ['klɑːsmeɪt] Mitschüler/in, Klassenkamerad/in ı

classroom ['klɑːsruːm] Klassenzimmer ı

clean [kliːn]:
1. sauber machen, putzen ı
2. sauber ıı 4 (72)

clear [klɪə] klar, deutlich ıı 2 (40)

clever ['klevə] klug, schlau ı

cliff [klɪf] Klippe ıı 6 (102)

climb [klaɪm] klettern; hinaufklettern (auf) ıı 1 (20)

clock [klɒk] (Wand-, Stand-, Turm-) Uhr ı

close [kləʊz] schließen ıı 3 (48/49)

closely ['kləʊsli]: **look closely** genau hinschauen ıı 4 (81)

clothes (pl) [kləʊðz] Kleidung, Kleidungsstücke ı

cloud [klaʊd] Wolke ıı 1 (8)

cloudy ['klaʊdi] bewölkt ıı 1 (8)

clown [klaʊn] Clown ıı 5 (99)

club [klʌb] Klub ı **join a club** in einen Klub eintreten; sich einem Klub anschließen ı

°**coal** [kəʊl] Kohle ı

coast [kəʊst] Küste ı

coat [kəʊt] Mantel ıı 4 (76)

cocoa ['kəʊkəʊ] Kakao ıı 4 (80)

coin [kɔɪn] Münze ı

cola ['kəʊlə] Cola ı

cold [kəʊld]:
1. kalt ı **be cold** frieren ı
2. **have a cold** eine Erkältung haben, erkältet sein ıı 6 (108)

collect [kə'lekt] sammeln ı

colon ['kəʊlən] Doppelpunkt ıı 2 (35)

colour ['kʌlə] Farbe ı

°**column** ['kɒləm] Spalte ı

come [kʌm], **came, come** kommen ı **come home** nach Hause kommen ı **come in** hereinkommen ı °**come in** (guitars, etc.) einsetzen **Come on, Dad.** Na los, Dad! / Komm, Dad! ı

comedy ['kɒmədi] Comedyshow, Komödie ıı 2 (41)

comma ['kɒmə] Komma ıı 2 (35)

°**compare** [kəm'peə] vergleichen ı

competition [ˌkɒmpə'tɪʃn] Wettbewerb ıı 5 (94)

computer [kəm'pjuːtə] Computer ı

concert ['kɒnsət] Konzert ıı 2 (38)

consonant ['kɒnsənənt] Konsonant, Mitlaut ıı 6 (112)

context ['kɒntekst] (Satz-, Text-) Zusammenhang, Kontext ıı 1 (19)

conversation [ˌkɒnvə'seɪʃn] Gespräch, Unterhaltung ıı 5 (99)

°**cook** [kʊk] kochen, zubereiten ı

cool [kuːl]:
1. cool ı
2. kühl ıı 2 (34)

copy ['kɒpi]:
1. kopieren, abschreiben ı
2. Kopie; Exemplar ıı 6 (104)

corner ['kɔːnə] Ecke ı **corner shop** Laden an der Ecke; Tante-Emma-Laden ı **on the corner of Church Road and London Road** Church Road, Ecke London Road ıı 3 (46)

cornflakes ['kɔːnfleɪks] Cornflakes ı

correct [kə'rekt]:
1. richtig, korrekt ıı 2 (40)
2. korrigieren, verbessern ıı 4 (73)

cost [kɒst], **cost, cost** kosten ıı 3 (48/49)

costume ['kɒstjuːm] Kostüm, Verkleidung ıı 5 (84)

cottage ['kɒtɪdʒ] Häuschen, Cottage ıı 4 (80)

cough [kɒf]: **have a cough** Husten haben ıı 6 (108)

could [kʊd, kəd]:
1. **he could …** er konnte … ı **we couldn't …** ['kʊdnt] wir konnten

two hundred and eleven **211**

Dictionary

nicht … I
2. What could be better? Was könnte besser sein? II 2 (40)
count [kaʊnt] zählen I **count to ten** bis zehn zählen
country [ˈkʌntri] Land (Staat) II 1 (10)
countryside [ˈkʌntrisaɪd] Landschaft, (ländliche) Gegend II 4 (66)
county [ˈkaʊnti] Grafschaft (in Großbritannien) I
course [kɔːs] Kurs, Lehrgang I
°**court** [kɔːt]: **tennis court** Tennisplatz
courtyard [ˈkɔːtjɑːd] Innenhof II 6 (104)
cousin [ˈkʌzn] Cousin, Cousine I
°**cover** [ˈkʌvə]: **inside cover** Umschlaginnenseite
cow [kaʊ] Kuh II 4 (67)
crab [kræb] Krebs I
crash [kræʃ] crashen II 1 (10)
cream [kriːm] Sahne I °**cream tea** Mahlzeit mit Tee, Scones, Marmelade und Sahne
°**creative** [kriˈeɪtɪv] kreativ
crib sheet [ˈkrɪb ʃiːt] (infml) Spickzettel, Merkzettel II 1 (13)
cricket [ˈkrɪkɪt] Cricket I
°**crier** [ˈkraɪə]: **town crier** Stadtausrufer/in
cross [krɒs] überqueren; sich kreuzen II 3 (46)
°**cross out** [ˌkrɒs ˈaʊt] durchstreichen
crowd [kraʊd] (Menschen-) Menge II 5 (84)
crown [kraʊn] Krone II 6 (115)
cry [kraɪ] schreien; weinen II 4 (76)
°**cult** [kʌlt] Kult; Kult-
cup [kʌp]: **a cup of tea** eine Tasse Tee I
cupboard [ˈkʌbəd] Schrank I
°**curry** [ˈkʌri] Curry (Gericht)
cut [kʌt], **cut, cut** schneiden II 3 (58)
Cut! Schnitt! (beim Filmen) II 3 (58)

D

dad [dæd] Papa, Vati I
dance [dɑːns]:
1. tanzen I
2. Tanz II 2 (42)
dance floor [ˈdɑːns flɔː] Tanzfläche II 2 (42)
dancer [ˈdɑːnsə] Tänzer/in II 2 (28)
danger [ˈdeɪndʒə] Gefahr II 6 (114)
dangerous [ˈdeɪndʒərəs] gefährlich I
dark [dɑːk] dunkel I

daughter [ˈdɔːtə] Tochter II 1 (14)
day [deɪ] Tag I **all day** den ganzen Tag II 5 (98) **day of the week** Wochentag I **go on day trips** Tagesausflüge machen II 1 (12)
dead [ded] tot I
dear [dɪə]:
1. Oh dear! Oje! II 4 (70)
2. dear liebe(r, s) II 6 (110)
December [dɪˈsembə] Dezember I
decide [dɪˈsaɪd] beschließen, sich entscheiden; sich interessieren (für) II 4 (75)
°**deck** [dek] Deck, Terrasse
°**decorate** [ˈdekəreɪt] verzieren
deep [diːp] tief II 5 (98)
deer [dɪə] Reh, Hirsch II 4 (78)
°**defend sb./sth. (against sb./sth.)** [dɪˈfend] jn./etwas verteidigen (gegen jn./etwas) II 5 (94)
°**degree** [dɪˈɡriː] Grad
delicious [dɪˈlɪʃəs] köstlich, lecker II 4 (72)
demonstration [ˌdemənˈstreɪʃn] Demonstration, Vorführung II 5 (90)
dentist [ˈdentɪst] Zahnarzt/-ärztin II 6 (108)
°**describe sth. (to sb.)** [dɪˈskraɪb] (jm.) etwas beschreiben II 3 (55)
°**description** [dɪˈskrɪpʃn] Beschreibung
design and technology [dɪˌzaɪn ənd tekˈnɒlədʒi] Design und Technik I
designer [dɪˈzaɪnə] Designer/in II 2 (38)
desk [desk] Schreibtisch I
dessert [dɪˈzɜːt] Nachtisch, Nachspeise I
destroy [dɪˈstrɔɪ] zerstören II 5 (94)
°**detail** [ˈdiːteɪl] Detail, Einzelheit
°**Devil, devil** [ˈdevl] Teufel
dialogue [ˈdaɪəlɒɡ] Dialog II 2 (31)
diary [ˈdaɪəri] Tagebuch; Kalender I
dictionary [ˈdɪkʃənri] alphabetisches Wörterverzeichnis, Wörterbuch I
did [dɪd] siehe **do**
die [daɪ] sterben I
different [ˈdɪfrənt] verschieden; anders I
°**diner** [ˈdaɪnə] einfaches Restaurant in den USA
dining room [ˈdaɪnɪŋ ruːm] Esszimmer I
dinner [ˈdɪnə] Abendessen, Abendbrot I **have dinner** zu Abend essen I
director [dəˈrektə] Regisseur/in II 5 (90)
dirty [ˈdɜːti] schmutzig II 4 (72)

disappear [ˌdɪsəˈpɪə] verschwinden II 3 (58)
°**disaster** [dɪˈzɑːstə] Desaster, Katastrophe
disco [ˈdɪskəʊ] Disko II 2 (42)
°**discuss sth.** [dɪˈskʌs] über etwas diskutieren, etwas besprechen
°**dish** [dɪʃ] Gericht
dishes (pl) [ˈdɪʃɪz]: **wash the dishes** das Geschirr abwaschen, spülen II 1 (24)
dislikes [dɪsˈlaɪks]: **likes and dislikes** (pl) Vorlieben und Abneigungen I
divorced [dɪˈvɔːst] geschieden I
do [duː], **did, done** machen, tun I **do sport** Sport treiben I **Don't go.** [dəʊnt] Geh nicht. I **he doesn't have time** er hat keine Zeit I
doctor [ˈdɒktə] Arzt/Ärztin, Doktor II 6 (108)
dog [dɒɡ] Hund I
°**dome** [dəʊm] Kuppel
done [dʌn] siehe **do**
°**donkey** [ˈdɒŋki] Esel
door [dɔː] Tür I °**back door** Hintertür °**front door** Vordertür
doorbell [ˈdɔːbel] Türklingel II 2 (28)
double [ˈdʌbl] Doppel- I
down [daʊn] hinunter, herunter; nach unten I **down there** dort unten II 3 (58) **up and down** auf und ab; rauf und runter I
downstairs [ˌdaʊnˈsteəz] unten; nach unten (im Haus) I
draft [drɑːft] Entwurf II 3 (56)
°**dragon** [ˈdræɡən] Drache
drama [ˈdrɑːmə] Schauspiel; darstellende Kuns II 2 (42)
drank [dræŋk] siehe **drink**
draw [drɔː], **drew, drawn** zeichnen I
drawing [ˈdrɔːɪŋ] Zeichnung I
drawn [drɔːn] siehe **draw**
dream [driːm]:
1. Traum I
°**2.** träumen
dress [dres] Kleid I
dress up [ˌdres ˈʌp]:
1. sich verkleiden II 5 (84)
2. sich schick anziehen II 5 (84)
drew [druː] siehe **draw**
drink [drɪŋk]:
1. (drank, drunk) trinken I
2. Getränk I
drive [draɪv], **drove, driven** (mit dem Auto) fahren II 5 (86)
driven [ˈdrɪvn] siehe **drive**

212 two hundred and twelve

English – German

drop sth. [drɒp] etwas fallen lassen II 2 (42)

drove [drəʊv] *siehe* **drive**

drum [drʌm] Trommel I **drums** *(pl)* Schlagzeug I **play the drums** Schlagzeug spielen I

drunk [drʌŋk] *siehe* **drink**

°**dues** [djuːz]: **I've paid my dues** *etwa:* Ich habe für meine Missetaten gebüßt.

°**during** ['djʊərɪŋ] während

DVD [ˌdiːviːˈdiː] DVD I

E

each [iːtʃ] jeder, jede, jedes (einzelne) II 6 (104)

ear [ɪə] Ohr I

early ['ɜːli] früh I

earphones *(pl)* ['ɪəfəʊnz] Ohrhörer, Kopfhörer II 2 (30)

earth [ɜːθ] Erde *(der Planet)* II 2 (34) **on earth** auf der Erde II 2 (34)

easy ['iːzi] leicht, einfach I

eat [iːt], **ate, eaten** essen I

eaten ['iːtn] *siehe* **eat**

edit ['edɪt] bearbeiten; schneiden *(Film, Video)* I

e.g. [ˌiːˈdʒiː] z.B. (zum Beispiel) II 5 (89)

egg [eg] Ei II 4 (72)

eight [eɪt] acht I

either ['aɪðə, 'iːðə]: **not ... either** auch nicht II 4 (81)

elephant ['elɪfənt] Elefant I

eleven [ɪ'levn] elf I

°**else** [els]: **anyone else** sonst jemand **What else ...?** Was sonst?

email ['iːmeɪl] E-Mail I

°**empty** ['empti] sich leeren

encore ['ɒŋkɔː] Zugabe II 5 (86)

end [end] Ende, Schluss I °**in the end** schließlich, am Ende, zum Schluss

ending ['endɪŋ] Ende, (Ab-)Schluss II 5 (99)

enemy ['enəmi] Feind/in II 6 (114)

English ['ɪŋglɪʃ] Englisch; englisch I **in English** auf Englisch I

°**enjoy** [ɪn'dʒɔɪ] genießen

enough [ɪ'nʌf] genug I

enter ['entə] betreten, hineingehen in II 6 (104)

°**entertaining** [ˌentə'teɪnɪŋ] unterhaltsam

entry ['entri] Eintrag, Eintragung *(im Tagebuch, Wörterbuch)* II 5 (99)

°**especially** [ɪ'speʃəli] besonders

etc. (et cetera) [et'setərə] usw. (und so weiter) II 4 (67)

°**euro** ['jʊərəʊ] Euro

even ['iːvn] sogar II 2 (36) **not even** (noch) nicht einmal II 4 (81)

even if ['iːvn_ɪf] selbst wenn II 5 (98)

evening ['iːvnɪŋ] Abend I **in the evening** abends, am Abend I **this evening** heute Abend II 1 (14)

event [ɪ'vent] Ereignis II 5 (90)

ever ['evə] jemals II 1 (14) **better than ever** besser als je zuvor II 5 (90) **for ever** (für) immer; ewig II 4 (76)

every day/colour/boat ['evri] jeder Tag / jede Farbe / jedes Boot I

everybody ['evribɒdi] jeder; alle I

everyday ['evrideɪ] Alltags- I

everyone ['evriwʌn] jeder; alle I

everything ['evriθɪŋ] alles II 2 (35)

everywhere ['evriweə] überall II 4 (76)

example [ɪg'zɑːmpl] Beispiel II 1 (14)

except [ɪk'sept] außer, bis auf II 2 (42)

excited [ɪk'saɪtɪd] aufgeregt, gespannt I

exciting [ɪk'saɪtɪŋ] aufregend, spannend I

exclamation mark [ˌeksklə'meɪʃn mɑːk] Ausrufezeichen II 2 (35)

Excuse me, ... [ɪk'skjuːz miː] Entschuldigung, ... / Entschuldigen Sie, ... II 3 (46)
▶ S. 187 „Entschuldigung"

exercise ['eksəsaɪz] Aufgabe, Übung I

exercise book ['eksəsaɪz bʊk] Schulheft, Übungsheft I

°**exit** ['eksɪt, 'egzɪt] *(von der Bühne)* abgehen *(Theater)*

expensive [ɪk'spensɪv] teuer I

explain sth. to sb. [ɪk'spleɪn] jm. etwas erklären, erläutern I

°**explosion** [ɪk'spləʊʒn] Explosion I

eye [aɪ] Auge I

F

face [feɪs] Gesicht I

fair [feə] fair, gerecht I

fall [fɔːl], **fell, fallen** fallen, stürzen; hinfallen I **fall asleep** einschlafen I **fall in love (with sb.)** sich verlieben (in jn.)

fallen ['fɔːlən] *siehe* **fall**

°**falls** *(pl)* [fɔːlz] Wasserfälle

family ['fæməli] Familie I **the Blackwell family** (die) Familie Blackwell I °**family name** Familienname, Nachname **family**

tree (Familien-)Stammbaum I **host family** Gastfamilie II 1 (18)

famous (for) ['feɪməs] berühmt (für, wegen) II 5 (94) °**world-famous** weltberühmt

fan [fæn] Fan, Anhänger/in I

fantastic [fæn'tæstɪk] fantastisch I

far [fɑː] weit (entfernt) I **so far** bis jetzt; bis hierher II 2 (36) °**far and wide** weit und breit

farm [fɑːm] Bauernhof, Farm I

farmer ['fɑːmə] Bauer/Bäuerin, Landwirt/in I

fashion ['fæʃn] Mode II 2 (38)

fast [fɑːst]:
1. schnell I
°**2.** fasten

fat [fæt] dick, fett I

father ['fɑːðə] Vater I

favourite ['feɪvərɪt]: **my favourite animal** mein Lieblingstier I

February ['februəri] Februar I

fed [fed] *siehe* **feed**

feed [fiːd], **fed, fed** füttern I **feeding time** Fütterungszeit I

°**feedback** ['fiːdbæk] Rückmeldung, Feedback

feel [fiːl], **felt, felt** fühlen; sich fühlen I **I feel sick.** Mir ist schlecht. II 6 (105) **I don't feel well** Ich fühle mich nicht gut. / Mir geht's nicht gut. II 6 (105)
▶ S. 204 ill – sick – well

feeling ['fiːlɪŋ] Gefühl I

feet [fiːt] *Plural von* **foot** II 4 (66)

fell [fel] *siehe* **fall**

felt [felt] *siehe* **feel**

felt pen [felt 'pen] Filzstift II 3 (48/49)

fence [fens] Zaun II 4 (81)

ferry ['feri] Fähre I

festival ['festɪvl] Fest, Festival II 5 (84)

few [fjuː]: **a few** ein paar, einige II 2 (30)

field [fiːld] Feld, Acker, Weide II 4 (66) °**playing field** Spielfeld

fight [faɪt], **fought, fought** kämpfen I **fight sb.** jn. bekämpfen II 3 (54)

fighter ['faɪtə] Kämpfer/in II 2 (28)

file [faɪl]: **background file** *Hintergrundinformation(en)* I **grammar file** *Zusammenfassung der Grammatik jeder Unit* I **skills file** *Übersicht über Lern- und Arbeitstechniken* I

film [fɪlm]:
1. filmen I
2. Film I

final ['faɪnl] Finale, Endspiel I

two hundred and thirteen **213**

Dictionary

find [faɪnd], **found, found** finden ı
Find someone who … Finde
jemanden, der … ı **find sth. out**
etwas herausfinden II 2 (32) °**find
out about sth.** sich über etwas in-
formieren
fine [faɪn] fein II 2 (39) **Fine,
thanks.** Gut, danke. ı
finger [ˈfɪŋgə] Finger II 6 (108)
finish [ˈfɪnɪʃ]:
1. enden ı
2. finish sth. etwas beenden; mit
etwas fertig werden/sein ı
°**3. finish sth.** etwas vervollständigen; etwas abschließen
finished [ˈfɪnɪʃt]: **We're finished.**
Wir sind fertig. ı
fire [ˈfaɪə] Feuer II 1 (25)
fireplace [ˈfaɪəpleɪs] Kamin II 4 (80)
firework [ˈfaɪəwɜːk] Feuerwerkskörper II 5 (84)
fireworks (pl) [ˈfaɪəwɜːks] Feuerwerk II 5 (84)
first [fɜːst] zuerst, als Erstes ı **at
first** zuerst, anfangs, am Anfang
II 1 (10) **the first day** der erste Tag ı
fish [fɪʃ], pl **fish** Fisch ı
five [faɪv] fünf ı
flag [flæg] Fahne, Flagge II 5 (84)
flash [flæʃ] Lichtblitz II 2 (42) **a
flash of lightning** ein Blitz II 5 (98)
flat [flæt] Wohnung ı
flew [fluː] siehe **fly**
floor [flɔː]:
1. Fußboden ı
2. Stock(werk) II 6 (110)
flower [ˈflaʊə] Blume; Blüte
II 3 (48/49)
flown [fləʊn] siehe **fly**
fly [flaɪ], **flew, flown** fliegen II 5 (92)
°**flyer** [ˈflaɪə] Flyer, Flugblatt
°**foal** [fəʊl] Fohlen
°**foil** [fɔɪl] Folie (Alufolie)
°**folder** [ˈfəʊldə] Mappe
follow [ˈfɒləʊ] folgen ı **Follow me.**
Folg(t) mir. ı °**the following …**
die folgenden …
food [fuːd] Essen; Lebensmittel;
Futter ı
foot [fʊt], pl **feet** [fiːt] Fuß II 4 (66)
football [ˈfʊtbɔːl] Fußball ı
footprint [ˈfʊtprɪnt] Fußabdruck
II 4 (66)
for [fɔː, fə] für ı **for ever** (für)
immer; ewig II 4 (76) **for example**
zum Beispiel II 1 (14) **What's for
lunch?** Was gibt es zum Mittagessen? ı **for miles** meilenweit II 4 (76)

What's for homework? Was haben
wir als Hausaufgabe auf? ı
foreground [ˈfɔːgraʊnd] Vordergrund
II 4 (66)
forest [ˈfɒrɪst] Wald II 1 (8)
forget [fəˈget], **forgot, forgotten**
vergessen ı
forgot [fəˈgɒt] siehe **forget**
forgotten [fəˈgɒtn] siehe **forget**
fork [fɔːk] Gabel II 2 (42)
form (of) [fɔːm] Form (von) ı
forward [ˈfɔːwəd]: **look forward to
sth.** sich auf etwas freuen II 1 (20)
fought [fɔːt] siehe **fight**
found [faʊnd] siehe **find**
°**fountain** [ˈfaʊntɪn] Fontäne
four [fɔː] vier ı
°**frame** [freɪm] Rahmen
free [friː]:
1. frei ı **free time** Freizeit, freie
Zeit ı **free-time activities** Freizeitaktivitäten ı
2. kostenlos II 1 (18)
French [frentʃ] Französisch ı
fresh [freʃ] frisch II 6 (108)
Friday [ˈfraɪdeɪ, ˈfraɪdi] Freitag ı
friend [frend] Freund/in ı
friendly [ˈfrendli] freundlich ı
fries (pl) [fraɪz] Pommes frites II 1 (24)
frog [frɒg] Frosch ı
from [frɒm, frəm] aus, von ı **from
… to …** von … bis … ı
front [frʌnt] Vorderseite ı **in front
of** vor (räumlich) **to the front**
nach vorne II 5 (86) °**front door**
Vordertür
frown [fraʊn] die Stirn runzeln
II 6 (110)
fruit [fruːt] Obst, Früchte; Frucht ı
fruit salad Obstsalat ı
°**frying pan** [ˈfraɪɪŋ pæn] Bratpfanne
full (of) [fʊl] voll II 4 (80) **full
sentence** ganzer Satz II 5 (89)
full stop [ˌfʊl ˈstɒp] Punkt II 2 (35)
fun [fʌn] Spaß ı **have fun** Spaß
haben, sich amüsieren ı °**a fun
place** ein Ort, an dem man Spaß
haben kann **That sounds fun.**
Das klingt nach Spaß. ı **Was it fun?**
Hat es Spaß gemacht? ı
funny [ˈfʌni] witzig, komisch ı
fun park [ˈfʌn pɑːk] Vergnügungspark II 1 (8)
°**fur** [fɜː] Pelz, Fell ı
further [ˈfɜːðə] weiter II 3 (58)
furthest [ˈfɜːðɪst] am weitesten
II 3 (58)

future [ˈfjuːtʃə]:
1. Zukunft II 1 (22)
2. zukünftige(r, s) II 1 (22)

G

°**galley** [ˈgæli] Kombüse, Bordküche
game [geɪm] Spiel ı
garage [ˈgærɑːʒ, ˈgærɪdʒ] Garage ı
garden [ˈgɑːdn] Garten ı
gardening [ˈgɑːdnɪŋ] Gärtnern,
Gartenarbeit ı
gate [geɪt] Tor, Pforte, Gatter II 3 (58)
°**gatehouse** [ˈgeɪthaʊs] Pförtnerhaus
gave [geɪv] siehe **give**
gel [dʒel] Gel II 2 (42)
geography [dʒiˈɒgrəfi] Geografie ı
German [ˈdʒɜːmən] Deutsch; deutsch
ı **in German** auf Deutsch ı
get [get], **got, got:**
1. bekommen ı **Did you get it?**
(infml) Hast du es verstanden? / Hast
du es mitbekommen? ı **get sth.**
(sich) etwas besorgen, (sich) etwas
holen II 2 (32)
2. gelangen, (hin)kommen ı **get in
touch (with sb.)** (mit jm.) Kontakt
aufnehmen ı sich (mit jm.) in Verbindung setzen II 1 (18) **get in(to) a
car/taxi** (in ein Auto/Taxi) einsteigen II 5 (86) **get on a bus/train/
plane** (in einen Bus/Zug, in ein Flugzeug) einsteigen II 5 (86)
3. get off (the bus/boat) (aus
dem Bus/Boot) aussteigen ı **get
out (of a car)** (aus einem Auto) aussteigen II 5 (86)
4. get on vorankommen, zurechtkommen II 2 (32)
5. get up aufstehen ı
6. get angry/cold/… wütend/
kalt/… werden ı **get ready (for)**
sich fertig machen (für), sich vorbereiten (auf) II 2 (32)
▶ S. 185 get
▶ S. 206 German „werden"
ghost [gəʊst] Geist, Gespenst ı
giraffe [dʒəˈrɑːf] Giraffe ı
girl [gɜːl] Mädchen ı
give [gɪv], **gave, given:**
1. geben ı °**give a concert** ein
Konzert geben
2. give a talk (about) einen Vortrag / eine Rede halten (über) ı
3. give sb. a lift jn. mitnehmen
II 5 (90)
4. give sb. a hug jn. umarmen
II 1 (25)

214 two hundred and fourteen

English – German

given ['gɪvn] *siehe* **give**

glass [glɑːs] Glas II 4 (72) **a glass of water** ein Glas Wasser II 4 (72)

glasses (pl) ['glɑːsɪz] (eine) Brille II 2 (42)

glove [glʌv] Handschuh II 5 (86)

glue [gluː] Klebstoff I

glue stick ['gluː stɪk] Klebestift I

go [gəʊ], **went, gone:**
1. gehen; fahren I **go by car/bus/ ...** mit dem Auto/Bus/... fahren I **go camping** zelten gehen II 1 (8) **go down** untergehen (Sonne) I **go for a walk** spazieren gehen, einen Spaziergang machen I **go home** nach Hause gehen I **go in** hineingehen II 2 (31) **go on** weiterreden, fortfahren; weitermachen I **go on day trips** Tagesausflüge machen II 1 (12) **go on holiday** in Urlaub fahren II 1 (10) **go sailing** segeln; segeln gehen I **go shopping** einkaufen gehen I °**go out for a meal** essen gehen **go with sth.** zu etwas gehören, zu etwas passen I **Here we go.** Los geht's. / Jetzt geht's los. I **I'm going to sing a song.** Ich werde ein Lied singen. / Ich habe vor ein Lied zu singen. II 2 (30)
2. Have a go. Versuch's mal. I
3. go green/hard/bad/mad grün/hart/schlecht/verrückt werden II 6 (110) **go red** rot werden, erröten II 6 (110)
▶ S. 206 German „werden"
°**4.** machen (Geräusch)

goat [gəʊt] Ziege II 4 (67)

°**goddess** ['gɒdes] Göttin

go-kart ['gəʊ kɑːt] Gokart II 1 (10)

gold [gəʊld]:
1. Gold I
2. golden, Gold- II 5 (99)

°**golden** ['gəʊldən] golden

gone [gɒn] *siehe* **go** °**has gone** ist fort, ist weg(gegangen)

good [gʊd]:
1. gut I **be good at kung fu** gut sein in Kung-Fu; gut Kung-Fu können I **Good luck!** Viel Glück! I **Good morning.** Guten Morgen. I
2. brav II 3 (54)

Goodbye. [ˌgʊd'baɪ] Auf Wiedersehen. I

good-looking [ˌgʊd'lʊkɪŋ] gutaussehend II 2 (42)

goods (pl) [gʊdz] Waren, Güter I

got [gɒt]:
1. *siehe* **get**
2. Have you got ...? Haben Sie

...? / Hast du ...? / Habt ihr ...? II 3 (48/49)

gram (g) [græm] Gramm II 3 (52)

grammar file ['græmə ˌfaɪl] Zusammenfassung der Grammatik I

°**Grammy award** ['græmi əˌwɔːd] Grammy Award (US-Musikpreis)

grandfather ['grænfɑːðə] Großvater I

grandma ['grænmɑː] Oma I **at Grandma's (house/flat)** bei Oma II 6 (105)

grandmother ['grænmʌðə] Großmutter I

grandpa ['grænpɑː] Opa I

grandparents (pl) ['grænpeərənts] Großeltern I

grass [grɑːs] Gras; Rasen II 4 (66)

grave [greɪv] Grab II 4 (81)

°**gravy** ['greɪvi] Soße

great [greɪt] großartig I

green [griːn] grün I

°**greetings** (pl) ['griːtɪŋz] Grüße

grew [gruː] *siehe* **grow**

grey [greɪ] grau I

groan [grəʊn]:
1. Stöhnen II 6 (105)
2. stöhnen II 6 (105)

ground [graʊnd] (Erd-)Boden II 4 (80)

group (of) [gruːp] Gruppe I

grow [grəʊ], **grew, grown:**
1. anbauen, anpflanzen I
2. wachsen II 4 (81)

grown [grəʊn] *siehe* **grow**

guard [gɑːd] Wachposten, Wache II 6 (104)

guess [ges] raten, erraten, schätzen I **Guess what, Dad ...** Stell dir vor, Papa ... / Weißt du was, Papa ... I

guide [gaɪd] Fremdenführer/in; Reiseleiter/in II 6 (104)

guinea pig ['gɪni pɪg] Meerschweinchen I

guitar [gɪ'tɑː] Gitarre I **play the guitar** Gitarre spielen I

gym [dʒɪm] Turnhalle I

gymnastics [dʒɪm'næstɪks] Gymnastik, Turnen I

H

had [hæd] *siehe* **have**

hair [heə] Haar, Haare I

half [hɑːf], *pl* **halves** [hɑːvz] Halbzeit I **half past ten** halb elf (10.30 / 22.30) I °**an hour and a half** eineinhalb Stunden °**half an hour** eine halbe Stunde

hall [hɔːl]: **town hall** Rathaus II 2 (38)

hamburger ['hæmbɜːgə] Hamburger II 1 (24)

hamster ['hæmstə] Hamster II 2 (35)

hand [hænd]:
1. Hand I **Clap your hands.** Klatscht in die Hände. II 2 (36)
2. hand sth. in etwas abgeben; etwas einreichen II 6 (104)

hang [hæŋ], **hung, hung:** hängen II 3 (56) °**hang up** aufhängen

happen (to) ['hæpən] geschehen, passieren (mit) II 3 (54)

happy ['hæpi] glücklich, froh I

harbour ['hɑːbə] Hafen I

hard [hɑːd] schwer, schwierig; hart I **go hard** (bread) hart werden II 6 (110)
▶ S. 206 German „werden"

°**harmonica** [hɑː'mɒnɪkə] Mundharmonika

has [hæz]: **he/she has** er/sie hat I

hat [hæt] Hut II 5 (86)

have [hæv, həv], **had, had** haben I **May I have a word with you?** Kann ich Sie kurz sprechen? II 5 (94) **Have a go.** Versuch's mal. I **have breakfast** frühstücken I **have dinner** zu Abend essen I **have fun** Spaß haben, sich amüsieren I **have lunch** zu Mittag essen I **have to do** tun müssen I **I'll have a tea/ burger/...** Ich nehme einen Tee/ Hamburger/... (beim Essen, im Restaurant) II 6 (113)
▶ S. 185 German „groß"
▶ S. 203 must – needn't – mustn't

have got [hæv 'gɒt, həv 'gɒt], **had, had** haben II 3 (48/49) **Have you got ...?** Haben Sie ...? / Hast du ...? / Habt ihr ...? II 3 (48/49)

hay [heɪ] Heu II 4 (68)

he [hiː] er I

head [hed] Kopf I

headache ['hedeɪk]: **have a headache** Kopfschmerzen haben II 6 (108)

hear [hɪə], **heard, heard** hören I °**Hear ye!** (altmodisch) Hört!

heard [hɜːd] *siehe* **hear**

heart [hɑːt] Herz II 5 (98) °**learn sth. by heart** etwas auswendig lernen

heavy ['hevi] schwer (von Gewicht) II 4 (72) **heavy rain** starker Regen, heftiger Regen II 5 (98)

held [held] *siehe* **hold**

Hello. [hə'ləʊ] Hallo. / Guten Tag. I

Dictionary

help [help]:
1. Hilfe ।
2. helfen ।
helper ['helpə] Helfer/in II 2 (28)
her [hɜː, hə]:
1. ihr, ihre । **her best friend** ihr bester Freund / ihre beste Freundin ।
2. sie; ihr ।
here [hɪə] hier; hierher । **Here we go.** Los geht's. / Jetzt geht's los. ।
Here you are. Bitte sehr. / Hier bitte. II 1 (15) **near here** (hier) in der Nähe । **over here** hier herüber II 5 (86) **up here** hier oben; nach hier oben II 3 (58)
°**hero** ['hɪərəʊ] Held/in
hers [hɜːz] ihrer, ihre, ihrs II 2 (36)
▶ S. 186 Possessivpronomen
hid [hɪd] siehe **hide**
hidden ['hɪdn] siehe **hide**
hide [haɪd], **hid, hidden** sich verstecken, etwas verstecken ।
high [haɪ] hoch ।
highlight ['haɪlaɪt] hervorheben, markieren (mit Textmarker) II 3 (56)
hill [hɪl] Hügel ।
him [hɪm] ihn; ihm ।
°**hip hop** ['hɪp ˌhɒp] Hip-Hop ।
°**hire** ['haɪə] Leihgebühr ।
his [hɪz]:
1. his friend sein Freund / seine Freundin ।
2. seiner, seine, seins II 2 (36)
▶ S. 186 Possessivpronomen
hiss [hɪs] zischen II 6 (105)
°**historical** [hɪ'stɒrɪkl] historisch
history ['hɪstri] Geschichte ।
hit [hɪt], **hit, hit:**
1. prallen, stoßen gegen ।
2. schlagen II 1 (15)
3. treffen II 6 (107)
°**4.** Hit
hobby ['hɒbi] Hobby ।
hold [həʊld], **held, held** halten ।
°**hold sth. up** etwas aufhalten, etwas hochhalten **Hold on a minute.** Bleib / Bleiben Sie am Apparat. (am Telefon) II 1 (12)
hole [həʊl] Loch II 3 (59)
holiday ['hɒlədeɪ] Urlaub II 1 (10) **be on holiday** in Urlaub sein II 1 (10) **go on holiday** in Urlaub fahren II 1 (10)
holidays (pl) ['hɒlədeɪz] Ferien ।
home [həʊm] Heim, Zuhause । **at home** daheim, zu Hause । **come/go home** nach Hause kommen/gehen ।
°**homeless** ['həʊmləs] obdachlos

hometown [ˌhəʊm'taʊn] Heimatstadt ।
homework ['həʊmwɜːk] Hausaufgabe(n) । **Do your homework.** Mach deine Hausaufgaben. । **What's for homework?** Was haben wir als Hausaufgabe auf? ।
honour ['ɒnə] Ehre II 4 (81)
°**Hooray!** [hʊ'reɪ] Hurra!
hope [həʊp] hoffen ।
horse [hɔːs] Pferd ।
hospital ['hɒspɪtl] Krankenhaus II 6 (108)
host family ['həʊst fæməli] Gastfamilie II 1 (18)
°**hostel** ['hɒstl] Herberge, Wohnheim ।
hot [hɒt] heiß ।
hotel [həʊ'tel] Hotel II 1 (8)
hour ['aʊə] Stunde । °**an hour and a half** eineinhalb Stunden °**half an hour** eine halbe Stunde ।
house [haʊs] Haus ।
how [haʊ] wie । **How are you?** Wie geht's? / Wie geht es dir/euch? । **How do you like it?** Wie findest du es (sie/ihn)? / Wie gefällt es (sie/er) dir? । **How many?** Wie viele? । **How much?** Wie viel? । **How much are ...?** Was kosten ...? । **How much is ...?** Was kostet ...? । **How old are you?** Wie alt bist du? ।
°**however** [haʊ'evə] jedoch ।
°**hug** [hʌg]:
1. jn. umarmen II 3 (59)
2. give sb. a hug jn. umarmen II 1 (25)
°**huge** [hjuːdʒ] riesig
hundred ['hʌndrəd]: **a/one hundred** einhundert ।
hung [hʌŋ] siehe **hang**
hungry ['hʌŋgri]: **be hungry** hungrig sein, Hunger haben ।
hurry ['hʌri] eilen; sich beeilen II 3 (59) **hurry up** sich beeilen ।
hurt [hɜːt], **hurt, hurt:** schmerzen, wehtun; verletzen II 4 (76)
▶ S. 196 hurt
hyphen ['haɪfən] Bindestrich II 2 (35)

I

I [aɪ] ich । **I'm from Plymouth.** Ich bin/komme aus Plymouth. । **I'm two years old.** Ich bin zwei Jahre alt. । °**I spy with my little eye** entspricht dem Spiel "Ich sehe was, was du nicht siehst"
ice [aɪs] Eis II 6 (108)

ice cream [ˌaɪs 'kriːm] (Speise-)Eis ।
°**ice rink** ['aɪs rɪŋk] Eislaufbahn ।
iced tea [ˌaɪst 'tiː] Eistee II 6 (113)
ICT [ˌaɪ siː 'tiː] Informations- und Kommunikationstechnologie ।
idea [aɪ'dɪə] Idee; Vorstellung ।
if [ɪf] wenn, falls II 1 (10) **even if** selbst wenn II 5 (98)
ill [ɪl] krank II 6 (105)
▶ S. 204 ill – sick – well
°**illustration** [ˌɪlə'streɪʃn] Illustration ।
imagine sth. [ɪ'mædʒɪn] sich etwas vorstellen ।
important [ɪm'pɔːtnt] wichtig ।
impossible [ɪm'pɒsəbl] unmöglich II 4 (76)
in [ɪn] in । **be in** zu Hause sein II 1 (10) **come in** hereinkommen । **in 1580** im Jahr 1580 । **in a loud voice** mit lauter Stimme II 3 (54) °**in class** im Unterricht । **in front of** vor (räumlich) । **in German/English** auf Deutsch/Englisch । **in the afternoon** nachmittags, am Nachmittag । **in the attic** auf dem Dachboden । °**in the end** schließlich, am Ende, zum Schluss **in the evening** abends, am Abend । **in the middle** in der Mitte । **in the morning** morgens, vormittags, am Morgen/Vormittag । **in the photo/ picture** auf dem Foto/Bild । **in the world** auf der Welt II 1 (8)
°**including** [ɪn'kluːdɪŋ] inklusive, einschließlich
Indian ['ɪndiən] Inder/in; indisch II 5 (90)
°**indoor** ['ɪndɔː]: **indoor people** Leute, die lieber drinnen sind
information (about/on) (no pl) [ˌɪnfə'meɪʃn] Information(en) (über) । **Information and Communications Technology** Informations- und Kommunikationstechnologie ।
°**inn** [ɪn] Gasthof ।
°**insect** ['ɪnsekt] Insekt ।
inside [ˌɪn'saɪd]:
1. drinnen; nach drinnen ।
2. inside sth. innerhalb von etwas II 6 (108)
°**3. inside cover** Umschlaginnenseite
instead [ɪn'sted] stattdessen II 4 (81)
°**instruction** [ɪn'strʌkʃn] Anweisung ।
instrument ['ɪnstrəmənt] Instrument ।
interested ['ɪntrəstɪd]: **be interested (in)** interessiert sein (an) II 4 (75)

English – German

interesting ['ɪntrəstɪŋ] interessant I
interrupt [ˌɪntə'rʌpt] unterbrechen
II 5 (99)
interview ['ɪntəvjuː]:
1. Interview II 6 (115)
2. interviewen, befragen I
into ['ɪntʊ]: **into the kitchen** in die
Küche (hinein) I
introduce sth./sb. (to sb.)
[ˌɪntrə'djuːs] etwas/jn. (jm.) vorstellen II 5 (93)
°**introduction** [ˌɪntrə'dʌkʃn] Einleitung
invade (a country) [ɪn'veɪd] (in ein
Land) einmarschieren II 5 (95)
invitation (to) [ˌɪnvɪ'teɪʃn]
Einladung (zu, nach) I
invite sb. (to) [ɪn'vaɪt] jn. einladen
(zu) II 1 (14)
irregular [ɪ'regjələ] unregelmäßig
II 3 (55)
is [ɪz]: **Is it Monday?** Ist es Montag? I **Is that you?** Bist du's? /
Bist du das? I **The camera is ...**
Die Kamera kostet ... I
island ['aɪlənd] Insel I
isn't ['ɪznt]: **he/she/it isn't (= is
not)** er/sie/es ist nicht ... I
it [ɪt] er, sie, es I
it's ... (= it is) [ɪts] er/sie/es ist ... I
its name [ɪts] sein Name / ihr Name I

J

jacket ['dʒækɪt] Jacke II 1 (23)
°**jacket potato** Backkartoffel I
jam [dʒæm] Marmelade I
January ['dʒænjuəri] Januar I
jeans *(pl)* [dʒiːnz] Jeans I
°**jewel** ['dʒuːəl] Juwel I
jigsaw ['dʒɪgsɔː] Puzzle II 4 (77)
job [dʒɒb]:
1. Job, (Arbeits-)Stelle I:
2. Aufgabe II 4 (71)
join a club [dʒɔɪn] in einen Klub eintreten; sich einem Klub anschließen I
joke [dʒəʊk] Witz I
journey ['dʒɜːni] Reise, Fahrt II 5 (87)
judo ['dʒuːdəʊ] Judo I
juggle sth. ['dʒʌgl] mit etwas jonglieren II 5 (86)
juggler ['dʒʌglə] Jongleur/in II 5 (86)
juice [dʒuːs] Saft II 3 (52)
July [dʒu'laɪ] Juli I
jump [dʒʌmp]:
1. springen I **jump up** aufspringen, hochspringen II 3 (54)
2. Sprung I

June [dʒuːn] Juni I
just [dʒʌst]:
1. (einfach) nur, bloß I
2. gerade (eben), soeben II 4 (68)
just after ... gleich nachdem ...;
kurz nachdem ... II 3 (48/49) **just
then** genau in dem Moment; gerade
dann II 3 (54)
3. just like genau wie ... II 1 (20)

K

°**keep** [kiːp] behalten
°**keeper** ['kiːpə]: **animal keeper**
Tierwärter/in
key [kiː]:
1. Schlüssel II 4 (68)
2. Schlüssel- II 5 (88)
keyword ['kiːwɜːd] Schlüsselwort I
kid [kɪd] Kind I
kill [kɪl] töten II 6 (105)
kilogram, kilo (kg) ['kɪləgræm,
'kiːləʊ] Kilogramm, Kilo I
kilometre (km) ['kɪləmiːtə,
kɪ'lɒmɪtə] Kilometer I **square
kilometre** Quadratkilometer II 2 (33)
kind [kaɪnd]:
1. a kind of ... eine Art (von) ... I:
2. freundlich, nett II 4 (80)
king [kɪŋ] König II 6 (104)
kiss [kɪs] küssen; sich küssen II 6 (114)
kit [kɪt] Ausrüstung I
kitchen ['kɪtʃɪn] Küche I
knee [niː] Knie II 6 (108)
kneel [niːl], **knelt, knelt** knien
II 6 (115)
knelt [nelt] *siehe* **kneel**
knew [njuː] *siehe* **know**
knife [naɪf], *pl* **knives** [naɪvz]
Messer II 2 (42)
knight [naɪt] Ritter II 5 (94) °**make
sb. a knight** jn. zum Ritter schlagen
°**knock sth. over** [ˌnɒk_'əʊvə] etwas
umstoßen
know [nəʊ], **knew, known** wissen;
kennen I **I don't know.** Ich weiß
(es) nicht. I **know about sth.** sich
mit etwas auskennen; über etwas Bescheid wissen II 3 (50) **..., you know.**
..., weißt du. / ..., wissen Sie. I
known [nəʊn] *siehe* **know**
kung fu [ˌkʌŋ 'fuː] Kung Fu I

L

label ['leɪbl]:
1. beschriften; etikettieren II 2 (32)

2. Beschriftung; Schild, Etikett
II 2 (32)
lain [leɪn] *siehe* **lie**
lake [leɪk] (Binnen-)See I
lamb [læm] Lamm II 4 (72)
lamp [læmp] Lampe I
land [lænd]:
1. landen, an Land gehen II 1 (24)
2. Land II 1 (24)
language ['læŋgwɪdʒ] Sprache I
large [lɑːdʒ] groß II 2 (32)
▶ S. 185 German „groß"
°**lassi** ['læsi] Lassi *(vorwiegend indisches Joghurtgetränk)*
last [lɑːst]:
1. last weekend/Friday letztes
Wochenende / letzten Freitag I **last
year's ...** das ... vom letzten Jahr
II 2 (28)
2. at last endlich, schließlich I
late [leɪt] spät I **You're late.** Du
bist spät dran. / Du bist zu spät. I
stay up late lang aufbleiben II 5 (91)
later ['leɪtə] später I
°**Latin** ['lætɪn] Latein, lateinisch I
laugh [lɑːf] lachen I
lay [leɪ] *siehe* **lie**
learn [lɜːn] lernen I °**learn sth. by
heart** etwas auswendig lernen
least ['liːst]: **at least** zumindest,
wenigstens II 5 (90)
leave [liːv], **left, left:**
1. verlassen; zurücklassen I
2. lassen II 4 (69) **leave a message**
eine Nachricht hinterlassen II 1 (10)
leave sth. etwas übrig lassen II 4 (69)
°**leave sth. out** etwas auslassen
3. (weg)gehen; abfahren II 4 (69)
▶ S. 194 (to) leave
left [left]:
1. *siehe* **leave**
2. linke(r, s); (nach) links II 3 (46) **on
the left** links/auf der linken Seite
II 3 (46)
▶ S. 189 left – right
leg [leg] Bein I
legend ['ledʒənd] Legende, Sage
II 6 (104)
°**leisure** ['leʒə]: **leisure centre**
Freiheitzentrum
°**lemon** ['lemən] Zitrone I
°**Lent** [lent] Fastenzeit I
°**leopard** ['lepəd] Leopard I
lesson ['lesn] (Unterrichts-)Stunde I
before lessons vorm Unterricht I
▶ S. 193 before
let [let] lassen I **Let me show you
...** Lass mich dir ... zeigen. I **Let's
...** Lass(t) uns ... I **Let's go to**

two hundred and seventeen **217**

Dictionary

England. Lass(t) uns nach England gehen/fahren. ı
letter ['letə]:
1. Brief ı
2. Buchstabe ı
°**letterbox** ['letəbɒks] Briefkasten ı
°**letterboxing** ['letəbɒksɪŋ] *Spiel für draußen, bei dem mit Hilfe von Karte u. Kompass versteckte Behälter gefunden werden müssen*
library ['laɪbrəri] Bibliothek, Bücherei ı
lie [laɪ], **lay, lain** liegen ıı 2 (41)
life [laɪf], *pl* **lives** [laɪvz] Leben ı
life jacket ['laɪf dʒækɪt] Schwimmweste ı
lift [lɪft] Mitfahrgelegenheit ıı 5 (90)
give sb. a lift jn. mitnehmen ıı 5 (90)
light [laɪt]:
1. Licht ı
2. **(lit, lit)** anzünden ıı 5 (84) **light sth. up** etwas erhellen *(aufleuchten lassen)* ıı 5 (99)
lightning *(no pl)* ['laɪtnɪŋ] Blitz ıı 5 (98) **a flash of lightning** ein Blitz ıı 5 (98)
like [laɪk]:
1. mögen, gernhaben ı **I like ...** Ich mag ... ı **I don't like ...** Ich mag ... nicht. / Ich mag kein ... ı **I'd like ...** Ich hätte gern ... / Ich möchte ... ı **I'd like to go** Ich möchte gehen / Ich würde gern gehen ı
2. **like boys** wie Jungen ı **just like** genau wie ... ıı 1 (20) **like that** so *(auf diese Weise)* ı **like this** so ıı 2 (40) **What's she like?** Wie ist sie? / Wie ist sie so? ı **What was it like?** Wie war es? ıı 1 (10)
likes and dislikes *(pl)* [ˌlaɪks_ən 'dɪslaɪks] Vorlieben und Abneigungen ı
line [laɪn] Zeile ı
°**link** [lɪŋk] Link, Verknüpfung, Verbindung ı
lion ['laɪən] Löwe ı
lip [lɪp] Lippe ıı 3 (59)
list [lɪst] Liste ı
listen ['lɪsn] zuhören, horchen ı **listen to sb.** jm. zuhören ı **listen to sth.** sich etwas anhören ı **Listen, Justin.** Hör zu, Justin. ı
listener ['lɪsənə] Zuhörer/in ıı 2 (28)
lit [lɪt] *siehe* **light**
°**literature** ['lɪtrətʃə] Literatur ı
°**litre** ['liːtə] Liter ı
litter bin ['lɪtə bɪn] Abfalleimer ıı 1 (23)
little ['lɪtl] klein ı

live [lɪv] leben; wohnen ı °**Long live ...** Es lebe ... / Lang lebe ...
living room ['lɪvɪŋ ruːm] Wohnzimmer ı
°**loch** [lɒx, lɒk] *(Binnen-)See in Schottland*
°**logbook** ['lɒgbʊk] Logbuch, Fahrtenbuch
lonely ['ləʊnli] einsam ı
long [lɒŋ] lang ı **(the) longest ...** der/die/das längste ...; am längsten ıı 2 (32) °**Long live ...** Es lebe ... / Lang lebe ...
look [lʊk] schauen ı **Look, ...** Sieh mal, ... / Schau mal, ... ı **look after sb.** auf jn. aufpassen; sich um jn. kümmern ıı 1 (15) **look at** anschauen, ansehen ı **look closely** genau hinschauen ıı 4 (81) **look for sth.** etwas suchen ı **look forward to sth.** sich auf etwas freuen ıı 1 (20) **look happy/angry/...** glücklich/ wütend/... aussehen ı °**look sth. up** etwas nachschlagen ı **look up** hochsehen, aufschauen ıı 1 (25)
°**Lord Mayor** [ˌlɔːd 'meə] Oberbürgermeister/in ı
lose [luːz], **lost, lost** verlieren ıı 4 (72)
lost [lɒst] *siehe* **lose**
lot [lɒt]: **a lot** viel ı **That helped us a lot.** Das hat uns sehr geholfen. ı **lots of ...** viel ..., viele ... ı
loud [laʊd] laut ı **in a loud voice** mit lauter Stimme ıı 3 (54)
°**lounge** [laʊndʒ] Wohnzimmer ı
love [lʌv]:
1. lieben, sehr mögen ı **I'd love to ...** Ich würde sehr gern ... ıı 4 (72)
2. **Love, ...** Alles Liebe, ... *(Briefschluss)* ıı 1 (14)
°3. **fall in love (with sb.)** sich verlieben (in jn.)
lovely ['lʌvli] schön, hübsch, herrlich, entzückend ıı 2 (36)
°**low** [ləʊ] niedrig ı **lower** untere(r, s) ı
luck [lʌk]: **Good luck!** Viel Glück! ı
lucky ['lʌki]: **be lucky** Glück haben ıı 1 (15) **Lucky you.** Du Glückspilz. ıı 1 (15)
lunch [lʌntʃ] Mittagessen ı **have lunch** zu Mittag essen ı **What's for lunch?** Was gibt es zum Mittagessen? ı
lunchtime ['lʌntʃtaɪm] Mittagszeit ı **at lunchtime** mittags ı

M

mad [mæd] verrückt ı **go mad** verrückt werden
▶ S. 206 German „werden"
made [meɪd]:
1. *siehe* **make**
2. **be made of sth.** aus etwas (gemacht) sein ıı 5 (97)
magazine [ˌmægə'ziːn] Zeitschrift ı
magic ['mædʒɪk] magisch, Zauber- ıı 3 (54)
mail [meɪl] E-Mail ıı 4 (71)
main [meɪn] Haupt- ıı 5 (94)
°**mainland** ['meɪnlænd] Festland ı
°**majesty** ['mædʒəsti]: **Your majesty** Eure Majestät ı
make [meɪk], **made, made:**
1. machen; herstellen ı **make a mistake** einen Fehler machen ıı 3 (57) **make a wish** sich etwas wünschen ı **make friends** Freunde finden ı **make notes (on sth.)** (sich) Notizen machen (über/zu etwas) *(zur Vorbereitung)* ıı 1 (13) °**make sth. better** etwas verbessern ı °**make sth. look nice** dafür sorgen, dass etwas schön aussieht ı **make sb. sth.** jn. zu etwas machen ıı 3 (54) **make sure that ...** sich vergewissern, dass ...; darauf achten, dass ...; dafür sorgen, dass ... ıı 2 (35)
°2. bilden ı
make-up ['meɪk_ʌp] Make-up ıı 2 (42)
mall [mɔːl] (großes) Einkaufszentrum ı
man [mæn], *pl* **men** [men] Mann ı
°**mango lassi** [ˌmæŋgəʊ 'læsi] Mangolassi *(vorwiegend indisches Joghurtgetränk)* ı
many ['meni] viele ı **How many?** Wie viele? ı
map [mæp] Landkarte; Stadtplan ı **on the map** auf der Landkarte; auf dem Stadtplan ı
°**maple syrup** [ˌmeɪpl 'sɪrəp] Ahornsirup ı
March [mɑːtʃ] März ı
mark [mɑːk]:
1. markieren ıı 4 (74) **mark sth. up** etwas markieren, kennzeichnen ıı 4 (74)
°2. Spur ı
market ['mɑːkɪt] Markt ı
married (to) ['mærɪd] verheiratet (mit) ı
°**marry** ['mæri] heiraten ı
°**marshmallows** *(pl)* [ˌmɑːʃ'mæləʊz] Marshmallows, Mäusespeck ı

218 two hundred and eighteen

English – German

°**mashed** [mæʃt]: **mashed potatoes** (pl) Kartoffelbrei

°**mask** [mɑːsk] Maske

°**massage** ['mæsɑːʒ] Massage

master ['mɑːstə] Meister/in I

match [mætʃ]:
1. Spiel, Wettkampf, Match I
°2. **match sth. (to sth.)** etwas (zu etwas) zuordnen

maths [mæθs] Mathematik I

matter: What's the matter? ['mætə] Was ist denn? / Was ist los? I

May [meɪ] Mai I

may [meɪ] dürfen II 5 (95) **May I have a word with you?** Kann ich Sie kurz sprechen? II 5 (95)

maybe ['meɪbi] vielleicht I

mayor [meə] Bürgermeister/in II 5 (84) °**lord mayor** Oberbürgermeister/in

me [miː] mich; mir I **Me too.** Ich auch. I

°**meal** [miːl] Mahlzeit, Essen **go out for a meal** essen gehen

mean [miːn], **meant, meant:**
1. bedeuten II 1 (17)
2. meinen II 2 (32)

meaning ['miːnɪŋ] Bedeutung II 1 (19)

meant [ment] siehe **mean**

meat [miːt] Fleisch I

mediation [ˌmiːdi'eɪʃn] Sprachmittlung, Mediation I

°**medieval** [ˌmedi'iːvl] mittelalterlich

meet [miːt], **met, met:**
1. treffen; kennenlernen I **Meet your classmates.** Triff deine Mitschüler/innen. / Lerne deine Mitschüler/innen kennen. I **Nice to meet you.** Freut mich, dich/euch/Sie kennenzulernen. I
2. sich treffen I

melt [melt] schmelzen II 6 (110)

memory ['meməri] Erinnerung II 1 (25)

men [men] Plural von **man** I

°**menu** ['menjuː] Speisekarte

message ['mesɪdʒ] Nachricht II 1 (8) **text message** SMS II 1 (18)

met [met] siehe **meet**

°**methinks** (altmodisch) [mɪ'θɪŋks] mich dünkt; ich denke

metre ['miːtə] Meter I

middle ['mɪdl] Mitte I **in the middle** in der Mitte I

midnight ['mɪdnaɪt] Mitternacht I

°**might** [maɪt]: **you might need ...** du brauchst vielleicht …, du könntest vielleicht … brauchen

mile [maɪl] Meile (ca. 1,6 km) II 4 (76) **for miles** meilenweit II 4 (76)

milk [mɪlk] Milch I

million ['mɪljən] Million II 5 (92)

°**mince** [mɪns] Hackfleisch

°**mind map** ['maɪnd mæp] Mindmap

mine [maɪn] meiner, meine, meins II 2 (32)
▶ S. 186 Possessivpronomen

minibus ['mɪnibʌs] Kleinbus I

minute ['mɪnɪt] Minute I **wait a minute** Warte einen Moment. / Moment mal. I

mirror ['mɪrə] Spiegel II 5 (98)

miss [mɪs] verpassen I

Miss [mɪs]: **Miss Bell** Frau Bell (übliche Anrede von Lehrerinnen) I

missing ['mɪsɪŋ]: **the missing words** die fehlenden Wörter I **be missing** fehlen II 4 (72)

mist [mɪst] (leichter) Nebel, Dunst(schleier) II 4 (66)

mistake [mɪ'steɪk] Fehler II 2 (33) **make a mistake** einen Fehler machen II 3 (57)

°**mix** [mɪks] anmischen, anrühren

°**mixture** ['mɪkstʃə] Mischung

mobile (phone) [ˌməʊbaɪl 'fəʊn] Mobiltelefon, Handy I

model ['mɒdl] Model II 2 (38)

moment ['məʊmənt] Moment I **at the moment** gerade, im Moment I

Monday ['mʌndeɪ, 'mʌndi] Montag I **on Monday** am Montag I

money ['mʌni] Geld I

monkey ['mʌŋki] Affe I

monster ['mɒnstə] Monster I

month [mʌnθ] Monat I

moon [muːn] Mond I **at full moon** bei Vollmond II 4 (81)

moor [mɔː, mʊə] Hochmoor II 4 (68)

°**moose** [muːs] Elch

more [mɔː] mehr I °**no more** nicht (mehr) wieder **more beautiful (than)** schöner (als) II 2 (36) **one more photo** noch ein Foto; ein weiteres Foto II 4 (72)

morning ['mɔːnɪŋ] Morgen, Vormittag I **Good morning.** Guten Morgen. I **in the morning** morgens, vormittags, am Morgen/Vormittag I **tomorrow morning** morgen früh, morgen Vormittag II 1 (10)

most [məʊst]: **most people** die meisten Menschen **most of them** die meisten von ihnen II 2 (42) **(the) most beautiful** der/die/das schönste …; am schönsten II 2 (36)

°**mostly** ['məʊstli] hauptsächlich, meistens

mother ['mʌðə] Mutter I

mountain ['maʊntən] Berg II 1 (8)

mouth [maʊθ] Mund; Maul I

move [muːv]:
1. bewegen; sich bewegen I
2. **move (to)** umziehen (nach) II 1 (14) **move in** einziehen II 4 (81) **move into a house** einziehen in ein Haus… II 4 (81)
▶ S. 197 (to) move

°**movement** ['muːvmənt] Bewegung

MP3 player [ˌem piː 'θriː ˌpleɪə] MP3-Spieler I

Mr Schwarz ['mɪstə] Herr Schwarz I

Mrs Schwarz ['mɪsɪz] Frau Schwarz I

much [mʌtʃ] viel I **How much …?** Wie viel …? I **How much are …?** Was kosten …? I **How much is …?** Was kostet …? I

mud [mʌd] Schlamm, Matsch II 4 (69)

mug [mʌg]: **a mug (of)** ein Becher II 4 (80)

mum [mʌm] Mama, Mutti I

museum [mju'ziːəm] Museum I

music ['mjuːzɪk] Musik I °**classical music** klassische Musik

musical ['mjuːzɪkl] Musical II 2 (28)

°**musician** [mju'zɪʃn] Musiker/in

must [mʌst] müssen II 1 (19) **you mustn't do it** ['mʌsnt] du darfst es nicht tun II 6 (104)
▶ S. 203 must – needn't – mustn't

my [maɪ] mein/e I **My birthday is in May.** Ich habe im Mai Geburtstag. I **My birthday is on 5th August.** Ich habe am 5. August Geburtstag. I **My name is …** Ich heiße … I

N

name [neɪm]:
1. Name I **My name is …** Ich heiße … I **What's your name?** Wie heißt du? / Wie heißt ihr? I
°2. nennen; benennen

narrow ['nærəʊ] schmal, eng II 6 (104)

°**national** ['næʃnəl] national

°**natural** ['nætʃrəl] natürlich

°**nature** ['neɪtʃə] Natur

navy ['neɪvi] Marine I

near [nɪə] in der Nähe von, nahe (bei) I **near here** (hier) in der Nähe I

nearby ['nɪəbaɪ]: **a nearby town** eine nahegelegene Stadt II 4 (81)

neck [nek] Hals II 6 (108)

need [niːd] brauchen, benötigen I **need to do sth.** etwas tun müssen II 3 (48/49) **you needn't do**

two hundred and nineteen **219**

Dictionary

it [ˈniːdnt] du musst es nicht tun II 6 (104)
▶ S. 203 must – needn't – mustn't

°**negative** [ˈnegətɪv] negativ

neighbour [ˈneɪbə] Nachbar/in II 1 (14)

nervous [ˈnɜːvəs] nervös, aufgeregt II 2 (30)

°**networking** [ˈnetwɜːkɪŋ]: **social networking site** *eine Website zur Bildung und Unterhaltung sozialer Netzwerke*

never [ˈnevə] nie, niemals I

new [njuː] neu I

news (no pl) [njuːz]:
  1. Nachrichten I
  2. Neuigkeiten II 1 (20)

New Year's Eve [ˌnjuː jɪəz_ˈiːv] Silvester II 5 (84)

next [nekst]: **next year's ...** das ... vom nächsten Jahr II 2 (28) **the next picture/question** das nächste Bild / die nächste Frage I °**What('s) next?** Was kommt als Nächstes?

next to [ˈnekst tʊ] neben II 1 (24)

nice [naɪs] nett, schön I **Nice to meet you.** Freut mich, dich/euch/ Sie kennenzulernen. I

night [naɪt] Nacht I **at night** nachts, in der Nacht I

°**nightmare** [ˈnaɪtmeə] Albtraum I

nine [naɪn] neun I

no [nəʊ]:
  1. nein I **No, that's wrong.** Nein, das ist falsch. / Nein, das stimmt nicht. I
  2. kein, keine I

nobody [ˈnəʊbədi] niemand I

nod [nɒd] nicken II 4 (80)

noisy [ˈnɔɪzi] laut, lärmend, voller Lärm II 6 (112)

°**no more** [ˌnəʊ ˈmɔː] nicht (mehr) wieder I

no one [ˈnəʊ wʌn] niemand I

°**noodle** [ˈnuːdl] Nudel I

nose [nəʊz] Nase I

not [nɒt] nicht I **he/she/it is not** er/sie/es ist nicht ... I **not till three** erst um drei, nicht vor drei II 5 (86) **not ... yet** noch nicht I

note [nəʊt] Notiz, Mitteilung I **make notes (on/about sth.)** (sich) Notizen machen (über/zu etwas) *(zur Vorbereitung)* II 1 (13) **take notes (on/about sth.)** (sich) Notizen machen (über/zu etwas) *(beim Lesen oder Zuhören)* II 5 (89)

nothing [ˈnʌθɪŋ] (gar) nichts I

November [nəʊˈvembə] November I

now [naʊ] nun, jetzt I **right now** jetzt gerade II 1 (24)
▶ S. 183 right

number [ˈnʌmbə] Zahl, Nummer, Ziffer I

O

o [əʊ] Null (in Telefonnummern) I

object [ˈɒbdʒɪkt, ˈɒbdʒekt] Objekt II 1 (17)

ocean [ˈəʊʃn] Ozean I

o'clock [əˈklɒk]: **at 1 o'clock** um 1 Uhr / um 13 Uhr I

October [ɒkˈtəʊbə] Oktober I

°**octopus** [ˈɒktəpəs] Krake I

of [ɒv, əv] von I

of course [əv ˈkɔːs] natürlich, selbstverständlich I

offer [ˈɒfə] anbieten II 5 (90)

often [ˈɒfn, ˈɒftən] oft I

°**ogre** [ˈəʊgə] Ungeheuer I

oh [əʊ]: **Oh, it's you.** Ach, du bist es. I

old [əʊld] alt I **How old are you?** Wie alt bist du? I

on [ɒn] auf I **on earth** auf der Erde II 2 (34) **on Monday** am Montag I **on Monday afternoon** am Montagnachmittag I **on the map** auf der Landkarte; auf dem Stadtplan I **on the phone** am Telefon II 1 (12) **on the plane** im Flugzeug II 2 (34) **on the radio** im Radio I °**on the road (to)** unterwegs (nach) **walk/run/ sail/... on** weitergehen/-laufen/ -segeln/... II 1 (20)

once [wʌns] einmal II 4 (68) **once a week/year** einmal pro Woche/Jahr II 4 (68) °**once again** nochmals I

one [wʌn] eins I °**one at a time** eins nach dem anderen **one by one** einzeln; einer nach dem anderen II 2 (42) **one night/day** eines Nachts/Tages II 4 (80) **one-syllable** einsilbige(r, s) II 2 (38) **a white one** ein weißer / eine weiße / ein weißes II 6 (113) **this one** diese(r, s) II 6 (113) **two black ones** zwei schwarze II 6 (113) **Which one?** Welche(r, s)? II 6 (113)
▶ S. 206 one/ones

online [ˌɒnˈlaɪn] online II 1 (18)

only [ˈəʊnli]:
  1. nur, bloß I **the only ...** der/ die/das einzige ...; die einzigen... II 3 (59)
  2. erst I

onto [ˈɒntʊ] auf (... hinauf) I

open [ˈəʊpən]:
  1. öffnen, aufmachen I; sich öffnen I
  2. geöffnet, offen I

opposite [ˈɒpəzɪt] gegenüber (von) II 3 (46)

or [ɔː] oder I

orange [ˈɒrɪndʒ]:
  1. orange I
  2. Orange, Apfelsine I

order [ˈɔːdə]:
  1. Reihenfolge I
  2. bestellen II 1 (24)

°**organize** [ˈɔːgənaɪz] organisieren I

°**original** [əˈrɪdʒənəl] ursprünglich I

other [ˈʌðə] andere(r, s) I

otter [ˈɒtə] Otter II 4 (78)

our [aʊə] unser/e I

ours [ˈaʊəz] unserer, unsere, unseres II 2 (32)
▶ S. 186 Possessivpronomen

out [aʊt]:
  1. heraus, hinaus, nach draußen II 1 (15) **out and about** unterwegs II 3 (46)
  2. **be out** nicht zu Hause sein, nicht da sein II 1 (10)
  3. **out of ...** [ˈaʊt_əv] aus ... (heraus/hinaus) I

outdoor [ˈaʊtdɔː] Außen-, im Freien II 1 (20)

outside [ˌaʊtˈsaɪd] draußen; nach draußen I **outside Rosie's Diner** vor Rosie's Diner, außerhalb von Rosie's Diner II 1 (24)

°**oven** [ˈʌvn] Ofen, Backofen I

over [ˈəʊvə]:
  1. über I **run over (to)** hinüberrennen (zu/nach) II 5 (90) **over to ...** hinüber zu/nach ... I **over here** hier herüber II 5 (86) **over there** da drüben, dort drüben II 4 (68)
  2. **over 4 years** über 4 Jahre; mehr als 4 Jahre I
  3. **be over** vorbei / zu Ende sein I

own [əʊn]:
  1. besitzen II 4 (68)
  2. **my own room/...** mein eigenes Zimmer/... II 1 (25)
  3. **on my/your/their/... own** allein II 2 (36)

P

p [piː] *Abkürzung für „pence", „penny"* I

packet [ˈpækɪt] Packung, Päckchen II 3 (52)

English – German

page [peɪdʒ] Seite ı **What page are we on?** Auf welcher Seite sind wir? ı

paid [peɪd] *siehe* **pay**

paint [peɪnt] (an)streichen; (an)malen II 5 (94)

painted ['peɪntɪd] bemalt, angemalt II 5 (98)

pair [peə]: **a pair (of)** ein Paar II 4 (72)

pancake ['pænkeɪk] Pfannkuchen II 1 (24)

paper ['peɪpə]:
1. Zeitung ı
2. Papier ı °**a piece of paper** ein Stück Papier

parade [pə'reɪd] Parade, Umzug II 5 (84)

paragraph ['pærəgrɑːf] Absatz *(in einem Text)* ı

parents *(pl)* ['peərənts] Eltern ı

park [pɑːk] Park ı

°**parliament** ['pɑːləmənt] Parlament

part [pɑːt] Teil ı **part of the body** Körperteil II 6 (108) **take part in sth.** an etwas teilnehmen II 5 (84)

partner ['pɑːtnə] Partner/in ı

party ['pɑːti] Party ı

pass [pɑːs]:
1. pass sth./sb. an etwas/jm. vorbeigehen/vorbeifahren II 4 (76)
2. pass sth. around etwas herumgeben, herumreichen II 5 (86)
▶ S. 197 around

past [pɑːst]:
1. Vergangenheit ı
2. half past ten halb elf (10.30 / 22.30) ı **quarter past ten** Viertel nach zehn (10.15 / 22.15) ı
3. vorbei (an), vorüber (an) II 3 (46)

°**pasty** ['pæsti] Pastete *(Fleisch und Gemüse in Teig)*

path [pɑːθ] Pfad, Weg II 4 (76)

pause [pɔːz] innehalten, pausieren; eine Pause einlegen II 2 (35)

paw [pɔː] Pfote, Tatze II 2 (39)

pay (for sth.) [peɪ], **paid, paid** (etwas) bezahlen II 5 (98)

PE [ˌpiː_'iː] Sportunterricht, Turnen ı

°**peace** [piːs] Frieden ı

peaceful ['piːsfl] friedlich II 5 (113)

°**pearl** [pɜːl] Perle ı

pedestrian zone [pə'destriən zəʊn] Fußgängerzone II 3 (48/49)

pen [pen] Kugelschreiber, Stift, Füller ı

pence [pens] Pence *(Plural von* **penny)** ı

pencil ['pensl] Bleistift ı

pencil case ['pensl keɪs] Federmäppchen ı

people ['piːpl] Leute, Menschen ı

pepper ['pepə] Pfeffer ı

perfect ['pɜːfɪkt] perfekt, ideal ı

°**perform** [pə'fɔːm] vorführen

°**permission** [pə'mɪʃn] Erlaubnis ı

person ['pɜːsn] Person ı

°**personal assistant** [ˌpɜːsənl_ə'sɪstənt] persönliche(r) Assistent/in

phone [fəʊn]:
1. Telefon ı **answer the phone** ans Telefon gehen II 1 (10) **on the phone** am Telefon II 1 (12)
2. phone sb. jn. anrufen II 1 (10)

phone call ['fəʊn kɔːl] *(kurz auch:* **call**) Anruf; Telefongespräch II 1 (10)

photo ['fəʊtəʊ] Foto ı **in the photo** auf dem Foto ı **take photos** fotografieren, Fotos machen ı

phrase [freɪz] Ausdruck, (Rede-) Wendung ı

Physical Education [ˌfɪzɪkl_ˌedʒu'keɪʃn] Sportunterricht, Turnen ı

piano [pi'ænəʊ] Klavier, Piano ı **play the piano** Klavier spielen ı

pick sb. up [ˌpɪk_'ʌp] jn. abholen II 5 (97)

pick sth. up [ˌpɪk_'ʌp] etwas aufheben (vom Boden), etwas hochheben II 5 (97)

picnic ['pɪknɪk] Picknick ı

picture ['pɪktʃə] Bild ı **in the picture** auf dem Bild ı

°**pie** [paɪ] Pastete ı

°**piece** [piːs] Stück ı **a piece of paper** ein Stück Papier ı

°**pier** [pɪə] Seebrücke ı

pig [pɪg] Schwein ı

pink [pɪŋk] pink, rosa ı

°**pixie** ['pɪksi] *Wesen aus der englischen Mythologie, ähnlich wie Kobolde und Feen*

pizza ['piːtsə] Pizza ı

place [pleɪs] Ort, Platz, Stelle ı

plan [plæn]:
1. Plan ı
2. planen II 5 (84)

plane [pleɪn] Flugzeug II 2 (34) **get on a plane** in ein Flugzeug einsteigen II 5 (86) **on the plane** im Flugzeug II 2 (34)
▶ S. 185 get

planet ['plænɪt] Planet ı

plant [plɑːnt]:
1. Pflanze II 1 (8)
2. pflanzen II 4 (81)

plaster ['plɑːstə] (Heft-)Pflaster II 6 (108)

plastic ['plæstɪk] Plastik, Kunststoff II 3 (48/49)

plate [pleɪt] **a plate of ...** ein Teller ... ı

play [pleɪ]:
1. spielen ı **play the drums** Schlagzeug spielen ı **play the guitar** Gitarre spielen ı **play the piano** Klavier spielen ı
2. abspielen *(CD, DVD)* ı
3. Theaterstück ı

°**playing field** ['pleɪɪŋ fiːld] Spielfeld ı

player ['pleɪə] Spieler/in ı

please [pliːz] bitte ı

pm: 4 pm [ˌpiː_'em] 4 Uhr nachmittags / 16 Uhr ı

pocket ['pɒkɪt] Tasche *(Manteltasche, Hosentasche usw.)* II 1 (23)

poem ['pəʊɪm] Gedicht II 4 (67)

°**poetry** ['pəʊətri] Lyrik, Dichtung, Poesie

point [pɔɪnt]:
1. Punkt ı
2. point to sth. auf etwas zeigen, deuten ı
3. point sth. at sb. etwas auf jn. richten ı

°**poisonous** ['pɔɪzənəs] giftig ı

°**police officer** [pə'liːs_ˌɒfɪsə] Polizist/in ı

policeman [pə'liːsmən] Polizist ı

pony ['pəʊni] Pony II 4 (66)

pool [puːl] Schwimmbad, Schwimmbecken ı

poor [pɔː, pʊə] arm ı

°**pop (music)** [pɒp] Popmusik ı

°**popular** ['pɒpjələ] populär, beliebt ı

postcard ['pəʊstkɑːd] Postkarte II 1 (18)

poster ['pəʊstə] Poster ı

post office ['pəʊst_ˌɒfɪs] Postamt II 3 (46)

potato [pə'teɪtəʊ], *pl* **potatoes** Kartoffel ı °**jacket potato** Backkartoffel **roast potatoes** *(pl)* im Backofen in Fett gebackene Kartoffeln ı

pound [paʊnd] Pfund *(britische Währung)* ı

pour [pɔː] gießen II 5 (99)

practice ['præktɪs] Übung ı

practise ['præktɪs] üben, trainieren ı °**practise doing sth.** üben, etwas zu tun

prepare sth. [prɪ'peə] etwas vorbereiten ı

two hundred and twenty-one **221**

Dictionary

present ['preznt]:
1. Geschenk I
2. Gegenwart II 2 (31)

present sth. (to sb.) [prɪ'zent] (jm.) etwas präsentieren, vorstellen II 5 (93)

presentation [ˌprezn'teɪʃn] Präsentation, Vorstellung II 5 (93)

pretty ['prɪti] hübsch II 4 (80)

price [praɪs] (Kauf-)Preis I

prince [prɪns] Prinz II 6 (104)

princess [ˌprɪn'ses, 'prɪnses] Prinzessin II 6 (104)

prison ['prɪzn] Gefängnis I

°**private** ['praɪvət]: **private school** Privatschule

prize [praɪz] Preis, Gewinn II 1 (15)

probably ['prɒbəbli] wahrscheinlich II 5 (86)

problem ['prɒbləm] Problem I

profile ['prəʊfaɪl] Profil; Beschreibung, Porträt I

programme ['prəʊɡræm] Programm (auch im Theater usw.); (Radio-, Fernseh-)Sendung I **What programmes …?** Welche Programme …? / Welche Art von Programmen …? I

project ['prɒdʒekt] Projekt II 1 (8)

°**projector** [prə'dʒektə] Projektor, Beamer

promise ['prɒmɪs] versprechen II 5 (86)

pronunciation [prəˌnʌnsi'eɪʃn] Aussprache I

°**props** (pl) [prɒps] Requisiten

pull [pʊl] ziehen I **pull sth. out** etwas herausziehen II 2 (30)

pullover ['pʊləʊvə] Pullover II 5 (86)

punctuation [ˌpʌŋktʃu'eɪʃn] Zeichensetzung II 2 (35)
▶ S. 186 Punctuation

puppet ['pʌpɪt] Marionette, Handpuppe II 5 (94)

purple ['pɜːpl] violett, lila I

push [pʊʃ] drücken, schieben, stoßen I

put [pʊt], **put, put** legen, stellen, (etwas wohin) tun I **put sth. on** etwas anziehen (Kleidung); etwas aufsetzen (Hut, Helm) II 5 (86) °**put sth. together** etwas zusammenstellen °**Put up your hand.** Melde dich. / Heb deine Hand.

°**puzzle** ['pʌzl] Rätsel

Q

quarter ['kwɔːtə]: **quarter past ten** Viertel nach zehn (10.15 / 22.15) I **quarter to eleven** Viertel vor elf (10.45 / 22.45) I

queen [kwiːn] Königin II 5 (87)

question ['kwestʃən] Frage I **question mark** Fragezeichen II 2 (35)

°**questionnaire** [ˌkwestʃə'neə] Fragebogen

queue [kjuː] Schlange stehen, sich anstellen II 2 (28)

quick [kwɪk] schnell II 4 (72)

quiet ['kwaɪət] ruhig, still, leise I

quiz [kwɪz] Quiz, Ratespiel I

R

rabbit ['ræbɪt] Kaninchen I

race [reɪs]:
1. Rennen, (Wett-)Lauf II 1 (10):
°2. rennen
°3. rasen

radio ['reɪdiəʊ] Radio I **on the radio** im Radio I

rain [reɪn]:
1. Regen II 1 (8) **heavy rain** starker Regen, heftiger Regen II 5 (98)
2. regnen II 1 (8)

raincoat ['reɪnkəʊt] Regenmantel II 4 (76)

°**raindrop** ['reɪndrɒp] Regentropfen

rainforest ['reɪnfɒrɪst] Regenwald II 1 (8)

rainy ['reɪni] regnerisch II 1 (11)

raise money (for sth.) [reɪz] Geld sammeln (für etwas) II 5 (84)

rally ['ræli] Rallye II 3 (46)

ran [ræn] siehe **run**

rang [ræŋ] siehe **ring**

rat [ræt] Ratte I

read [riːd], **read** [red], **read** [red] lesen I

reader ['riːdə] Leser/in II 2 (28)

ready ['redi] bereit, fertig I

real ['riːəl] echt, wirklich II 6 (104)

really ['rɪəli] echt, wirklich I

reason ['riːzn] Grund, Begründung II 6 (105)

recipe ['resəpi] (Koch-)Rezept II 5 (94)

°**record** ['rekɔːd] Schallplatte

recorder [rɪ'kɔːdə] Blockflöte II 2 (38)

red [red] rot I **go red** rot werden, erröten II 6 (110)
▶ S. 206 German „werden"

°**registration** [ˌredʒɪ'streɪʃn] Durchgang durch die Klassenliste, um die Anwesenheit zu überprüfen

regular ['reɡjələ] regelmäßig II 3 (55)

°**rehearsal** [rɪ'hɜːsl] Probe

°**rehearse** [rɪ'hɜːs] proben

°**relax** [rɪ'læks] sich entspannen

religion [rɪ'lɪdʒən] Religion I

remember sth. [rɪ'membə] sich an etwas erinnern I

repeat [rɪ'piːt] wiederholen II 5 (94)

report [rɪ'pɔːt] Bericht, Reportage II 6 (110)

°**reporter** [rɪ'pɔːtə] Reporter/in

rescue ['reskjuː]:
1. retten II 3 (59)
°2. **rescue centre** Rettungsstelle, Rettungsstation

responsible [rɪ'spɒnsəbl] verantwortlich II 3 (54)

°**rest** [rest] Rest

°**restaurant** ['restrɒnt] Restaurant

revision [rɪ'vɪʒn] Wiederholung (des Lernstoffs) II 1 (11)

rhyme [raɪm] Reim; Vers I

rich [rɪtʃ] reich I

ridden ['rɪdn] siehe **ride**

ride [raɪd]:
1. Fahrt I
2. **(rode, ridden)** reiten; (Rad) fahren II 4 (73) **ride a bike** Fahrrad fahren I

riding ['raɪdɪŋ] Reiten I

right [raɪt]:
1. richtig I **sb. is right** jemand hat Recht I **Yes, that's right.** Ja, das ist richtig. / Ja, das stimmt. I
2. rechte(r, s); (nach) rechts II 3 (46) **on the right** rechts/auf der rechten Seite II 3 (46)
3. **right now** jetzt gerade II 1 (24)
4. **…, right?** …, nicht wahr? II 1 (15)
5. **right behind you** direkt hinter dir, genau hinter dir II 1 (24) **right after you** gleich nach dir II 1 (24)
▶ S. 183 right
▶ S. 189 left – right

ring [rɪŋ]:
1. **(rang, rung)** klingeln, läuten II 2 (28)
2. Ring II 5 (99)

river ['rɪvə] Fluss I

road [rəʊd] Straße I **at 8 Beach Road** in der Beach Road 8 I **in Beach Road** in der Beach Road I

°**roast** [rəʊst] rösten, braten

roast beef [ˌrəʊst 'biːf] Rinderbraten I

222 two hundred and twenty-two

English – German

roast potatoes (pl)
[ˌrəʊst pəˈteɪtəʊz] *im Backofen in Fett gebackene Kartoffeln* ı
rock [rɒk]:
  1. Fels, Felsen ı
  2. rock (music) Rockmusik ıı 5 (86)
rocky [ˈrɒki] felsig, steinig ıı 1 (24)
rode [rəʊd] *siehe* **ride**
role [rəʊl] Rolle *(in einem Theaterstück, Film)* ıı 6 (110)
roll [rəʊl] rollen ıı 1 (15)
°**Roman** [ˈrəʊmən] römisch; Römer, Römerin
roof [ruːf] Dach ıı 3 (58)
room [ruːm] Zimmer, Raum ı
°**roommate** [ˈruːmmeɪt] Zimmergenosse/Zimmergenossin
round [raʊnd]:
  1. round the world um die Welt ıı 2 (38)
  °**2. all year round** das ganze Jahr ı
  °**3. round up ponies** Ponys zusammentreiben ı
roundabout [ˈraʊndəbaʊt] Kreisverkehr ıı 3 (46)
°**route** [ruːt] Route ı
royal [ˈrɔɪəl] königlich ıı 6 (110)
rubber [ˈrʌbə] Radiergummi ı
rubbish [ˈrʌbɪʃ] Müll, Abfall ıı 5 (97)
rucksack [ˈrʌksæk] Rucksack ı
ruin [ˈruːɪn] Ruine ıı 4 (80)
rule [ruːl] Regel, Vorschrift ıı 1 (18)
ruler [ˈruːlə] Lineal ı
run [rʌn], **ran, run** rennen, laufen ı
  run after sb. hinter jm. herrennen ı
  run around herumrennen, umherrennen ıı 4 (81)   **run on** weiterlaufen ıı 1 (20)   **run over (to)** (zu/nach …) hinüberrennen ıı 5 (90)
  ▶ S. 197 around
rung [rʌŋ] *siehe* **ring** ıı 6 (104)
runner [ˈrʌnə] Läufer/in ıı 2 (28)

S

sad [sæd] traurig ı
°**sadness** [ˈsædnəs] Traurigkeit ı
said [sed] *siehe* **say**
sail [seɪl] segeln ıı 5 (87)   **go sailing** segeln; segeln gehen ı   **sailing boat** Segelboot ı
salad [ˈsæləd] Salat *(als Gericht oder Beilage)* ı   **fruit salad** Obstsalat ı
°**sale** [seɪl] Verkauf ı
°**salt** [sɔːlt] Salz ı
samba [ˈsæmbə] Samba ı
same [seɪm]: **the same as …** der-/die-/dasselbe wie … ı

°**sanctuary** [ˈsæŋktʃuəri] (Natur-, Tier, Vogel-)Schutzgebiet, Schutzgehege ı
sand [sænd] Sand ı
sandwich [ˈsænwɪtʃ, ˈsænwɪdʒ] Sandwich, (zusammengeklapptes) belegtes Brot ı
sang [sæŋ] *siehe* **sing**
sat [sæt] *siehe* **sit**
Saturday [ˈsætədeɪ, ˈsætədi] Samstag, Sonnabend ı   **on Saturday afternoon** am Samstagnachmittag ı
°**sauna** [ˈsɔːnə, ˈsaʊnə] Sauna ı
save [seɪv] retten ı   °**be saved** gerettet werden ı
saw [sɔː] *siehe* **see**
say [seɪ], **said, said** sagen ı   **Say hello to … for me.** Grüß … von mir. ıı 1 (8)
scan (a text) [skæn] einen Text schnell nach bestimmten Wörtern/Informationen absuchen ıı 3 (53)
°**scare** [skeə] erschrecken ı
scared [skeəd] verängstigt ıı 2 (35)
scary [ˈskeəri] unheimlich, gruselig ı
scene [siːn] Szene ı
school [skuːl] Schule ı   **at school** in der Schule ı   **before school** vor der Schule *(vor Schulbeginn)* ı   **in front of the school** vor der Schule *(vor dem Schulgebäude)* ı   **school bag** Schultasche ı
  ▶ S. 193 before
science [ˈsaɪəns] Naturwissenschaft ı
scone [skɒn, skəʊn] *kleines rundes Milchbrötchen, leicht süß* ı
score [skɔː] einen Treffer erzielen, ein Tor schießen ı
scream [skriːm] schreien ıı 6 (105)
screen [skriːn] Bildschirm ıı 1 (24)
°**sculpture** [ˈskʌlptʃə] Skulptur ı
sea [siː] Meer ı
seagull [ˈsiːgʌl] Möwe ı
seal [siːl] Robbe ı
°**seaman** [ˈsiːmən], *pl* **seamen** [ˈsiːmən] Matrose, Seemann ı
°**seaside** [ˈsiːsaɪd]:
  1. Meeresküste, Strand ı
  2. Meeres-; am Meer ı
seat [siːt] Sitz, Platz ıı 6 (105)
second [ˈsekənd]:
  1. zweite(r, s) ı   **second biggest** zweitgrößte(r, s) ıı 2 (32)
  2. Sekunde ıı 5 (98)
°**secret** [ˈsiːkrət] geheim ı
see [siː] **(saw, seen)** sehen; besuchen ı; *(Arzt)* aufsuchen ıı 6 (108)
  See you. [ˈsiː ju, ˈsiː jə] Bis gleich. / Bis bald. ı   **…, you see.** …, weißt du. ıı 5 (90)

seen [siːn] *siehe* **see**
sell [sel], **sold, sold** verkaufen ı
send [send], **sent, sent: send sth. to sb.** jm. etwas schicken, senden ı
sent [sent] *siehe* **send**
sentence [ˈsentəns] Satz ı   **full sentence** ganzer Satz ıı 5 (89)
September [sepˈtembə] September ı
set [set] Satz, Set ıı 3 (48/49)
°**set square** [ˈset skweə] Geodreieck®
seven [ˈsevn] sieben ı
shadow [ˈʃædəʊ] Schatten ıı 1 (24)
shake [ʃeɪk], **shook, shaken** schütteln ıı 2 (42)
shaken [ˈʃeɪkn] *siehe* **shake**
°**shape** [ʃeɪp] Form, Gestalt ı
shark [ʃɑːk] Hai ı
sharpener [ˈʃɑːpnə] Anspitzer ı
she [ʃiː] sie ı
sheep [ʃiːp], *pl* **sheep** Schaf ıı 4 (67)
shelf [ʃelf], *pl* **shelves** [ʃelvz] Regal ı
°**shepherd** [ˈʃepəd] Schafhirte/-hirtin ı
ship [ʃɪp] Schiff ı
shirt [ʃɜːt] Hemd ıı 5 (86)
shocked [ʃɒkt] schockiert, entsetzt ıı 1 (20)
shoe [ʃuː] Schuh ı
shook [ʃʊk] *siehe* **shake**
shop [ʃɒp]:
  1. Laden ı   **corner shop** Laden an der Ecke; Tante-Emma-Laden ı   **shop assistant** Verkäufer/in ıı 3 (48/49)
  2. einkaufen ıı 2 (28)
shopper [ˈʃɒpə] (Ein-)Käufer/in ıı 2 (28)
shopping [ˈʃɒpɪŋ]: **do the/some shopping** einkaufen gehen; Einkäufe erledigen ıı 3 (48/49)   **go shopping** einkaufen gehen ı   **shopping centre** Einkaufszentrum ıı 3 (46)   **shopping mall** (großes) Einkaufszentrum ı
shore [ʃɔː] Ufer, Strand ıı 3 (58)
short [ʃɔːt] kurz ı
shorts (pl) [ʃɔːts] Shorts, kurze Hose ı
should [ʃʊd, ʃəd]: **You should …** Du solltest … / Ihr solltet … / Sie sollten … ıı 2 (30)
shoulder [ˈʃəʊldə] Schulter ıı 5 (99)
shout [ʃaʊt]:
  1. schreien, rufen ı
  °**2.** Ruf ı
show [ʃəʊ]:
  1. (showed, shown) zeigen ı
  2. Show, Vorstellung ıı 2 (30)
  °**talent show** Castingshow, Talentschau ı
shown [ʃəʊn] *siehe* **show**

two hundred and twenty-three   **223**

Dictionary

shy [ʃaɪ] schüchtern, scheu II 2 (41)

sick [sɪk] krank I **be sick** sich übergeben II 6 (105) **I feel sick.** Mir ist schlecht. II 6 (105) **I'm going to be sick.** Ich muss mich übergeben. II 6 (105)

▶ S. 204 ill – sick – well

side [saɪd] Seite II 2 (30)   °**side by side** [saɪd] nebeneinander, Seite an Seite

sights (pl) [saɪts] Sehenswürdigkeiten I

sign [saɪn] Schild; Zeichen I

silky [ˈsɪlki] seidig I

silly [ˈsɪli]:
1. albern; blöd I
2. Dummerchen I

similar (to sth./sb.) [ˈsɪmələ] (etwas/jm.) ähnlich II 1 (19)

sing [sɪŋ], **sang, sung** singen I

singer [ˈsɪŋə] Sänger/in II 2 (28)

single [ˈsɪŋgl] ledig, alleinstehend I

°**sir** [sɜː] Sir (höfliche Anrede, z. B. für Kunden, Vorgesetzte oder Lehrer)

sister [ˈsɪstə] Schwester I

sit [sɪt], **sat, sat** sitzen; sich setzen I   **sit down** sich hinsetzen I

°**site** [saɪt]: **social networking site** eine Website zur Bildung und Unterhaltung sozialer Netzwerke

six [sɪks] sechs I

size [saɪz] Größe II 2 (40)   **What size tea would you like?** Wie groß soll der/dein Tee sein? II 6 (113)

skates [skeɪts] Inlineskates I

skating [ˈskeɪtɪŋ] Inlineskaten, Rollschuhlaufen I

skill [skɪl] Fertigkeit II 6 (109)   **skills file** Übersicht über Lern- und Arbeitstechniken I   **study skills** Lern- und Arbeitstechniken I

skirt [skɜːt] Rock II 5 (86)

sky [skaɪ] Himmel II 1 (25)

°**skype** [skaɪp] per Skype telefonieren

sleep [sliːp], **slept, slept** schlafen I   °**sleeping beauty** Dornröschen („schlafende Schöne")

sleepover [ˈsliːpəʊvə] Schlafparty I

slept [slept] siehe **sleep**

slow [sləʊ] langsam I   **he shook his head slowly** er schüttelte langsam den Kopf II 3 (54)

small [smɔːl] klein I

smell [smel] riechen I   **smell sth.** an etwas riechen I   **smell good** gut riechen II 4 (72)

smile [smaɪl] lächeln I   **smile at sb.** jn. anlächeln I

smiley [ˈsmaɪli] Smiley I

smuggle [ˈsmʌgl] schmuggeln I

smuggler [ˈsmʌglə] Schmuggler/in I

smuggling [ˈsmʌglɪŋ] der Schmuggel, das Schmuggeln I

snack [snæk] Snack, Imbiss I

snake [sneɪk] Schlange I

sneeze [sniːz] niesen I

snow [snəʊ] Schnee II 2 (38)

°**snow leopard** [ˌsnəʊ ˈlepəd] Schneeleopard

°**snowy** [ˈsnəʊi] schneebedeckt

so [səʊ]:
1. also; deshalb, daher I
2. **so cool/nice** so cool/nett I   **so far** bis jetzt; bis hierher II 2 (36)
3. **So?** Und? / Na und? I
4. **so that / so** sodass, damit II 1 (25)

°**social** [ˈsəʊʃl]: **social networking site** eine Website zur Bildung und Unterhaltung sozialer Netzwerke

°**society** [səˈsaɪəti] Gesellschaft, Verein

sock [sɒk] Socke II 3 (52)

sofa [ˈsəʊfə] Sofa I

soft [sɒft] weich I   **in a soft voice** sanft II 5 (98)   **she sang softly** sie sang leise II 5 (98)

sold [səʊld] siehe **sell**

°**soldier** [ˈsəʊldʒə] Soldat/in I

solo [ˈsəʊləʊ] Solo- II 5 (98)

some [sʌm] einige, ein paar; etwas I

somebody [ˈsʌmbədi] jemand I

someone [ˈsʌmwʌn] jemand I

something [ˈsʌmθɪŋ] etwas I

sometimes [ˈsʌmtaɪmz] manchmal I

°**somewhere** [ˈsʌmweə] irgendwo

son [sʌn] Sohn II 1 (14)

song [sɒŋ] Lied, Song I

soon [suːn] bald I

sore [sɔː] wund II 6 (108)   **have a sore throat** Halsschmerzen haben II 6 (108)

sorry [ˈsɒri]: **(I'm) sorry.** Tut mir leid. / Entschuldigung. I   **I'm sorry about ...** Es tut mir leid wegen ... I

▶ S. 187 „Entschuldigung"

sound [saʊnd]:
1. klingen, sich anhören I
2. Geräusch; Klang I
°3. Laut I
°4. Meerenge, Sund I

°**sound system** [ˈsaʊnd sɪstm] Tonanlage

soup [suːp] Suppe I

°**Southwest** [ˌsaʊθˈwest] Südwesten I

souvenir [ˌsuːvəˈnɪə] Andenken, Souvenir II 3 (53)

spaghetti [spəˈgeti] Spagetti I

Spanish [ˈspænɪʃ] spanisch II 5 (94)

speak [spiːk], **spoke, spoken** sprechen I; reden II 2 (28)   **speak to sb.** mit jm. sprechen II 1 (10)

speaker [ˈspiːkə] Sprecher/in I; Redner/in II 2 (28)

special [ˈspeʃl] besondere(r, s) II 5 (84)

speech [spiːtʃ] (offizielle) Rede II 5 (94)

°**speech bubble** [ˈspiːtʃ bʌbl] Sprechblase

spell [spel] buchstabieren I

°**spend** [spend], **spent, spent** **spend time** Zeit verbringen I

°**spicy** [ˈspaɪsi] würzig, scharf gewürzt I

spoke [spəʊk] siehe **speak**

spoken [spəʊkn] siehe **speak**

spoon [spuːn] Löffel II 2 (42)

sport [spɔːt] Sport; Sportart I   **do sport** Sport treiben I

spot [spɒt] Fleck, Punkt I

spring [sprɪŋ]:
1. Frühling I
°2. Quelle I

°**spy** [spaɪ] spähen   **I spy with my little eye** entspricht dem Spiel „Ich sehe was, was du nicht siehst"

°**square** [skweə]: **set square** Geodreieck

square kilometre, sq km [skweə] Quadratkilometer II 2 (33)

stage [steɪdʒ] Bühne II 2 (36)

stairs (pl) [steəz] Treppe; Treppenstufen II 2 (39)

stall [stɔːl] (Markt-)Stand II 3 (48/49)

stamp [stæmp] Stempel II 4 (75)

stand [stænd], **stood, stood** stehen; sich (hin)stellen II 2 (42)

star [stɑː]:
1. (Film-, Pop-)Star I
°2. Stern I

start [stɑːt] anfangen, beginnen I

°**statement** [ˈsteɪtmənt] Aussage I

station [ˈsteɪʃn] Bahnhof II 3 (46)

stay [steɪ] bleiben I   **stay in touch (with sb.)** (mit jm.) Kontakt halten; (mit jm.) in Verbindung bleiben II 1 (18)   **stay up late** lang aufbleiben II 5 (91)

steer [stɪə] steuern, lenken I

step [step] Schritt I

stick [stɪk], **stuck, stuck: stick sth. into sth.** etwas in etwas stechen, stecken II 2 (42)

sticky [ˈstɪki] klebrig II 6 (106)

still [stɪl]:
1. (immer) noch I
2. trotzdem, dennoch II 1 (14)

°**stir-fry** [stɜːˈfraɪ] Gericht aus kurz scharf angebratenen Zutaten

stomach [ˈstʌmək] Magen II 6 (105)

224   two hundred and twenty-four

English – German

stone [stəʊn] Stein II 6 (114)

stood [stʊd] *siehe* **stand**

stop [stɒp]:
1. anhalten, stoppen I **Stop it!** *(infml)* Hör auf (damit)! / Lass das! II 6 (105)
2. Halt; Station, Haltestelle II 1 (8)

storm [stɔːm] Sturm, Unwetter, Gewitter II 5 (90)

story ['stɔːri] Geschichte, Erzählung I

straight [streɪt]: **straight on** geradeaus weiter II 3 (46) °**straight towards sb.** direkt auf jn. zu

strange [streɪndʒ] seltsam, komisch I

strawberry ['strɔːbəri] Erdbeere II 6 (110)

street [striːt] Straße I **at 14 Dean Street** in der Deanstraße 14 **in Dean Street** in der Dean Street I **street artist** Straßenkünstler/in II 5 (86)

strong [strɒŋ] stark, kräftig II 4 (72)

stuck [stʌk] *siehe* **stick**

student ['stjuːdənt] Schüler/in; Student/in I

studio ['stjuːdiəʊ] Studio I

study ['stʌdi]: **study skills** Lern- und Arbeitstechniken I **study poster** Lernposter II 3 (56)

sub-clause ['sʌbklɔːz] Nebensatz I

subject ['sʌbdʒɪkt, 'sʌbdʒekt]:
1. Schulfach I
2. Subjekt II 1 (17)

subtitle ['sʌbtaɪtl] Untertitel I

°**successful** [sək'sesfl] erfolgreich I

suddenly ['sʌdnli] plötzlich, auf einmal I

°**sugar** ['ʃʊgə] Zucker I

summer ['sʌmə] Sommer I

sun [sʌn] Sonne I

Sunday ['sʌndeɪ, 'sʌndi] Sonntag I

sung [sʌŋ] *siehe* **sing**

sunglasses *(pl)* ['sʌnglɑːsɪz] (eine) Sonnenbrille II 2 (42)

sunny ['sʌni] sonnig II 1 (8)

°**supermarket** ['suːpəmɑːkɪt] Supermarkt I

sure [ʃʊə, ʃɔː] sicher II 1 (14) **make sure that ...** sich vergewissern, dass ...; darauf achten, dass ...; dafür sorgen, dass ... II 2 (35)

surprise [sə'praɪz] Überraschung II 1 (14)

surprised [sə'praɪzd] überrascht I

swam [swæm] *siehe* **swim**

°**swap** [swɒp] tauschen I

sweet [swiːt] süß II 4 (72)

sweets *(pl)* [swiːts] Süßigkeiten II 6 (105)

swim [swɪm]**, swam, swum** schwimmen I

swimmer ['swɪmə] Schwimmer/in I

swimming pool ['swɪmɪŋ puːl] Schwimmbad, Schwimmbecken I

sword [sɔːd] Schwert I

swum [swʌm] *siehe* **swim**

syllable ['sɪləbl] Silbe II 2 (38) **one-/ two-syllable** ein-/zweisilbig II 2 (38)

symbol ['sɪmbl] Symbol II 5 (89)

°**syrup** ['sɪrəp] Sirup

T

table ['teɪbl]:
1. Tisch I **table tennis** Tischtennis II 1 (15)
2. Tabelle I

take [teɪk]**, took, taken** nehmen, mitnehmen; (weg-, hin)bringen I; *(Zeit)* brauchen; dauern II 4 (75) **take notes (on/about sth.)** (sich) Notizen machen (über/zu etwas) *(beim Lesen oder Zuhören)* II 5 (89) **take part in sth.** an etwas teilnehmen II 5 (84) **take photos** fotografieren, Fotos machen **take sb. by the arm** jn. am Arm nehmen II 3 (54) **take sth. off** etwas ausziehen *(Kleidung)*; etwas absetzen *(Hut, Helm)* II 5 (86) **take sth. out** etwas herausnehmen II 2 (32) °**take turns (to do sth.)** sich abwechseln (etwas zu tun) ▶ S. 180 German „bringen"

takeaway ['teɪkəweɪ] *Restaurant/ Imbissgeschäft, das auch Essen zum Mitnehmen verkauft; Essen zum Mitnehmen* II 6 (113)

taken ['teɪkən] *siehe* **take**

talented ['tæləntɪd] begabt, talentiert II 2 (36)

°**talent show** ['tælənt ʃəʊ] Castingshow, Talentschau I

talk [tɔːk]:
1. Vortrag, Referat, Rede I **give a talk (about)** einen Vortrag / eine Rede halten (über) I
2. **talk (to)** reden (mit), sich unterhalten (mit) I

tall [tɔːl] groß *(Person)*; hoch *(Gebäude, Baum)* II 2 (34) ▶ S. 185 German „groß"

tap [tæp] tippen, *(vorsichtig)* klopfen II 6 (105)

task [tɑːsk] Aufgabe I

taste [teɪst] schmecken I

tasty ['teɪsti] lecker II 5 (94)

taxi ['tæksi] Taxi II 5 (86)

tea [tiː] *leichte Nachmittags- oder Abendmahlzeit* II 1 (14)

teacher ['tiːtʃə] Lehrer/in I

team [tiːm] Team, Mannschaft I

tear [tɪə] Träne II 1 (20)

teaspoon ['tiːspuːn] Teelöffel II 2 (42)

teeth [tiːθ] *Plural von* **tooth**

telephone ['telɪfəʊn] Telefon I

tell [tel]**, told, told: tell sb. about sth.** jm. von etwas erzählen; jm. über etwas berichten I **tell sb. the way (to ...)** jm. den Weg (nach ...) beschreiben II 3 (46)

temperature ['temprətʃə] Temperatur, Fieber II 6 (108) **have a temperature** Fieber haben II 6 (108)

ten [ten] zehn I

tennis ['tenɪs] Tennis I **table tennis** Tischtennis II 1 (15) °**tennis court** Tennisplatz

tent [tent] Zelt II 1 (24)

term [tɜːm] Trimester II 1 (20)

terrible ['terəbl] schrecklich, furchtbar II 6 (108)

text [tekst]:
1. Text I
2. *(auch* **text message***)* SMS II 1 (18)
3. **text sb.** jm. eine SMS schicken I

than [ðæn, ðən]: **bigger than** größer als II 2 (32)

thanks ['θæŋks] Danke. I **thanks to Maya** dank Maya II 3 (59)

Thank you. ['θæŋk juː] Danke. I **Thank you for listening.** Danke, dass ihr zugehört habt. / Danke für eure Aufmerksamkeit. II 5 (93)

that [ðæt, ðət]:
1. **it shows that ...** es zeigt, dass ... I
2. **that group** die Gruppe (dort), jene Gruppe I
3. **that's** das ist I
4. der/die/das; die *(Relativpronomen)* II 3 (48/49)
5. **that's why** deshalb, darum II 3 (58)

the [ðə] der, die, das; die I

theatre ['θɪətə] Theater II 2 (38)

their [ðeə] ihr I **their first day** ihr erster Tag I

theirs [ðeəz] ihrer, ihre, ihrs II 2 (36) ▶ S. 186 Possessivpronomen

them [ðem, ðəm] sie; ihnen I

theme [θiːm] Thema II 5 (84)

then [ðen] dann I **just then** genau in dem Moment; gerade dann II 3 (54)

there [ðeə] da, dort; dahin, dorthin I **down there** dort unten II 3 (58) **over there** da drüben, dort drüben II 4 (68) **There are ...** Es sind ... / Es

Dictionary

gibt … ı **There's …** Es ist/gibt … ı

thermometer [θəˈmɒmɪtə] Thermometer ıı 6 (108)

these [ðiːz] diese, die (hier) ı

they [ðeɪ] sie *(Plural)* ı **they're (= they are)** sie sind … ı

thief [θiːf], *pl* **thieves** [θiːvz] Dieb/in ı

thing [θɪŋ] Sache, Ding, Gegenstand ı

think [θɪŋk]**, thought, thought** denken, glauben ı **think of sth.** sich etwas ausdenken; an etwas denken ı

third [θɜːd] dritte(r, s) ı **third biggest** drittgrößte(r, s) ıı 2 (32)

thirsty [ˈθɜːsti]: **be thirsty** durstig sein, Durst haben ı

this [ðɪs]:

1. This is … Dies ist … / Das ist … ı

2. this place/break/subject dieser Ort / diese Pause / dieses Fach ı **this time** dieses Mal ıı 1 (25) **this afternoon/evening/…** heute Nachmittag/Abend/… ıı 1 (14) **this year's …** das diesjährige … ıı 2 (28)

those [ðəʊz] die … dort; jene … ı

thought [θɔːt] *siehe* **think**

°**thousand** [ˈθaʊznd] Tausend ı

three [θriː] drei ı

threw [θruː] *siehe* **throw**

throat [θrəʊt] Hals, Kehle ıı 6 (108) **have a sore throat** Halsschmerzen haben ıı 6 (108)

through [θruː] durch ı

throw [θrəʊ]**, threw, thrown** werfen ı

thrown [θrəʊn] *siehe* **throw**

thunder [ˈθʌndə] Donner ıı 5 (98)

Thursday [ˈθɜːzdeɪ, ˈθɜːzdi] Donnerstag ı

ticket [ˈtɪkɪt]:

1. Eintrittskarte ı

2. Fahrkarte ı

till [tɪl]: **till 1 o'clock** bis 1 Uhr ı **not till three** erst um drei, nicht vor drei ıı 5 (86)

time [taɪm]:

1. Zeit; Uhrzeit ı **feeding time** Fütterungszeit ı **free time** Freizeit, freie Zeit ı **free-time activities** Freizeitaktivitäten ı °**of all time** aller Zeiten ı **What time is it?** Wie spät ist es? ı

2. Mal ıı 1 (25) **this time** dieses Mal ıı 1 (25) °**one at a time** eins nach dem anderen

timetable [ˈtaɪmteɪbl] Stundenplan ı

tin [tɪn] Dose ıı 3 (52)

tip [tɪp] Tipp ı

tired [ˈtaɪəd] müde ı

title [ˈtaɪtl] Titel, Überschrift ı

to [tu, tə]:

1. zu, nach ı **count to ten** bis zehn zählen **from … to …** von … bis … ı **to the front** nach vorne ıı 5 (86)

2. Nice to meet you. Freut mich, dich/euch/Sie kennenzulernen. ı

3. quarter to eleven Viertel vor elf (10.45 / 22.45) ı

4. um zu ıı 1 (24)

today [təˈdeɪ] heute ı

toe [təʊ] Zeh ıı 6 (108)

°**toffee** [ˈtɒfi] Toffee ı

together [təˈgeðə] zusammen ı

toilet [ˈtɔɪlət] Toilette ı

told [təʊld] *siehe* **tell**

tomato [təˈmɑːtəʊ] Tomate ıı 3 (52)

tomorrow [təˈmɒrəʊ] morgen ıı 1 (10) **tomorrow morning** morgen früh, morgen Vormittag ıı 1 (10)

tongue [tʌŋ] Zunge ıı 6 (108)

tongue-twister [ˈtʌŋˌtwɪstə] Zungenbrecher ıı 5 (94)

°**tonight** [təˈnaɪt] heute Abend/Nacht ı

too [tuː]:

1. auch ı

2. too late/cold/big/… zu spät/kalt/groß/… ı

took [tʊk] *siehe* **take**

tooth [tuːθ], *pl* **teeth** [tiːθ] Zahn ıı 5 (98)

toothache [ˈtuːθeɪk]: **have a toothache** Zahnschmerzen haben ıı 6 (108)

top [tɒp]:

1. Spitze ıı 1 (24) **at the top (of)** oben, am oberen Ende, an der Spitze (von) ıı 4 (66)

2. Spitzen-, oberste(r, s) ı

3. Top, Oberteil ı

topic [ˈtɒpɪk] Thema, Themengebiet ıı 3 (56)

°**tor** [tɔː] *kahler Hügel in Südwestengland*

torch [tɔːtʃ]:

1. Taschenlampe ıı 1 (25)

2. Fackel ıı 5 (86)

°**toss** [tɒs]: **toss a pancake** einen Pfannkuchen hochwerfen und wenden ı

touch [tʌtʃ]:

1. berühren, anfassen ı

2. get in touch (with sb.) (mit jm.) Kontakt aufnehmen; sich (mit jm.) in Verbindung setzen ıı 1 (18) **stay in touch (with sb.)** (mit jm.) Kontakt

halten; (mit jm.) in Verbindung bleiben ıı 1 (18)

▶ S. 185 get

tour (of) [ˈtʊər_əv] Rundgang, Rundfahrt, Reise (durch) ı

tourist [ˈtʊərɪst] Tourist/in ı

°**tournament** [ˈtʊənəmənt] Turnier ı

°**towards sb.** [təˈwɔːdz] jm. entgegen **straight towards sb.** direkt auf jn. zu

tower [ˈtaʊə] Turm ı

town [taʊn] Stadt ı °**town crier** Stadtausrufer/in **town hall** Rathaus ıı 2 (38)

toy [tɔɪ] Spielzeug ı

tractor [ˈtræktə] Traktor ıı 4 (68)

traditional [trəˈdɪʃənl] traditionell ıı 5 (94)

train [treɪn]:

1. Zug ıı 4 (75) **get on a train** in einen Zug einsteigen ıı 5 (86)

2. trainieren ıı 4 (78)

▶ S. 185 get

trainer [ˈtreɪnə] Turnschuh ı

training [ˈtreɪnɪŋ] Training(sstunde) ı

°**tram** [træm] Tram, Straßenbahn ı

translate [trænsˈleɪt] übersetzen ıı 5 (88)

travel [ˈtrævl] reisen ı

traveller [ˈtrævələ] Reisende(r) ı

tree [triː] Baum ı

°**triangle** [ˈtraɪæŋgl] Dreieck ı

trick [trɪk] Kunststück, Trick ıı 3 (54)

trip [trɪp] Ausflug; Reise ı **go on day trips** Tagesausflüge machen ıı 1 (12)

trophy [ˈtrəʊfi] Pokal; Trophäe ı

trouble [ˈtrʌbl]: **be in trouble** in Schwierigkeiten sein; Ärger kriegen ı

trousers *(pl)* [ˈtraʊzəz] Hose ıı 5 (86)

▶ S. 199 Clothes

true [truː] wahr ı

truth [truːθ] Wahrheit ıı 6 (114)

try [traɪ] (aus)probieren; versuchen ı

T-shirt [ˈtiːʃɜːt] T-Shirt ı

Tuesday [ˈtjuːzdeɪ, ˈtjuːzdi] Dienstag ı **on Tuesday** am Dienstag ı

tulip [ˈtjuːlɪp] Tulpe ıı 4 (80)

tunnel [ˈtʌnl] Tunnel ıı 6 (106)

turn [tɜːn]:

1. (It's) my turn. Ich bin dran / an der Reihe. ı °**take turns** sich abwechseln *(etwas zu tun)*

2. turn around sich umdrehen; wenden, umdrehen ı **turn to sb.** sich jm. zuwenden; sich an jn. wenden

English – German

II 6 (105)
▶ S. 197 around
3. turn sth. on etwas einschalten ı
turn sth. off etwas ausschalten
II 1 (25)
4. turn left/right (nach) links/
rechts abbiegen II 3 (46)
▶ S. 189 left – right
TV [ˌtiːˈviː] Fernsehen, Fernsehgerät ı
twelve [twelv] zwölf ı
twice [twaɪs] zweimal II 4 (68)
twins (pl) [twɪnz] Zwillinge ı
two [tuː] zwei ı **two-syllable**
zweisilbig II 2 (38)

U

°**ugly** [ˈʌgli] hässlich
umbrella [ʌmˈbrelə] Regenschirm ı
uncle [ˈʌŋkl] Onkel ı
under [ˈʌndə] unter ı
°**underground** [ˌʌndəˈgraʊnd]
U-Bahn
underline [ˌʌndəˈlaɪn] unterstreichen
II 3 (56)
understand [ˌʌndəˈstænd]**, understood, understood** verstehen ı
understood [ˌʌndəˈstʊd] siehe
understand
unhappy [ʌnˈhæpi] unglücklich
II 1 (21)
uniform [ˈjuːnɪfɔːm] Uniform ı
unit [ˈjuːnɪt] Kapitel, Lektion ı
°**unite** [juˈnaɪt] vereinigen ı
°**unpack** [ˌʌnˈpæk] auspacken ı
until [ənˈtɪl] bis II 4 (76)
up [ʌp] hinauf, herauf; (nach) oben ı
up and down auf und ab; rauf und
runter ı **up here** hier oben; nach
hier oben II 3 (58) **up to** bis (zu)
II 3 (59)
°**upper** [ˈʌpə] obere(r, s)
upstairs [ˌʌpˈsteəz] oben; nach oben
(im Haus) ı
us [ʌs, əs] uns ı
use [juːz] benutzen, verwenden ı
usually [ˈjuːʒuəli] meistens,
normalerweise, gewöhnlich ı

V

valley [ˈvæli] Tal II 4 (66)
vegetables (pl) [ˈvedʒtəblz] Gemüse
ı
vegetarian [ˌvedʒəˈteəriən]:
1. Vegetarier/in II 6 (113)
2. vegetarisch II 6 (113)

verse [vɜːs] Vers, Strophe II 4 (77)
very [ˈveri] sehr ı
video [ˈvɪdiəʊ] Video ı
video camera [ˈvɪdiəʊ ˌkæmərə]
Videokamera ı
view (of) [vjuː] Aussicht, Blick (auf)
II 3 (58)
village [ˈvɪlɪdʒ] Dorf ı
°**vinegar** [ˈvɪnɪgə] Essig ı
visit [ˈvɪzɪt]:
1. besuchen ı
2. Besuch ı
visitor [ˈvɪzɪtə] Besucher/in,
Gast II 3 (46)
vocabulary [vəˈkæbjələri] Vokabelverzeichnis, Wörterverzeichnis ı
voice [vɔɪs] Stimme ı **in a loud
voice** mit lauter Stimme II 3 (54)
volleyball [ˈvɒlibɔːl] Volleyball ı
vowel [ˈvaʊəl] Vokal, Selbstlaut
II 6 (112)

W

waist [weɪst] Taille II 3 (59)
wait (for) [weɪt] warten (auf) ı
wait a minute Warte einen
Moment. / Moment mal. ı **I can't
wait to see …** Ich kann es kaum
erwarten, … zu sehen II (8)
wake up [ˌweɪk_ˈʌp]**, woke up,
woken up:**
1. aufwachen ı
2. wake sb. up jn. (auf)wecken
II 2 (41)
walk [wɔːk]:
1. Spaziergang ı **go for a walk**
spazieren gehen, einen Spaziergang
machen ı
2. (zu Fuß) gehen ı **walk around**
herumlaufen, umherspazieren II 4 (81)
walk on weitergehen II 1 (20)
▶ S. 197 around
wall [wɔːl] Mauer; Wand II 3 (54)
wander [ˈwɒndə] herumlaufen;
herumirren II 4 (80)
want [wɒnt]: **want sth.** etwas
(haben) wollen ı **want to do
sth.** etwas tun wollen ı
°**war** [wɔː] Krieg ı
warm [wɔːm] warm ı
was [wɒz, wəz]:
1. siehe **be**
2. I wish I was there. Ich wünschte,
ich wäre da. II 2 (42)
wash [wɒʃ]: **wash the dishes** (pl)
das Geschirr abwaschen, spülen
II 1 (24)

watch [wɒtʃ]:
1. Armbanduhr ı
2. sich etwas anschauen; beobachten
ı **watch TV** fernsehen ı **Watch
out!** Pass auf! / Vorsicht! ı
water [ˈwɔːtə] Wasser ı
waterfall [ˈwɔːtəfɔːl] Wasserfall
II 4 (75)
wave [weɪv] Welle II 1 (8)
way [weɪ]:
1. Weg ı **ask sb. the way** jn. nach
dem Weg fragen II 3 (46) **on the way
to …** auf dem Weg zu/nach … ı
tell sb. the way (to …) jm. den
Weg (nach …) beschreiben II 3 (46)
this way/that way hier entlang/
dort entlang; in die Richtung II 4 (69)
°**2.** Art, Weise
we [wiː] wir ı
wear [weə]**, wore, worn** tragen
(Kleidung) ı
weather [ˈweðə] Wetter II 1 (8)
website [ˈwebsaɪt] Website ı
Wednesday [ˈwenzdeɪ, ˈwenzdi]
Mittwoch ı °**Ash Wednesday**
Aschermittwoch
week [wiːk] Woche ı
weekend [ˌwiːkˈend] Wochenende ı
at the weekend am Wochenende ı
weigh [weɪ] wiegen ı
Welcome to Plymouth. [ˈwelkəm]
Willkommen in Plymouth. ı
well [wel]:
1. gut II 3 (54); (gesundheitlich) gut,
gesund II 6 (105) **I don't feel well**
Ich fühle mich nicht gut. / Mir geht's
nicht gut. II 6 (105)
▶ S. 204 ill – sick – well
2. Well, … Nun, … / Also, … / Na
ja, … ı
went [went] siehe **go**
were [wɜː, wə] siehe **be**
wet [wet] nass ı
whale [weɪl] Wal ı
what? [wɒt] was? ı **What about
you?** Und du/ihr? / Und was ist mit
dir/euch? ı **What about …?** Wie
wäre es mit …? II 1 (10) **What
colour …?** Welche Farbe …? ı
What is the story about? Wovon
handelt die Geschichte? Worum geht
es in der Geschichte? ı **What
programmes …?** Welche Programme …? / Welche Art von Programmen
…? ı **What size tea would you
like?** Wie groß soll der/dein Tee sein?
II 6 (113) **What time is it?** Wie spät
ist es? ı **What would you like to
eat?** Was möchtest du essen? ı

two hundred and twenty-seven **227**

Dictionary

What's your name? Wie heißt du? I **What's for lunch?** Was gibt es zum Mittagessen? I **What's for homework?** Was haben wir als Hausaufgabe auf? I °**What's next?** Was kommt als Nächstes? **What's she like?** Wie ist sie? / Wie ist sie so? I
wheel [wiːl]: **big wheel** Riesenrad I
°**wheelchair** [ˈwiːltʃeə] Rollstuhl
when [wen]:
1. wenn I
2. als I
3. **when?** wann? I
where? [weə] wo? / wohin? / woher? I
which [wɪtʃ]:
1. **which?** welche(r, s)? I
2. der/die/das; die *(Relativpronomen)* II 3 (48/49)
while [waɪl]:
1. während II 6 (105)
°2. Weile **for a while** eine Zeit lang, eine Weile
whisper [ˈwɪspə] flüstern II 3 (58)
whistle [ˈwɪsl] pfeifen II 5 (99)
white [waɪt] weiß I
who [huː]:
1. **Who is there?** Wer ist da? I **Who did you tell?** Wem hast du es erzählt? II 1 (14) **Who does Sam know?** Wen kennt Sam? II 1 (14)
2. der/die/das; die *(Relativpronomen)* II 3 (48/49)
whole [həʊl] ganze(r, s), gesamte(r, s) II 5 (99)
whose? [huːz] wessen? II 2 (39)
why [waɪ] warum I **that's why** deshalb, darum II 3 (58)
°**wicked** [ˈwɪkɪd] böse, schlecht
°**wide** [waɪd] breit **far and wide** weit und breit
wild [waɪld] wild II 1 (25)
will [wɪl]: **we'll miss the girls (= we will miss the girls)** wir werden die Mädchen verpassen II 5 (86) **I'll have a tea/burger/…** Ich nehme einen Tee/Hamburger/… *(beim Essen, im Restaurant)* II 6 (113)
win [wɪn], **won, won** gewinnen I
wind [wɪnd] Wind II 1 (8)
window [ˈwɪndəʊ] Fenster I
windy [ˈwɪndi] windig II 1 (8)
winner [ˈwɪnə] Gewinner/in, Sieger/in I
winter [ˈwɪntə] Winter I
wise [waɪz] weise II 6 (115)
wish [wɪʃ]:
1. Wunsch I **make a wish** sich etwas wünschen I

2. wünschen II 2 (42) **I wish I was there.** Ich wünschte, ich wäre da. II 2 (42)
°**witch** [wɪtʃ] Hexe
with [wɪð]
1. mit I
2. bei I
without [wɪˈðaʊt] ohne I
°**wizard** [ˈwɪzəd] Zauberer
woke [wəʊk] siehe **wake**
woken [ˈwəʊkən] siehe **wake**
woman [ˈwʊmən], *pl* **women** [ˈwɪmɪn] Frau I
won [wʌn] siehe **win**
won't [wəʊnt]: **she won't come (= she will not come)** sie wird nicht kommen II 5 (86)
wood [wʊd] Holz II 3 (59)
°**woodland** [ˈwʊdlənd] Wald(gelände)
word [wɜːd] Wort I **May I have a word with you?** Kann ich Sie kurz sprechen? II 5 (94) **word order** Wortstellung I
wordbank [ˈwɜːdˌbæŋk] „Wortspeicher" I
wore [wɔː] siehe **wear**
work [wɜːk]
1. arbeiten I °**work sth. out** etwas herausfinden/herausarbeiten
2. Arbeit I
workbook [ˈwɜːkbʊk] Arbeitsheft I
worker [ˈwɜːkə] Arbeiter/in II 2 (28)
worksheet [ˈwɜːkʃiːt] Arbeitsblatt II 2 (32)
workshop [ˈwɜːkʃɒp] Workshop, Lehrgang II 5 (94)
world [wɜːld] Welt II 1 (8) **in the world** auf der Welt II 1 (8)
°**world-famous** [ˌwɜːld ˈfeɪməs] weltberühmt
worm [wɜːm] Wurm I
worn [wɔːn] siehe **wear**
worried [ˈwʌrid] besorgt, beunruhigt I
worry (about) [ˈwʌri] sich Sorgen machen (wegen, um) II 3 (54)
worse [wɜːs] schlechter, schlimmer II 2 (164)
°**worship sb.** [ˈwɜːʃɪp] jn. anbeten
worst [wɜːst] der/die/das schlechteste/schlimmste …; am schlechtesten/schlimmsten II 2 (164)
would [wʊd]: **I would choose Sam** ich würde Sam wählen II 6 (110) **What would you like to eat?** Was möchtest du essen? I **I'd (= I would) like …** Ich möchte … I

write [raɪt], **wrote, written** schreiben I **write sth. down** etwas aufschreiben II 6 (104)
°**writer** [ˈraɪtə] Schreiber/in; Schriftsteller/in
°**writing** [ˈraɪtɪŋ] Inschrift
written [ˈrɪtn] siehe **write**
wrong [rɒŋ]:
1. falsch, verkehrt I **No, that's wrong.** Nein, das ist falsch. / Nein, das stimmt nicht. I
2. **sb. is wrong** jemand irrt sich; jemand hat Unrecht I
3. **What's wrong with you?** Was fehlt dir?; Was ist los mit dir? II 6 (105)
wrote [rəʊt] siehe **write**

Y

°**Yay!** [jeɪ] Juhu!
°**ye** [jiː]: **Hear ye!** *(altmodisch)* Hört!
year [jɪə]:
1. Jahr I **last/next year's …** das … vom letzten/nächsten Jahr II 2 (28) **this year's …** das diesjährige … II 2 (28) °**all year round** das ganze Jahr
2. Jahrgang(sstufe) I
yellow [ˈjeləʊ] gelb I
yes [jes] ja I **Yes, that's right.** Ja, das ist richtig. / Ja, das stimmt. I
▶ S. 183 right
yesterday [ˈjestədeɪ, ˈjestədi] gestern I
yet [jet]: **not … yet** noch nicht I **Have you … yet?** Hast du schon …? II 4 (72)
yoga [ˈjəʊgə] Yoga I
yoghurt [ˈjɒgət] Joghurt I
you [juː] du; Sie; ihr; dir; dich; euch; Ihnen I
young [jʌŋ] jung I
your [jɔː, jə] dein/e; euer/eure; Ihr/Ihre I
yours [jɔːz] deiner, deine, deins; eurer, eure, eures II 2 (36)
▶ S. 186 Possessivpronomen
yourself [jɔːˈself]: **about yourself** über dich selbst I
yummy [ˈjʌmi] *(infml)* lecker I

Z

°**zebra** [ˈzebrə] Zebra I
zoo [zuː] Zoo I

228 two hundred and twenty-eight

German – English

Das **German – English Dictionary** enthält den **Lernwortschatz** der Bände 1 und 2 von *English G Access*. Es kann dir eine erste Hilfe sein, wenn du vergessen hast, wie etwas auf Englisch heißt.

Wenn du wissen möchtest, wo das entsprechende englische Wort zum ersten Mal in *English G Access* vorkommt, dann kannst du im **English – German Dictionary** (S. 208 – 228) nachschlagen.

Im **German – English Dictionary** werden folgende **Abkürzungen** verwendet:

sth. = something (etwas)   sb. = somebody (jemand)   jn. = jemanden   jm. = jemandem
pl = *plural* (Mehrzahl)   *infml* = *informal* (umgangssprachlich)

▶ Der Pfeil weist auf Kästen im **Vocabulary** (S. 178 – 207) hin, in denen du weitere Informationen zu diesem Wort findest.

A

ab: auf und ab up and down [ˌʌp_ən ˈdaʊn]

abbiegen: (nach) links/rechts abbiegen turn left/right [tɜːn]
▶ S. 189 left – right

Abend evening [ˈiːvnɪŋ] **am Abend** in the evening **zu Abend essen** have dinner [ˈdɪnə]

Abendbrot, Abendessen dinner [ˈdɪnə]

abends in the evening [ˈiːvnɪŋ]

Abenteuer adventure [ədˈventʃə]

aber but [bʌt], [bət] **Aber egal, …** Anyway, … [ˈeniweɪ]

abfahren leave [liːv]
▶ S. 194 (to) leave

Abfall rubbish [ˈrʌbɪʃ]

Abfalleimer litter bin [ˈlɪtə bɪn]

abgeben: etwas abgeben *(einreichen)* hand sth. in [ˌhænd_ˈɪn]

abholen: jn. abholen pick sb. up [ˌpɪk_ˈʌp]

Abkürzung *(Kurzform eines Wortes)* abbreviation [əˌbriːviˈeɪʃn]

Abneigungen: Vorlieben und Abneigungen likes and dislikes *(pl)* [ˌlaɪks_ən ˈdɪslaɪks]

Absatz *(in einem Text)* paragraph [ˈpærəɡrɑːf]

Abschluss ending [ˈendɪŋ]

abschreiben copy [ˈkɒpi]

absetzen: etwas absetzen *(Hut, Helm)* take sth. off [ˌteɪk_ˈɒf]

abspielen *(CD usw.)* play [pleɪ]

abwaschen: das Geschirr abwaschen wash the dishes *(pl)* [ˈdɪʃɪz]

acht eight [eɪt]

achten: darauf achten, dass … make sure that …

Acker field [fiːld]

Adjektiv adjective [ˈædʒɪktɪv]

adoptiert, Adoptiv- adopted [əˈdɒptɪd]

Adresse address [əˈdres]

Adverb adverb [ˈædvɜːb]

Affe monkey [ˈmʌŋki]

ähnlich: etwas/jm. ähnlich similar to sth./sb. [ˈsɪmələ]

Aktivität activity [ækˈtɪvəti]

albern silly [ˈsɪli]

alle all [ɔːl]; *(jeder)* everyone [ˈevriwʌn], everybody [ˈevribɒdi]

allein alone [əˈləʊn]; *(ohne Hilfe)* on my/your/their/… own [əʊn]

alleinstehend *(ledig)* single [ˈsɪŋɡl]

alles everything [ˈevriθɪŋ]; all [ɔːl]

Alltags- everyday [ˈevrideɪ]

als 1. *(zeitlich)* when [wen]; *(während)* as [æz], [əz]
2. als Kind as a child
3. als Erstes first [fɜːst]
4. älter als older than [ðæn], [ðən]
▶ S. 206 as …

also 1. *(deshalb, daher)* so [səʊ]
2. Also, … Well, … [wel]

alt old [əʊld] **Wie alt bist du?** How old are you? **… ist so alt wie du** … is your age [eɪdʒ]

Alter age [eɪdʒ] **… ist in deinem Alter** … is your age [eɪdʒ]

am 1. *(in Ortsangaben)* at [æ], [ət]
am Meer by the sea [baɪ] **am Telefon** on the phone
2. *(in Zeitangaben)* **am Abend** in the evening **am Montag/Dienstag/…** on Monday/Tuesday/… **am Morgen** in the morning **am Nachmittag** in the afternoon **am Samstagmorgen** on Saturday afternoon **am Wochenende** at the weekend

Ameise ant [ænt]

amüsieren: sich amüsieren have fun [fʌn]

an *(in Ortsangaben)* at [æ], [ət] **an britischen Schulen** at British schools

anbauen *(anpflanzen)* grow [ɡrəʊ]

anbieten offer [ˈɒfə]

Andenken souvenir [ˌsuːvəˈnɪə]

andere(r, s) other [ˈʌðə] **ein anderer …/eine andere …/ein anderes …** another … [əˈnʌðə] **einer nach dem anderen** one by one

ändern; sich ändern change [tʃeɪndʒ]

anders *(verschieden)* different [ˈdɪfrənt]

anfangen start [stɑːt]; begin [bɪˈɡɪn]

anfangs at first [ət ˈfɜːst]

anfassen touch [tʌtʃ]

angemalt painted [ˈpeɪntɪd]

angreifen attack [əˈtæk]

anhalten stop [stɒp]

anhören: 1. sich etwas anhören listen to sth. [ˈlɪsn]
2. sich gut anhören *(gut klingen)* sound good [saʊnd]

ankommen arrive [əˈraɪv]

anlächeln: jn. anlächeln smile at sb. [smaɪl]

anmalen paint [peɪnt]

anordnen *(in eine bestimmte Ordnung bringen)* arrange [əˈreɪndʒ]

anpflanzen grow [ɡrəʊ]

Anruf phone call [ˈfəʊn kɔːl], *(kurz auch:)* call

anrufen call [kɔːl]; phone [fəʊn]

Anrufer/in caller [ˈkɔːlə]

anschauen: sich etwas anschauen watch sth. [wɒtʃ]; look at sth. [lʊk]

anschließen: sich einem Klub anschließen join a club [dʒɔɪn]

Anschrift address [əˈdres]

ansehen: sich etwas ansehen watch sth. [wɒtʃ]; look at sth. [lʊk]

Anspitzer sharpener [ˈʃɑːpnə]

anstellen: sich anstellen *(Schlange stehen)* queue [kjuː]

anstreichen paint [peɪnt]

Antwort answer [ˈɑːnsə]

antworten answer [ˈɑːnsə]

anziehen: etwas anziehen *(Kleidung)* put sth. on [ˌpʊt_ˈɒn] **sich schick anziehen** dress up [ˌdres_ˈʌp]

anzünden light [laɪt]

Apfel apple [ˈæpl]

Dictionary

Apfelsine orange [ˈɒrɪndʒ]
Apparat: Bleib/Bleiben Sie am Apparat. Hold on a minute. [ˌhəʊld_ˈɒn], *(oft auch kurz:)* Hold on.
April April [ˈeɪprəl]
Aquarienhaus aquarium [əˈkweəriəm]
Aquarium aquarium [əˈkweəriəm]
Arbeit work [wɜːk]; *(Job, Stelle)* job [dʒɒb]
arbeiten work [wɜːk]
Arbeiter/in worker [ˈwɜːkə]
Arbeitsblatt worksheet [ˈwɜːkʃiːt]
Arbeitsheft workbook [ˈwɜːkbʊk]
Ärger kriegen/haben be in trouble [ˈtrʌbl]
arm poor [pɔː], [pʊə]
Arm arm [ɑːm]   **jn. am Arm nehmen** take sb. by the arm
Armbanduhr watch [wɒtʃ]
Art: eine Art (von) … a kind of … [kaɪnd]
Artikel article [ˈɑːtɪkl]
Arzt/Ärztin doctor [ˈdɒktə]
Atem, Atemzug breath [breθ]
auch: auch aus Berlin from Berlin too [tuː]; also from Berlin [ˈɔːlsəʊ]
Ich auch. Me too.   **auch nicht** not … either [ˈaɪðə], [ˈiːðə]
auf on [ɒn]   **auf das Boot (hinauf)** onto the boat [ˈɒntu]   **auf dem Bild/Foto** in the picture/photo
auf dem Dachboden in the attic
auf dem Weg zu/nach … on the way to …   **auf der Landkarte/dem Stadtplan** on the map   **auf der Welt** in the world   **auf Englisch** in English   **auf einmal** suddenly [ˈsʌdnli]   **auf und ab** up and down
Auf welcher Seite sind wir? What page are we on?   **Auf Wiedersehen.** Goodbye.
aufbleiben: lange aufbleiben stay up late
Aufgabe task; exercise [ˈeksəsaɪz]; job
aufgeregt *(gespannt)* excited [ɪkˈsaɪtɪd]; *(nervös)* nervous [ˈnɜːvəs]
aufheben: etwas aufheben *(vom Boden)* pick sth. up [ˌpɪk_ˈʌp]
aufhören: Hör auf (damit)! Stop it! *(infml)*
aufmachen open [ˈəʊpən]
aufnehmen: (mit jm.) Kontakt aufnehmen get in touch (with sb.) [tʌtʃ]
aufpassen: auf jn. aufpassen look after sb.
aufregend *(spannend)* exciting [ɪkˈsaɪtɪŋ]

aufrufen: die Namen aufrufen call out the names
aufschauen *(hochsehen)* look up [lʊk_ˈʌp]
aufschreiben: etwas aufschreiben write sth. down [ˌraɪt ˈdaʊn]
aufsetzen: etwas aufsetzen *(Hut, Helm)* put sth. on [ˌpʊt_ˈɒn]
aufspringen jump up [ˌdʒʌmp_ˈʌp]
aufstehen get up [ˌget_ˈʌp]
aufsuchen *(Arzt)* see
auftauchen *(erscheinen)* appear [əˈpɪə]
aufwachen wake up [ˌweɪk_ˈʌp]
aufwecken: jn. aufwecken wake sb. up [ˌweɪk_ˈʌp]
Auge eye [aɪ]
Augenblick moment [ˈməʊmənt]
August August [ˈɔːgəst]
aus from [frɒm], [frəm]   **aus … heraus/hinaus** out of … [ˈaʊt_əv]   **aus etwas (gemacht) sein** be made of sth.
ausblasen: etwas ausblasen blow sth. out [ˌbləʊ_ˈaʊt]
ausdenken: sich etwas ausdenken think of sth. [θɪŋk]
Ausdruck *(Redewendung)* phrase [freɪz]
Ausflug trip [trɪp]
auskennen: sich mit etwas auskennen know about sth.
ausprobieren try [traɪ]
auspusten: etwas auspusten blow sth. out [ˌbləʊ_ˈaʊt]
Ausrufezeichen exclamation mark [ˌekskləˈmeɪʃn mɑːk]
Ausrüstung kit [kɪt]
ausschalten: etwas ausschalten turn sth. off [ˌtɜːn_ˈɒf]
aussehen: glücklich/wütend/… aussehen look happy/angry/…
Außen- *(im Freien)* outdoor [ˈaʊtdɔː]
außer *(bis auf)* except [ɪkˈsept]
außerhalb von … outside … [ˌaʊtˈsaɪd]
Aussicht, Blick (auf) view (of) [vjuː]
Aussprache pronunciation [prəˌnʌnsiˈeɪʃn]
aussteigen get off [ˌget_ˈɒf]   **aus einem Bus/Boot aussteigen** get off a bus/boat   **aus einem Auto aussteigen** get out of a car
aussuchen: (sich) etwas aussuchen choose sth. [tʃuːz]
auswählen: etwas auswählen choose sth. [tʃuːz]
ausziehen: etwas ausziehen *(Kleidung)* take sth. off [ˌteɪk_ɒf]

Auto car [kɑː]   **mit dem Auto fahren** go by car
Autor/in author [ˈɔːθə]

B

Bad bath [bɑːθ]
Badezimmer bathroom [ˈbɑːθruːm]
Bahnhof station [ˈsteɪʃn]
bald soon [suːn]   **Bis bald.** See you.
Ball ball [bɔːl]
Band *(Musikgruppe)* band [bænd]
Bär bear [beə]
Bart beard [bɪəd]
Basketball basketball [ˈbɑːskɪtbɔːl]
bauen build [bɪld]
Bauer/Bäuerin farmer [ˈfɑːmə]
Bauernhof farm [fɑːm]
Baum tree [triː]
beantworten answer [ˈɑːnsə]
bearbeiten *(Texte, Videos)* edit [ˈedɪt]
Becher mug [mʌg]   **ein Becher …** a mug of …
bedeuten mean [miːn]
Bedeutung meaning [ˈmiːnɪŋ]
beeilen: sich beeilen hurry (up) [ˌhʌri_ˈʌp]
beenden: etwas beenden finish sth. [ˈfɪnɪʃ]
befragen: jn. befragen interview sb. [ˈɪntəvjuː]
begabt talented [ˈtæləntɪd]
beginnen start [stɑːt]; begin [bɪˈgɪn]
Begründung reason [ˈriːzn]
bei *(in Ortsangaben)* at [æt], [ət]   **bei den Blackwells zu Hause** at the Blackwells' house   **bei Oma** at Grandma's   **bei jm. sein** be with sb.
beide both [bəʊθ]
Bein leg [leg]
beinahe almost [ˈɔːlməʊst]
Beispiel example [ɪgˈzɑːmpl]   **zum Beispiel (z.B.)** for example (e.g.) [ˌiː ˈdʒiː] *(from Latin* exempli gratia*)*
beißen bite [baɪt]
bekämpfen: jn. bekämpfen fight sb. [faɪt]
bekommen get [get]
▶ S. 185 (to) get
bellen bark [bɑːk]
bemalt painted [ˈpeɪntɪd]
benötigen need [niːd]
benutzen use [juːz]
beobachten watch [wɒtʃ]
Bereich area [ˈeəriə]
bereit ready [ˈredi]
bereits already [ɔːlˈredi]
Berg mountain [ˈmaʊntən]

230 two hundred and thirty

German – English

Bericht report [rɪˈpɔːt]
berichten: jm. etwas berichten tell sb. about sth. [tel]
berühmt (für, wegen) famous (for) [ˈfeɪməs]
berühren touch [tʌtʃ]
beschäftigt sein *(viel zu tun haben)* be busy [ˈbɪzi]
Bescheid: über etwas Bescheid wissen know about sth.
beschließen decide [dɪˈsaɪd]
beschreiben: (jm.) etwas beschreiben describe sth. (to sb.) [dɪˈskraɪb]
jm. den Weg (nach …) beschreiben tell sb. the way (to …)
beschriften *(etikettieren)* label [ˈleɪbl]
Beschriftung *(Etikett)* label [ˈleɪbl]
Besetzung *(Theaterstück)* cast [kɑːst]
besitzen own [əʊn]
besondere(r, s) special [ˈspeʃl]
besorgen: (sich) etwas besorgen get sth.
► S. 185 (to) get
besorgt worried [ˈwʌrid]
besser better [ˈbetə]
beste(r, s) best [best]
bestellen order [ˈɔːdə]
Besuch visit [ˈvɪzɪt]
besuchen: jn. besuchen visit sb. [ˈvɪzɪt]; see sb. [siː]
Besucher/in visitor [ˈvɪzɪtə]
betreten *(hineingehen)* enter [ˈentə]
Bett bed [bed]
beunruhigt worried [ˈwʌrid]
Beutel bag [bæg]
bevor before [bɪˈfɔː]
► S. 193 before
bewegen; sich bewegen move [muːv]
bewölkt cloudy [ˈklaʊdi]
bezahlen pay [peɪ] **etwas bezahlen** pay for sth. [peɪ]
Bibliothek library [ˈlaɪbrəri]
Bild picture [ˈpɪktʃə] **auf dem Bild** in the picture
Bildschirm screen [skriːn]
Bildunterschrift caption [ˈkæpʃn]
billig cheap [tʃiːp]
Bindestrich hyphen [ˈhaɪfən]
bis 1. till [tɪl]; until [ənˈtɪl] **bis zwölf Uhr** till/until twelve o'clock
bis jetzt so far **Bis gleich. / Bis bald.** See you. **bis zehn zählen** count to ten **bis (zu)** up to **von … bis …** from … to …
2. bis auf *(außer)* except [ɪkˈsept]
bisschen: ein bisschen a bit [ə ˈbɪt]
bitte 1. *(in Fragen und Aufforderungen)* please [pliːz]

2. Bitte sehr. / Hier bitte. Here you are.
bitten: jemanden bitten, etwas zu tun ask sb. to do sth. [ɑːsk] **um etwas bitten** ask for sth.
blau blue [bluː]
bleiben stay [steɪ] **(mit jm.) in Verbindung bleiben** stay in touch (with sb.) [tʌtʃ] **Bleib/Bleiben Sie am Apparat.** Hold on a minute. [ˌhəʊld ˈɒn], *(oft auch kurz:)* Hold on.
Bleistift pencil [ˈpensl]
Blick (auf) view (of) [vjuː]
Blitz(e) lightning *(no pl)* [ˈlaɪtnɪŋ]
ein Blitz a flash of lightning
Blockflöte recorder [rɪˈkɔːdə]
blöd *(albern)* silly [ˈsɪli]
Blog *(Weblog, digitales Tagebuch)* blog [blɒg]
blond blond *(bei Frauen oft:* blonde) [blɒnd]
bloß only [ˈəʊnli]; *(einfach nur)* just [dʒʌst]
Blume flower [ˈflaʊə]
Blüte flower [ˈflaʊə]
Boden ground [graʊnd]
Boot boat [bəʊt]
böse auf jn. angry with sb. [ˈæŋgri]
brauchen need [niːd]; *(Zeit)* take [teɪk] **du brauchst es nicht zu tun** you needn't do it [ˈniːdnt]
► S. 203 must – needn't – mustn't
braun brown [braʊn]
brav good
brechen *(kaputt gehen)* break [breɪk]
Brief letter [ˈletə]
Brille glasses *(pl)* [ˈglɑːsɪz]
bringen *(mit-, herbringen)* bring [brɪŋ]; *(weg-, hinbringen)* take [teɪk]
► S. 180 German "bringen"
britisch British [ˈbrɪtɪʃ]
Brot bread [bred]
Brücke bridge [brɪdʒ]
Bruder brother [ˈbrʌðə]
Brust(korb) chest [tʃest]
Buch book [bʊk]
Bücherei library [ˈlaɪbrəri]
Buchhandlung bookshop [ˈbʊkʃɒp]
Buchstabe letter [ˈletə]
buchstabieren spell [spel]
Bühne stage [steɪdʒ]
Burg castle [ˈkɑːsl]
Bürgermeister/in mayor [meə]
Bus bus **mit dem Bus fahren** go by bus

C

Café café [ˈkæfeɪ]
Camping camping [ˈkæmpɪŋ]
Champion champion [ˈtʃæmpiən]
Chaos chaos [ˈkeɪɒs]
Chor choir [ˈkwaɪə]
Clown clown [klaʊn]
Cola cola [ˈkəʊlə]
Comedyshow comedy [ˈkɒmədi]
Computer computer [kəmˈpjuːtə]
cool cool [kuːl]
Cornflakes cornflakes [ˈkɔːnfleɪks]
Cottage cottage [ˈkɒtɪdʒ]
Cousin, Cousine cousin [ˈkʌzn]

D

da, dahin *(dort, dorthin)* there [ðeə]
da sein *(zu Hause sein)* be in **nicht da sein** *(nicht zu Hause sein)* be out
Dach roof [ruːf]
Dachboden attic [ˈætɪk] **auf dem Dachboden** in the attic
daheim at home [ət ˈhəʊm]
daher *(deshalb)* so [səʊ]
damit so that, *(oft auch kurz:)* so
Danke. Thank you. [ˈθæŋk juː]; Thanks. [θæŋks] **dank Maya** thanks to Maya **Danke, gut.** Fine, thanks.
Danke, dass ihr zugehört habt. Thank you for listening.
dann then [ðen]
darstellende Kunst drama [ˈdrɑːmə]
darum that's why
das *(Artikel)* the [ðə]
das *(Relativpronomen)* **1.** *(für Dinge)* which; that
2. *(für Personen)* who; that
das (dort) *(Singular)* that [ðæt]; *(Plural)* those [ðəʊz] **das Auto dort** that car
dass that [ðæt], [ðət] **es zeigt, dass …** it shows that …
dasselbe wie … the same as … [seɪm]
dauern *(Zeit brauchen)* take [teɪk]
Deck deck [dek]
dein(e) … your … [jɔː], [jə]
deiner, deine, deins yours [jɔːz]
► S. 186 Possessivpronomen
Demonstration demonstration [ˌdemənˈstreɪʃn]
denken think [θɪŋk] **an etwas denken** think of sth.
denn: Was ist denn? What's the matter? [ˈmætə]
dennoch still [stɪl]

two hundred and thirty-one **231**

Dictionary

der (Artikel) the [ðə]
der (Relativpronomen) **1.** (für Personen) who; that
2. (für Dinge) which; that
der ... (dort) (Singular) that ...
[ðæt]; (Plural) those ... [ðəʊz] **der
... (hier)** (Singular) this ... [ðɪs];
(Plural) these ... [ðiːz]
derselbe wie ... the same as ...
[seɪm]
deshalb so [səʊ]; that's why
Design design [dɪˈzaɪn]
Designer/in designer [dɪˈzaɪnə]
deuten: auf etwas deuten (zeigen)
point to sth. [pɔɪnt]
deutlich clear(ly) [klɪə], [ˈklɪəli]
Deutsch; deutsch German [ˈdʒɜːmən]
Dezember December [dɪˈsembə]
Dialog dialogue [ˈdaɪəlɒg]
dich you [juː]
dick fat [fæt]
die (Artikel) the [ðə]
die (Relativpronomen) **1.** (für Personen) who; that
2. (für Dinge) which; that
die ... (dort) (Singular) that ... [ðæt];
(Plural) those ... [ðəʊz] **die ...
(hier)** (Singular) this ... [ðɪs]; (Plural) these ... [ðiːz]
Dieb/in thief [θiːf], pl thieves [θiːvz]
Dienstag Tuesday [ˈtjuːzdeɪ, ˈtjuːzdi]
dies (hier) (Singular) this [ðɪs]; (Plural) these [ðiːz]
**diese(r, s): dieser Ort / diese
Pause / dieses Fach** this place/
break/subject **diese Leute** these
people **Diese(r, s) hier.** This one.
▶ S. 206 one/ones
dieselbe(n) wie ... the same as ...
[seɪm]
**diesjährige(r, s): das diesjährige
Musical/Theaterstück/...** this
year's musical/play/...
Ding thing [θɪŋ]
dir you [juː]
Disko disco [ˈdɪskəʊ]
Donner thunder [ˈθʌndə]
Donnerstag Thursday [ˈθɜːzdeɪ, -di]
Doppel- double [ˈdʌbl]
Doppelpunkt colon [ˈkəʊlən]
Dorf village [ˈvɪlɪdʒ]
dort, dorthin there [ðeə] **dort entlang** that way [weɪ] **dort unten**
down there
Dose tin [tɪn]
dran: Ich bin dran. (It's) my turn.
[tɜːn]
draußen outside [ˌaʊtˈsaɪd] **nach
draußen** out(side)

drei three [θriː]
drinnen inside [ˌɪnˈsaɪd] **nach drinnen** inside
dritte(r, s) third [θɜːd]
drittgrößte(r, s) third biggest
drüben: da drüben, dort drüben
over there
drücken (schieben, stoßen) push [pʊʃ]
du you [juː]
Dummerchen silly [ˈsɪli]
dunkel dark [daːk]
Dunst(schleier) mist [mɪst]
durch through [θruː]
dürfen can [kæn], [kən]; may [meɪ]; be
allowed to [əˈlaʊd] **du darfst es
nicht tun** you mustn't do it [ˈmʌsnt]
▶ S. 203 must – needn't – mustn't
Durst haben be thirsty [ˈθɜːsti]
durstig sein be thirsty [ˈθɜːsti]
DVD DVD [ˌdiːviˈdiː]

E

eben: gerade eben just [dʒʌst]
echt (wirklich) real [ˈriːl]
Ecke corner [ˈkɔːnə] **Church Road,
Ecke London Road** on the corner of
Church Road and London Road
Laden an der Ecke („Tante-Emma-
Laden") corner shop [ˈkɔːnə ʃɒp]
egal: Aber egal, ... (Wie dem auch
sei) Anyway, ... [ˈeniweɪ]
Ehre honour [ˈɒnə]
Ei egg [eg]
Eierkuchen pancake [ˈpænkeɪk]
**eigene(r, s): mein eigener Film /
mein eigenes Zimmer / ...** my own
film/room/... [əʊn]
eilen; sich beeilen hurry (up) [ˈhʌri]
Eimer bucket [ˈbʌkɪt]
ein(e) (Artikel) a, an [ə], [ən] **ein
anderer .../eine andere .../ein
anderes ...** another ... [əˈnʌðə]
einer nach dem anderen one by
one **eines Nachts/Tages** one
night/day **ein paar** a few [əˈfjuː];
some [sʌm], [səm]
einbringen (Heu) bring in
einfach 1. (nicht schwierig) easy
[ˈiːzi]
2. einfach nur just [dʒʌst]
einhundert a hundred, one hundred
[ˈhʌndrəd]
einige a few [əˈfjuː]; some [sʌm],
[səm]
einigen: sich auf etwas einigen
agree on sth. [əˈgriː]

Einkäufe erledigen do the/some
shopping [ˈʃɒpɪŋ]
einkaufen shop [ʃɒp] **einkaufen
gehen** go shopping [ˈʃɒpɪŋ]; do the
shopping / do some shopping
Einkaufszentrum shopping centre
[ˈʃɒpɪŋ sentə]; shopping mall [ˈʃɒpɪŋ
mɔːl], (kurz auch:) mall
einladen: jn. einladen (zu) invite sb.
(to) [ɪnˈvaɪt]
Einladung (zu, nach) invitation (to)
[ˌɪnvɪˈteɪʃn]
einlegen: eine Pause einlegen
pause [pɔːz]
einmal 1. once [wʌns] **noch einmal** again [əˈgen]
2. auf einmal (plötzlich) suddenly
[ˈsʌdnli]
3. (noch) nicht einmal not even
einmarschieren: in ein Land einmarschieren invade a country
[ɪnˈveɪd]
einreichen: etwas einreichen hand
sth. in [ˌhænd ˈɪn]
eins one [wʌn]
einsam lonely [ˈləʊnli]
einschalten: etwas einschalten turn
sth. on [ˌtɜːn ˈɒn]
einschlafen fall asleep [ˌfɔːl əˈsliːp]
einsilbig (aus einer Silbe bestehend)
one-syllable [ˈsɪləbl]
einsteigen: in ein Auto/Taxi einsteigen get in(to) a car/taxi **in
einen Bus/einen Zug/ein Flugzeug einsteigen** get on a bus/train/
plane
Eintrag, Eintragung (im Tagebuch,
Wörterbuch) entry [ˈentri]
eintreffen arrive [əˈraɪv]
eintreten (in Zimmer usw.) enter
[ˈentə] **in einen Klub eintreten**
join a club [dʒɔɪn]
Eintrittskarte ticket [ˈtɪkɪt]
einziehen move in **in ein Haus einziehen** move into a house
▶ S. 197 (to) move
**einzige(r, s): der/die/das einzige
...; die einzigen...** the only ...
[ˈəʊnli]
Eis ice [aɪs]; (Speiseeis) ice cream [ˌaɪs
ˈkriːm]
Eistee iced tea
Elefant elephant [ˈelɪfənt]
elf eleven [ɪˈlevn]
Eltern parents [ˈpeərənts]
E-Mail email [ˈiːmeɪl]; mail
Ende end [end]; (Abschluss) ending
am oberen Ende (von) at the top
(of) **am unteren Ende (von)** at

German – English

the bottom (of) ['bɒtəm]   **zu Ende sein** be over ['əʊvə]
enden finish ['fɪnɪʃ]
endlich *(schließlich)* at last [ət 'lɑːst]
Endspiel final ['faɪnl]
eng *(schmal)* narrow ['nærəʊ]
Englisch; englisch English ['ɪŋglɪʃ]
**entlang: die Straße/den Fluss/...
entlang** along the street/the river/... [ə'lɒŋ]   **dort entlang** that way
entscheiden: sich entscheiden decide [dɪ'saɪd]
Entschuldigung.   1. *(Tut mir leid.)* (I'm) sorry. ['sɒri]
2. Entschuldigung, ... / Entschuldigen Sie, ... *(Darf ich mal stören?)* Excuse me, ... [ɪk'skjuːz miː]
▶ S. 180 "Entschuldigung"
entsetzt shocked [ʃɒkt]
Entwurf draft [drɑːft]
er   1. *(männliche Person)* he [hiː]
2. *(Ding; Tier)* it [ɪt]
Erdbeere strawberry ['strɔːbəri]
Erdboden ground [graʊnd]
Erde *(der Planet)* earth [ɜːθ] *(oft auch: Earth)*   **auf der Erde** on earth
Ereignis event [ɪ'vent]
erhellen *(aufleuchten lassen)* light up [ˌlaɪt 'ʌp]
erinnern: sich an etwas erinnern remember sth. [rɪ'membə]
Erinnerung memory ['meməri]
erkältet sein have a cold [kəʊld]
Erkältung: eine Erkältung haben have a cold [kəʊld]
erklären: jm. etwas erklären explain sth. to sb. [ɪk'spleɪn]
erläutern: jm. etwas erläutern explain sth. to sb. [ɪk'spleɪn]
erraten guess [ges]
erröten go red
erscheinen *(auftauchen)* appear [ə'pɪə]
erst only ['əʊnli]   **erst um drei** *(nicht vor drei)* not till three
erste(r, s) first [fɜːst]   **als Erstes** first   **der erste Tag** the first day
erwarten: Ich kann es kaum erwarten, ... zu sehen. I can't wait to see ...
erzählen (von) tell (about) [tel]
Erzählung story ['stɔːri]
erzielen: einen Treffer erzielen score [skɔː]
es it [ɪt]   **es ist ... / es gibt ...** there's ...   **es sind ... / es gibt ...** there are ...   **Ach, du bist es.** Oh, it's you.   **Bist du es?** Is that you?

essen eat [iːt]   **zu Abend/Mittag essen** have dinner/lunch
Essen *(Lebensmittel)* food [fuːd]
Esszimmer dining room ['daɪnɪŋ ruːm]
Etikett label ['leɪbl]
etikettieren label ['leɪbl]
etwas   1. something ['sʌmθɪŋ]; *(in Fragen)* anything ['eniθɪŋ]
2. *(ein bisschen)* some [sʌm], [səm]; a bit [ə 'bɪt]
euch you [juː]
euer .../eure ... your ... [jɔː], [jə]
eurer, eure, eures yours [jɔːz]
▶ S. 186 Possessivpronomen
ewig *(für immer)* for ever [fər 'evə]
Exemplar copy ['kɒpi]

F

Fackel torch [tɔːtʃ]
Fahne *(Flagge)* flag [flæg]
Fähre ferry ['feri]
fahren go [gəʊ]; *(ein Auto/mit dem Auto)* drive [draɪv]   **in Urlaub fahren** go on holiday   **mit dem Bus/Auto/Zug fahren** go by bus/car/train   **Rad fahren** ride a bike
Fahrkarte ticket ['tɪkɪt]
Fahrrad bike [baɪk]
Fahrt journey ['dʒɜːni]; ride [raɪd]
fair fair [feə]
fallen fall [fɔːl]   **etwas fallen lassen** drop sth. [drɒp]
falls if [ɪf]
falsch wrong [rɒŋ]   **Nein, das ist falsch.** No, that's wrong.
Familie family ['fæməli]   **Familie Blackwell** the Blackwell family
Fan fan [fæn]
fangen catch [kætʃ]
fantastisch fantastic [fæn'tæstɪk]
Farbe colour ['kʌlə]
Farm farm [fɑːm]
fast almost ['ɔːlməʊst]
Februar February ['februəri]
Federmäppchen pencil case ['pensl keɪs]
fehlen be missing ['mɪsɪŋ]   **die fehlenden Wörter** the missing words   **Was fehlt Justin/dir?** *(Was ist los?)* What's wrong with Justin/you?
Fehler mistake [mɪ'steɪk]   **einen Fehler machen** make a mistake
Feier celebration [ˌselɪ'breɪʃn]
feiern celebrate ['selɪbreɪt]
fein fine [faɪn]
Feind/in enemy ['enəmi]
Feld field [fiːld]

Fels, Felsen rock [rɒk]
felsig rocky ['rɒki]
Fenster window ['wɪndəʊ]
Ferien holidays *(pl)* ['hɒlədeɪz]
fernsehen watch TV [ˌwɒtʃ tiː'viː]
Fernsehen, Fernsehgerät TV [ˌtiː'viː]
fertig   1. mit etwas fertig werden/sein finish sth. ['fɪnɪʃ]   **Wir sind fertig.** *(Wir haben es erledigt.)* We're finished. ['fɪnɪʃt]
2. *(bereit)* ready ['redi]   **Wir sind fertig.** *(Wir sind bereit.)* We're ready.   **sich fertig machen (für)** get ready (for)
Fertigkeit skill [skɪl]
Fest, Festival festival ['festɪvl]
fett fat [fæt]
Feuer fire ['faɪə]
Feuerwerk fireworks *(pl)* ['faɪəwɜːks]
Feuerwerkskörper firework ['faɪəwɜːk]
Fieber temperature ['temprətʃə]
Fieber haben have a temperature
Figur *(in Roman, Film, Theaterstück usw.)* character ['kærəktə]
Film film [fɪlm]
filmen film [fɪlm]
Filzstift felt pen [ˌfelt 'pen]
Finale final ['faɪnl]
finden find [faɪnd]   **Freunde finden** make friends   **Wie findest du ...?** How do you like ...?
Finger finger ['fɪŋgə]
Fisch fish [fɪʃ], *pl* fish
Flagge flag [flæg]
Flasche bottle ['bɒtl]
Fleck spot [spɒt]
Fleisch meat [miːt]
fliegen fly [flaɪ]
Flugzeug plane [pleɪn]   **im Flugzeug** on the plane
Fluss river ['rɪvə]
flüstern whisper ['wɪspə]
folgen follow ['fɒləʊ]
Form (von) form (of) [fɔːm]
fort away [ə'weɪ]
fortfahren *(weiterreden)* go on [ˌgəʊ_'ɒn]
Foto photo ['fəʊtəʊ]   **auf dem Foto** in the photo   **Fotos machen** take photos
Fotoapparat camera ['kæmərə]
fotografieren take photos [ˌteɪk 'fəʊtəʊz]
Frage question ['kwestʃn]   **eine Frage stellen** ask a question
fragen ask [ɑːsk]   **jn. nach dem Weg fragen** ask sb. the way

two hundred and thirty-three   **233**

Dictionary

Fragezeichen question mark ['kwestʃən maːk]

Französisch; französisch French [frentʃ]

Frau **1.** woman ['wʊmən], *pl* women ['wɪmɪn]

2. Frau Schwarz Mrs Schwarz ['mɪsɪz]

3. *(übliche Anrede von Lehrerinnen)* **Frau Bell** Miss Bell [mɪs]

frei free [friː]

Freitag Friday ['fraɪdeɪ], ['fraɪdi]

Freizeit free time [ˌfriː 'taɪm]

Freizeitaktivitäten free-time activities [ˌfriːtaɪm ˌæk'tɪvətiz]

Fremdenführer/in guide [gaɪd]

freuen: sich auf etwas freuen look forward to sth. ['fɔːwəd] **Freut mich, dich/euch/Sie kennenzulernen.** Nice to meet you.

Freund/in friend [frend] **Freunde finden** make friends

freundlich friendly ['frendli; kind [kaɪnd]

friedlich peaceful ['piːsfl]

frieren be cold [kəʊld]

frisch fresh [freʃ]

froh *(glücklich)* happy ['hæpi]

Frosch frog [frɒg]

Frucht fruit [fruːt]

früh early ['ɜːli]

Frühling spring [sprɪŋ]

Frühstück breakfast ['brekfəst]

frühstücken have breakfast

fühlen; sich fühlen feel [fiːl] **Ich fühle mich nicht gut.** I don't feel well.

Füller pen [pen]

fünf five [faɪv]

für for [fɔː], [fə]

furchtbar terrible ['terəbl]; awful ['ɔːfl]

fürchterlich terrible ['terəbl]; awful ['ɔːfl]

Fuß foot [fʊt], *pl* feet [fiːt] **zu Fuß gehen** walk [wɔːk]

Fußabdruck footprint ['fʊtprɪnt]

Fußball football ['fʊtbɔːl]

Fußboden floor [flɔː]

Fußgängerzone pedestrian zone [pə'destrɪən zəʊn]

Futter food [fuːd]

füttern feed [fiːd]

Fütterungszeit feeding time ['fiːdɪŋ taɪm]

G

Gabel fork [fɔːk]

ganz allein all alone

ganze(r, s) whole [həʊl] **das ganze Plymouth, ganz Plymouth** all of Plymouth **den ganzen Tag** all day **die ganze Zeit** all the time **ganzer Satz** full sentence

gar nichts nothing ['nʌθɪŋ]

Garage garage ['gærɑːʒ], ['gærɪdʒ]

Garten garden ['gɑːdn]

Gartenarbeit gardening ['gɑːdnɪŋ]

Gärtnern gardening ['gɑːdnɪŋ]

Gastfamilie host family ['həʊst fæməli]

Gatter gate [geɪt]

gebackene Kartoffeln *(im Backofen in Fett gebacken)* roast potatoes [rəʊst pə'teɪtəʊz]

Gebäude building ['bɪldɪŋ]

geben give [gɪv] **Es gibt ...** *(Singular)* There's ...; *(Plural)* There are ... **Gibt es (irgendwelche) ...?** Are there any ...? ['eni] **Was gibt es zum Mittagessen?** What's for lunch?

Gebiet area ['eəriə]

gebrochen broken ['brəʊkən]

Geburtstag birthday ['bɜːθdeɪ] **Ich habe am 5. Mai Geburtstag.** My birthday is on 5th May. **Ich habe im Mai Geburtstag.** My birthday is in May. **Wann hast du Geburtstag?** When's your birthday?

Gedicht poem ['pəʊɪm]

Gefahr danger ['deɪndʒə]

gefährlich dangerous ['deɪndʒərəs]

gefallen: Wie gefällt dir ...? How do you like ...?

Gefängnis prison ['prɪzn]

Gefühl feeling ['fiːlɪŋ]

gegen **1.** against [ə'genst] **2. gegen 18 Uhr** around 6 pm [ə'raʊnd]
▶ S. 197 around

Gegend area ['eəriə]; *(Landschaft)* countryside ['kʌntrisaɪd]

gegenüber (von) opposite ['ɒpəzɪt]

Gegenwart present ['preznt]

gehen go [gəʊ]; *(zu Fuß gehen)* walk [wɔːk]; *(weggehen, verlassen)* leave [liːv] **an Land gehen** land **ans Telefon gehen** answer the phone **einkaufen gehen** go shopping **Los geht's. / Jetzt geht's los.** Here we go. **nach Hause gehen** go home **segeln gehen** go sailing ['seɪlɪŋ] **spazieren gehen** go for a walk

[wɔːk] **Wie geht's? / Wie geht es dir/euch/Ihnen?** How are you? **Mir geht's nicht gut.** I don't feel well. **Worum geht es in der Geschichte?** What is the story about? **Es geht um eine Möwe.** It's about a seagull.

gehören: zu etwas gehören *(zu etwas passen)* go with sth.

Geist ghost [gəʊst]

gelangen *(hinkommen)* get [get]
▶ S. 185 (to) get

Gel gel [dʒel]

gelangweilt sein be/feel bored [bɔːd]

gelb yellow ['jeləʊ]

Geld money ['mʌni] **Geld sammeln (für)** raise money (for) [reɪz]

gemacht: aus etwas gemacht sein be made of sth.

Gemüse vegetables *(pl)* ['vedʒtəblz]

genannt werden *(heißen)* be called [kɔːld]

genau **1. genau in dem Moment** just then **genau wie ...** just like ... ['dʒʌst laɪk]
2. genau hinschauen look closely ['kləʊsli]

genial brilliant ['brɪliənt]

genug enough [ɪ'nʌf]

geöffnet open ['əʊpən]

Geografie geography [dʒi'ɒgrəfi]

gerade *(im Moment)* at the moment ['məʊmənt] **gerade dann** just then **gerade eben** just [dʒʌst] **jetzt gerade** *(in diesem Moment)* right now
▶ S. 183 right

geradeaus weiter straight on [streɪt 'ɒn]

Geräusch sound [saʊnd]

gern: Ich tanze/singe/... gern. I like dancing/singing/... **Ich hätte gern ...** I'd like ... [ˌaɪd 'laɪk] (= I would like ...) **Ich würde gern gehen.** I'd like to go. **Ich würde sehr gern bleiben.** I'd love to stay. **Was hättest du gern?** What would you like? [wʊd]

gernhaben like [laɪk]

gesamte(r, s) whole [həʊl]

Geschäft *(Laden)* shop [ʃɒp]

geschehen (mit) happen (to) ['hæpən]

Geschenk present ['preznt]

Geschichte **1.** *(vergangene Zeiten)* history ['hɪstri] **2.** *(Erzählung)* story ['stɔːri]

geschieden divorced [dɪ'vɔːst]

Geschirr: das Geschirr abwaschen, spülen wash the dishes *(pl)* ['dɪʃɪz]

German – English

Gesicht face [feɪs]

gespannt *(aufgeregt)* excited [ɪkˈsaɪtɪd]

Gespenst ghost [gəʊst]

Gespräch talk; *(Unterhaltung)* conversation [ˌkɒnvəˈseɪʃn]

gestern yesterday [ˈjestədeɪ], [-di]

gesund well [wel]   **Ich bin wieder gesund.** I'm well again.

▶ S. 204 ill – sick – well

Getränk drink [drɪŋk]

gewinnen win [wɪn]

Gewinn *(Preis)* prize [praɪz]

Gewinner/in winner [ˈwɪnə]

Gewitter storm [stɔːm]

gewöhnlich *(normalerweise)* usually [ˈjuːʒuəli]

gießen pour [pɔː]

Giraffe giraffe [dʒəˈrɑːf]

Gitarre guitar [gɪˈtɑː]   **Gitarre spielen** play the guitar

glänzend *(großartig)* brilliant [ˈbrɪliənt]

Glas glass [glɑːs]   **ein Glas Wasser** a glass of water

glauben believe [bɪˈliːv]; *(denken)* think [θɪŋk]

gleich nachdem ... just after ...

Glocke bell [bel]

Glück: Glück haben be lucky   **Viel Glück!** Good luck! [lʌk]

glücklich happy [ˈhæpi]

Glückspilz: Du Glückspilz. Lucky you. [ˈlʌki]

Gokart go-kart [ˈgəʊ kɑːt]

Gold gold [gəʊld]

golden, Gold- gold [ˈgəʊld]

Grab grave [greɪv]

Grafschaft *(in Großbritannien)* county [ˈkaʊnti]

Gramm gram [græm]

Gras grass [grɑːs]

grau grey [greɪ]

groß big [bɪg]; large [lɑːdʒ]; *(Person)* tall [tɔːl]   **Wie groß soll der/dein Tee sein?** What size tea would you like?

▶ S. 185 German "groß"

großartig great [greɪt]; brilliant [ˈbrɪliənt]

Größe size [saɪz]

Großeltern grandparents [ˈgrænpeərənts]

Großmutter grandmother [ˈgrænmʌðə]

Großstadt city [ˈsɪti]

Großvater grandfather [ˈgrænfɑːðə]

grün green [griːn]

Grund *(Begründung)* reason [ˈriːzn]

Gruppe group (of) [gruːp]; *(Band)* band [bænd]

gruselig scary [ˈskeəri]

Gruß: Liebe Grüße, ... *(Briefschluss)* Love, ...

grüßen: Grüß ... von mir. Say hello to ... for me.

gucken look [lʊk]

gut good [gʊd]; *(gesundheitlich)* well; *(Adverb)* well [wel]   **gut sein in Kung-Fu / gut Kung-Fu können** be good at kung fu   **Danke, gut.** Fine, thanks.   **Guten Morgen.** Good morning. [gʊd ˈmɔːnɪŋ]   **Guten Tag.** Hello. [həˈləʊ]   **Mir geht's nicht gut. / Ich fühle mich nicht gut.** I don't feel well.

▶ S. 204 ill – sick – well

gutaussehend good-looking [ˌgʊdˈlʊkɪŋ]

Güter goods *(pl)* [gʊdz]

Gymnastik gymnastics [dʒɪmˈnæstɪks]

H

Haar, Haare hair [heə]

haben have [hæv], [həv]; have got   **Durst haben** be thirsty [ˈθɜːsti]   **Glück haben** be lucky   **Hunger haben** be hungry [ˈhʌŋgri]   **Ich habe im Mai Geburtstag.** My birthday is in May.   **jemand hat Recht** someone is right   **jemand hat Unrecht** someone is wrong   **viel zu tun haben** *(beschäftigt sein)* be busy [ˈbɪzi]   **Wann hast du Geburtstag?** When's your birthday?

▶ S. 190 German "haben"

Hafen harbour [ˈhɑːbə]

Hai shark [ʃɑːk]

halb elf (10.30 / 22.30) half past ten [ˈhɑːf pɑːst]

Halbzeit half [hɑːf], *pl* halves [hɑːvz]

Hallo. Hello. [həˈləʊ]

Hals neck [nek]; *(Kehle)* throat [θrəʊt]

Halsschmerzen haben have a sore throat [ˌsɔː ˈθrəʊt]

Halt stop [stɒp]

halten hold [həʊld]   **einen Vortrag/ eine Rede halten (über)** give a talk (about)   **(mit jm.) Kontakt halten** stay in touch (with sb.) [tʌtʃ]

Haltestelle stop [stɒp]

Hamburger hamburger [ˈhæmbɜːgə]; burger

Hamster hamster [ˈhæmstə]

Hand hand [hænd]

handeln: Es handelt von einer Möwe. It's about a seagull.   **Wovon handelt die Geschichte?** What is the story about?

Handpuppe puppet [ˈpʌpɪt]

Handschuh glove [glʌv]

Handy mobile phone [ˌməʊbaɪl ˈfəʊn], *(kurz auch:)* mobile

hängen hang [hæŋ]

hart hard [hɑːd]   **hart werden** go hard

▶ S. 206 German "werden"

Haupt- main [meɪn]

Haus house [haʊs]   **nach Hause gehen** go home   **nach Hause kommen** come home   **zu Hause** at home   **zu Hause sein** be in   **nicht zu Hause sein** be out

Hausaufgabe(n) homework [ˈhəʊmwɜːk]   **Hausaufgaben machen** do my / your / ... homework   **Was haben wir als Hausaufgabe auf?** What's for homework?

Häuschen *(Cottage)* cottage [ˈkɒtɪdʒ]

heftig: heftiger Regen heavy rain [ˈhevi]

Heftpflaster plaster [ˈplɑːstə]

Heim *(Zuhause)* home [həʊm]

Heimatstadt hometown [ˌhəʊmˈtaʊn]

heiß hot [hɒt]

heißen *(genannt werden)* be called [kɔːld]   **Ich heiße ...** My name is ...   **Wie heißt du?** What's your name?

helfen help [help]

Helfer/in helper [ˈhelpə]

hell bright [braɪt]

Hemd shirt [ʃɜːt]

herauf up [ʌp]

heraus out [aʊt]   **aus ... heraus** out of ... [ˈaʊt‿əv]

heraus-: herausfinden find out   **herausnehmen** take out   **herausziehen** pull out

Herbst autumn [ˈɔːtəm]

hereinkommen come in [ˌkʌm‿ˈɪn]

Herr Schwarz Mr Schwarz [ˈmɪstə]

herrennen: hinter jm. herrennen run after sb. [ˌrʌn‿ˈɑːftə]

herrlich lovely [ˈlʌvli]

herum: um ... herum around ... [əˈraʊnd]   **um 18 Uhr herum** *(gegen 18 Uhr)* around 6 pm

▶ S. 197 around

herum-: herumgeben pass around [ˌpɑːs‿əˈraʊnd]   **herumirren** wander [ˈwɒndə]   **herumlaufen** walk around; wander   **herumreichen** pass around   **herumrennen** run around

▶ S. 197 around

two hundred and thirty-five   **235**

Dictionary

herunter down [daʊn]

hervorheben (mit Textmarker) highlight ['haɪlaɪt]

Herz heart [hɑːt]

Heu hay [heɪ]

heute today [tə'deɪ]   **heute Nachmittag/Abend/...** this afternoon/evening/...

hier here [hɪə]   **Hier bitte.** (Bitte sehr.) Here you are.   **hier in der Nähe** near here   **hier herüber** over here   **hier oben** up here

hierher here [hɪə]   **bis hierher** (bis jetzt) so far

Hilfe help [help]

Himmel sky [skaɪ]

hinauf up [ʌp]   **auf das Boot hinauf** onto the boat ['bʊntʊ]

hinaufklettern (auf) climb [klaɪm]

hinaus out [aʊt]   **aus ... hinaus** out of ... ['aʊt‿əv]

hinbringen take [teɪk]
▶ S. 180 German "bringen"

hinein: in die Küche hinein into the kitchen ['ɪntʊ]

hineingehen go in; (eintreten) enter ['entə]

hinfallen fall [fɔːl]

hinkommen (gelangen) get [get]
▶ S. 185 (to) get

hinsetzen: sich hinsetzen sit down [ˌsɪt 'daʊn]

hinstellen: sich hinstellen stand [stænd]

hinten: von hinten from behind [bɪ'haɪnd]

hinter behind [bɪ'haɪnd]   **hinter jm. herrennen** run after sb. [ˌrʌn‿ə'ftə]   **aus dem hinteren Teil des Buses** from the back of the bus

Hintergrund background ['bækgraʊnd]

hinterlassen: eine Nachricht hinterlassen leave a message [ˌliːv‿ə 'mesɪdʒ]

hinüberrennen (zu/nach ...) run over (to) ['əʊvə]

hinunter down [daʊn]

Hirsch deer, pl deer [dɪə]

Hobby hobby ['hɒbi]

hoch high [haɪ]; (Gebäude, Baum) tall [tɔːl]
▶ S. 185 German "groß"

Hochmoor moor [mɔː], [mʊə]

hochsehen (aufschauen) look up [lʊk‿'ʌp]

hochspringen jump up

hoffen hope [həʊp]

Höhle cave [keɪv]

holen: (sich) etwas holen get sth.
▶ S. 185 (to) get

Holz wood [wʊd]

horchen listen ['lɪsn]

hören hear [hɪə]

Hose trousers (pl) ['traʊzəz]
▶ S. 199 Clothes

Hotel hotel [həʊ'tel]

hübsch pretty ['prɪti]; (schön, wunderbar) lovely ['lʌvli]

Hügel hill [hɪl]

Hund dog [dɒg]

Hunger haben be hungry ['hʌŋgri]

hungrig sein be hungry ['hʌŋgri]

Husten haben have a cough [kɒf]

Hut hat [hæt]

I

ich I [aɪ]   **Ich auch.** Me too.

ideal (perfekt) perfect ['pɜːfɪkt]

Idee idea [aɪ'dɪə]

ihm him [hɪm]; (bei Dingen, Tieren) it

ihn him [hɪm]; (bei Dingen, Tieren) it

ihnen them [ðem], [ðəm]

Ihnen (höfliche Anredeform) you [juː]

ihr (Plural von „du") you [juː]

ihr: Hilf ihr. Help her. [hɜː]

ihr(e) ... (vor Nomen; besitzanzeigend)
 1. (zu „she") her ... [hɜː, hə]
 2. (zu „it") its ... [ɪts]
 3. (zu „they") their ... [ðeə]

Ihr(e) ... (vor Nomen; besitzanzeigend) (zur höflichen Anredeform „you") your ... [jɔː, jə]

ihrer, ihre, ihrs (zu „she") hers [hɜːz]; (zu „they") theirs [ðeəz]
▶ S. 186 Possessivpronomen

Ihrer, Ihre, Ihrs (höfliche Anredeform) yours [jɔːz]
▶ S. 186 Possessivpronomen

im: im Jahr 1580 in 1580   **im Flugzeug** on the plane   **im Radio** on the radio

Imbiss snack [snæk]

immer always ['ɔːlweɪz]   **für immer** for ever [fər 'evə]   **immer noch** still [stɪl]   **immer wieder** again and again

in in [ɪn]; (in Ortsangaben auch oft:) at [æt], [ət]   **in der Beach Road** in Beach Road   **in der Beach Road 8** at 8 Beach Road   **in der Dean Street** in Dean Street   **in der Dean Street 14** at 14 Dean Street   **in der Nacht** at night   **in der Nähe von** near   **in der Schule** at school   **in**

die Küche (hinein) into the kitchen

in England in England   **in Ordnung** all right   **in Schwierigkeiten sein** be in trouble ['trʌbl]

Inder/in Indian ['ɪndiən]

indisch Indian ['ɪndiən]

Information(en) (über) information (about) (no pl) [ˌɪnfə'meɪʃn]

Informations- und Kommunikationstechnologie ICT [ˌaɪ siː 'tiː] (Information and Communication Technology)

Inlineskaten skating ['skeɪtɪŋ]

Inlineskates skates [skeɪts]

innehalten pause [pɔːz]

Innenhof courtyard ['kɔːtjɑːd]

Innere(r, s): im Innern von ... inside ... [ˌɪn'saɪd]

innerhalb von ... inside ... [ˌɪn'saɪd]

Insel island ['aɪlənd]

Instrument instrument ['ɪnstrəmənt]

interessant interesting ['ɪntrəstɪŋ]

interessieren: sich interessieren (für) be interested (in) ['ɪntrəstɪd]

interessiert sein (an) be interested (in) ['ɪntrəstɪd]

Internat boarding school ['bɔːdɪŋ skuːl]

Interview interview ['ɪntəvjuː]

interviewen: jn. interviewen interview sb. ['ɪntəvjuː]

irgendetwas? anything? ['eniθɪŋ]

irgendjemand? anybody? / anyone? ['enibɒdi, 'eniwʌn]

irgendwelche: Gibt es irgendwelche ...? Are there any ...? ['eni]

irren: jemand irrt sich (jemand hat Unrecht) someone is wrong [rɒŋ]

J

ja yes [jes]   **Ja, das ist richtig. / Ja, das stimmt.** Yes, that's right.
▶ S. 183 right

Jacke, Jackett jacket ['dʒækɪt]

Jahr year [jɪə]

Jahrgang, Jahrgangsstufe year [jɪə]

Jahrhundert century ['sentʃəri]

Januar January ['dʒænjuəri]

je: besser als je zuvor better than ever

Jeans jeans (pl) [dʒiːnz]

jede(r, s) ... every ... ['evri]; (jede(r, s) einzelne) each ... [iːtʃ]

Jedenfalls, ... (Wie dem auch sei) Anyway, ... ['eniweɪ]

jeder (alle) everyone ['evriwʌn], everybody ['evribɒdi]

German – English

jemals ever ['evə] **Bist du jemals in … gewesen?** Have you ever been to …?

jemand somebody / someone ['sʌmbədi, 'sʌmwʌn]; (in Fragen) anybody? / anyone? ['enibɒdi, 'eniwʌn] **Finde jemanden, der …** Find someone who …

jene(r, s): jener Ort / jene Fähre / jenes Kleid that place/ferry/dress **jene Leute** those people

jetzt now [naʊ] **jetzt gerade** right now **bis jetzt** so far

Job job [dʒɒb]

Joghurt yoghurt ['jɒgət]

Jongleur/in juggler ['dʒʌglə]

jonglieren: mit etwas jonglieren juggle sth. ['dʒʌgl]

jubeln cheer [tʃɪə]

Judo judo ['dʒuːdəʊ]

Jugendliche(r) kid [kɪd] (infml)

Juli July [dʒu'laɪ]

jung young [jʌŋ]

Junge boy [bɔɪ]

Juni June [dʒuːn]

K

Käfig cage [keɪdʒ]

Kakao cocoa ['kəʊkəʊ]

Kalender diary ['daɪəri]

kalt cold [kəʊld]

Kamera camera ['kæmərə]

Kameramann cameraman, pl -men ['kæmrəmən]

Kamin fireplace ['faɪəpleɪs]

Kampf (Schlacht) battle ['bætl]

kämpfen fight [faɪt] **gegen jn. kämpfen** fight sb.

Kämpfer/in fighter ['faɪtə]

Kaninchen rabbit ['ræbɪt]

Kantine canteen [kæn'tiːn]

Kapitän/in captain ['kæptɪn]

Kappe cap [cæp]

kaputt broken ['brəʊkən] **kaputt gehen** break [breɪk] **etwas kaputt machen** break sth.

Karren cart [kɑːt]

Karte (an) card (to) [kɑːd]

Kartoffel potato [pə'teɪtəʊ], pl potatoes

Käse cheese [tʃiːz]

Kasse (in Geschäften) cash desk ['kæʃ desk]

Kästchen box [bɒks]

Kasten box [bɒks]

Katze cat [kæt]

kaufen buy [baɪ]

Käufer/in shopper ['ʃɒpə]

kaum: Ich kann es kaum erwarten, … zu sehen I can't wait to see …

Kehle throat [θrəʊt]

kein(e) no [nəʊ] **Es gibt/sind keine …** There aren't any … ['eni] **Ich bin kein Junge.** I'm not a boy. **Ich mag kein Grün.** I don't like green. **er hat keine Zeit** he doesn't have time

Keks biscuit ['bɪskɪt]

kennen know [nəʊ]

kennenlernen meet [miːt] **Freut mich, dich/euch/Sie kennenzulernen.** Nice to meet you.

kennzeichnen: etwas kennzeichnen mark sth. up [‚mɑːk_'ʌp]

Kerze candle ['kændl]

Kette chain [tʃeɪn]

Kilogramm, Kilo (kg) kilogram ['kɪləgræm], kilo ['kiːləʊ] (kg)

Kilometer (km) kilometre ['kɪləmiːtə], [kɪ'lɒmɪtə] (km)

Kind child [tʃaɪld], pl children ['tʃɪldrən]; (infml auch:) kid [kɪd]

Kino cinema ['sɪnəmə]

Kirche church [tʃɜːtʃ]

Kiste box [bɒks]

Klang sound [saʊnd]

klar (deutlich) clear [klɪə]

Klasse class [klɑːs]

Klassenkamerad/in classmate ['klɑːsmeɪt]

Klassenzimmer classroom ['klɑːsruːm]

klatschen (Beifall) clap [klæp] **Klatscht in die Hände.** Clap your hands.

Klavier piano [pi'ænəʊ] **Klavier spielen** play the piano

Klebestift glue stick ['gluː stɪk]

klebrig sticky ['stɪki]

Klebstoff glue [gluː]

Kleid dress [dres]

Kleidung, Kleidungsstücke clothes (pl) [kləʊðz]

klein little ['lɪtl]; small [smɔːl]

klettern climb [klaɪm]

Klingel bell [bel]

klingeln ring [rɪŋ]

klingen sound [saʊnd]

Klippe cliff [klɪf]

klopfen (tippen) tap [tæp]

Klub club [klʌb] **in einen Klub eintreten / sich einem Klub anschließen** join a club [dʒɔɪn]

klug clever ['klevə]

Knie knee [niː]

knien kneel [niːl]

komisch 1. (lustig) funny ['fʌni] 2. (seltsam, merkwürdig) funny; strange [streɪndʒ]

Komma comma ['kɒmə]

kommen come [kʌm]; (gelangen, hinkommen) get [get] **Ich komme aus Plymouth.** I'm from Plymouth. **Komm, Dad!** (Na los, Dad!) Come on, Dad. **nach Hause kommen** come home

Komödie comedy ['kɒmədi]

König king [kɪŋ]

Königin queen [kwiːn]

königlich royal ['rɔɪəl]

können can [kæn], [kən] **ich kann nicht … / du kannst nicht …** usw. I can't … / you can't … etc. [kɑːnt] **gut Kung-Fu können** be good at kung fu

konnte(n): ich konnte … / du konntest … usw. I could … / you could … etc. [kʊd] **ich konnte nicht … / du konntest nicht …** usw. I couldn't … / you couldn't … etc. [kʊdnt]

könnte(n): Was könnte besser sein? What could be better? [kʊd], [kəd]

Konsonant consonant ['kɒnsənənt]

Kontakt: (mit jm.) Kontakt aufnehmen get in touch (with sb.) [tʌtʃ] **(mit jm.) Kontakt halten** stay in touch (with sb.)

Kontext (Text-, Satzzusammenhang) context ['kɒntekst]

Kontrolle (Überprüfung) check [tʃek]

kontrollieren (überprüfen) check [tʃek]

Konzert concert ['kɒnsət]

Kopf head [hed]

Kopfschmerzen haben have a headache ['hedeɪk]

Kopie copy ['kɒpi]

kopieren copy ['kɒpi]

Korb basket ['bɑːskɪt]

Körper body ['bɒdi]

Körperteil part of the body

korrekt correct [kə'rekt]

korrigieren correct [kə'rekt]

kosten cost [kɒst] **Die Kamera kostet …** The camera is … **Die DVDs kosten …** The DVDs are … **Was/Wie viel kostet …?** How much is …? **Was/Wie viel kosten …?** How much are …?

kostenlos free

köstlich delicious [dɪ'lɪʃəs]

Kostüm costume ['kɒstjuːm]

kräftig strong [strɒŋ]

Dictionary

krank sick [sɪk]; ill [ɪl]
▶ S. 204 ill – sick – well
Krankenhaus hospital ['hɒspɪtl]
Krebs *(Tier)* crab [kræb]
Kreis circle ['sɜːkl]
Kreisverkehr roundabout
 ['raʊndəbaʊt]
kreuzen; sich kreuzen cross [krɒs]
Kreuzotter adder ['ædə]
Kricket cricket ['krɪkɪt]
Krone crown [kraʊn]
Küche kitchen ['kɪtʃɪn]
Kuchen cake [keɪk]
Kugelschreiber pen [pen]
Kuh cow [kaʊ]
kühl cool [kuːl]
kümmern: sich um jn. kümmern
 look after sb.
Kunst art [ɑːt]
Künstler/in artist ['ɑːtɪst]
Kunststoff plastic ['plæstɪk]
Kunststück trick [trɪk]
kurz short [ʃɔːt] **kurz nachdem
 …** just after … **Kann ich Sie kurz
 sprechen?** May I have a word with
 you?
küssen; sich küssen kiss [kɪs]
Küste coast [kəʊst]

L

lächeln smile [smaɪl]
lachen laugh [lɑːf]
Laden shop [ʃɒp] **Laden an der
 Ecke** *(„Tante-Emma-Laden")* corner
 shop ['kɔːnə ʃɒp]
Lamm lamb [læm]
Lampe lamp [læmp]
Land *(auch als Gegensatz zur Stadt)*
 country ['kʌntri]; *(Grund und Boden)*
 land [lænd] **an Land gehen** land
landen land [lænd]
Landkarte map ['mæp] **auf der
 Landkarte** on the map
Landschaft *(ländliche Gegend)*
 countryside ['kʌntrisaɪd]
Landwirt/in farmer ['fɑːmə]
lang long [lɒŋ] **lange aufbleiben**
 stay up late
langsam slow [sləʊ] **er schüttelte
 langsam den Kopf** he shook his
 head slowly ['sləʊli]
langweilen: sich langweilen be/feel
 bored [bɔːd]
langweilig boring ['bɔːrɪŋ]
Lärm: voller Lärm noisy ['nɔɪzi]
lärmend noisy ['nɔɪzi]

lassen 1. let **Lass mich dir …
 zeigen.** Let me show you …
 Lass(t) uns … Let's …
 2. leave [liːv] **Lass bitte das Fenster offen.** Leave the window open,
 please. **etwas übrig lassen (für
 jn.)** leave sth. (for sb.) **etwas fallen lassen** drop sth. [drɒp]
 3. Lass das! *(Hör auf damit)* Stop it!
 (infml)
▶ S. 194 (to) leave
laufen run [rʌn]
Läufer/in runner ['rʌnə]
laut loud [laʊd]; *(unangenehm laut)*
 noisy ['nɔɪzi] **laut (vor)lesen**
 read aloud [ə'laʊd] **mit lauter
 Stimme** in a loud voice
läuten ring [rɪŋ]
Leben life [laɪf], *pl* lives [laɪvz]
leben *(wohnen)* live [lɪv]
lecker delicious [dɪ'lɪʃəs]; tasty
 ['teɪsti]; yummy ['jʌmi] *(infml)*
ledig *(alleinstehend)* single ['sɪŋgl]
legen *(hinlegen, ablegen)* put [pʊt]
Legende legend ['ledʒənd]
Lehrer/in teacher ['tiːtʃə]
Lehrgang workshop ['wɜːkʃɒp]
leicht *(einfach)* easy ['iːzi]
leid: Es tut mir leid (wegen …) I'm
 sorry (about …)
leise quiet ['kwaɪət] **sie sang
 leise** she sang softly ['sɒftli]
lenken steer [stɪə]
lernen learn [lɜːn]
Lernposter study poster ['stʌdi
 pəʊstə]
lesen read [riːd]
Leser/in reader ['riːdə]
letzte(r, s) last [lɑːst] **letztes Wochenende / letzten Freitag** last
 weekend/Friday **das Musical/The-
 aterstück/… vom letzten Jahr**
 last year's musical/play/…
leuchtend bright [braɪt]
Leute people ['piːpl]
Licht light [laɪt]
Lichtblitz flash [flæʃ]
**Liebe: Alles Liebe, … / Liebe
 Grüße, …** *(Briefschluss)* Love, …
liebe(r, s) dear [dɪə]
lieben love [lʌv]
Lieblings-: mein Lieblingstier my
 favourite animal ['feɪvərɪt]
Lied song [sɒŋ]
liegen lie [laɪ]
lila purple ['pɜːpl]
Lineal ruler ['ruːlə]

linke(r, s) left [left] **auf der linken
 Seite** on the left **nach links** left
 (nach) links abbiegen turn left
▶ S. 189 left – right
Lippe lip [lɪp]
Liste list [lɪst]
Loch hole [həʊl]
Löffel spoon [spuːn]
los: Los geht's. / Jetzt geht's los.
 Here we go. **Was ist los?** What's
 the matter? ['mætə] **Was ist los mit
 Justin/dir?** *(Was fehlt Justin/dir?)*
 What's wrong with Justin/you?
Löwe lion ['laɪən]
Luft air [eə]

M

machen *(tun)* do [duː]; *(herstellen)*
 make [meɪk] **aus etwas gemacht
 sein** be made of sth. **einen Fehler
 machen** make a mistake **einen
 Spaziergang machen** go for a walk
 [wɔːk] **Fotos machen** take photos
 Hat es Spaß gemacht? Was it fun?
 jn. zu etwas machen make sb. sth.
 sich fertig machen (für) get ready
 (for) ['redi]
Mädchen girl [gɜːl]
Magen stomach ['stʌmək]
magisch magic ['mædʒɪk]
Mai May [meɪ]
Make-up make-up ['meɪk_ʌp]
mal: (vorher) schon mal before
 [bɪ'fɔː] **Warst du schon mal hier?**
 Have you been here before?
▶ S. 193 before
Mal time [taɪm] **dieses Mal** this
 time
malen paint [peɪnt]
Mama mum [mʌm]
manchmal sometimes ['sʌmtaɪmz]
Mann man [mæn], *pl* men [men]
Mannschaft team [tiːm]
Mantel coat [kəʊt]
Marine navy ['neɪvi]
Marionette puppet ['pʌpɪt]
markieren mark (up) [mɑːk]; *(mit
 Textmarker)* highlight ['haɪlaɪt]
Markt market ['mɑːkɪt]
Marmelade jam [dʒæm]
März March [mɑːtʃ]
Mathematik maths [mæθs]
Matsch mud [mʌd]
Mauer wall [wɔːl]
Maul mouth [maʊθ]
Meer sea [siː] **am Meer** by the sea

German – English

Meerschweinchen guinea pig ['gɪni pɪg]

mehr more [mɔː] **nicht mehr** not … any more

Meile *(ca. 1,6 km)* mile [maɪl]

meilenweit for miles [maɪlz]

mein(e) … my … [maɪ]

meinen *(sagen wollen)* mean [miːn]

meiner, meine, meins mine [maɪn]
▶ S. 186 Possessivpronomen

meisten: die meisten Menschen most people [məʊst] **die meisten von ihnen** most of them

meistens usually ['juːʒuəli]

Meister/in master ['maːstə]; *(Champion)* champion ['tʃæmpiən]

Menge *(Menschenmenge)* crowd [kraʊd]

Mensa *(Kantine)* canteen [kænˈtiːn]

Menschen people ['piːpl]

Merkzettel crib sheet ['krɪb ʃiːt] *(infml)*

Messer knife [naɪf], *pl* knives [naɪvz]

Meter metre ['miːtə]

mich me [miː]

Milch milk [mɪlk]

Million million ['mɪljən]

Minute minute ['mɪnɪt]

mir me [miː]

mit with [wɪð] **mit dem Bus/Auto fahren** go by bus/car

Mitfahrgelegenheit lift [lɪft]

Mitlaut *(Konsonant)* consonant ['kɒnsənənt]

Mitschüler/in classmate ['klaːsmeɪt]

Mittag: zu Mittag essen have lunch [lʌntʃ]

Mittagessen lunch [lʌntʃ]

mittags at lunchtime ['lʌntʃtaɪm]

Mittagszeit lunchtime ['lʌntʃtaɪm]

Mitte middle ['mɪdl]; *(Zentrum)* centre ['sentə]

Mitternacht midnight ['mɪdnaɪt]

Mittwoch Wednesday ['wenzdeɪ, -di]

Mitwirkende *(Besetzung in Theaterstück, Film)* cast [kaːst]

Mobiltelefon mobile phone [ˌməʊbaɪl 'fəʊn], *(kurz auch:)* mobile

möchte: Ich möchte … (haben) I'd like … [ˌaɪd 'laɪk] (= I would like …) **Ich möchte gehen.** I'd like to go. **Was möchtest du (haben)?** What would you like? [wʊd] **Was möchtest du essen?** What would you like to eat?

Mode fashion ['fæʃn]

Model model ['mɒdl]

mögen like [laɪk] **Ich mag …** I like … **Ich mag Grün nicht. / Ich mag**

kein Grün. I don't like green. ['dəʊnt laɪk]

Moment moment ['məʊmənt] **im Moment** at the moment **Warte einen Moment. / Moment mal.** Wait a minute.

Monat month [mʌnθ]

Mond moon [muːn]

Monster monster ['mɒnstə]

Montag Monday ['mʌndeɪ, 'mʌndi]

morgen tomorrow [təˈmɒrəʊ] **morgen früh, morgen Vormittag** tomorrow morning

Morgen *(Vormittag)* morning ['mɔːnɪŋ] **am Morgen** in the morning

morgens in the morning ['mɔːnɪŋ]

Möwe seagull ['siːgʌl]

MP3-Player, MP3-Spieler MP3 player [ˌempiːˈθriː ˌpleɪə]

müde tired ['taɪəd]

Müll rubbish ['rʌbɪʃ]

Mund mouth [maʊθ]

Münze coin [kɔɪn]

Museum museum [mjuˈziːəm]

Musical musical ['mjuːzɪkl]

Musik music ['mjuːzɪk]

müssen have to ['hæv tə]; need to ['niːd tə]; must [mʌst] **du musst es nicht tun** you don't have to do it; you don't need to do it; you needn't do it ['niːdnt]
▶ S. 203 must – needn't – mustn't

Mutter mother ['mʌðə]

Mutti mum [mʌm]

N

Na: Na ja, … Well, … [wel] **Na los, Dad!** *(Komm, Dad!)* Come on, Dad. **Na und?** So? [səʊ]

nach **1.** *(örtlich)* to [tu], [tə] **nach draußen** outside [ˌaʊtˈsaɪd] **nach drinnen** inside [ˌɪnˈsaɪd] **nach Hause gehen/kommen** go/come home **nach oben** up; *(im Haus)* upstairs [ˌʌpˈsteəz] **nach unten** down; *(im Haus)* downstairs [ˌdaʊnˈsteəz] **nach vorn** to the front **einer nach dem anderen** one by one **2.** *(zeitlich)* after ['aːftə] **nach dem Frühstück** after breakfast **Viertel nach zehn (10.15 / 22.15)** quarter past ten ['kwɔːtə paːst]

Nachbar/in neighbour ['neɪbə]

nachdem after ['aːftə] **gleich nachdem … / kurz nachdem …** just after …

Nachmittag afternoon [ˌaːftəˈnuːn] **am Nachmittag** in the afternoon

nachmittags in the afternoon [ˌaːftəˈnuːn]

Nachricht message ['mesɪdʒ] **eine Nachricht hinterlassen** leave a message [ˌliːv ˌə 'mesɪdʒ]

Nachrichten news *(no pl)* [njuːz]

Nachspeise dessert [dɪˈzɜːt]

nächste(r, s) next [nekst] **das nächste Bild / die nächste Frage** the next picture/question **das Musical/Theaterstück/… vom nächsten Jahr** next year's musical/play/…

Nacht night [naɪt] **in der Nacht** at night

Nachtisch dessert [dɪˈzɜːt]

nachts at night [ət 'naɪt]

Nähe: in der Nähe von near [nɪə] **hier in der Nähe** near here

nahe (bei) near [nɪə]

nahegelegen: eine nahegelegene Stadt a nearby town ['nɪəbaɪ]

Name name [neɪm] **Mein Name ist Silky.** My name is Silky.

Nase nose [nəʊz]

nass wet [wet]

natürlich *(selbstverständlich)* of course [əv 'kɔːs]

Naturwissenschaft science ['saɪəns]

neben next to ['nekst tʊ]

Nebensatz sub-clause ['sʌbklɔːz]

nehmen take [teɪk] **jn. am Arm nehmen** take sb. by the arm

nein no [nəʊ] **Nein, das ist falsch. / Nein, das stimmt nicht.** No, that's wrong.

nennen *(rufen, bezeichnen)* call [kɔːl]

nervös nervous ['nɜːvəs]

nett nice [naɪs]; kind [kaɪnd]

neu new [njuː]

Neuigkeiten news [njuːz]

neun nine [naɪn]

nicht not [nɒt] **auch nicht** not … either ['aɪðə], ['iːðə] **Geh nicht.** Don't go. [dəʊnt] **Ich mag Grün nicht.** I don't like green. **Ich weiß (es) nicht.** I don't know. **nicht mehr** not … any more **nicht vor drei** not till three **…, nicht wahr?** …, right? **noch nicht** not … yet [jet] **(noch) nicht einmal** not even

nichts not … anything ['eniθɪŋ]

nicken nod [nɒd]

nie never ['nevə] **(vorher) noch nie** not … before, never … before
▶ S. 193 before

niemals never ['nevə]

two hundred and thirty-nine **239**

Dictionary

niemand no one ['nəʊ wʌn], nobody ['nəʊbədi]; not ... anybody/anyone ['enibɒdi, 'eniwʌn]

niesen sneeze [sni:z]

noch: noch ein Foto one more photo [mɔ:]; another photo [ə'nʌðə] **noch einmal** again [ə'gen] **noch nicht** not ... yet [jet] **noch nicht einmal** not even **immer noch** still [stɪl] **(vorher) noch nie** not/never before
▶ S. 193 before

normalerweise usually ['ju:ʒuəli]

Notiz note [nəʊt] **(sich) Notizen machen** (beim Lesen oder Zuhören) take notes **(sich) Notizen machen (über/zu etwas)** (zur Vorbereitung) make notes (on sth.)

November November [nəʊ'vembə]

Null (in Telefonnummern) o [əʊ]

Nummer number

nun now [nəʊ] **Nun, ...** Well, ... [wel]

nur only ['əʊnli]; (einfach nur) just [dʒʌst]

O

oben (an der Spitze, am oberen Ende) at the top (of); (im Haus) upstairs [ˌʌp'steəz] **hier oben** up here **nach oben** up; (im Haus) upstairs

Objekt object ['ɒbdʒekt]

Obst fruit [fru:t]

Obstsalat fruit salad [ˌfru:t 'sæləd]

oder or [ɔ:]

offen open ['əʊpən]

öffnen; sich öffnen open ['əʊpən]

oft often ['ɒfn], ['ɒftən]

ohne without [wɪ'ðaʊt]

Ohr ear [ɪə]

Ohrhörer earphones (pl) ['ɪəfəʊnz]

Oje! Oh dear! [dɪə]

okay OK [ˌəʊ'keɪ]; all right [ɔ:l 'raɪt]

Oktober October [ɒk'təʊbə]

Oma grandma ['grænmɑ:]

Onkel uncle ['ʌŋkl]

online online [ˌɒn'laɪn]

Opa grandpa ['grænpɑ:]

Orange orange ['ɒrɪndʒ]

orange(farben) orange ['ɒrɪndʒ]

Ordnung: in Ordnung (okay) all right [ɔ:l 'raɪt]; OK [ˌəʊ'keɪ]

Ort place [pleɪs]

Otter otter ['ɒtə]

Ozean ocean ['əʊʃn]

P

paar: ein paar a few [ə 'fju:]; some [sʌm], [səm]

Paar: ein Paar a pair (of) [peə]

Päckchen packet ['pækɪt]

Packung packet ['pækɪt]

Papa dad [dæd]

Papier paper ['peɪpə]

Parade parade [pə'reɪd]

Park park [pɑ:k]

Partner/in partner ['pɑ:tnə]

Party party ['pɑ:ti]

Pass auf! (Vorsicht!) Watch out! [ˌwɒtʃ 'aʊt]

passen: zu etwas passen (zu etwas gehören) go with sth.

passieren (mit) happen (to) ['hæpən]

Pause break [breɪk] **eine Pause einlegen** pause [pɔ:z]

pausieren pause [pɔ:z]

Pence pence [pens]

perfekt perfect ['pɜ:fɪkt]

Person person ['pɜ:sn]; (in Roman, Film, Theaterstück usw.) character ['kærəktə]

Pfad path [pɑ:θ]

Pfannkuchen pancake ['pænkeɪk]

Pfeffer pepper ['pepə]

pfeifen whistle ['wɪsl]

Pferd horse [hɔ:s]

Pflanze plant [plɑ:nt]

pflanzen plant [plɑ:nt]

Pflaster (Heftpflaster) plaster ['plɑ:stə]

Pforte (Gatter) gate [geɪt]

Pfote paw [pɔ:]

Pfund (britische Währung) pound (£) [paʊnd]

Piano piano [pi'ænəʊ]

Picknick picnic ['pɪknɪk]

piepen beep [bi:p]

pink pink [pɪŋk]

Pizza pizza ['pi:tsə]

Plan plan [plæn]

planen plan [plæn]

Planet planet ['plænɪt]

Plastik plastic ['plæstɪk]

Platz place [pleɪs]

Plätzchen (Keks) biscuit ['bɪskɪt]

plötzlich suddenly ['sʌdnli]

Pokal (Trophäe) trophy ['trəʊfi]

Polizist/in police officer [pə'li:s ˌɒfɪsə]

Pommes frites chips (pl) [tʃɪps]; (American English) fries (pl) [fraɪz]

Pony pony ['pəʊni]

Porträt (Personenbeschreibung) profile ['prəʊfaɪl]

Postamt post office ['pəʊst ˌɒfɪs]

Poster poster ['pəʊstə]

Postkarte postcard ['pəʊstkɑ:d]

Praline chocolate ['tʃɒklət]

prallen: gegen etwas prallen hit sth. [hɪt]

Präsentation presentation [ˌprezn'teɪʃn]

präsentieren: (jm.) etwas präsentieren present sth. (to sb.) [prɪ'zent]

Preis 1. (Kaufpreis) price [praɪs] 2. (Gewinn) prize [praɪz]

preiswert (billig) cheap [tʃi:p]

Prinz prince [prɪns]

Prinzessin princess [ˌprɪn'ses], ['prɪnses]

pro: einmal/zweimal pro Woche/Jahr once/twice a week/year

probieren try [traɪ]

Problem problem ['prɒbləm]

Profil (Personenbeschreibung, Porträt) profile ['prəʊfaɪl]

Programm programme ['prəʊgræm]

Projekt project ['prɒdʒekt]

prüfen (überprüfen) check [tʃek]

Publikum audience ['ɔ:diəns]

Pullover pullover ['pʊləʊvə]

Punkt point [pɔɪnt]; (Satzzeichen) full stop [ˌfʊl 'stɒp]; (Fleck) spot [spɒt]

putzen clean [kli:n]

Puzzle jigsaw ['dʒɪgsɔ:]

Q

Quadratkilometer (km²) square kilometre (sq km) [ˌskweə kɪ'lɒmɪtə]

Quiz quiz [kwɪz]

R

Rad (Fahrrad) bike [baɪk] **Rad fahren** ride a bike [ˌraɪd ə 'baɪk]

Radiergummi rubber ['rʌbə]

Radio radio ['reɪdiəʊ] **im Radio** on the radio

Rallye rally ['ræli]

Rasen grass [grɑ:s]

raten guess [ges]

Rathaus town hall [ˌtaʊn 'hɔ:l]

Ratte rat [ræt]

rauf und runter up and down [ˌʌp ən 'daʊn]

Recht: jemand hat Recht someone is right
▶ S. 183 right

rechte(r, s) right [raɪt] **auf der rechten Seite** on the right **nach**

240 two hundred and forty

German – English

rechts right **(nach) rechts abbie-gen** turn right
▶ S. 189 left – right
Rede talk [tɔːk]; *(offiziell)* speech [spiːtʃ] **eine Rede halten (über)** give a talk (about)
reden talk [tɔːk]; speak [spiːk]
Redner/in speaker [ˈspiːkə]
Referat talk [tɔːk] **ein Referat hal-ten (über)** give a talk (about)
Refrain chorus [ˈkɔːrəs]
Regal shelf [ʃelf], *pl* shelves [ʃelvz]
Regel rule [ruːl]
regelmäßig regular [ˈregjələ]
Regen rain [reɪn]
Regenmantel raincoat [ˈreɪnkəʊt]
Regenschirm umbrella [ʌmˈbrelə]
Regenwald rainforest [ˈreɪnfɒrɪst]
Regisseur/in director [dəˈrektə]
regnen rain [reɪn]
regnerisch rainy [ˈreɪni]
Reh deer, *pl* deer [dɪə]
reich rich [rɪtʃ]
Reihe: Ich bin an der Reihe. (It's) my turn. [tɜːn]
Reihenfolge order [ˈɔːdə]
Reim rhyme [raɪm]
Reise trip [trɪp]; journey [ˈdʒɜːni]
Reiseleiter/in guide [gaɪd]
reisen travel [ˈtrævl]
Reisende(r) traveller [ˈtrævələ]
reiten ride [raɪd]
Reiten riding [ˈraɪdɪŋ]
Religion religion [rɪˈlɪdʒən]
rennen run [rʌn]
Rennen race [reɪs]
Reportage report [rɪˈpɔːt]
retten save [seɪv]; *(in Sicherheit brin-gen)* rescue [ˈreskjuː]
Rezept *(Kochrezept)* recipe [ˈresəpi]
richten: etwas auf jn. richten point sth. at sb. [pɔɪnt]
richtig right [raɪt]; correct [kəˈrekt] **Ja, das ist richtig.** Yes, that's right.
▶ S. 183 right
Richtung: in die Richtung that way [weɪ]
riechen smell [smel] **an etwas rie-chen** smell sth. **gut riechen** smell good
Riesenrad big wheel [bɪg ˈwiːl]
Rinderbraten roast beef [ˌrəʊst ˈbiːf]
Ring ring [rɪŋ]
Ritter knight [naɪt]
Robbe seal [siːl]
Rock skirt [skɜːt]
Rockmusik rock (music) [rɒk]
Rolle *(in einem Theaterstück, Film)* role [rəʊl]

rollen roll [rəʊl]
rosa pink [pɪŋk]
rot red [red] **rot werden** go red
▶ S. 206 German "werden"
Rücken back [bæk]
Rucksack rucksack [ˈrʌksæk]
rufen call [kɔːl]; shout [ʃaʊt]
ruhig *(leise)* quiet [ˈkwaɪət]
Ruine ruin [ˈruːɪn]
Rundgang, Rundfahrt (durch) tour (of) [ˈtʊər_əv]
runter: rauf und runter up and down [ˌʌp_ən ˈdaʊn]
runzeln: die Stirn runzeln frown [fraʊn]

S

Sache thing [θɪŋ]
Saft juice [djuːs]
Sage *(Legende)* legend [ˈledʒənd]
sagen say [seɪ]
Sahne cream [kriːm]
Salat *(Gericht, Beilage)* salad [ˈsæləd]
Samba samba [ˈsæmbə]
sammeln collect [kəˈlekt] **Geld sammeln (für etwas)** raise money (for sth.) [reɪz]
Samstag Saturday [ˈsætədeɪ, ˈsætədi]
Sand sand [sænd]
Sandwich sandwich [ˈsænwɪtʃ, ˈsænwɪdʒ]
sanft: mit sanfter Stimme in a soft voice
Sänger/in singer [ˈsɪŋə]
Satz sentence [ˈsentəns]
sauber clean [cliːn] **sauber machen** clean [kliːn]
Schach chess [tʃes]
Schaf sheep, *pl* sheep [ʃiːp]
Schatten *(einer Person, eines Gegen-standes)* shadow [ˈʃædəʊ]
schauen look [lʊk]
Schauspiel *(darstellende Kunst)* drama [ˈdrɑːmə]
Schauspieler/in actor [ˈæktə]
schauspielern act [ækt]
scheu shy [ʃaɪ]
Scheune barn [bɑːn]
schick: sich schick anziehen dress up [ˌdres_ˈʌp]
schicken: jm. etwas schicken send sth. to sb. [send] **einem Freund/einer Freundin eine SMS schicken** text a friend [tekst]
schieben push [pʊʃ]
schießen: ein Tor schießen score [skɔː]

Schiff ship [ʃɪp]
Schild sign [saɪn]; *(Etikett)* label
Schinkenspeck bacon [ˈbeɪkən]
Schirm umbrella [ʌmˈbrelə]
Schlacht battle [ˈbætl]
schlafen sleep [sliːp]; *(nicht wach sein)* be asleep [əˈsliːp]
Schlafparty sleepover [ˈsliːpəʊvə]
Schlafzimmer bedroom [ˈbedruːm]
schlagen hit [hɪt]
Schlagzeug drums *(pl)* [drʌmz] **Schlagzeug spielen** play the drums
Schlamm mud [mʌd]
Schlange snake [sneɪk] **Schlange stehen** queue [kjuː]
schlau clever [ˈklevə]
schlecht bad [bæd] **schlechter** worse [wɜːs] **der/die/das schlech-teste ...; am schlechtesten** worst [wɜːst] **schlecht werden** *(Lebens-mittel)* go bad **Mir ist schlecht.** I feel sick.
▶ S. 204 ill – sick – well
▶ S. 206 German "werden"
schließen, zumachen close [kləʊz]
schließlich at last [ət ˈlɑːst]
schlimm bad [bæd] **schlimmer** worse [wɜːs] **der/die/das schlimmste ...; am schlimms-ten** worst [wɜːst]
Schloss castle [ˈkɑːsl]
Schluss end [end]; *(Abschluss)* end-ing [ˈendɪŋ]
Schlüssel key [kiː]
Schlüsselwort keyword [ˈkiːwɜːd]
schmal narrow [ˈnærəʊ]
schmecken taste [teɪst]
schmelzen melt [melt]
schmerzen hurt [hɜːt]
▶ S. 196 hurt
Schmetterling butterfly [ˈbʌtəflaɪ]
Schmuggel; das Schmuggeln smuggling [ˈsmʌglɪŋ]
schmuggeln smuggle [ˈsmʌgl]
Schmuggler/in smuggler [ˈsmʌglə]
schmutzig dirty [ˈdɜːti]
Schnee snow [snəʊ]
schneiden cut [kʌt]; *(Film, Video be-arbeiten)* edit [ˈedɪt]
schnell fast [fɑːst]; quick [kwɪk]
Schnitt! *(beim Filmen)* Cut! [kʌt]
schockiert shocked [ʃɒkt]
Schokolade chocolate [ˈtʃɒklət]
schön beautiful [ˈbjuːtɪfl]; *(nett)* nice [naɪs]; *(herrlich, wunderbar)* lovely [ˈlʌvli]

two hundred and forty-one **241**

Dictionary

schon already [ɔːl'redi] **Hast du schon …?** Have you … yet? [jet] **(vorher) schon mal** before
▶ S. 193 before
Schrank cupboard ['kʌbəd]
schrecklich terrible ['terəbl]; awful ['ɔːfl]
schreiben write [raɪt]
Schreibtisch desk [desk]
schreien shout [ʃaʊt]; cry [kraɪ]; scream [skriːm]
Schritt step [step]
schüchtern shy [ʃaɪ]
Schuh shoe [ʃuː]
Schule school [skuːl] **in der Schule** at school
Schüler/in student ['stjuːdənt]
Schulfach (school) subject ['sʌbdʒɪkt]
Schulheft (Übungsheft) exercise book ['eksəsaɪz bʊk]
Schultasche school bag ['skuːl bæg]
Schulter shoulder ['ʃəʊldə]
Schüssel bowl [bəʊl]
schütteln shake [ʃeɪk] **er schüttel-te den Kopf** he shook his head
schwarz black [blæk]
Schwein pig [pɪg]
schwer 1. (von Gewicht) heavy ['hevi]
2. (schwierig) hard [hɑːd]
Schwert sword [sɔːd]
Schwester sister ['sɪstə]
schwierig hard [hɑːd]
Schwimmbad, Schwimmbecken (swimming) pool [puːl]
schwimmen swim [swɪm]
Schwimmer/in swimmer ['swɪmə]
Schwimmweste life jacket ['laɪf dʒækɪt]
sechs six [sɪks]
See 1. (Binnensee) lake [leɪk]
2. (die See, das Meer) sea [siː]
Segelboot sailing boat ['seɪlɪŋ bəʊt]
segeln sail [seɪl] **segeln gehen** go sailing ['seɪlɪŋ]
sehen see [siː]
Sehenswürdigkeiten sights (pl) [saɪts]
sehr very ['veri] **Das hat uns sehr geholfen.** That helped us a lot.
seidig silky ['sɪlki]
sein (Verb) be [biː]
sein(e) … (vor Nomen; besitzanzeigend)
1. (zu „he") his … [hɪz]
2. (zu „it") its … [ɪts]
seiner, seine, seins his [hɪz]
▶ S. 186 Possessivpronomen

Seite 1. side [saɪd] **auf der linken Seite** on the left **auf der rechten Seite** on the right
2. (Buchseite) page [peɪdʒ] **Auf welcher Seite sind wir?** What page are we on?
Sekunde second ['sekənd]
selbst wenn even if ['iːvn_ɪf]
Selbstlaut (Vokal) vowel ['vaʊəl]
selbstverständlich of course [əv 'kɔːs]
seltsam strange [streɪndʒ]
senden: jm. etwas senden send sth. to sb. [send]
Sendung (im Radio, Fernsehen) programme ['prəʊgræm]
September September [sep'tembə]
Sessel armchair ['ɑːmtʃeə]
Set set [set]
setzen: sich setzen sit [sɪt] **sich (mit jm.) in Verbindung setzen** get in touch (with sb.) [tʌtʃ]
Shorts (kurze Hose) shorts (pl) [ʃɔːts]
Show show [ʃəʊ]
sicher sure [ʃʊə], [ʃɔː]
sie 1. (Einzahl; weibliche Person) she [ʃiː] **Frag sie.** Ask her. [hɜː]
2. (Einzahl; Ding, Tier) it [ɪt]
3. (Mehrzahl) they [ðeɪ] **Frag sie.** Ask them. [ðem, ðəm]
Sie (höfliche Anredeform) you [juː, ju]
sieben seven ['sevn]
Sieger/in winner ['wɪnə]
Silbe syllable ['sɪləbl]
Silvester New Year's Eve [ˌnjuː jɪəz_'iːv]
singen sing [sɪŋ]
Sitz seat [siːt]
sitzen sit [sɪt]
SMS text message ['tekst mesɪdʒ], (kurz auch:) text **einem Freund/einer Freundin eine SMS schicken** text a friend
Snack snack [snæk]
so 1. (auf diese Weise) like that / like this
2. (nicht) so groß wie (not) as big as [æz], [əz]
3. so cool/nett/leise/… so cool/nice/quiet/… [səʊ]
Socke sock [sɒk]
sodass so that, (oft auch kurz:) so
soeben just [dʒʌst]
Sofa sofa ['səʊfə]
sogar even ['iːvn]
Sohn son [sʌn]
sollen: Du solltest … / Ihr solltet … You should … [ʃʊd], [ʃəd]
Solo- solo ['səʊləʊ]

Sommer summer ['sʌmə]
Sonnabend Saturday ['sætədeɪ, -di]
Sonne sun [sʌn]
Sonnenbrille sunglasses (pl) ['sʌnglɑːsɪz]
sonnig sunny ['sʌni]
Sonntag Sunday ['sʌndeɪ, 'sʌndi]
Sorge: sich Sorgen machen (wegen, um) worry (about) ['wʌri]
sorgen: dafür sorgen, dass … make sure that …
Souvenir souvenir [ˌsuːvə'nɪə]
Spagetti spaghetti [spə'geti]
spanisch Spanish ['spænɪʃ]
spannend (aufregend) exciting [ɪk'saɪtɪŋ]
Spaß fun [fʌn] **Spaß haben** have fun [fʌn] **Hat es Spaß gemacht?** Was it fun?
spät late [leɪt] **Du bist spät dran. / Du bist zu spät.** You're late. **Wie spät ist es?** What time is it?
später later ['leɪtə]
spazieren gehen go for a walk [wɔːk]
Spaziergang walk [wɔːk] **einen Spaziergang machen** go for a walk
Spickzettel crib sheet ['krɪb ʃiːt] (infml)
Spiegel mirror ['mɪrə]
Spiel game [geɪm]; (Wettkampf, Match) match [mætʃ]
spielen play [pleɪ] **Gitarre spielen** play the guitar **Klavier spielen** play the piano **Schlagzeug spielen** play the drums
Spieler/in player ['pleɪə]
Spielzeug toy [tɔɪ]
Spitze top [tɒp] **an der Spitze (von)** at the top (of)
Sport; Sportart sport [spɔːt] **Sport treiben** do sport
Sportunterricht PE [ˌpiː_'iː] (Physical Education)
Sprache language ['læŋgwɪdʒ]
sprechen (mit jm.) speak (to sb.) [spiːk] **Kann ich Sie kurz sprechen?** May I have a word with you?
Sprecher/in speaker ['spiːkə]
springen jump [dʒʌmp]
Sprung jump [dʒʌmp]
spülen: das Geschirr spülen wash the dishes (pl) [ˌwɒʃ ðə 'dɪʃɪz]
Stadt town [taʊn]; (Großstadt) city ['sɪti]
Stadtplan map [mæp] **auf dem Stadtplan** on the map
Stammbaum family tree ['fæməli triː]
Stand (Marktstand) stall [stɔːl]
Star star [stɑː]

German – English

stark strong [strɒŋ] **starker Regen** heavy rain ['hevi]
Station (Haltestelle) stop [stɒp]
stattdessen instead [ɪn'sted]
stechen: etwas in etwas stechen stick sth. into sth. [stɪk]
stecken: etwas in etwas stecken stick sth. into sth. [stɪk]
stehen stand [stænd] **Schlange stehen** queue [kju:]
Stein stone [stəʊn]
steinig rocky ['rɒki]
Stelle place [pleɪs]; (Job, Arbeitsstelle) job [dʒɒb]
stellen (hinstellen, abstellen) put [pʊt] **eine Frage stellen** ask a question
Stempel stamp [stæmp]
sterben die [daɪ]
steuern steer [stɪə]
Stiefel boot [bu:t]
Stift (zum Schreiben) pen [pen]
still quiet ['kwaɪət]
Stimme voice [vɔɪs] **mit lauter Stimme** in a loud voice
stimmen: Ja, das stimmt. Yes, that's right. [raɪt] **Nein, das stimmt nicht.** No, that's wrong. [rɒŋ]
  ▶ S. 183 right
Stirn: die Stirn runzeln frown [fraʊn]
Stock(werk) floor [flɔ:]
stöhnen groan [grəʊn]
Stöhnen groan [grəʊn]
stoppen stop [stɒp]
stoßen push [pʊʃ] **gegen etwas stoßen** hit sth. [hɪt]
strahlend (leuchtend hell) bright [braɪt]
Strand beach [bi:tʃ]
Straße street [stri:t]; road [rəʊd]
Straßenkünstler/in street artist
Strophe verse [vɜ:s]
Student/in student ['stju:dənt]
Studio studio ['stju:diəʊ]
Stuhl chair [tʃeə]
Stunde hour ['aʊə]; (Unterrichtsstunde) lesson ['lesn]
Stundenplan timetable ['taɪmteɪbl]
Sturm storm [stɔ:m]
stürzen fall [fɔ:l]
Subjekt subject ['sʌbdʒekt]
suchen: etwas suchen look for sth. ['lʊk fɔ:]
Suppe soup [su:p]
süß sweet [swi:t]
Süßigkeiten sweets (pl) [swi:ts]
Symbol symbol ['sɪmbl]
Szene scene [si:n]

T

Tabelle table ['teɪbl]
Tafel board [bɔ:d]
Tag day [deɪ]
Tagebuch diary ['daɪəri]
Tagesausflüge machen go on day trips
Taille waist [weɪst]
Tal valley ['væli]
talentiert talented ['tæləntɪd]
Tante aunt [ɑ:nt]
Tante-Emma-Laden corner shop ['kɔ:nə ʃɒp]
Tanz dance [dɑ:ns]
tanzen dance [dɑ:ns]
Tänzer/in dancer ['dɑ:nsə]
Tanzfläche dance floor ['dɑ:ns flɔ:]
Tasche bag [bæg]; (Manteltasche, Hosentasche usw.) pocket ['pɒkɪt]
Taschenlampe torch [tɔ:tʃ]
Tasse: eine Tasse ... a cup of ... [kʌp]
Tatze paw [pɔ:]
Team team [ti:m]
Technik, Technologie technology [tek'nɒlədʒi]
Tee tea [ti:]
Teelöffel teaspoon ['ti:spu:n]
Teil part [pɑ:t] **aus dem hinteren Teil des Buses** from the back of the bus
teilnehmen: an etwas teilnehmen take part in sth. [ˌteɪk 'pɑ:t]
Telefon telephone ['telɪfəʊn], (kurz auch:) phone **am Telefon** on the phone **ans Telefon gehen** answer the phone
Telefonat call [kɔ:l]
Telefongespräch (Anruf) phone call ['fəʊn kɔ:l], (kurz auch:) call
Teller: ein Teller ... a plate of ... [pleɪt]
Temperatur temperature ['temprətʃə]
Tennis tennis ['tenɪs]
Termin appointment [ə'pɔɪntmənt]
teuer expensive [ɪk'spensɪv]
Text text [tekst] **einen Text schnell nach bestimmten Wörtern/Informationen absuchen** scan a text [skæn]
Theater theatre ['θɪətə]
Theaterstück play [pleɪ]
Thema theme [θi:m]; topic ['tɒpɪk]
Thermometer thermometer [θə'mɒmɪtə]
tief deep [di:p]
Tier animal ['ænɪml]
Tipp tip [tɪp]

tippen (vorsichtig klopfen) tap [tæp]
Tisch table ['teɪbl]
Tischtennis table tennis
Titel title ['taɪtl]
Tochter daughter ['dɔ:tə]
Toilette toilet ['tɔɪlət]
Tomate tomato [tə'mɑ:təʊ], pl tomatoes
Top (Oberteil) top [tɒp]
Tor 1. (Pforte, Gatter) gate [geɪt] 2. **ein Tor schießen** score [skɔ:]
tot dead [ded]
töten kill [kɪl]
Tourist/in tourist ['tʊərɪst]
traditionell traditional [trə'dɪʃənl]
tragen (Kleidung) wear [weə]
trainieren practise ['præktɪs]; train [treɪn]
Training training ['treɪnɪŋ]
Traktor tractor ['træktə]
Träne tear [tɪə]
Traum dream [dri:m]
traurig sad [sæd]
treffen; sich treffen meet [mi:t] **etwas treffen** hit sth.
Treffer: einen Treffer erzielen score [skɔ:]
Treppe; Treppenstufen stairs (pl) [steəz]
Trick trick [trɪk]
Trimester term [tɜ:m]
trinken drink [drɪŋk]
Trommel drum [drʌm]
Trophäe trophy ['trəʊfi]
trotzdem still [stɪl]
Tschüs. Bye. [baɪ]
T-Shirt T-shirt ['ti:ʃɜ:t]
Tulpe tulip ['tju:lɪp]
tun do [du:] **etwas tun müssen** have to do sth.; need to do sth. **etwas tun wollen** want to do sth. [wɒnt] **Tut mir leid.** (I'm) sorry. **viel zu tun haben** be busy ['bɪzi]
Tunnel tunnel ['tʌnl]
Tür door [dɔ:]
Türklingel doorbell ['dɔ:bel]
Turm tower ['taʊə]
Turnen gymnastics [dʒɪm'næstɪks]; (Sportunterricht) PE [ˌpi: 'i:] (Physical Education)
Turnhalle gym [dʒɪm]
Turnschuh trainer ['treɪnə]

U

üben practise ['præktɪs]
über 1. (räumlich) over ['əʊvə] **(quer) über das Moor/die Straße**

two hundred and forty-three **243**

Dictionary

across the moor/the street [ə'krɒs]
2. *(mehr als)* over ['əʊvə]   **über 400 Jahre** over 400 years
3. über mich/dich/… about me/ you/… [ə'baʊt]   **über dich selbst** about yourself [jɔː'self]
überall everywhere ['evriweə]
übergeben: Ich muss mich übergeben. I'm going to be sick.
▶ S. 204 ill – sick – well
überprüfen check [tʃek]
Überprüfung check [tʃek]
überqueren cross [krɒs]
überrascht surprised [sə'praɪzd]
Überraschung surprise [sə'praɪz]
Überschrift title ['taɪtl]
übersetzen translate [træns'leɪt]
übrig: etwas übrig lassen (für jn.) leave sth. (for sb.) [liːv]
▶ S. 194 (to) leave
Übung exercise ['eksəsaɪz]
Übungsheft exercise book ['eksəsaɪz bʊk]
Ufer *(eines Sees)* shore [ʃɔː]
Uhr   1. *(Armbanduhr)* watch [wɒtʃ]; *(Wand-, Stand-, Turmuhr)* clock [klɒk]
2. 4 Uhr morgens 4 am [,eɪ_'em]
4 Uhr nachmittags / 16 Uhr 4 pm [,piː_'em]   **um 1 Uhr / 13 Uhr** at 1 o'clock [ə'klɒk]
Uhrzeit time [taɪm]
um   1. *(örtlich)* **um … (herum)** around … [ə'raʊnd]   **um die Welt** round the world [raʊnd]
2. *(zeitlich)* **um 1 Uhr / 13 Uhr** at 1 o'clock [ə'klɒk]   **um 18 Uhr herum** *(gegen 18 Uhr)* around 6 pm
3. um zu to [tu], [tə]
▶ S. 197 around
umarmen: jn. umarmen hug sb. [hʌg]; give sb. a hug [hʌg]
umdrehen *(wenden)* turn around [,tɜːn_ə'raʊnd]   **sich umdrehen** turn around
umher: in der Bücherei / auf dem Strand umher around the library/ the beach [ə'raʊnd]
▶ S. 197 around
umher-: umherrennen run around [,rʌn_ə'raʊnd]   **umherspazieren** walk around
▶ S. 197 around
umsehen: sich (auf der Farm) umsehen look around (the farm)
umziehen (nach) move (to) [muːv]
▶ S. 197 (to) move
Umzug *(Parade)* parade [pə'reɪd]

und and [ænd, [ənd]   **Und du? / Und was ist mit dir?** What about you?   **Und? / Na und?** So? [səʊ]
Unfall: einen Unfall haben crash [kræʃ]
ungefähr about [ə'baʊt]
unglücklich unhappy [ʌn'hæpi]
unheimlich scary ['skeəri]
Uniform uniform ['juːnɪfɔːm]
unmöglich impossible [ɪm'pɒsəbl]
Unrecht: jemand hat Unrecht someone is wrong [rɒŋ]
unregelmäßig irregular [ɪ'regjələ]
uns us [ʌs], [əs]
unser(e) … our … ['aʊə]
unserer, unsere, unseres ours ['aʊəz]
▶ S. 186 Possessivpronomen
unten *(am unteren Ende)* at the bottom (of) ['bɒtəm]; *(im Haus)* downstairs [,daʊn'steəz]   **dort unten** down there   **nach unten** down; *(im Haus)* downstairs
unter under ['ʌndə]
unterbrechen interrupt [,ɪntə'rʌpt]
untergehen *(Sonne)* go down [daʊn]
unterhalten: sich unterhalten (mit) talk (to) [tɔːk]
Unterhaltung conversation [,kɒnvə'seɪʃn]
unterstreichen underline [,ʌndə'laɪn]
Untertitel subtitle ['sʌbtaɪtl]
unterwegs out and about
Unwetter storm [stɔːm]
Urlaub holiday ['hɒlədeɪ]   **in Urlaub fahren** go on holiday   **in Urlaub sein** be on holiday
usw. (und so weiter) etc. (et cetera) [et'setərə]

V

Vater father ['fɑːðə]
Vati dad [dæd]
Vegetarier/in vegetarian [,vedʒə'teəriən]
vegetarisch vegetarian [,vedʒə'teəriən]
Verabredung appointment [ə'pɔɪntmənt]
verändern; sich verändern change [tʃeɪndʒ]
verängstigt scared [skeəd]
verantwortlich responsible [rɪ'spɒnsəbl]
verbessern *(korrigieren)* correct [kə'rekt]

verbeugen: sich verbeugen bow [baʊ]
Verbindung: sich (mit jm.) in Verbindung setzen get in touch (with sb.) [tʌtʃ]   **(mit jm.) in Verbindung bleiben** stay in touch (with sb.)
Vergangenheit past [pɑːst]
vergessen forget [fə'get]
vergewissern: sich vergewissern, dass … make sure that …
Vergnügungspark fun park
verheiratet (mit) married (to) ['mærɪd]
verkaufen sell [sel]
Verkäufer/in shop assistant ['ʃɒp_ə,sɪstənt], *(kurz auch:)* assistant
verkehrt wrong [rɒŋ]
verkleiden: sich verkleiden dress up [,dres_'ʌp]
Verkleidung costume ['kɒstjuːm]
verlassen leave [liːv]
▶ S. 194 (to) leave
verletzen hurt [hɜːt]
▶ S. 196 hurt
verletzt hurt [hɜːt]
▶ S. 196 hurt
verlieren lose [luːz]
verneigen: sich verneigen bow [baʊ]
verpassen miss [mɪs]
verrückt mad [mæd]   **verrückt werden** go mad
▶ S. 206 German "werden"
Vers *(Reim)* rhyme [raɪm]; *(Strophe)* verse [vɜːs]
verschieden different ['dɪfrənt]
verschwinden disappear [,dɪsə'pɪə]
versprechen promise ['prɒmɪs]
verstecken; sich verstecken hide [haɪd]
verstehen understand [,ʌndə'stænd]   **Hast du es verstanden?** Did you get it? *(infml)*
versuchen try [traɪ]   **Versuch's mal.** Have a go.
verteidigen: jn./etwas verteidigen (gegen jn./etwas) defend sb./sth. (against sb./sth.) [dɪ'fend]
verwenden use [juːz]
Video video ['vɪdiəʊ]
Videokamera video camera ['vɪdiəʊ kæmrə]
viel a lot (of); lots (of); much [mʌtʃ]   **Viel Glück!** Good luck! [lʌk]   **viel zu tun haben** be busy ['bɪzi]   **Wie viel kosten …?** How much are …?   **Wie viel kostet …?** How much is …?
viele a lot (of); lots (of); many ['meni]
vielleicht maybe ['meɪbi]

German – English

vier four [fɔː]

Viertel: Viertel nach zehn (10.15/ 22.15) quarter past ten ['kwɔːtə pɑːst] **Viertel vor elf (10.45/ 22.45)** quarter to eleven ['kwɔːtə tʊ]

violett purple ['pɜːpl]

Vogel bird [bɜːd]

Vokal vowel ['vaʊəl]

voll full (of) [fʊl]

Volleyball volleyball ['vɒlibɔːl]

Vollmond full moon [fʊl 'muːn]

von of [ɒv], [əv]; from [frɒm], [frəm] **ein Lied von …** a song by … [baɪ] **von … bis …** from … to …

vor 1. *(örtlich)* in front of [ɪn 'frɒnt_əv] **vor der Schule** *(vor dem Schulgebäude)* in front of the school; *(außerhalb der Schule)* outside the school [ˌaʊt'saɪd] 2. *(zeitlich)* before [bɪ'fɔː] **vor der Schule** *(vor Schulbeginn)* before school **vorm Unterricht** before lessons **vor zwei Tagen** two days ago [ə'gəʊ] **Viertel vor elf (10.45/ 22.45)** quarter to eleven ['kwɔːtə tʊ]

vorankommen *(zurechtkommen)* get on [ˌget_'ɒn]

vorbei (an) past [pɑːst]

vorbei sein *(zu Ende sein)* be over ['əʊvə]

vorbei-: an etwas/jm. vorbeigehen/vorbeifahren pass sth./sb. [pɑːs]

vorbereiten: etwas vorbereiten prepare sth. [prɪ'peə] **sich vorbereiten (auf)** get ready (for) ['redi]

Vordergrund foreground ['fɔːgraʊnd]

Vorderseite front [frʌnt]

Vorführung *(Demonstration)* demonstration [ˌdemən'streɪʃn]

vorhaben: Ich habe vor ein Lied zu singen. I'm going to sing a song.

vorher: vorher schon mal before **vorher noch nie** not … before, never … before
▶ S. 193 before

Vorlieben und Abneigungen likes and dislikes *(pl)* [ˌlaɪks_ən 'dɪslaɪks]

Vormittag morning ['mɔːnɪŋ]

vorn: nach vorn to the front [frɒnt]

Vorschrift *(Regel)* rule [ruːl]

Vorsicht! *(Pass auf!)* Watch out! [ˌwɒtʃ_'aʊt]

vorsichtig careful ['keəfl]

vorspielen: etwas vorspielen act sth. out [ˌækt_'aʊt]

Vorspielen *(Theater)* audition [ɔː'dɪʃn]

Vorsprechen *(Theater)* audition [ɔː'dɪʃn]

vorstellen 1. **(jm.) etwas vorstellen** *(präsentieren)* present sth. (to sb.) [prɪ'zent] 2. **jn. (jm.) vorstellen** introduce sb. (to sb.) [ˌɪntrə'djuːs] 3. **sich etwas vorstellen** imagine sth. [ɪ'mædʒɪn] **Stell dir vor, Dad …** Guess what, Dad …

Vorstellung 1. *(Idee)* idea [aɪ'dɪə] 2. *(Präsentation)* presentation [ˌprezn'teɪʃn] 3. *(Show)* show [ʃəʊ]

Vortrag talk [tɔːk] **einen Vortrag halten (über)** give a talk (about)

vorüber: vorbei (an), vorüber (an) past [pɑːst]

W

Wache, Wachposten guard [gɑːd]

wachsen grow [grəʊ]

wählen *(aussuchen)* choose [tʃuːz]

wahr true [truː] **…, nicht wahr?** …, right?
▶ S. 183 right

während as [æz], [əz]; while [waɪl]

Wahrheit truth [truːθ]

wahrscheinlich probably ['prɒbəbli]

Wal whale [weɪl]

Wald forest ['fɒrɪst]

Wand wall [wɔːl]

wann? when? [wen] **Wann hast du Geburtstag?** When's your birthday.

Waren *(Güter)* goods *(pl)* [gʊdz]

warm warm [wɔːm]

warten (auf) wait (for) [weɪt] **Warte einen Moment.** Wait a minute.

warum? why? [waɪ]

was? what? [wɒt] **Was gibt es zum Mittagessen?** What's for lunch? **Was haben wir als Hausaufgabe auf?** What's for homework? **Was hättest du gern? / Was möchtest du?** What would you like? **Was ist denn? / Was ist los?** What's the matter? **Und was ist mit dir?** What about you?

Wasser water ['wɔːtə]

Wasserfall waterfall ['wɔːtəfɔːl]

Website website ['websaɪt]

Wechselgeld change [tʃeɪndʒ]

wecken: jn. wecken wake sb. up [ˌweɪk_'ʌp]

weg away [ə'weɪ]

Weg way [weɪ]; *(Pfad)* path [pɑːθ] **auf dem Weg zu/nach …** on the way to … **jm. den Weg (nach …) beschreiben** tell sb. the way (to …) **jn. nach dem Weg fragen** ask sb. the way

wegen: Es tut mir leid wegen … I'm sorry about …

weggehen leave [liːv]
▶ S. 194 (to) leave

wehtun hurt [hɜːt]
▶ S. 196 hurt

weich soft [sɒft]

Weide field [fiːld]

weil because [bɪ'kɒz]

weinen cry [kraɪ]

weise wise [waɪz]

weiß white [waɪt]

weit (entfernt) far [fɑː] **weiter** further ['fɜːðə] **am weitesten** furthest ['fɜːðɪst]

weiter: geradeaus weiter straight on [streɪt_'ɒn]

weiter-: weitergehen/-laufen/-segeln/… walk/run/sail/… on **weitermachen** go on **weiterreden** go on

welche(r, s) 1. **Auf welcher Seite sind wir?** What page are we on? **Welche Farbe …?** What colour …? 2. *(aus einer begrenzten Anzahl)* which [wɪtʃ] **Welche Klubs …?** (= *Welche von diesen Klubs …?)* Which clubs …?

Welle wave [weɪv]

Welt world [wɜːld] **auf der Welt** in the world

wem? who? **Wem hast du es erzählt?** Who did you tell?

wen? who? **Wen kennt Sam?** Who does Sam know?

wenden 1. *(umkehren)* turn around [ˌtɜːn_ə'raʊnd] 2. **sich an jn. wenden** turn to sb.

wenigstens at least [ət 'liːst]

wenn 1. *(zeitlich)* when [wen] 2. *(falls)* if [ɪf] **selbst wenn** even if ['iːvn_ɪf]

wer? who? [huː] **Wer kennt Sam?** Who knows Sam?

werden become [bɪ'kʌm] **rot werden** go red **wütend/kalt werden** get angry/cold **hart/schlecht/ verrückt werden** go hard/bad/mad
▶ S. 185 (to) get
▶ S. 206 German "werden"

werfen throw [θrəʊ]

wessen? whose? [huːz]

two hundred and forty-five **245**

Dictionary

Wettbewerb competition [ˌkɒmpəˈtɪʃn]
Wetter weather [ˈweðə]
Wettkampf *(Match)* match [mætʃ]
wichtig important [ɪmˈpɔːtnt]
wie 1. *(Fragewort)* how [haʊ] **Wie alt bist du?** How old are you? **Wie findest du …? / Wie gefällt dir …?** How do you like …? **Wie geht's? / Wie geht es dir/euch?** How are you? **Wie heißt du?** What's your name? **Wie ist sie (so)?** What's she like? **Wie spät ist es?** What time is it? **Wie viel kosten …?** How much are …? **Wie viel kostet …?** How much is …? **Wie war es?** What was it like? **Wie wäre es mit …?** What about …? **Wie dem auch sei, …** Anyway, … [ˈeniweɪ]
2. wie Jungen like boys [laɪk]
genau wie … just like …
3. der-/die-/dasselbe wie … the same as … [æz], [əz] **(nicht) so groß wie** (not) as big as
wieder again [əˈgen] **immer wieder** again and again
wiederholen repeat [rɪˈpiːt]
Wiederholung *(des Lernstoffs)* revision [rɪˈvɪʒn]
wiegen weigh [weɪ]
wild wild [waɪld]
Willkommen in Plymouth. Welcome to Plymouth. [ˈwelkəm]
Wind wind [wɪnd]
windig windy [ˈwɪndi]
Winter winter [ˈwɪntə]
wir we [wiː]
wirklich really [ˈrɪəli]
wissen know [nəʊ] **…, weißt du. / …, wissen Sie.** …, you know. [nəʊ]; …, you see. **Weißt du was, Dad …** Guess what, Dad … **über etwas Bescheid wissen** know about sth.
Witz joke [dʒəʊk]
witzig funny [ˈfʌni]
wo? where? [weə]
Woche week [wiːk]
Wochenende weekend [ˌwiːkˈend] **am Wochenende** at the weekend
Wochentag day of the week
Woher kommst du? Where are you from?
wohin? where? [weə]
Wohlfahrtsorganisation charity [ˈtʃærəti]
Wohltätigkeit, wohltätige Zwecke charity [ˈtʃærəti]
wohnen *(leben)* live [lɪv]

Wohnung flat [flæt]; apartment [əˈpɑːtmənt]
Wohnwagen caravan [ˈkærəvæn]
Wohnzimmer living room [ˈlɪvɪŋ ruːm]
Wolke cloud [klaʊd]
wollen: etwas haben wollen want sth. [wɒnt] **etwas tun wollen** want to do sth.
Workshop workshop [ˈwɜːkʃɒp]
Wort word [wɜːd]
Wortstellung word order [ˈwɜːd ˌɔːdə]
Wovon handelt die Geschichte? What is the story about?
wund sore [sɔː]
Wunsch wish [wɪʃ]
wünschen wish [wɪʃ] **Ich wünschte, ich wäre da.** I wish I was there. **sich etwas wünschen** make a wish
würde: Ich würde gern … I'd like to … **Ich würde sehr gern …** I'd love to …
Wurm worm [wɜːm]
wütend (auf jn.) angry (with sb.) [ˈæŋgri]

Y

Yoga yoga [ˈjəʊgə]

Z

Zahl number [ˈnʌmbə]
zählen count [kaʊnt] **bis zehn zählen** count to ten
z.B. (zum Beispiel) e.g. [ˌiː ˈdʒiː] *(from Latin* exempli gratia)
Zahn tooth [tuːθ], *pl* teeth [tiːθ]
Zahnarzt/-ärztin dentist [ˈdentɪst]
Zahnschmerzen haben have a toothache [ˈtuːθeɪk]
Zauber- magic [ˈmædʒɪk]
Zaun fence [fens]
Zeh toe [təʊ]
zehn ten [ten]
Zeichen sign [saɪn]
Zeichensetzung punctuation [ˌpʌŋktʃuˈeɪʃn]
▶ S. 186 Punctuation
zeichnen draw [drɔː]
Zeichnung drawing [ˈdrɔːɪŋ]
zeigen show [ʃəʊ] **auf etwas zeigen** point to sth. [pɔɪnt] **es zeigt, dass …** it shows that …
Zeile line [laɪn]
Zeit time [taɪm] **die ganze Zeit** all the time
Zeitschrift magazine [ˌmægəˈziːn]

Zeitung paper [ˈpeɪpə]
Zelt tent [tent]
zelten gehen go camping [ˈkæmpɪŋ]
Zeltplatz campsite [ˈkæmpsaɪt]
Zentrum centre [ˈsentə]
zerbrechen break [breɪk]
zerbrochen broken [ˈbrəʊkən]
zerstören destroy [dɪˈstrɔɪ]
Ziege goat [gəʊt]
ziehen pull [pʊl]
Ziffer number [ˈnʌmbə]
zischen hiss [hɪs]
Zoo zoo [zuː]
zu 1. *(örtlich)* to [tu], [tə]
2. zu spät/kalt/groß/… too late/cold/big/… [tuː]
3. Es ist Zeit zu gehen. It's time to go. **Nice to meet you.** Freut mich, dich/euch/Sie kennenzulernen.
zuerst first [fɜːst]; *(anfangs)* at first [ət ˈfɜːst]
Zug train [treɪn]
Zugabe encore [ˈɒŋkɔː]
Zuhause home [həʊm]
zuhören listen [ˈlɪsn] **Hör(t) mir zu.** Listen to me.
Zuhörer/in listener [ˈlɪsənə]
Zukunft future [ˈfjuːtʃə]
zukünftige(r, s) future [ˈfjuːtʃə]
zum Beispiel for example [fər_ɪgˈzɑːmpl]
zumachen close [kləʊz]
zumindest at least [ət ˈliːst]
Zunge tongue [tʌŋ]
Zungenbrecher tongue-twister [ˈtʌŋˌtwɪstə]
zurechtkommen get on [ˌget_ˈɒn]
zurück back [bæk]
zurücklassen leave [liːv]
▶ S. 194 (to) leave
zusammen together [təˈgeðə]
Zusammenhang *(Text-, Satzzusammenhang)* context [ˈkɒntekst]
Zuschauer/innen *(Publikum)* audience [ˈɔːdiəns]
zustimmen: jm. zustimmen agree with sb. [əˈgriː]
zuvor: besser als je zuvor better than ever
zuwenden: sich jm. zuwenden turn to sb. [ˈtɜːn]
zwei two [tuː]
zweimal twice [twaɪs]
zweisilbig two-syllable [ˈsɪləbl]
zweite(r, s) second [ˈsekənd]
zweitgrößte(r, s) second biggest
Zwillinge twins *(pl)* [twɪnz]
zwischen between [bɪˈtwiːn]
zwölf twelve [twelv]

List of names

Family names / Surnames
(Familiennamen)

Alfred ['ælfrɪd]
Bell [bel]
Bennett ['benɪt]
Blackwell ['blækwel]
Buloni [bu'ləʊni]
Cobb [kɒb]
Cooper ['kuːpə]
Cyrus ['saɪrəs]
Detweiler ['detwaɪlə]
Dewberry ['djuːbəri]
DiCamillo [ˌdikə'mɪləʊ]
Doe [dəʊ]
Drake [dreɪk]
Dump [dʌmp]
Elton ['eltən]
Fawkes [fɔːks]
Pascoe ['pæskəʊ]
Petrock ['petrɒk]
Potter ['pɒtə]
Sen [sen]
Skinner ['skɪnə]
Smith [smɪθ]
Taylor ['teɪlə]
Tizzard ['tɪzəd]
Willis ['wɪlɪs]
Wilson ['wɪlsn]
Wu [wuː]

First names (Vornamen)

Abby ['æbi]
Amar ['æmə, ˌʌmə]
Amber ['æmbə]
Arthur ['ɑːθə]
Conan ['kəʊnən]
Dunlap ['dʌnlæp]
Fiona [fi'əʊnə]
Francis ['frɑːnsɪs]
Gertrude ['gɜːtruːd]
Ginny ['dʒɪni]
Gloria ['glɔːriə]
Guinevere ['gwɪnəvɪə]
Guy [gaɪ]
Hector ['hektə]
Igraine [ɪ'greɪn, iː'greɪn]
India ['ɪndiə]
Jack [dʒæk]
James [dʒeɪmz]
Jessie ['dʒesi]
Jill [dʒɪl]
Jim [dʒɪm]
Jo [dʒəʊ]
Justin ['dʒʌstɪn]
Kate [keɪt]
Kay [keɪ]
Leo ['liːəʊ]
Lucy ['luːsi]

Mary ['meəri]
Maya ['maɪə]
Merlin ['mɜːlɪn]
Miley ['maɪli]
Mukesh ['mʊkeʃ]
Oliver ['ɒlɪvə]
Opal ['əʊpl]
Paul [pɔːl]
Phil [fɪl]
Richard ['rɪtʃəd]
Robbie ['rɒbi]
Rosie ['rəʊzi]
Ruby ['ruːbi]
Ryan ['raɪən]
Sam [sæm]
Samuel ['sæmjuəl]
Sarah ['seərə]
Stevie ['stiːvi]
Susan ['suːzn]
Tiny ['taɪni]
Uther ['uːθə]

Place names (Ortsnamen)

Alaska [ə'læskə]
the **Alps** [ælps] *die Alpen*
America [ə'merɪkə]
Aquae Sulis
  [ˌækwaɪ 'suːlɪs]
Armada Way
  [ɑːˌmɑːdə 'weɪ]
Asia ['eɪʒə] *Asien*
the **Atlantic Ocean**
  [ətˌlæntɪk 'əʊʃn] *Atlantik*
the **Barbican** ['bɑːbɪkən]
  (Kanonenbastion)
Bath [bɑːθ]
Baxter State Park
  [ˌbækstə steɪt 'pɑːk]
Becky Falls [ˌbeki 'fɔːlz]
Ben Nevis [ˌben 'nevɪs]
Berlin [bɜː'lɪn]
Boston ['bɒstən]
Britain ['brɪtn]
  Großbritannien
the **Broadway** ['brɔːdweɪ]
Buckingham Palace
  [ˌbʌkɪŋəm 'pæləs]
Carrantuohill [ˌkærən 'tuːl]
Coombe Dean [ˌkuːm 'diːn]
Cornwall ['kɔːnwɔːl]
Covent Garden
  [ˌkɒvənt 'gɑːdn]
Dartmoor ['dɑːtmɔː]
Dean Cross Road
  [ˌdiːn krɒs 'rəʊd]
Devon ['devn]
Disneyland ['dɪznilænd]
Drury Lane [ˌdrʊəri 'leɪn]

Eden ['iːdn]
Empire State Building
  [ˌempaɪə 'steɪt ˌbɪldɪŋ]
England ['ɪŋglənd]
Eton College [ˌiːtn 'kɒlɪdʒ]
Exeter ['eksɪtə]
Florida ['flɒrɪdə]
Germany ['dʒɜːməni]
  Deutschland
Great Britain [ˌgreɪt 'brɪtn]
  Großbritannien
the **Hoe** [həʊ]
  (Hügel in Plymouth)
Horn Cross, Horn Lane
  [ˌhɔːn 'krɒs], [ˌhɔːn 'leɪn]
India ['ɪndiə] *Indien*
King's Tor [ˌkɪŋz 'tɔː]
Loch Awe [lɒx 'ɔː]
Loch Lomond
  [lɒx 'ləʊmənd]
Loch Ness [lɒx 'nes]
London ['lʌndən]
Madagascar [ˌmædə'gæskə]
  Madagaskar
Maine [meɪn]
Massachusetts
  [ˌmæsə'tʃuːsɪts]
Merrivale ['meriveɪl]
Mount Katahdin
  [ˌmaʊnt kə'tɑːdɪn]
New York [ˌnjuː 'jɔːk]
Northern Ireland
  [ˌnɔːðən 'aɪələnd]
  Nordirland
Nuremberg ['njʊərəmbɜːg]
  Nürnberg
Olney ['ɒlni]
Plymouth ['plɪməθ]
Plymouth Pavilions
  [ˌplɪməθ pə'vɪliənz]
Plymouth Sound
  [ˌplɪməθ 'saʊnd]
Plymstock ['plɪmstɒk]
Radford Park
  [ˌrædfəd 'pɑːk]
the **River Plym** [plɪm]
the **River Severn** ['sevn]
the **River Thames** [temz]
the **River Trent** [trent]
Rome [rəʊm]
Scary Tor [ˌskeəri 'tɔː]
Scotland ['skɒtlənd]
  Schottland
Smeaton's Tower
  [ˌsmiːtnz 'taʊə]
Snowdon ['snəʊdn]
St Mary's Church
  [sənt ˌmeərɪz 'tʃɜːtʃ]
  Marienkirche

Sudan [su'dɑːn]
Sweden [swiːdn] *Schweden*
Sutton ['sʌtn]
Tavistock ['tævɪstɒk]
Tinside Lido
  [ˌtɪnsaɪd 'laɪdəʊ, 'liːdəʊ]
Tintagel [tɪn'tædʒəl]
Torbay [ˌtɔː'beɪ]
Turkey ['tɜːki]
Turkish Riviera
  [ˌtɜːkɪʃ ˌrivi'eərə]
the **UK** [ˌjuː 'keɪ] (= **Great
  Britain and Northern
  Ireland**) *das Vereinigte
  Königreich*
the **USA** [ˌjuː es 'eɪ] *die
  Vereinigten Staaten von
  Amerika*
Wales [weɪlz]
Watley ['wɒtli]
Wembury
  ['wembri, 'wembəri]
Weston-super-Mare
  [ˌwestn ˌsuːpə 'meə]
Windermere ['wɪndəmɪə]
  (auch: Lake Windermere)
Wycombe Abbey
  [ˌwɪkəm 'æbi]

Other names
(Andere Namen)

Cap'n Jaspers
  [ˌkæpn 'dʒæspəz]
Celt [kelt] *Kelte/Keltin*
Diwali [di'vɑːli]
Footloose ['fʊtluːs]
  (etwa: ungebunden)
Haytor Hoppa
  [heɪˌtɔː 'hɒpə]
Hogwarts ['hɒgwɔːts]
Morph [mɔːf]
Pendragon [ˌpen'drægən]
Rolling Stones
  [ˌrəʊlɪŋ 'stəʊnz]
Shrek [ʃrek]
Silky ['sɪlki]
Sir Charles [sə 'tʃɑːlz]
Skip [skɪp]
Spiderman ['spaɪdəmæn]
Spot [spɒt]
Sulis ['suːlɪs]
Talking Heads
  [ˌtɔːkɪŋ 'hedz]
Theatre Royal
  [ˌθɪətə 'rɔɪəl]
U2 [ˌjuː 'tuː]
Winn-Dixie [wɪn 'dɪksi]

Irregular verbs

infinitive	simple past	past participle	
(to) **be**	*I/he/she/it* **was**; *you/we/you/they* **were**	**been**	sein
(to) **become**	**became**	**become**	werden
(to) **begin**	**began**	**begun**	beginnen, anfangen
(to) **bite** [aɪ]	**bit** [ɪ]	**bitten** [ɪ]	beißen
(to) **blow** sth. **out**	**blew**	**blown**	etwas auspusten, ausblasen
(to) **break** [eɪ]	**broke**	**broken**	brechen; zerbrechen
(to) **bring**]	**brought**	**brought**	(mit-, her)bringen
(to) **build**	**built**	**built**	bauen
(to) **buy**	**bought**	**bought**	kaufen
(to) **catch**	**caught**	**caught**	fangen
(to) **choose** [uː]	**chose** [əʊ]	**chosen** [əʊ]	aussuchen, (aus)wählen; sich aussuchen
(to) **come**	**came**	**come**	kommen
(to) **cost**	**cost**	**cost**	kosten
(to) **cut**	**cut**	**cut**	schneiden
(to) **do**	**did**	**done** [ʌ]	tun, machen
(to) **draw**	**drew**	**drawn**	zeichnen
(to) **drive** [aɪ]	**drove** [əʊ]	**driven** [ɪ]	*(mit dem Auto)* fahren
(to) **drink**	**drank**	**drunk**	trinken
(to) **eat**	**ate** [et, eɪt]	**eaten**	essen
(to) **fall**	**fell**	**fallen**	fallen, stürzen; hinfallen
(to) **feed**	**fed**	**fed**	füttern
(to) **feel**	**felt**	**felt**	fühlen; sich fühlen
(to) **fight**	**fought**	**fought**	(be)kämpfen
(to) **find**	**found**	**found**	finden
(to) **fly**	**flew**	**flown**	fliegen
(to) **forget**	**forgot**	**forgotten**	vergessen
(to) **get**	**got**	**got**	bekommen; holen, besorgen; werden; gelangen, (hin)kommen
(to) **give**	**gave**	**given**]	geben
(to) **go**	**went**	**gone** [ɒ]	gehen
(to) **grow**	**grew**	**grown**	wachsen; anbauen, anpflanzen
(to) **hang**	**hung**	**hung**	hängen
(to) **have**	**had**	**had**	haben
(to) **hear** [ɪə]	**heard** [ɜː]	**heard** [ɜː]	hören
(to) **hide** [aɪ]	**hid** [ɪ]	**hidden** [ɪ]	verstecken; sich verstecken
(to) **hit**	**hit**	**hit**	schlagen
(to) **hold**	**held**	**held**	halten
(to) **hurt**	**hurt**	**hurt**	schmerzen, wehtun; verletzen
(to) **kneel** [niːl]	**knelt** [nelt]	**knelt** [nelt]	knien
(to) **know** [nəʊ]	**knew** [njuː]	**known** [nəʊn]	wissen; kennen
(to) **leave** [iː]	**left**	**left**	(weg)gehen; abfahren; (zurück)lassen; verlassen
(to) **lie**	**lay**	**lain**	liegen
(to) **light** [aɪ]	**lit** [ɪ]	**lit** [ɪ]	anzünden
(to) **lose** [uː]	**lost** [ɒ]	**lost** [ɒ]	verlieren
(to) **make**	**made**	**made**	machen; herstellen
(to) **mean** [iː]	**meant** [e]	**meant** [e]	bedeuten; meinen
(to) **meet** [iː]	**met** [e]	**met**	treffen; sich treffen; kennenlernen
(to) **pay**	**paid**	**paid**	bezahlen
(to) **put**	**put**	**put**	*(etwas wohin)* tun, legen, stellen
(to) **read** [iː]	**read** [e]	**read** [e]	lesen
(to) **ride** [aɪ]	**rode**	**ridden** [ɪ]	reiten; *(Rad)* fahren

Irregular verbs · English sounds

infinitive	simple past	past participle	
(to) **ring**	**rang**	**rung**	klingeln, läuten
(to) **run**	**ran**	**run**	rennen, laufen
(to) **say** [eɪ]	**said** [e]	**said** [e]	sagen
(to) **see**	**saw**	**seen**	sehen
(to) **sell**	**sold**	**sold**	verkaufen
(to) **send**	**sent**	**sent**	schicken, senden
(to) **shake**	**shook**	**shaken**	schütteln
(to) **sing**	**sang**	**sung**	singen
(to) **sit**	**sat**	**sat**	sitzen; sich setzen
(to) **sleep**	**slept**	**slept**	schlafen
(to) **speak** [iː]	**spoke**	**spoken**	sprechen
(to) **stand**	**stood**	**stood**	setzen; sich (hin)stellen
(to) **stick**	**stuck**	**stuck**	stechen, stecken
(to) **swim**	**swam**	**swum**	schwimmen
(to) **take**	**took**	**taken**	nehmen, mitnehmen; (weg-, hin)bringen; dauern, *(Zeit)* brauchen
(to) **tell**	**told**	**told**	erzählen, berichten
(to) **think**	**thought**	**thought**	denken, glauben
(to) **throw**	**threw**	**thrown**	werfen
(to) **understand**	**understood**	**understood**	verstehen
(to) **wake up**	**woke up**	**woken up**	aufwachen; (auf)wecken
(to) **wear** [eə]	**wore** [ɔː]	**worn** [ɔː]	tragen *(Kleidung)*
(to) **win**	**won** [ʌ]	**won** [ʌ]	gewinnen
(to) **write**	**wrote**	**written**	schreiben

English sounds

[iː] gr**ee**n, h**e**, s**ea**
[i] happ**y**, monk**ey**
[ɪ] b**i**g, **i**n, **e**xpensive
[e] r**e**d, y**e**s, ag**ai**n, br**ea**kfast
[æ] c**a**t, **a**nimal, **a**pple, bl**a**ck
[ɑː] cl**a**ss, **a**sk, c**a**r, p**a**rk
[ɒ] s**o**ng, **o**n, d**o**g, wh**a**t
[ɔː] d**oo**r, **o**r, b**a**ll, f**ou**r, m**o**rning
[uː] bl**ue**, r**u**ler, t**oo**, tw**o**, y**ou**
[ʊ] b**oo**k, g**oo**d, p**u**llover
[ʌ] m**u**m, b**u**s, c**o**lour
[ɜː] g**i**rl, **ea**rly, h**e**r, w**o**rk, T-sh**i**rt
[ə] **a** partner, **a**gain, tod**a**y

[eɪ] n**a**me, **ei**ght, pl**a**y, gr**ea**t
[aɪ] t**i**me, r**i**ght, m**y**, **I**
[ɔɪ] b**oy**, t**oi**let, n**oi**se
[əʊ] **o**ld, n**o**, r**oa**d, yell**ow**
[aʊ] t**ow**n, n**ow**, h**ou**se
[ɪə] h**ere**, y**ea**r, id**ea**
[eə] wh**ere**, p**air**, sh**are**, th**eir**
[ʊə] t**our**

[b] **b**oat, ta**b**le, ver**b**
[p] **p**ool, **p**a**p**er, sho**p**
[d] **d**ad, win**d**ow, goo**d**
[t] **t**en, le**tt**er, a**t**
[g] **g**ood, a**g**ain, ba**g**
[k] **c**at, **k**itchen, ba**ck**
[m] **m**um, **m**an, re**m**ember
[n] **n**o, o**n**e, te**n**
[ŋ] so**ng**, you**ng**, u**n**cle, tha**n**ks
[l] he**ll**o, **l**ike, o**l**d, sma**ll**
[r] **r**ed, **r**uler, f**r**iend, so**rr**y
[w] **w**e, **wh**ere, **o**ne
[j] **y**ou, **y**es, **u**niform
[f] **f**amily, a**f**ter, lau**gh**
[v] ri**v**er, **v**ery, se**v**en, ha**v**e
[s] **s**i**s**ter, po**s**ter, ye**s**
[z] plea**s**e, **z**oo, qui**z**, hi**s**, mu**s**ic
[ʃ] **sh**op, sta**ti**on, Engli**sh**
[ʒ] televi**s**ion, u**s**ually
[tʃ] **t**ea**ch**er, **ch**ild, wa**tch**
[dʒ] **G**ermany, **j**ob, pro**j**ect, oran**ge**
[θ] **th**anks, **th**ree, ba**th**room
[ð] **th**e, **th**is, fa**th**er, wi**th**
[h] **h**ere, **wh**o, be**h**ind
[x] lo**ch**

> ●
> Am besten kannst du dir die Aussprache der einzelnen Lautzeichen einprägen, wenn du dir zu jedem Zeichen ein einfaches Wort merkst – das [iː] ist der **green**-Laut, das [eɪ] ist der **name**-Laut usw.

True and false friends

True friends (Wahre Freunde)

Es gibt viele Wörter, die im Englischen und im Deutschen sehr ähnlich sind – das sind die „wahren Freunde". Manchmal gibt es allerdings Unterschiede in der Schreibung oder der Aussprache, die man beachten muss.

action [ˈækʃn] Aktion
activity [ækˈtɪvəti] Aktivität
address [əˈdres] Adresse
April [ˈeɪprəl] April
aquarium [əˈkweəriəm] Aquarium
arm [ɑːm] Arm
article [ˈɑːtɪkl] Artikel
August [ˈɔːgəst] August
ball [bɔːl] Ball
band [bænd] Band, Musikgruppe
basketball [ˈbɑːskɪtbɔːl] Basketball
before [bɪˈfɔː] bevor
begin [bɪˈgɪn] beginnen
blond [blɒnd] blond
bring [brɪŋ] bringen
burger [ˈbɜːgə] Hamburger
bus [bʌs] Bus
café [ˈkæfeɪ] Café
camera [ˈkæmərə] Kamera
camping [ˈkæmpɪŋ] Camping, Zelten
clown [klaʊn] Clown
club [klʌb] Klub
cola [ˈkəʊlə] Cola
comedy [ˈkɒmədi] Comedyshow
comma [ˈkɒmə] Komma
computer [kəmˈpjuːtə] Computer
concert [ˈkɒnsət] Konzert
consonant [ˈkɒnsənənt] Konsonant
context [ˈkɒntekst] Kontext
cool [kuːl] cool
copy [ˈkɒpi] Kopie
cornflakes [ˈkɔːnfleɪks] Cornflakes
correct [kəˈrekt] korrekt
cost [kɒst] kosten
costume [ˈkɒstjuːm] Kostüm
cousin [ˈkʌzn] Cousin, Cousine

crash [kræʃ] crashen
cricket [ˈkrɪkɪt] Cricket
deck [dek] Deck (eines Schiffes)
demonstration [ˌdemənˈstreɪʃn] Demonstration
designer [dɪˈzaɪnə] Designer/in
dialogue [ˈdaɪəlɒg] Dialog
disco [ˈdɪskəʊ] Disko
doctor [ˈdɒktə] Doktor
DVD [diːviːˈdiː] DVD
elephant [ˈelɪfənt] Elefant
email [ˈiːmeɪl] E-Mail
end [end] Ende
fair [feə] fair, gerecht
fall [fɔːl] fallen
family [ˈfæməli] Familie
fan [fæn] Fan, Anhänger/in
farm [fɑːm] Farm, Bauernhof
film [fɪlm] Film
final [ˈfaɪnl] Finale
find [faɪnd] finden
fine [faɪn] fein
finger [ˈfɪŋgə] Finger
fish [fɪʃ] Fisch
flag [flæg] Flagge
form [fɔːm] Form
garage [ˈgærɑːʒ, ˈgærɪdʒ] Garage
garden [ˈgɑːdn] Garten
gel [dʒel] Gel
giraffe [dʒəˈrɑːf] Giraffe
glass [glɑːs] Glas
go-kart [ˈgəʊ kɑːt] Gokart
gold [gəʊld] Gold
gram [græm] Gramm
grass [grɑːs] Gras
guitar [gɪˈtɑː] Gitarre

gymnastics [dʒɪmˈnæstɪks] Gymnastik
hamburger [ˈhæmbɜːgə] Hamburger
hamster [ˈhæmstə] Hamster
hand [hænd] Hand
hobby [ˈhɒbi] Hobby
hotel [həʊˈtel] Hotel
house [haʊs] Haus
instrument [ˈɪnstrəmənt] Instrument
interview [ˈɪntəvjuː] Interview
jeans [dʒiːnz] Jeans
job [dʒɒb] Job, Arbeitsstelle
judo [ˈdʒuːdəʊ] Judo
kilogram [ˈkɪləgræm] Kilogramm
kilometre [ˈkɪləmiːtə] Kilometer
kung fu [ˌkʌŋ ˈfuː] Kung Fu
lamp [læmp] Lampe
land [lænd] Land
legend [ˈledʒənd] Legende
lip [lɪp] Lippe
list [lɪst] Liste
make-up [ˈmeɪk ʌp] Make-up
man [mæn] Mann
mediation [ˌmiːdiˈeɪʃn] Mediation
metre [ˈmiːtə] Meter
million [ˈmɪljən] Million
minute [ˈmɪnɪt] Minute
model [ˈmɒdl] Model
moment [ˈməʊmənt] Moment
monster [ˈmɒnstə] Monster
museum [mjuˈziːəm] Museum
music [ˈmjuːzɪk] Musik
musical [ˈmjuːzɪkl] Musical
name [neɪm] Name
object [ˈɒbdʒekt] Objekt
ocean [ˈəʊʃn] Ozean

250 two hundred and fifty

True and false friends

online [ˌɒnˈlaɪn] online
orange [ˈɒrɪndʒ] orange
otter [ˈɒtə] Otter
parade [pəˈreɪd] Parade
park [pɑːk] Park
partner [ˈpɑːtnə] Partner/in
party [ˈpɑːti] Party
perfect [ˈpɜːfɪkt] perfekt
person [ˈpɜːsn] Person
photo [ˈfəʊtəʊ] Foto
picnic [ˈpɪknɪk] Picknick
pink [pɪŋk] pink, rosa
pizza [ˈpiːtsə] Pizza
plan [plæn] Plan
planet [ˈplænɪt] Planet
pony [ˈpəʊni] Pony
poster [ˈpəʊstə] Poster
prince [prɪns] Prinz
problem [ˈprɒbləm] Problem
programme [ˈprəʊɡræm] Programm
project [ˈprɒdʒekt] Projekt
quiz [kwɪz] Quiz, Ratespiel
radio [ˈreɪdiəʊ] Radio
rally [ˈræli] Rallye
religion [rɪˈlɪdʒən] Religion
ring [rɪŋ] Ring
rock (music) [rɒk] Rockmusik
roll [rəʊl] rollen

rucksack [ˈrʌksæk] Rucksack
ruin [ˈruːɪn] Ruine
samba [ˈsæmbə] Samba
sand [sænd] Sand
sandwich [ˈsænwɪtʃ] Sandwich
scene [siːn] Szene
second [ˈsekənd] Sekunde
set [set] Set, Satz
shorts [ʃɔːts] Shorts, kurze Hose
show [ʃəʊ] Show, Vorstellung
sing [sɪŋ] singen
snack [snæk] Snack, Imbiss
sofa [ˈsəʊfə] Sofa
solo [ˈsəʊləʊ] Solo-
song [sɒŋ] Lied, Song
sport [spɔːt] Sport
star [stɑː] (Film-, Pop-)Star
stop [stɒp] anhalten, stoppen
student [ˈstjuːdənt] Student/in
studio [ˈstjuːdiəʊ] Studio
subject [ˈsʌbdʒekt] Subjekt
symbol [ˈsɪmbl] Symbol
tea [tiː] Tee
team [tiːm] Team, Mannschaft
telephone [ˈtelɪfəʊn] Telefon
tennis [ˈtenɪs] Tennis
theatre [ˈθɪətə] Theater
theme [θiːm] Thema

thermometer [θəˈmɒmɪtə] Thermometer
title [ˈtaɪtl] Titel
toilet [ˈtɔɪlət] Toilette
tomato [təˈmɑːtəʊ] Tomate
top [tɒp] Top, Oberteil
tourist [ˈtʊərɪst] Tourist/in
tractor [ˈtræktə] Traktor
traditional [trəˈdɪʃənl] traditionell
train [treɪn] trainieren
trick [trɪk] Trick, Kunststück
T-shirt [ˈtiːʃɜːt] T-Shirt
tunnel [ˈtʌnl] Tunnel
uniform [ˈjuːnɪfɔːm] Uniform
vegetarian [ˌvedʒəˈteəriən] Vegetarier/in
video [ˈvɪdiəʊ] Video
volleyball [ˈvɒlibɔːl] Volleyball
warm [wɔːm] warm
website [ˈwebsaɪt] Website
wild [waɪld] wild
wind [wɪnd] Wind
winter [ˈwɪntə] Winter
workshop [ˈwɜːkʃɒp] Workshop
yoga [ˈjəʊɡə] Yoga
yoghurt [ˈjɒɡət] Joghurt
zoo [zuː] Zoo

Some words look the same, but they don't mean the same.

The English word *become* means **werden**, not **bekommen**.

False friends (Falsche Freunde)

! Leider gibt es auch einige Wörter, die im Englischen und Deutschen ähnlich klingen oder aussehen, aber eine ganz andere Bedeutung haben.
Hier sind einige Beispiele für *false friends*:

English	German	German	English
also	= auch	also	= **so; Well …**
become	= werden	bekommen	= **get**
boot	= Stiefel	Boot	= **boat**
build	= bauen	bilden	= **make, form**
chips	= Pommes frites	Kartoffelchips	= **crisps**
fire	= Feuer	Feier	= **celebration**
kind	= freundlich	Kind	= **child**
handy	= praktisch	Handy	= **mobile**
listen	= zuhören	Listen	= **lists**
map	= Landkarte	Mappe	= **folder**
mist	= Nebel	Mist *(Unsinn)*	= **rubbish**

English	German	German	English
snake	= Schlange	Schnecke	= **snail**
stay	= bleiben	stehen	= **stand**
where	= wo	wer	= **who**
while	= während	weil	= **because**

TIP
Wenn du nicht sicher bist, ob du *true friends* oder *false friends* vor dir hast, dann schau in einem guten Wörterbuch nach.

Early finisher – answers

Unit 1

1 *Justin's **father** lives in the USA.*
2 *Abby gave a name **to a seal: Silky**.*
3 *The Bennetts have **two children: Sam and Lily**.*
4 *Lucy and her **friend Maya** were at **Lucy's** grandparents' farm in the summer.*

Unit 2

*RIVER**S***
      ***W**ALES*
      ***E**NGLAND*
*SCOTLAN**D***
    *LAK**E***
      ***N**ESS*

Unit 3

Mögliche Lösungen (108)

a few, am, after, are, area, arm, art, as, ask, at, ate, dad, dark, dead, desk, do, draft, drama, draw, dream, drew, drop, drum, ear, eat, far, farm, farmer, fast, fat, fed, for, forest, fork, form, four, from, mad, made, make, map, market, mean, meat, more, mouse, must, or, order, out, part, past, pause, paw, PE, pm, poster, put, read, red, rode, sad, sat, saw, sea, set, so, so far, sofa, soft, some, soup, speak, sport, spot, star, start, stop, sure, swam, sword, take, task, taste, tea, team, tear, term, to, top, tour, tower, true, two, up, us, use, wake up, warm, we, wear, wet, woke, word, wore, work, worker, worm

Unit 4

hay – barn – sheep – valley – cottage – mountain – footprint

Unit 5

Every school in Britain tries to raise money on Red Nose Day. The money that our school made is for homeless people. So what did we do? Of course, we had a non-uniform day. Most students dressed up. Three of my friends and I wore banana costumes. So everyone gave £1.30. You pay £1 if you don't wear a uniform and the red noses cost 30p. We also had a school talent show. The people who watched had to pay 20p (or more). I played the guitar, but I didn't win a prize. :-(In my year (Year 8) we had a cake sale. We made lots of funny red cakes and we raised £57.62.

Quellenverzeichnis

Illustrationen

Roland Beier, Berlin (S. 140 Mitte; 141; 143; 145; 148 – 153 oben; 154; 163 2. v. oben; 164 re.; 170 unten li.; 178 oben; 179 – 180; 182 unten – 192; 198 – 199; 201 – 202; 204 unten – 205; 207 oben); **Carlos Borrell**, Berlin (vordere u. hintere Umschlaginnenseite); **Cornelsen Schulverlage GmbH**, Berlin (S. 13 icons oben, Bild A, Bild B (u. 147 unten); 26 oben; 29 unten re., unten li.; 57 unten); 146–147; **Judy Brown**, Sutton (S. 19); **Tobias Dahmen**, Utrecht, Niederlande, www.tobidahmen.de (S. 6; 8 oben; 9; 11 Mitte li., unten; 12 oben; 13 unten; 14 – 17 oben (M); 18; 22 oben; 27; 33 – 34 oben; 35; 38 – 40; 46 – 47; 53 – 56; 60; 62 – 65; 70; 73 oben; 82; 84; 87; 88; 92 – 93; 100 – 101; 106 (u. 132) – 108; 118 – 121; 127 unten; 135; 140 oben, unten; 142; 144; 153 unten; 155; 156 – 163 oben, 2. v. unten, unten; 164 li.; 165 – 169; 170 Mitte, unten re.; 171 – 175; 250 – 251); **Elke Hanisch**, Köln (S. 8 unten; 17 unten; 26; 34 unten; 80 (M) – 81; 91); **Jeongsook Lee**, Heidelberg (S. 178 unten; 182 oben; 204 oben; 207 unten); **M.B. Schulz**, Düsseldorf (S. 11 oben, Mitte Mitte, Mitte re.; 12 unten; 20; 22 Mitte, unten (u. 123); 42 – 43; 48; 52 (u. 127 oben); 58; 69 (M); 71 (u. 128); 73 unten; 95; 104; 109)

Bildquellen

action press, Hamburg (S. 21 oben, unten: REX FEATURES LTD.); **akg images**, Berlin (S. 142 mosque: Bildarchiv Monheim); **Alamy**, Abingdon (S. 9 unten: Corbis Super RF; S. 26 unten: Ball Miwako; S. 37 Mitte li.: VQA Images; S. 38 re.: STOCK4B GmbH; S. 39: Mim Friday; S. 46: Europe / Peter Forsberg; S. 66 oben: Penny Tweedie; S. 72 Hintergrund barn (M): Walter Quirtmair; S. 76 Hintergrund tor (M): natureslight; S. 77 (M): WILDLIFE GmbH; S. 85 Bild C re.: Jeremy Hoare; S. 86 (M): Arch White; S. 88: Caro; S. 89 (u. 130): Ian Lamond; S. 96 oben li.: Manor Photography, unten re.: DWD-photo; S. 99 Hintergrund (M): PhotoStock-Israel; S. 104 oben: P Tomlins, unten: Robert Harding Picture Library Ltd; S. 137 oben: Alistair Laming; S. 140 birdwatching: Radius Images, hiking: J.R. Bale, snorkeling: Susan E. Degginger, holiday camp: ITAR-TASS Photo Agency, guest house: MiRafoto.com, caravan site: Alvey & Towers Picture Library, youth hostel: imagebroker; S. 141 orchestra: Enigma, string quartet: Tony West; S. 142 hairdresser's, church: imagebroker, butcher's: Dennis Cox, baker's: Lightworks Media, pet shop: Lourens Smak, ice cream parlor: Zoonar GmbH, department store: Wild Places Photography/Chris Howes, kindergarten: Mark Dyball, underground station: Peter Horree, tram stop: Diadem Images/Jonathan Larsen, zebra crossing: David Davies, hospital: Jochen Tack, pub: Yadid Levy; S. 144 chilly: Image Source, St Martin's Day: imagebroker; S. 190 2. v. li.: studiomode; S. 197: Stephen Dorey ABIPP); **Avenue Images**, Hamburg (S. 67 oben: agefotostock / Sebastian Wasek; S. 142 health food store: agefotostock / Peter Erik Forsberg); **Becky Falls Woodland Park Ltd.**, Devon (S. 74); **Trevor Burrows** Photography Ltd, Plymouth (S. 4 Sam, Leo, Mitte li.; S. 5 Lucy; S. 6 Maya; S. 7 Justin; S. 10; S. 14 – 17 (M); S. 24 li.; S. 28 – 29 oben (M); S. 30; S. 31 unten re. u. li.; S. 32 – 33; S. 36 – 37 oben; S. 54; S. 68 oben; S. 69 (M); S. 72 (M); S. 76 (M); S. 80 (M); S. 84 oben, li., re.; S. 86 (M); S. 90; S. 98 (M); S. 99 Leo (M); S. 105; S. 110; S. 114 – 115; S. 154); **Cinetext**, Frankfurt/Main (S. 38 li.); **Corbis**, Düsseldorf (S. 9 Bild C: Reuters/LUKE MACGREGOR; S. 24 oben: Louis K. Meisel Gallery, Inc.; S. 37 Mitte re.: Neal Preston; S. 67 unten: JAI/Doug Pearson); **Cornelsen Schulverlage GmbH**, Berlin (S. 4 unten li.; S. 23; S. 40 unten – 41; S. 57; S. 75; S. 97; S. 113); **English Heritage** (S. 102 – 103); **Fotolia**, Berlin (S. 6 Mitte li.: Brigitte Meckle, unten li.: majeczka; S. 140 ice skating: Kathrin39; S. 142 doctor's: Heike Jestram); **Getty Images**, München (S. 25: WIN-Initiative; S. 37 unten: AFP; S. 44 2. v. oben li.: WireImage, 2. v. oben re.; S. 53: Pavel Losevsky; S. 66 unten: David Clapp; S. 85 Bild C li.: AFP; S. 140 B & B: James Braund; S. 144 sultry: Phil Boorman); **Stefanie Gira**, Berlin (S. 85 Bild B; S. 92); **images.de**, Berlin (S. 142: PhotoAlto); **iStockphoto**, Calgary (S. 24 unten: Kyslynskyy; S. 31 oben re.: nilsz; S. 44 oben: CEFutcher; S. 139: RyanJLane; S. 140 waterskiing: jentakespictures, mountaineering: Gorfer, bodyboarding: carrollphoto, surfing: djjohn, holiday home: LordRunar; S. 141 clarinet: CEFutcher, bass: DNF-Style, double bass: the4js; S. 142 restaurant: MMassel, newsagent's: Estherrr, greengrocer's: NikD90, dentist's: choja, fast food stand: Sigarru, bank: MichaelJay, car park: delectus, fire station: erlucho, police station: Kerrick; S. 143: beaver, fox,

Quellenverzeichnis

wolf: GlobalP, falcon: galdzer; S. 144 freezing cold: starekase, thunder: ninjaMonkeyStudio, thunderstorm: clintspencer, rainbow: gui00878, Christmas: alle12, Rosh Hashana: sbossert, Feast of the Sacrifice: burakpekakcan; S. 179 oben: PIKSEL, unten li.: duaneellison; S. 182: ejs9; S. 184: mattjeacock; S. 194 oben li.: LouisHiemstra, unten li.: chictype, unten re.: ZAtanasoski; S. 196 unten: CaroleGomez; S. 205 finger: hocus-focus); **jump Fotoagentur**, Hamburg (S. 140 sledging: Kristiane Vey); **Kuttig-Fotos**, Lüneburg (S. 144 Three Kings' Day: Siegfried Kuttig); **laif**, Köln (S.64: Polaris); **Petra Mai**, Dresden (S.137: Kinderstadtplan); **mauritius images GmbH**, Frankfurt/Main (S. 48 unten: Alamy); **Peekaboo Tours**, Dresden (S. 51 unten: Jana Krähe); **Photothek.net**, Berlin (S. 142 supermarket: Thomas Trutschel); **Jörg Rademacher**, Mannheim (S. 8 Bild A); **Shutterstock**, New York (S. 4 oben li.: Oleg Znamenskiy; S. 6 oben li.: Ron Ellis; S. 8 Bild E: Francesco Carucci; S. 9 oben li.: Leonux; S. 11: tuulijumala; S. 18 (u. 123): buchan; S. 29 unten (u. 44 2. v. unten): Featureflash; S. 31 oben li. (u. 94 Bild 2 fish and chips): ronfromyork; S. 38 Mitte: dotshock; S. 40 li., re.: Robert Spriggs, Mitte: Tatiana Popova; S. 44 unten: dwphotos; S. 51 Bild 1 (u. 126 Bild 1): Alexander Raths, Bild 2 (u. 126 Bild 2): pukach, Bild 3 (u. 126 Bild 3): Lim Yong Hian, Bild 4 (u. 126 Bild 4): Madlen, Bild 5 (u. 126 Bild 5): T-Design, Bild 6 (u. 126 Bild 6): Michaelpuche; S. 68 unten (M): cooperman; S. 79 oben (u. 129 u. 196 adder): Eric Isselee, unten: sima; S. 85 unten: sgm; S. 93: Hurst Photo; S. 94 Bild 2 board: Fedor Korolevskiy, hand: brem stocker, potatoe: Joe Gough, pasties: Malivan_Iuliia, curry: stocksolutions; S. 96 oben re.: Joe Gough, unten li.: Santibhavank P; S. 98 bag (M): mikeledray, umbrella (M): Stocksnapper; S. 111: joeborg; S. 136: scphoto60; S. 140 snowboarding: Ipatov, windsurfing: Sean Nel, skiing: gorillaimages, diving: C.K.Ma; S. 141 electric guitar: 4contrast_dot_com, choir: Shutterstock.com / Ferenc Szelepcsenyi, flute, cello: Fotokostic, saxophone: Anton Albert, violin: Katrina Brown; S. 142 traffic lights: dedi57, dry cleaner's: mangostock, petrol station: Gary James Calder, children's playground: Againstar, chemist's: Dmitry Kalinovsky; S. 143 ducks: panbazil, goose: Roman Samokhin, geese: DenisNata, stork, eagle, buzzard eagle, wild boar, red squirrel: Eric Isselee, wolves: Iakov Filimonov, grey squirrel: IrinaK, hedgehog: Galushko Sergey; S. 144 sunshine: rangizzz, rain shower: peresanz, stormy: Photobank gallery, dry: David Aleksandrowicz, rainy: andreiuc88, bright: Efired, foggy: PHOTO FUN, Valentine's Day: meviogra, Easter: Nicole Gordine, Germany: Robert Biedermann, Chanukkah: Sergey Pinaev, Sugar Feast: ersin ergin; Advent: Bernd Juergens, St Nicholas' Day: Africa Studio; S. 179 unten re.: Baloncici; S. 180: fritz16; S. 183 (u. 190 3. v. li.): Tobik; S. 190 Mitte: Sergio Foto, 2. v. re.: Ramon grosso dolarea, li.: GorillaAttack, 3. v. re.: tarasov, re.: Nattika; S. 192 oben re.: Villiers Steyn, li.: Lighthunter, unten li., Mitte, re.: Eric Isselee; S. 194 oben re.: Evgeny Karandaev, oben Mitte: Andrey Eremin; S. 196 otter: Eric Isselee, deer: Ekaterina V. Borisova, male deer: Anan Kaewkhammul; S. 204: Thorsten Rust; S. 205 girl: DenisNata, leg: Alan Poulson Photography, back: Africa Studio, boy: Indigo Fish)

Songs

S. 10: Song of Weston Super Mare, M+T: Paul Hobbs, produced by SCAMP studio

S. 52: Money (That's what I want), M + T: Janie Bradford, Berry Gordy

Titelbild

Trevor Burrows Photography Ltd, Plymouth

Special thanks to:

The staff and students at **Plymstock School**, Plymouth

Classroom English

Zu Beginn und am Ende des Unterrichts

Guten Morgen, Frau …	**Good morning, Mrs/Miss …** *(bis 12 Uhr)*
Guten Tag, Herr …	**Good afternoon, Mr …** *(ab 12 Uhr)*
Entschuldigung, dass ich zu spät komme.	**Sorry I'm late.**
Auf Wiedersehen! / Bis morgen.	**Goodbye. / See you tomorrow.**

Du brauchst Hilfe

Können Sie/Kannst du mir bitte helfen?	**Can you help me, please?**
Auf welcher Seite sind wir, bitte?	**What page are we on, please?**
Was heißt … auf Englisch/Deutsch?	**What's … in English/German?**
Können Sie/Kannst du mir bitte … buchstabieren?	**Can you spell …, please?**
Können Sie es bitte an die Tafel schreiben?	**Can you write it on the board, please?**

Hausaufgaben und Übungen

Tut mir leid, ich habe mein Schulheft nicht dabei.	**Sorry, I don't have my exercise book.**
Kann ich bitte vorlesen?	**Can I read, please?**
Ich verstehe diese Übung nicht.	**I don't understand this exercise.**
Ich kann Nummer 3 nicht lösen.	**I can't do number 3.**
Entschuldigung, ich bin noch nicht fertig.	**Sorry, I haven't finished.**
Ich habe … Ist das auch richtig?	**I have … Is that right too?**
Tut mir leid, das weiß ich nicht.	**Sorry, I don't know.**
Was haben wir (als Hausaufgabe) auf?	**What's for homework?**

Wenn es Probleme gibt

Kann ich es auf Deutsch sagen?	**Can I say it in German?**
Können Sie/Kannst du bitte lauter sprechen?	**Can you speak louder, please?**
Können Sie/Kannst du das bitte noch mal sagen?	**Can you say that again, please?**
Kann ich bitte das Fenster öffnen/zumachen?	**Can I open/close the window, please?**
Kann ich bitte zur Toilette gehen?	**Can I go to the toilet, please?**

Partnerarbeit

Kann ich mit Julian arbeiten?	**Can I work with Julian?**
Kann ich bitte dein Lineal/deinen Filzstift/… haben?	**Can I have your ruler/felt tip/…, please?**
Danke. / Vielen Dank.	**Thank you. / Thanks a lot.**
Du bist dran.	**It's your turn.**

Arbeitsanweisungen

Diese Arbeitsanweisungen findest du häufig im Schülerbuch.

Act out the song.	Spiel das Lied vor.
Add more words to the table.	Füge weitere Wörter zur Tabelle hinzu.
Ask/Answer the questions.	Stelle/Beantworte die Fragen.
Check/Compare with a partner.	Prüfe/Vergleiche mit einem Partner/einer Partnerin.
Choose the correct/right words.	Wähle die richtigen Wörter.
Copy the words from the box.	Schreibe die Wörter aus dem Kästchen ab.
Correct the sentences.	Verbessere/Korrigiere die Sätze.
Find this information.	Finde/Suche diese Informationen.
Find out about cities in Britain.	Informiere dich über Großstädte in Großbritannien.
Finish the table below.	Vervollständige die Tabelle unten.
Get more words from page 44.	Hole zusätzliche Wörter von Seite 44.
Give reasons.	Gib Gründe an.
Give your text to another pair.	Gebt euren Text einem anderen Paar.
Go on with new ideas.	Mach weiter mit neuen Ideen.
Hang the poster up in your classroom.	Hänge das Poster im Klassenzimmer auf.
Hold up the card.	Halte die Karte hoch.
Imagine you're Silky.	Stell dir vor, du bist Silky.
Label your drawing.	Beschrifte deine Zeichnung.
Learn the rhyme.	Lerne den Reim/Vers auswendig.
Leave space for your answers.	Lass Platz für deine Antworten.
Listen to Morph.	Hör Morph zu.
Look at page 10.	Sieh auf Seite 10 nach. / Sieh dir Seite 10 an.
Look at the picture.	Schau dir das Bild an.
Look up the word if you can't understand it.	Schlag das Wort nach, wenn du es nicht verstehst.
Make appointments with three partners.	Verabrede dich mit drei Partner/innen.
Make groups of three.	Bildet Dreiergruppen.
Match the words to the pictures.	Ordne die Wörter den Bildern zu.
Practise the words.	Übe die Wörter.
Put all the verbs in the right place.	Setze alle Verben an der richtigen Stelle ein.
Put the card into your MyBook.	Lege die Karte in dein MyBook.
Put up your hand.	Melde dich.
Read the dialogue out loud to your group.	Lies deiner Gruppe den Dialog laut vor.
Rewrite the text.	Schreibe den Text neu.
Scan the text to find these words.	Überfliege den Text und versuche, diese Wörter zu finden.
Sing along with the chorus.	Sing den Refrain mit.
Start a profile for Sam.	Fang ein Profil für Sam an.
Swap cards with another team.	Tauscht Karten mit einem anderen Team.
Take turns.	Wechselt euch ab.
Talk to different partners about the photo.	Rede mit verschiedenen Partner/innen über das Foto.
Talk to your partner like this: ...	Rede so mit deinem Partner/deiner Partnerin: ...
Think of a sentence.	Denk dir einen Satz aus.
Use these words: ...	Verwende diese Wörter: ...
Walk around the classroom.	Geh im Klassenzimmer herum.
Write down the letters in the right order.	Schreib die Buchstaben in der richtigen Reihenfolge auf.